Explorations in Marital and Family Therapy

**Selected Papers of
James L. Framo**

James L. Framo, Ph.D., is presently Professor in the Department of Psychology of Temple University in Philadelphia. An early worker in the field of marital and family therapy, he has given many workshops around the United States and in Mexico, Canada, Italy, Switzerland, Israel, and Australia. He is a coeditor (with Ivan Boszormenyi-Nagy) of *Intensive Family Therapy,* a classic that has been translated into five languages. He also edited *Family Interaction: A Dialogue Between Family Researchers and Family Therapists,* the proceedings of a landmark conference in the field, as well as coedited (with Robert J. Green) *Family Therapy: Major Contributions.* In addition, he has published numerous articles and chapters. He is a founding member and vice-president (1981) of the American Family Therapy Association, a diplomate of the American Board of Professional Psychology, a member of the Advisory Board of the Family Mediation Association, Advisory Editor of *Family Process*, and a fellow of the American Association for Marriage and Family Therapy.

Explorations in Marital and Family Therapy

Selected Papers of James L. Framo

James L. Framo, Ph.D.

Foreword by Murray Bowen, M.D.

Springer Publishing Company / New York

To the memory of my Mom and Dad,
Madeline and James; to my sisters,
Vi and Eleanor; to my brother, Michael;
to my wife, Mary; to the memory of my
sons, Jimmie and Michael; to my
daughters, Joan and Patty.

Copyright © 1982 by Springer Publishing Company, Inc.

Springer Publishing Company, Inc.
200 Park Avenue South
New York, New York 10003

82 83 84 85 86 / 10 9 8 7 6 5 4 3 2 1

Library of Congress Cataloging in Publication Data

Framo, James L.
  Explorations in marital and family therapy.

  Bibliography: p.
  Includes indexes.
  1. Family psychotherapy.   2. Marital
psychotherapy.   I. Title.
RC488.5.F7   616.89'156   81-18470
ISBN 0-8261-3400-9   AACR2
ISBN 0-8261-3401-7 (pbk.)

Printed in the United States of America

Contents

Part Four

Application to Intergenerational Processes

8

Family of Origin as a Therapeutic Resource for Adults
in Marital and Family Therapy: You Can and Should

9

The Integration of Marital Therapy With Sessions

10

Part Five

Professional and Personal Issues

11

12

Chronicle of a Struggle to Establish a Family Unit Within a

13

A Personal Viewpoint on Training in Marital

14

Foreword

This volume is important to anyone interested in family therapy. It contains the most significant writings of a pioneer who has been active in the professional and literary development of a vital new field. It is not often that one finds such a volume.

Jim Framo has been present and accounted for since the beginnings of family therapy when schizophrenia was its primary focus. He has traveled widely both nationally and internationally, he has personally known everyone important to the development of the field, and there has rarely been a time when he was not editing yet another book. He has used his literary talents to chronicle his own influential ideas and those of others in this evolving field. To have his writings all in one volume is a tribute to one of the old masters and a treasure to the reader.

Murray Bowen, M.D.
Clinical Professor and Director
Georgetown University Family Center

Introduction

In some quarters it is considered the culmination of narcissistic presumption to publish a book of one's collected papers. Such an endeavor assumes that one's work is worthy of reproduction, will last unto perpetuity, and puts one into a different class, whatever that class is. But self-deception can only go so far. In truth, the impetus for this book evolved from more commonplace, utilitarian sources. Students in family and marital therapy training programs, some of them doing dissertations or master's theses on my work, have expressed some frustration in trying to locate my papers, since they were published in so many scattered places. The primary stimulus for this book, then, was to bring together most of my published papers and chapters in one place for more efficient access. Versions of these papers were presented at the many workshops I have given in the United States and abroad; family therapists at these workshops have often asked if I would put out a volume such as this. The final incentive came from the publisher of this book, Dr. Ursula Springer, who encouraged me to assemble my collected papers, which she offered to publish.

Originally my structural plan for the book was one of chronological order (from 1965 to 1980), thereby revealing the development of my thinking over the years. But articles written at disparate periods and for different purposes do not necessarily follow a coherent progression. For the benefit of the readers' interest it seemed preferable to group the papers by subject matter (theory, application to families, application to marriage and divorce, application to intergenerational processes, and professional and personal issues), and to introduce each section with an explanation of the creation of those papers within their contexts. This book contains all the major papers I have written as of 1980, except for a chapter I wrote on systematic research on family dynamics (1965b), deleted because it was too outdated.

I hope that the various papers mingle well, considering that certain themes are threaded throughout all of my work. My orientation to marital and family theory and therapy emphasizes the depth, the dynamic aspects of family life, such as the psychology of intimate relationships, the interlocking of multi-person motivational systems, the relationship between the intrapsychic and the transactional, and the hidden transgenerational and historical forces that exercise their powerful influence on current intimate relationships.

I would like to express my appreciation to Janet Gibson for typing parts of this manuscript and for helping put it together.

I would like to take this opportunity to give credit to some of the family therapists who influenced my thinking and practice. Ivan Nagy and I worked together for 13 years, starting on a schizophrenia project that developed into one of the major family therapy centers. During those years Ivan and I had some great discussions from which I profited immensely. All of us on that project—Oscar Weiner, Gerry Spark, Gerry Lincoln Grossman, Leon Robinson, Dave Rubinstein, Jerry Zuk, and others—observed each other's treatment sessions, taught each other, fought and debated, and enhanced each other's development. Those were enriching, formative, fine years. I was also influenced by Nathan Ackerman, the grandfather of family therapy, whose line-bucking against the psychiatric establishment paved the way, and whose masterful clinical acumen I wanted to imitate. Murray Bowen's concepts, especially his creative leap about multigenerational processes, served as a guide for my own work with family of origin; Murray served as president, and I as vice-president, of the newly formed American Family Therapy Association. I have been influenced by Norman Paul's concepts on mourning. Virginia Satir and I conducted together a memorable workshop in Mexico City, some years ago; her deep knowledge about families and her boundless optimism allowed me to see the potentials in the worst family situations. I have benefited from Lyman Wynne's reasoned and unifying effect on the field. Finally, Carl Whitaker, the family therapist's family therapist, has probably influenced everybody; certainly he has stretched my imagination and helped me dare become looser, more real, with couples and families, and more comfortable with my own craziness. I would also like to acknowledge cotherapists I have worked with over the years.* To be sure, I have learned from family therapy orientations different from my own, and hope that in the future the various concepts will become more integrated.

Some years ago, during the course of a workshop I was conducting in Rome, a psychiatrist said, "I am so glad to hear that family therapy has become the dominant treatment method in the States." Of course, I had to reply quickly that my enthusiasm for my work had misrepresented its impact, because about 98% of clinical practice in social work, psychiatry, and psychology was still being conducted in traditional ways—that is, through the diagnosis and treatment of "emotionally disturbed" individuals. Since that time there has been an accelerating explosion of interest in conjoint family and marital therapy, with new books and articles coming out profusely, and training programs, workshops, and conferences proliferating on the subject. My previously estimated percentage of traditional practice would probably have to be lowered today.

As one of the early workers in the field I have been surprised at the growth we spawned; it seems that nearly everybody today wants to be a family therapist. I must confess that I have such proprietary concerns about family therapy that at

---

*Cotherapists I have worked with in recent years have been my wife, Mary D. Framo, M.S.S., Ph.D. candidate, Cheryl Keats, M.S.W., Joann Gillis-Donovan, Ph.D., Ann Gravagno, M.F.T., Peggy Tietz, M.S.W., and Gail Hogeboom Wilson, M.A., Ph.D. candidate.

times I have vague feelings of resentment toward newcomers, whom I unfairly regard as interlopers in "my" field. It has probably ever been true that so-called elder statesmen have mixed feelings of receptivity toward new ideas, and want to leave their own impress. I think the field expanded because professional helpers found that the family approach enabled them to deal at last with the real problems of people instead of psychiatric syndromes—that is, with clients' relationships with those who mattered most to them. Symptoms erupt when these relationships break down. By spreading the focus to intimate contexts, in which people really live, it was found that more meaningful and lasting therapeutic changes could be brought about. More than a technique or form of psychotherapy, however, family system theory has provided a new conceptual model of psychopathology and human relationships whose implications are only beginning to be recognized. Not only is family therapy now routinely included in psychotherapy textbooks, but it is in danger of becoming a doctrine and the new religion, even on the part of those who do not really understand what family therapy is all about. Nonetheless, I identify myself more as a family therapist than as a psychologist, and I do believe that family therapy is a separate profession rather than a subdivision of psychiatry, clinical psychology, or social work.

James Thurber, one of my favorite writers, once quoted Benvenuto Cellini as saying that a man should be at least 40 years old before he undertakes so fine an enterprise as that of setting down the story of his life. Well, these collected papers are not the story of my life, but they do represent a kind of attempt to come to grips with the existential questions one usually confronts at my stage of life. Ernest Becker, in *The Denial of Death,* says that all our actions, in one form or another, are designed to deny our own death. Those people who know me and the events of my personal life know why it is especially important to me that my name carry on.

For a number of years I have been working on another book, my magnum opus, containing an integrated and comprehensive account of my work. Since this book, too, signifies my legacy, it has become difficult to finish. When I can overcome my sense of self importance, recognize that ideas have a half-life of a few years, and when I can inhibit my stalling tactics (striving perfectionistically to discover the "last word" on a subject, sometimes welcoming interruptions, sharpening pencils over and over again, getting cups of coffee—all of which are familiar to writers), I will finish it. One of these days, that is.

James L. Framo

Part One

Theory

Chapter 1, "Family Theory and Therapy," was commissioned as an essay-editorial for a special issue of *The American Psychologist*, in honor of the International Year of the Child. *The American Psychologist* is the only journal of the American Psychological Association received by the entire variety of psychologists in the Association—academic, experimental, industrial, developmental, social, and others, as well as clinical. I accepted the invitation to prepare the paper in order to take advantage of the opportunity to reach the entire field of psychology with family system concepts. The paper presents a rather succinct review of some basic precepts of family theory and therapy, and was intended to stimulate a different kind of epistemology than that followed by most psychologists—comprising linear, acontextual thinking, and either totally focused on processes occurring within individuals or on the comparison of groups. The paper would have been written differently had it been directed toward a family therapy audience. Although written relatively late compared to other papers in this volume, its brief overview can serve as an introduction to the rest of the book.

"Symptoms From a Transactional Viewpoint," chapter 2, has a rather interesting history. It was originally prepared for a book entitled *Family Therapy in Transition*, edited by Nathan W. Ackerman, Judith Lieb, and John K. Pearce, and published by Little, Brown, and Company in 1970. Because of space limitations, Nate Ackerman asked me to cut out the first third of the chapter, which of course I was reluctant to do. One of the editors, John Pearce, said he felt the paper was important enough to include without limitation. However, other considerations had to prevail; the shortened paper was reprinted in *Progress in Group and Family Therapy*, edited by Clifford Sager and Helen Singer Kaplan and published by Brunner/Mazel in 1972. For the first time anywhere, the full paper is presented here in its entirety.

I consider this "symptom" paper to be my most important theoretical contribution. It provides the conceptual formulation on which is based its clinical application—the work I do with adults and their families of origin. This paper has had some moderate influence on the field, being required reading in a number of training institutions, including, I understand, some traditional programs in psychiatry, social work, and clinical psychology. It is comforting that some psychiatric residents are being influenced to think about the intimate context of the patients they see.

1

Family Theory
and Therapy (1979)

When I started to study academic psychology many years ago at Penn State, I could not understand why such processes as cognition, affect, and perception were treated as isolated functions, as if there were no interrelationships between them. Later on I was pleased to learn that psychologists had proved that need influences perception, but then I wondered why so few psychologists ever studied whole persons. Still later, it seemed to me that behavior does not occur in a vacuum; people behave and feel and perceive in situations, yet rarely were people in situations examined. Clinical psychology, I learned, was preoccupied with studying what went on inside people, giving only occasional passing attention to "environmental factors" and rarely examining what went on between people (except perhaps for group therapy). Social psychology would presumably be the discipline that would examine contexts, but curiously, practically all the studies done by social psychologists have been with ad hoc groups of strangers, that is, those with no past history or likelihood of a future together. The study of intimately related people and the rules and laws that govern their interaction has been largely ignored by social psychologists. (Rare exceptions are Carson, 1969; Davis, 1973; Levinger and Raush, 1976.)

Humans are ecologically situated in many contexts, the most important of which is the family. The family, however, is not just another context in a whole range of contexts. Its unique and massive effects, rooted in blood ties, not only have been past personality-forming influences but exercise powerful forces on one's current life and future destiny. The family shapes the fiber of people's beings

Reprinted with permission from the *American Psychologist*, 1979, *34*, 988–992. Copyright © 1979, American Psychological Association.

in a way no other social force can begin to realize. Peer groups, work settings, friendship networks, social class, age, race, sex, nationality, and religion can only have glancing effects compared with that of the family. You reserve for your family the best and the worst that is in you; toward these intimates you will show your greatest cruelty, yet for them you will make your greatest sacrifices. Family members, in turn, can frustrate and hurt you the most because you want and expect more from them, and they can also give you the kind of gratification for which no price is too high to pay.

The family as a human institution is universal and has survived through history as the most workable kind of living unit for mediating the culture in preparing the young for the next generation. Families provide the deepest satisfactions of living and an emotional refuge from harsh external realities. Whatever is human in people in their capacity to relate beyond their narcissism and to love comes from their family relationships. As every professional knows who deals with human suffering, however, family living can also paradoxically provide the context for tragedy and anguish of endless variety—the cruel rejections, marital discord or emptiness, murderous hostility, the child unloved or discriminated against, "parentification" of the child, jealousy, hatred, unrealized fulfillments, and outrages against the human spirit.

The genius of Freud led to profound understanding of the intrapsychic world of the individual, but his discouragement of involvement of family members in the treatment process established the practice of exclusion of the family in most forms of psychotherapy. Disturbed children have traditionally been diagnosed and treated in child psychiatry and clinical child psychology by the child-guidance model. This model, which was a real advance from viewing only the child's problems, consisted of the child being assessed alone by interview and tests, and the mother being seen alone collaterally, by a social worker, in order to get a history of the child. Rarely were fathers included, because it was believed "you can't get fathers." (It is interesting that the statues in front of child guidance clinics depict mothers and children, never fathers.) Even if both parents were seen, the focus was on the child's problems; the social worker, who had to deal with the bulk of the pathology, would gradually become aware, for example, of marital or in-law problems, but she would be given the clear message by the rest of the psychiatric team that her therapy efforts were secondary. All kinds of intelligence, personality, and specialized tests were devised to measure precisely what was wrong with the child, and the main thrust of therapy was given to the child by the child psychologist or child psychiatrist; the therapist would then do play therapy with the child and interpret to the child the meaning of his or her conflicts. Childhood psychoses, conduct disturbances, developmental disorders, neurotic and psychosomatic problems were handled in this fashion, and if the child needed a specialist (for example, for a learning disability), referrals were made. The emotionally disturbed child, usually caught in the midst of horrendous family situations, might cooperate, figuring, "Maybe if *I* get the help things might get better at home." Some of the kids had to be dragged to therapy and most were labeled for all time as "the patient." If word leaked out in school that they were seeing a psychiatrist they would be taunted by peers.

Bowen (1965) graphically described the "family projection process," whereby the problems in the family are transmitted to one scapegoated family member, usually a child, and are then fixed there with the unwitting assistance of the professional, who lends the stamp of official authenticity to the process:

> The parental problem is most often projected to the child by the mother, with the father supporting her viewpoint. She is an immature person with deep feelings of inadequacy who looks outside herself for the cause of her anxiety. The projection goes into fears and worries about the health and adequacy of the child. The projection searches out small inadequacies, defects, and functional failures in the child, focuses on them, and enlarges and exaggerates them into major deficiencies. . . . For the child, accepting the projection as a reality is a small price to pay for a calmer mother. Now the child *is* a little more inadequate. . . . The projection system can also utilize minor defects. Some of these require an examination and diagnosis by an expert to confirm the presence of the defect. Parents can go from one physician to another until the "feared" defect is finally confirmed by diagnosis. Any defect discovered in physical examination, laboratory tests, and psychological tests can facilitate the projection process. . . . One need listen to such a mother only a few minutes to hear her invoke outside opinions, diagnoses, and tests to validate the projection. . . . The usual psychiatric approach is to examine the patient, confirm the presence of the pathology with a diagnosis, and recommend appropriate treatment. The psychiatric consultation fits, step-by-step, with the family projection process. Thus, a time-proven principle of good medical practice serves to support the parental projection process in the family, to crystallize and fix emotional illness in the patient, and to help make the illness chronic and irreversible. . . . Social custom, laws governing sickness and mental illness, and our most basic, time-proven principles of medical practice are all oriented around the individual theory of disease. (pp. 224–228)

It is frightening to realize that professionals sometimes officially certify the family's process of designating a patient. One wonders how many mental health professionals have lent themselves, for instance, to family extrusion processes that populate children's and adolescent's institutions, mental hospitals, foster homes, boarding schools, prisons, and military academies. Case in point: A mother insisted on her child being tested because "there was something very wrong with him and maybe he needed to go to a place where he could be helped." Examination of the situation revealed that she was about to marry for the second time and wanted to "grab at her last chance for happiness," but her new husband-to-be said he wouldn't marry her as long as she kept her child.

The essence of individual psychotherapy is that the professional, using his or her trained skill, is expected to correct for crippling parental influences and, in some cases, to provide for the child what the parents will not or cannot give. Puzzling treatment failures led to reexamination of the principle of exclusion of the family when it was realized that when the child was treated, a part of the total problem was not visible, that treatment was often undermined by the family, and that the child could not change if the family did not.

About 25 years ago a few maverick psychiatrists, social workers, and psychologists flew in the face of established procedure and began seeing entire families together, thus beginning a quiet revolution. In the beginning the family was seen as a resource in treating the patient; at that time the family was viewed as a noxious influence to be neutralized. The creative step was to take this interference and use it: The family itself could be seen as needing help and as containing the potential for possible change which could be capitalized upon. The pioneer family therapists were slow in recognizing that they were on the threshold of a true paradigmatic shift in the conceptualization of human problems, a fundamental reorientation in thinking, philosophy, and attitude about the nature of psychopathology, relationships, and society (Kuhn, 1962). All traditional concepts of etiology, symptom formation, diagnosis, and treatment had to be broadened and recast. The family approach was not just another form of therapy or body of techniques but a new theory and way of looking at experience and behavior. In the past, science had to rely on second-hand information about the family, on reports given by family members seen separately, or on questionnaires. By observing the family interacting together in a clinical setting, phenomena began to be seen that had never before been known to be present, because the special microscope for their disclosure had not existed. A limited sample of these findings follows:

1.   When the family was observed as an interacting unit it was learned that the family is an intricate system with its own unique bondings, rules, homeostatic mechanisms, secret alliances, communication network, myths, regressive features, and dynamic influences from previous generations. Intimates can drive each other crazy, the problems are similar from one generation to the next, and adults use their spouses and children to live through inner conflicts derived from their families of origin (Framo, 1965a, 1976a).

2.   The psychopathology that seemed to exist only in the "identified patient" was found to be present, subclinically at least, in all family members and to be projected onto a scapegoat who cooperated with this role assignment and became the symptom bearer of a family-wide disturbance. Parts of the family pathology were found to be present in each member, like separate segments of a multilayered jigsaw puzzle.

3.   Seen in the context of the family, heretofore incomprehensible symptoms of the patient became decoded and made sense (that is, the child who refused to go to school, diagnosed as having "school phobia," had to stay home with

his depressed mother because he was afraid she was going to kill herself; he was also delegated to send messages to the absent father).

4. As the symptoms of the identified patient diminished, someone else in the family would develop symptoms. Psychopathology, seen previously as solely the outcome of internalized, insoluble intrapsychic conflicts, could balance family forces as well.

5. It was learned that the psychology of intimate relationships is very different from that of all other social relationships. Everyone is on the same level when dealing with close relationships, from the lowliest peasant to presidents of countries. You are a different person when you are with your family than you are with other people. In general, your immature personality features emerge.

6. Characteristics of individuals are peculiar to their context or system and can best be explained by analyzing the system, not just the individual.

7. In general systems theory, all systems are characterized by homeostasis, feedback loops, complementarity, and equifinality (tending toward a steady state). *Family* systems move toward diminishing or modifying personal change in relating to other family members; that is, the system resists individual efforts to change and prescribes the members' behaviors to adapt to the needs of the system. Anyone, for instance, who tries to change his or her role in a family will soon find out what this means.

8. Interlocking, multi-person motivational systems, whereby one person carries part of the motivations and psychology of another, are only beginning to be understood. Wherever two or more persons are in close relationship they collusively carry psychic functions for each other. The collusion can be benign: If you are scared I can afford to be brave; if you are responsible I can allow myself to be irresponsible; if you take the hard line I can take the soft line. The collusion can be more serious and unconscious: I will be your bad self and act out your impulses if you will never leave me.

9. Symptoms are formed, selected, faked, exchanged, maintained, and reduced as a function of the relationship context in which they are embedded (Framo, 1970). Psychopathology has been described in such standard individual terms as "strong sadistic impulses," "oral–passive needs," "inappropriate affect," "unrealistic ideas," "poor judgment," and "withdrawn." Such stereotyped statements, seen in every psychological report, have no meaning without knowledge of their place in the matrix in which they are displayed; the ideas are often not "unrealistic" and the affect not so "inappropriate" when they are observed in family interaction.

When I was asked to write this essay, the guideline stated that authors should focus on what we have learned about children and what we believe should be done to help children. In my judgment, the best way to help children is to help the whole family, including the extended family. (A child's symptoms, for instance, may be timed to the breakdown in a relationship between mother and grandmother or aunt.) Some children are caught up in a maelstrom of family disturbance, such as a custody battle between divorcing parents. To pluck the child, one minor element, out of that complex situation and send that child to the repair shop and then return that child to the same unchanged situation makes little sense to me. The real problems have been left untouched. Yet that is exactly how this situation is handled in many cases. In order to help an abused child one must help the abusing parent, who is usually enmeshed in a web of other family problems.

The following is a list of some reasons why the family-system approach is more effective and humane:

1. By evaluating whole families one can determine the place of the symptoms in the dynamic economy of the family system and be better able to determine who or what in the family needs treatment.
2. The family evaluation, because it involves contact with those asymptomatic people who (though they never seek treatment for themselves and see problems only in others) sometimes have a pathological impact on others, for the first time moves the helping professions into the vast hinterland of the heretofore unreachable of the population.
3. Keeping in mind that some symptomatic children or adolescents are often resistant to therapeutic exploration, the involvement of the family usually increases motivation for help and may avoid desperate acting out or graver symptomatology, which often serves as a means of forcing the family to do something.
4. Bringing in the whole family communicates the message that everyone has a part in the problem; the other family members, usually the parents, can be helped to take responsibility for their part in the process and no longer have to expiate guilt in a variety of ways.
5. By involving the family, treatment and remedial efforts can be more intelligently aimed and can consequently be given more rapidly than by traditional methods.

In their enthusiasm about what had been discovered, family therapists in the past had oversold themselves and others into believing it was effective in all situations. The history of all new therapies probably follows this course. When the family therapists came up against the truly formidable difficulties of changing families, they began to be more cautious about their claims. Family evaluations may always be useful, but they may not always be practical or feasible. We really do not yet know enough about this enormously complicated subject to state the range of indications and contraindications for family therapy or the circumstances under which it can be combined with other forms of treatment. Furthermore, even when family therapy is done, there are reasons why a child needs to be referred for specialized help, such as reading disorders, neuropsychological or neurological examinations, and determination of retardation. I have not given up altogether being a psychologist. However, I do prefer not to test a child alone for emotional problems; if testing is indicated at all I believe the whole family should be tested. Some instruments for family assessment have been advanced (Fisher, 1976). Innovative approaches to assessment of marital or family interaction have been developed, such as the Family Rorschach (Loveland, Wynne, and Singer, 1963) and Interaction Testing (Roman and Bauman, 1960). Some fascinating findings have resulted from the use of these methods. For instance, the Family Rorschach, in which the whole family is requested to discuss and agree on responses to the inkblots, reveals that thinking disorders of individuals are reflective of family styles of aberrant thinking (Wynne and Singer, 1963). Interaction Testing, in which husbands and wives take the Wechsler test together and agree on responses, has revealed that the joint IQs of troubled couples are often lower than the individual IQs. A brighter woman, dependent on her husband's good will, might agree to accept his intellectually inferior response. Such assessment procedures as these have not been widely used, largely because the tradition of clinical psychology is so firmly rooted in the study of the individual. An individual, acontextual orientation also explains why most research in psychology consists of subjects' responses to the investigator rather than subjects' responses to each other.

Over the years there have been many developments in the field of family therapy, most particularly an astonishing explosion of growth in the field. Twenty years ago there were 3 books in the field, and now there are over 100. The American Family Therapy Association has just come into existence. Treatment techniques have become much more sophisticated, and understanding of how family systems work has considerably increased. Family and marital therapy is used in many settings, and workshops on the subject continue to be crowded. Although little training is done in academic settings, there are now over 300 free-standing family therapy training institutes in the country. The theoretical aspects of family work have only begun to become a part of the mainstream of psychology, which is unfortunate because the study of family processes can make intelligible the behavior of people in other social systems. Some exciting experiments have been done with families, using innovative research methods (Framo, 1965b, 1972). There have also been enough outcome studies done on marital and family therapy to warrant an extensive review (Gurman and Kniskern, 1978) which indicated that "family therapy appears to be at least as effective and possibly more effective than individual therapy for a wide variety of problems, both apparent 'individual' difficulties and more obvious family conflicts" (p. 883).

The transactions of family therapy sessions graphically reveal that despite the comfort of family love and the deep satisfaction of family ritual and play, there occurs among people intimately related to one another a blind destructiveness unmatched in the entire spectrum of all human relationships. Parents tend to do to children what was once done to them, or in their efforts to undo what was done to them, will commit other wrongs to their children. Consequently, one sees children exploited, parentified, shamed, overindulged, infantilized, teased, humiliated, seduced, neglected, persecuted, and sometimes murdered. And since children cannot leave parents who have an unhappy marriage or who will die or collapse without them, many remain bound as captive objects, unable to leave and form families of their own. It is painful to witness the magic of childhood being crushed in those growing years that could be so wondrous. How many thousands of children lie awake at night, in terror over the turmoil in their homes? The family problems, which get repeated over generations, are preventable and can be aborted in this generation, since we have some of the conceptual and therapeutic tools that can alleviate some of the unnecessary suffering. The true Society for the Prevention of Cruelty to Children is treatment for the whole family.

2

Symptoms From a Family Transactional Viewpoint (1970)

The first psychiatric revolution, according to Zilboorg and Henry's *A History of Medical Psychology* (1941), occurred when mental disturbances, which for centuries had been seen as manifestations of supernatural power, evil spirits, or sorcery, were moved from the province of established legal authority, religion, and philosophy into the realm of medicine. This drastic reappraisal of disordered behavior and thinking had to go through the horrors of the Inquisition and the age of witchcraft before there was humanitarian recognition of mental aberrations as illness. We see traces of demonological thinking even today in attitudes toward mental illness, and it is doubtful that these attitudes will ever disappear; emotional problems are never private affairs and always have interpersonal disruptive power. Following recognition of mental disturbance as illness, the next great advance was the evolution of an observational branch of medicine, descriptive psychiatry, a movement which continues as the dominant force in clinical practice.

The second psychiatric revolution, of course, centered around the profound discoveries of Freud when, for the first time in human history, explanatory concepts were applied to disorders of behavior, experience, and feeling. Freud's dynamic, motivational approach brought the *person* into the study of mental illness, in that he tied in mental phenomena with the substance of human existence. Before Freud, once the struggle of bringing mental illness into medicine was over, elaborate schemes were developed to classify mental and behavior phe-

Reprinted with permission from N. W. Ackerman, J. Lieb, and J. K. Pearce (Eds.) *Family Therapy in Transition*. Boston: Little, Brown, 1970. Copyright © 1972, Little, Brown and Company. Also reprinted in C. J. Sager, and H. S. Kaplan, (Eds.) *Progress in Family Therapy*. New York: Brunner/ Mazel, 1972.

nomena, but these classifications were based on the model of physical disease, and they reduced man to a system of body functions. Nosological psychiatry had reached a dead end because the classification of illness did not lead to the kind of understanding which is necessary for treatment. With the development of Freud's concepts, mental processes began to make sense and become lawful: an emotional disorder was not just something that happened, or the result of Satanic influence or a diseased body organ, but came to be understood as part and parcel of being biological and human, of being sexual, of being aggressive, of needing, hoping, fearing, loving, and hating in a world which required socialization in order to survive. Freud's concept of the unconscious and the principle of psychological determinism aroused intense fear and hostility, however. Even today there are mental health professionals who disavow or give lip service to the unconscious, and cannot emotionally accept the idea, partially because the unconscious, by definition, is not acceptable. The phenomenon of ready aversion to the unconscious is similar, we have found, to the automatic repulsion and denial to which the family-system approach is subject, by professionals as well as families. (In one family we evaluated, referred by the courts, in which consummated incest had occurred, the fear of family exploration was so intense that the father and his wife preferred for the father to accept the possibility of a 30-year prison sentence rather than to continue with the family sessions.)

The momentous impact of psychoanalytic concepts on psychopathology was followed by a proliferation of investigations in a number of related fields, developments in psychoanalytic theory, nonpsychoanalytic personality theories, sociological theory, child development, group dynamics, cultural anthropology, social–psychological theory, communication theory, community psychiatry, general systems theory, and others. Developments in these fields are presently blending in a transactional approach which promises to lead to the third revolution in psychopathologic thought. Jackson (1967) recently gave explicit recognition to this movement when he stated that:

> We are on the edge of a new era in psychiatry and the related disciplines of psychology, social work, anthropology and sociology. In this new era we will come to look at human nature in a much more complex way than ever before. From this threshold the view is not of the individual *in vitro* but of the small or larger group within which any particular individual's behavior is adaptive. We will move from individual assessment to analysis of contexts, or more precisely, the *system* from which individual conduct is inseparable. (p. 139)

Consequently, behavior which is usually seen as disordered from the individual viewpoint can be viewed as accommodative, even necessary, in terms of the context within which the individual operates: the most vital context, for most people's lives, is, perforce, their family. To be sure, as Zilboorg has pointed out after surveying the long history of psychiatry, for each stage of history, mental illness has been defined in a manner which is congruent with the spirit and ethos of the age. It may well be that the family movement reflects, in part, an American emphasis on environmental reform, as Spiegel and Bell (1959) have pointed out. It is the opinion, of this writer, however, that if family therapy was just a form of treatment, it would merely take its place along with other forms of psychotherapy (individual, child, group, behavioral, gestalt, and so forth.)[1] The family approach is a fundamental reorientation in thinking, philosophy, and attitude about human nature, society, and psychopathology. As Bowen (1966) put it:

> Individual theory was built on a medical model with its concepts of etiology, the diagnosis of pathology in the patient, and treatment of sickness in the individual. . . . The study of the family provides a completely new order of theoretical models for thinking about man and his relationship to nature and the universe. . . . I believe that family can provide answers to the medical model dilemma of psychiatry, that family concepts may eventually become the basis for a new and different theory about emotional illness, and that this in turn will make its contribution to medical science and practice. (pp. 346, 348)

The purpose of this paper is to document, with theoretical and clinical observations of the present investigator and others, the point of view that psychological symptoms, rather than being viewed and treated as intrapsychic entities, can be better understood and ameliorated within the family transactional system.

Traditional View of Symptoms and Individual Classification

Viewed from an historical perspective, there is little question that Kraepelinian nosology performed an invaluable function. Kraepelin took masses of chaotic observations, made detailed descriptions, and classified clinical entities with such insight that they have stood up even into the modern era. Sophisticated professionals, who usually view Kraepelinian thinking as anachronistic, do not recognize its values: from the point of view of individual psychopathology, while there are always mixtures of symptoms, there is a tendency for certain ones to occur in clusters; the diagnoses do help professionals to communicate with each other in a kind of shorthand way; there are many generalizations one can make about a person diagnosed, say, as manic-depressive; without classification there can be no science, for the ordering of phenomena is not only necessary for developing

---

[1]Since family therapy is "in" these days, psychiatric training programs, schools of social work, departments of psychology, and other mental health agencies feel obliged to include it in their curricula as a kind of token gesture, without recognition of its broad connotations.

systematized knowledge, but for the practical purpose of collating statistical data for planning and research purposes.

Kraepelin's diagnostic system came under early criticism, largely on the basis of its assumption that mental illness was like physical illnesses, and also because the focus was not on the total personality of the patient, but on his "mind," which was divided into mental faculties described in terms of variation from arbitrarily defined normal faculties of perception, will, comprehension, and so forth. Among the notable efforts to broaden the very basis of diagnosis was Adolph Meyer's psychobiologic, "common-sense" approach, which included biological, psychological, and social factors. (Meyer was one of the first to emphasize the patient's reaction to his situation.) Curiously, Freud, while his work had great influence on demolishing static concepts of diagnosis, used the Kraepelinian labels of his time, admittedly however, in a casual manner. He was far more preoccupied with weightier matters—the reconstructive understanding of the causes of symptoms. One of the most penetrating analyses of the philosophy and present chaotic state of classification of mental illness was presented by Thomas Szasz (1959). Szasz maintains that taxonomic anarchy exists in our present state of psychiatric nosology, not only because different orders of phenomena (brain, mind, or behavior) are classified within the same system, without meaningful relationship between them, but also because classification is used in various kinds of psychiatric situations which sometimes subvert the purposes of diagnosis (thus, the social consequences vary according to which setting within which a diagnosis is made: private practice, the child-guidance clinic, the psychoanalytic training system, the military service, the mental hospital, the court of law, and the prison). Szasz points out that in the psychoanalytic situation, for example, the term "psychosis" refers only to certain mental mechanisms or patterns of human relationships, and does not refer to overt behavior or social judgment, whereas in the mental hospital or legal situation the same term could mean involuntary detention, and life or death. Szasz is not against classification itself, but suggests that taxonomic systems should be limited to a given order of phenomena, and methodologically defined in terms of the situational endeavor at hand.

Putting aside for the moment the issue of whether the environmental situation should be an integral part of individual diagnosis (Sargent et al., 1958), there is, indeed, little question that psychiatric labels have come to have loaded, negative social values attached to them. Diagnostic labels, which are supposed to be nonevaluative, are being utilized in the service of human needs in a way that was not originally intended, by professionals as well as laymen. The labels are frequently used as weapons, insults, or manipulative devices, often under the guise of benevolent or scientific motives.[2] Professionals not only characterize patients but their colleagues with diagnostic epithets (for example, "He's a paranoid bastard; a compulsive duck; a stingy, anal character; a psychopathic

---

[2]The role of humor, with its hostile and tension-relieving functions among the staff members of a mental hospital, was studied by Coser (1960).

liar," and so forth). Intimates, such as family members or spouses, are particularly adept at using psychiatric labels on each other. Then, too, psychiatric pigeonholing usually has served to hinder the explanation and deeper understanding of patients. Despite the admonition of Menninger (1962) that good psychiatric diagnosis is much more than the ascription of a name, but a complex set of conclusions, descriptive, analytic, and continuous, in most psychiatric installations there exists the interesting conference game of "Find the Diagnosis." How many hundreds of case conferences have been held where clinical interviews, case histories, observations, and psychological tests were utilized to support endless debates over whether the patient was a pseudoneurotic or ambulatory schizophrenic, a hysteric with borderline features, a paranoid schizophrenic, or what have you? At the very least, an awful lot of professional time is wasted this way; perhaps these conferences provide something for the professionals.[3] Presumably, the purpose of diagnosis is to give information about course, prognosis, and treatment, but how often does not diagnosis block understanding because of the myths that exist about many psychiatric conditions? Schizophrenia, for example, as Szasz has pointed out, has not only become a reified catchall and "explain-all" diagnosis, but usually carries along with it a host of associations—poor prognosis, hospitalization, no uncovering in psychotherapy, and so forth—which not only obstructs comprehension of what the patient is grappling with, but brings in a note of pessimism which prevents effective treatment.[4] Recognition of the negative social and professional consequences which can follow the assigning of a label is seen in the widespread practice of diagnosing a youngster as an "adjustment reaction of adolescence" rather than schizophrenic reaction, no matter how "schizophrenic" the adolescent may seem. No one is as sick as his case history, and most experienced psychotherapists rely on the face-to-face encounter rather than on what happened with the patient before. Besides, we all have friends whose pathological traits we ignore because they are our friends; under a psychiatric microscope anyone can look very sick.[5]

A more serious misapplication of psychiatric labeling, with far-reaching con-

[3]A particularly interesting phenomenon, observable if one gets to know those attending a series of diagnostic conferences, is the way each professional presses for his favorite diagnosis or dynamic formulation, which he sees in every patient (related, of course, to what the professional himself has been struggling with). This phenomenon ought to be researched systematically sometime.

[4]For an intriguing point of view on schizophrenia which represents a marked shift from traditional thinking, see Laing (1964).

[5]The foregoing observations suggest that if the healthy, adaptive features of the personality were included as a part of individual diagnosis, rather than exclusive emphasis on the pathological, social misuse of diagnosis would be lessened. Of course, there are many other reasons why positive concepts of mental health and the human potentials of a person should be an integral part of diagnostic classification as well as treatment. Investigators such as Allport (1955), Jahoda (1958), and Maslow (1962) are among those who have pioneered this approach. Ackerman (1966), in his chapter, "The Question of Cure," extends even further these concepts by stressing that treatment should not only be concerned with symptom removal and creative well-being, but that self-actualization is only likely to occur when the individual's group, the family, is included in the therapeutic process.

sequences, occurs as a function of the unwitting collusion between the family and the professional in diagnosing one person in the family as a patient with an illness. What is being discussed here is not just the ubiquitous transaction whereby each person in a disturbed close relationship will, because of fears about his own sanity, accuse the other of being crazy, but the process which begins when several members of a family jointly designate another member as the scapegoat "sick one." Bowen (1965) has described this "family projection process" with piercing acumen. There are some parents who unconsciously design a prescription for a child, for instance, to fulfill the sick role; the process may begin before the child is born, and even if the child's inherent personality structure is inimical to the particular mode of behavior prescribed, sooner or later he is "trained" to play the role. The concept of individual psychiatric diagnosis fits in beautifully with these family dynamics. A whole generation of parents, having dutifully absorbed the publicity of the mental health associations that stress recognition of signs of mental illness in the "loved one," frequently becomes learned in psychiatric classification. Since the diagnosis requires confirmation by a professional expert, the parents shop around for one who will officially authenticate the "dreaded" condition with psychiatric observations and psychological tests. (One wonders whether any child taken to a professional in private practice or a clinic has ever been given a clean bill of health.) The dynamics of some families require that one of its members be put away or sent out of the family; this cannot be done conscience-free without "scientific" backing. It is alarming to realize that psychiatrists, clinical psychologists, and social workers have sometimes lent themselves to family extrusion processes which populate foster homes, boarding schools, mental hospitals, prisons, military academies, and institutions for delinquents, the aged, and "mentally ill" children.

Critique of Psychoanalytic Views on Symptoms and on the Family

In a symposium on symptom formation, Lample-DeGroot and Arlow (1963) discussed both Freud's original views (Freud, 1926) plus recent psychoanalytic thinking on symptoms, and these papers were in turn discussed by six other psychoanalysts (Schur et al., 1964). These present remarks, which do not even pretend to give a complete account of the psychoanalytic view on symptoms, are oriented around the highlights of these symposium views as well as certain aspects of the psychoanalytic vantage point which have relevance for this paper.

First of all, psychoanalytic theory does reserve for the concept "symptom" a specific meaning having to do with neuroses. There are a variety of other psychiatric disturbances, according to psychoanalytic thought, which ordinarily are called symptoms, which are not symptoms in the neurotic sense, but inhibitions (such as restrictions in the sexual, eating, or work areas), learned maladaptive behaviors, pathological character traits, and other behavior disorders which may or may not be neurotic (including firesetting, exhibitionism, gambling, enuresis, inadequacy, withdrawal, rage reactions, learning and speech disturbances, criminality, and so forth). Neurotic symptoms are conceived as substitutes in fantasy for appropriate action, whereas character disorders are diagnosed in terms of the whole rhythm of a life where the stereotyped, repetitive patterns of behavior can become the equivalent of symptoms. The behavior disorders share with neurotic symptoms the feature that the unconscious conflicts are not subject to the ego's control. Such conditions as alcoholism, drug addiction, and sexual acting out are looked upon by psychoanalysis as addictive habits which are acquired as secondary complications of depression and character neurosis. Freud maintained that the term symptom should be reserved for the result of the failure of defense against the derivative of an instinctual drive, and there appears to be agreement among psychoanalysts on the following basic course of the process of symptom formation: instinctual demands perceived by the ego as danger—then signal anxiety—then conflict, with eventual emergence of a symptom, representing both substitute gratification and defense. There is also consensus that long and complex mental processes precede the actual eruption of a symptom.

That this fundamental definition is oversimplified is seen in the following sample of technical complications which various psychoanalytic theoreticians have postulated as to how symptoms are formed, attenuated, accentuated, and modified: constitutional intensity of drives; the developmental stage of ego formation; the differentiation of psychic structure required for intrapsychic conflict; the effects of psychic trauma on early ego formation; the stratification of dangers (internal and external) which determine the course of neurotic symptoms; how current experiences can reactivate instinctual regressive wishes which conflict with reality; how a symptom can be an isolated phenomenon which comes and goes, or it can be embedded in the ego for a lifetime, or it can be integrated into the ego organization to become a character trait; how fantasies represent specific versions of how the ego integrates the demands of the id, ego, and superego with reality considerations; the loss of ego functions which are drawn into the neurotic struggles; how symptoms may serve restitutive functions by leading to conflict solution; how symptoms may become libidinized; how symptoms serve secondary gain purposes; and how symptoms can serve adaptive as well as defensive purposes over the life course; and so forth. There do appear to be differences among psychoanalytic thinkers about symptom formation, particularly between those who refer more to Freud's original formulations and those who focus on the developments in ego psychology over the last few decades. These differences appear to revolve around such issues as whether conflict arises from intersystemic (*between* id, ego, superego), or intrasystemic sources (*within* the id, ego, and superego); the role of the external dangers; and the importance of ego functions in symptom formation (as in the case of the secondary anxiety which arises as a consequence of the ego's reaction to the symptom, or the issue of whether the role of the ego is limited to defense alone).

Granting that Freud's instinct theory has been historically considered as a profound contribution to the understanding of man, there has been considerable questioning over the years of the formulation that all symptoms are derived from the threatened emergence of an instinctual wish, and that the conflicts underlying symptom formation are all intrapsychic—that is, conflicts among the different parts of the mind of one person. The trend of psychoanalytic thinking toward examining factors outside the intrapsychic structure of the individual, what the psychoanalysts call "external dangers," is not just restricted to such cultural Neo-Freudians as Sullivan, Horney, Fromm, and Erikson. The psychoanalytic investigator Loewenstein, for example, states that "They (defenses) may remain mechanisms involving mainly the internal processes of the individual. Or they may, either to begin with or at a later stage, be entangled with external dangers and thus with external objects. . . . The enormous diversity of psychopathological phenomena forces us to conclude that while this intersystemic conflict is a necessary condition, it is not a sufficient one to account for the variety of phenomena we see." (Schur et al., 1964). (p. 156) The British psychoanalyst Fairbairn (1954) has recast psychoanalytic theory even more drastically by positing that the fundamental fact about human nature is not instinct gratification but the libidinal drive toward good object-relationships. He constructed a revised theory of the psychoses and psychoneuroses by postulating that schizoid and depressive states are the two fundamental types of reaction in bad-object relationships—the two basic or ultimate dangers to be escaped from—and that paranoia, obsessions, hysteria, and phobias are four different defensive techniques for dealing with bad internal objects. Fairbairn's concepts, the revolutionary nature of which have yet to be appreciated, provide one of the first theoretical models for traversing and integrating the internal and external worlds of man.

It would be inaccurate to state that orthodox psychoanalysis does not take external or reality factors into account in both the etiology and treatment of psychopathology. Neurotic symptoms are postulated as resulting when the ego resorts to pathological use of defenses in failing to synthesize instinctual impulses, the demands of the superego, and the demands of the environment. With characteristic perceptive genius Freud identified the fundamental extrinsic determinants of human distress when he classified the external dangers as loss of the object, loss of the penis (castration), loss of the object's love, and loss of the superego's love. All these external dangers, however, were seen as later displacements and determinants of the irreducible danger of a state of helplessness. Freud (1926) also emphasized that "an instinctual demand often only becomes an (internal) danger because its satisfaction would bring on an external danger—that is, because the internal danger represents an external one. On the other hand, the external (real) danger must also have managed to become internalized if it is to be significant for the ego." (pp. 167–168). When psychoanalysts are asked whether they consider the external or internal processes more important, they are likely to reply that they are of equal importance.

The foregoing notwithstanding, one gets the curious feeling in reading the psychoanalytic literature that the patient lives in a vacuum, that the intrapsychic world is pretty much of a closed system, and the environment is largely treated as a constant. To be sure, there are occasional references to such exogenous factors as the primal scene, or the effects of poor mothering upon ego development, or some unusual circumstance in the patient's life, and there is even recognition that neurotic parents bring up neurotic children. Most psychoanalysts, however, operationally function from the assumption that it is not the environment that makes people sick (even though Freud, in his philosophical writings on applied psychoanalysis, does discuss the deleterious effects of society on human adjustment), but that *people do it to themselves* via fantasy, and intrapsychic work, and elaboration of what goes on outside. It is taken for granted by psychoanalysts that people behave largely on the basis of their fantasies, which are highly distorted versions of outside events and people, particularly of the family members. A favorite story of psychoanalysts in this connection is the one about the little boy patient who describes his father as a vicious monster, and when the analyst meets the father he (the father) turns out to be a nice, meek, mild guy. Without disputing the validity of fantasy as a stimulus for behavior, of fantasy distortion and psychic elaboration, nonetheless there are other considerations which suggest that the psychoanalytic construction (the child's anticipation of retaliation because of death wishes toward the father) may not be the whole story:

1. Fathers meeting with the doctor of their children are likely to behave in a nice, mild, meek way. The degrees of behavioral freedom in this relationship-situation are quite limited.
2. Father's transference to his son (such as of destructive attitudes derived from his relationship to his own father) is likely to be revealed only under special conditions, and rarely outside the privacy of the home.
3. Father may indeed be meek and mild and never express sadism, or even anger, toward his son; as a matter of fact, father may never get angry at anyone, including his wife, and his son may be furious at father's abdication of his parental role, or the way father goes to him and asks, "What are you going to do about the way your mother treats me?"
4. Father's relationship to his son depends, in part, on the nature of his marriage relationship—which is not observable to the analyst.
5. One wonders whether the family emotional system can ever be reconstructed from the therapy productions of one person.

To elaborate on these points a bit, some psychoanalysts have stated that they do not need to see the family in order to know what is going on in the family situation, that they are able to filter through the misrepresentations of their patient and thus get a pretty good picture of what the family members are like. In one sense, psychoanalysts, because of the tremendous amount of detailed information they get from patients over a long period of time, are in a better position than anyone else to know and appreciate the psychic pain and suffering which arises from what people in close relationships do to each other. Yet, psychoanalysts do not see the families of their patients (particularly adult patients), and they presume that the family dynamics are internalized in the mind of the patient. Because they do not see family members together, they could not know that certain important behaviors and attitudes come into existence only in the actual physical presence of a close other.[6] Many of these attitudes and behaviors of a patient, moreover, are lived through and acted out in relationships and transactions with family members, and therefore are not reproduced in the transference relationship with the analyst.

Experience in family therapy has indicated that the developmental process in personality is of much longer duration than had been thought, and that symptoms or disordered behavior can be viewed as adaptive, nay, necessary responses to the intimate social systems with which the person is involved throughout all his life. The most powerful social influence is, perforce, the family, yet psychoanalytic theory has been ambiguous and contradictory about the role of the family in the etiology of emotional disturbance. Freud, admittedly, was the first person to recognize in a systematic way the parts that love, hate, jealousy, ambivalence, and generational differences which arise from the inherent nature of family relationships, play in the development of psychopathology. There was even a publication in 1921 of the psychoanalyst Flugel on *The Psychoanalytic Study of the Family.* Psychoanalytic theory, which utilizes a family dynamic in its nuclear concept of the oedipus complex, however, deals with the intrapsychic struggle over the oedipal wishes, or with its wider social aspects in the culture at large. In *Totem and Taboo, Civilization and Its Discontents,* and *Group Psychology* Freud proposed that the function of the oedipus complex was to protect the family from disruption—for only if incest and patricide are outlawed can the family and thus society survive. Yet though in one sense psychoanalytic thought sees the survival of man as dependent on the preservation of the family, the lack of focus on the transactional dynamics of the family itself represents a real gap in the theory—the gap existing between the individual and the wider culture.

As is well known, Freud initially accepted at face value the stories of incest and family violence which his patients told him, and later came to believe that these reports were based on fantasies created by unconscious instinctual forces. One wonders whether he set the tone for the pendulum to swing too far in that direction, just as he set the precedent for analysts not to get involved with the family of the patient. From time to time other psychoanalytic investigators have drawn attention to external family factors. For example, Ferenczi wrote of parental seduction, the imposition of adult genital love on the child. And Johnson and Szurek (1954), among the precursors of current family theory, utilizing the method of concurrent

---

[6]Gaarder (1965), a psychoanalyst, has presented evidence to suggest that there is one condition of the ego in which the internalized representation of the object exists in the *presence* of the object and another condition of the ego in which the internalized representation of a given object exists in the *absence* of the object.

treatment of patients and their parents (but not conjointly), found that murderous or incestuous or psychological assaults actually did occur with great frequency in their schizophrenic sample; the schizophrenic delusions were found to reflect these verified traumatic assaults (Beckett et al., 1956). Continuing their work with school phobias and antisocial behavior, Johnson and Szurek (1954) found that the parents consciously and unconsciously sanctioned and fostered the child's acting out of the parents' poorly integrated forbidden impulses. Although the parent got vicarious gratification of his impulses through the symptoms of the child, at the same time he was punitive toward the child for misbehaving (Johnson, 1953; Johnson and Szurek, 1954). Freud was certainly not oblivious of the actual reality of the family environment, particularly in his case histories. Still, even in the case histories there were some notable omissions; for example, he did not mention that during the course of Little Hans's treatment Hans's parents were in the process of getting a divorce and indeed did divorce when the treatment was over. For a reexamination of the case of Little Hans from the standpoint of family dynamics see Strean (1967).

Whatever the genesis of symptoms, psychoanalytic theory does touch upon the interpersonal effects of symptoms when it deals with the defenses against symptoms, spontaneous cures, and the concept of secondary gain. (As a matter of fact, psychoanalysts, when they hear about transactional phenomena, usually attempt to fit them into their framework under the category of secondary gain.) Classically, secondary gain comes into the picture once the symptoms are established; the concept refers to the process whereby symptoms get rewarded socially, help the patient avoid unpleasant duties, provoke sympathy, bring about dependency gratification, increase status, and so forth. Secondary gain maneuvers, whether conscious or unconscious, however, cannot function unless other people, particularly the close relationships, "cooperate"; symptomatic payoffs require a sympathetic medium. The transactional meaning of secondary gain will be explored later in this paper.

In the section which follows, an attempt will be made to document the theory that symptoms are formed, chosen, faked, traded, maintained, and removed as a function of the nature of the relationship context within which they are intimately embedded. In essence, some symptoms of individuals, rather than being viewed solely as compromises arising from internal conflicts between instinctual gratification and defense, can be seen as evolving from the universal conflict between the drive toward autonomy and loyalty to the relationship system. Symptoms can balance family forces as well as intrapsychic forces.

Background of the Family Transactional Viewpoint

The family transactional approach represents the blending of developments in social-psychological theory, psychoanalytic dynamic thinking and ego psychology, general systems theory, communication theory, child development, group dynamics, sociology of the family, and family therapy. The forerunners of this viewpoint, then, existed in a number of scientific theoretical and applied fields. Academic psychology, which has traditionally dealt with the individual as the focus of study, has fractionated variables from the whole person and studied them in isolation (as in the study of sensation, perception, affect, will, cognition, imagery, and so forth). Personality traits, learning capacities, intelligence are generally considered in academic psychology as properties of the individual, irrespective of social context and interpersonal meaning. John Dewey, who recognized that the individual cannot be separated from the group, once commented that all psychology is social psychology. In social psychology itself Kurt Lewin's field theory (1951) stressed that the determinants of behavior are a function of the life space or total psychological situation for an individual or a group. The pioneering work of Lewin was congruent with other movements in the social sciences, called by such various names as configurationism, situationalism, field theory, or the system approach. Dewey and Bentley (1949) provided a philosophical rationale for the transactional viewpoint. L. K. Frank (1957) expounded that "we need to think in terms of circular, reciprocal relations and feedbacks, both positive and negative, through which the component members of the field participate in and thereby create the field of the whole, which field in turn regulates and patterns their individual activities. This is a circular, reciprocal relation, not serial cause and effect, stimulus and response relation" (p. 12). A conference of social scientists, published in the book *Toward a Unified Theory of Human Behavior* (Grinker, 1956) further explored systems theory as a general integrative way of organizing biological, psychological, and cultural phenomena; all systems were considered by the conference participants as having the common properties of homeostasis, transaction (reciprocal relationship among all parts of the field, and not interaction, which is an effect of one system on another), and communication of information. From the transactional vantage point, human behavior is seen as evolving, not only from the past, but from the unitary nature of the individual-environment as a total process in space and time.

It follows from this point of view that the concept of causation acquires a different meaning, in that specific causes are not sought for specific events; even the principle of multiple determination is not adequate. Some day scientists may not even have in their vocabulary the expression, "What caused that?" Frank in his article, "Causation: An Episode in the History of Thought" (1934) stated that if social science were not so devoted to the causal principle there would be more readiness to entertain a less artificial and clumsy theory of human behavior. While things do not just happen, and therefore are caused in a sense, all events are considered as occurring within a configuration of transactional fields, fluid process, and concomitant variation. One neglected work in social psychology which makes a provocative attempt at integrating personal and situational phenomena within a single conceptual framework is Coutu's *Emergent Human Nature* (1949).

There have been some notable applications of these viewpoints in several different areas of study. The Kaiser Foundation research group, for instance, operating under the assumption that all behavior has some interpersonal meaning, developed a method for measuring the interpersonal purpose of any given action (Leary, 1957). Using 16 generic interpersonal mechanisms which reflected almost any motive which can be expressed by one human being to another, they studied the interpersonal reactions that individuals "pull" from others. One of their interesting findings was that people train others to respond to them in a certain way (e.g. to be exploited), often with astonishing rapidity. In the field of psychotherapy, Berne (1961) has developed a transactional approach to individual and social psychiatry; his constructs of adult, parent, and child ego states, and his analysis of scripts and repetitive sets of social maneuvers (games that people play with each other) have been significant contributions. Kobler and Stotland (1964), deviating from the usual view of suicide as stemming from forces within the individual (depression, suicidal drive, and others), did a transactional investigation of suicides which occurred in a mental hospital and found that the incidence increased as a function of the declining morale of a whole hospital. Suicide attempt was seen by them as a cry for help and a demand for change in a relationship, and if the response was hopeless and helpless actual suicide was more likely to occur. Sampson, Messinger, and Towne (1964), in a thorough, long-range study of schizophrenic women, found that the clinical condition of the patient should never be regarded as a phenomenon in itself, apart from the fabric of the patient's family life; the prehospitalization, hospitalization, and posthospitalization phases are interinvolved with a continuous, dynamic family process. These authors emphasize the need for studying the interaction between the implicit features of institutional practices and family processes (for instance, hospital procedures often reinforce regressive patterns by having the spouse sign out and be responsible for their partner while home on leave). Spiegel and Kluckhohn (1954), in the fields of family sociology and anthropology, utilized a transactional approach, to postulate that the mental illness of an individual can only be understood within a total system of subsystems which are complexly interrelated. They state that while a component system, such as the individual or the family or the culture, can be isolated and studied as an entity, none have any greater "reality" than the other. The intent of the present paper does not allow for a summary of the revolutionary contributions of family therapy itself. The literature in family therapy is beginning to grow (Ackerman, 1966; Bowen, 1961; Boszormenyi-Nagy and Framo, 1965; Friedman et al., 1965; Haley and Hoffman, 1967; Satir, 1964).

Introduction to the Family Transactional View of Symptoms

In this present section, departing from the conventional, simplistic view of psychological symptoms as stemming from a central illness process, some of the findings of family therapy experience will be used to present a new, more intricate conception of symptom formation, symptom choice, symptom maintenance, symptom sharing and exchange, and symptom reduction as a function of the interplay between individual and family relationship systems. It is, of course, impossible at this stage of understanding to study simultaneously the total range of a transactional field. The family context is focused upon here, not only because of its manageability, but because of the conviction that the family is the most vital, lasting, and influential force in human life. Such social contexts as the community, work, friendship networks, and school can never approach the unique and powerful effects of family,—not only because of its close blood ties and personality-forming influences but because of the special rules which apply to family relationships.

Many problems present themselves in shifting to this new frame of reference, not the least of which is the lack of a language to express field or contextual concepts. For instance, the very term "symptom" comes from an individual, medical framework, and in a certain sense it is inappropriate to apply this word to pathological phenomena of a system complex like the family. If one wished to conceptualize family pathology it would be necessary to have some standard or model of family health or "normality"—an immense undertaking which has hardly begun (Otto, 1963; Pollak, 1957). It certainly makes little sense to use for family diagnosis a diagnostic classification system developed from individual psychology.

In this paper the term symptom is used in the broadest sense, encompassing not only subjective complaints of individuals, but the observations of others (family members, associates, professionals) that something is wrong with someone's behavior, thinking, or feeling. People present their difficulties in the only way they know how, running the full spectrum of emotional pain or dissatisfaction with oneself or others, whether in the area of physical, personal, or social disturbance. This admittedly loose use of the term "symptom" has the shortcoming of being individually oriented, as well as lacking scientific specificity. Nonetheless, using "symptom" temporarily in this commodious way does reflect the way it is used operationally by both laymen and professionals, and enables the writer to communicate while attempting to bridge the transition from individual theory to family transactional theory.

Some Family Transactional Situations
Related to Symptom Production, Symptom Choice,
Symptom Maintenance and Reduction, Pseudosymptoms,
and the Sharing and Exchange of Symptoms

The following series of family-relationship situations is intended as suggestive rather than exhaustive, and no particular importance should be attached to the order or sequence, with the exception of the extended discussion of "irrational role assignment" in symptom production, which is considered fundamental. The situations, further, are not mutually exclusive. The case material excerpts do an injustice to the complexity of multiple dynamic levels which are simultaneously operating, and it should be recognized that each situation is abstracted from a transactional whole for illustrative purposes.

While the phenomena to be described are probably universal and present to some extent in all families, they function more pervasively and can be most strikingly observed in families described by Bowen (1966) as being at the lower end of his scale of differentiation. Furthermore, though, of course, symptoms appear in anyone, most of the situations to be cited focus on the symptoms of the children—usually the immediate stimulus which propels the family to seek help.

Symptom-Producing Family Situations

Irrational Role Assignment or Projective Transference Distortion

Human needs operate most forcefully in the family setting, with struggles over love, hate, rejection, hurt, gratification, and jealousy being a continuous dynamic process from one generation to the next. The implicit or explicit irrational[7] assignment of roles in the family (role being defined as a pattern or type of behavior which a person builds up in terms of what significant others expect or demand of him) reflects unconscious attempts by the parents to master, reenact, or externalize their intrapsychic conflicts about these powerful human needs, derived from relationship experiences in their family of origin. Before discussing further this concept of *interpersonal resolution of inner conflict,* it is necessary to take a brief sojourn into intrapsychic psychology. Among the theories which can provide an explanation of the genesis of irrational family role assignment and intrafamilial transference distortion, there is one model which to the present writer best fits the clinical facts. W. Fairbairn (1954), elaborating on some of Freud's and Melanie Klein's concepts, has postulated that man's need for a satisfying object relationship constitutes the fundamental motive of life. His object-relationship approach is contrasted with Freud's theory of the pleasure principle and instinctual gratification as primary in man; for Fairbairn, instinct is a function of the ego, pleasure is incidental to the object-seeking, and aggression is a reaction to frustration when the sought-after object denies satisfaction. When the parents' behavior is interpreted as rejection, desertion, or persecution, the child, unable to give up the external object or change it in outer reality, handles the frustration and disappointment by internalizing the loved-hated parent in order to master and control the object in the inner psychic world, where it is repressed and retained as an introject, a psychological representative. It is the emotional relationship be-

---

[7]Conscious, formal, instrumental family roles, described by sociologists, are not under discussion here because they are not very pertinent to psychopathology; it is the discrepancy between the irrational, informal role assignment and the natural family role that creates the difficulties.

tween the self and some external figure which is internalized, not feelings as such; moreover, these internal objects are not just fantasies but become sub-identities and part of the structure of the personality. The bad (unsatisfying, exciting-frustrating) object, according to Fairbairn, is split into the dependent, unrequited love need (libidinal ego) and the dangerous, rejecting object (antilibidinal ego). Good objects are retained as satisfying memories, and the ideal object, the nucleus of the original object divested of its exciting and frustrating elements, can be safely loved by the central ego as a desexualized and perfect object. The bad internal objects remain as "internal saboteurs" or warring forces in the inner world— furious, guilty, hungry, anxious, conflictual—consuming psychic energy which the central ego should have available for evaluation of reality and investment in external relationships. The earlier in life splitting occurs, and the more painful and frustrating the external-object world, the more dependence on the inner object world and incomplete the personality, a state of affairs with grave consequences for the development of psychopathology and symptom formation (thus, an individual with early personality splits—say, resulting from early loss of a parent—is likely to develop the symbiotic relationship dilemma: yearning for merger and fusion with those he loves so that they are part of each other, but then feeling possessed, tied, trapped, and losing his personality, thus having to break away for independence, resulting in feeling lost, isolated, lonely, and depressed). During the course of development of the individual, external, real figures may be assimilated in successive strata or by fusion into the existing bad-object situations; other people are seen only in terms of the individual's own libidinal wishes toward them, or as carrying his/her own guilt-laden, denied, split-off traits. More important for the present subject, life situations in outer reality are not only unconsciously interpreted in the light of the inner-object world, resulting in distorted expectations of other people, *but active, unconscious attempts are made to force and change close relationships into fitting the internal role models.*

This theoretical formulation, greatly oversimplified in this presentation (the reader is referred to the original sources),—while it sounds abstract and easy to caricature as "objects bouncing around in the psyche like little men," nonetheless is supported by innumerable clinical observations in that a variety of puzzling human predicaments become deciphered. For example, it helps explain why the psychology of intimate relationships is different from the psychology of other social relationships, and it sheds light on why some people have to select object attachments that bring them so much distress. It helps understanding of why so many people can become vocationally successful or accomplished in social-adjustment terms, yet be unable to tolerate the intimacy of a close relationship or form a viable marriage.[8] The inner psychological splitting of which Fairbairn

[8]Aldous Huxley's novel *Genius and the Goddess* (1955) gives a fascinating account of an internationally famous scientist's infantile behavior in the home. Research in the behavioral sciences, which usually uses social-adjustment criteria of maturity or mental health, should take into account how people function in their intimate family relationships as well as their capacity to function in the outside world. There are many renowned, gifted people with positions of great responsibility whose marriages or children are very disturbed.

speaks can have its real, external counterparts; individuals will seek representatives of the libidinal and antilibidinal objects in their external relationships. For instance, some people are able to maintain a love relationship with one person only if someone else is related to as the enemy (for instance, a woman fantasizes a love relationship with her psychotherapist while her husband is seen as a monster). Or one child in the family may get all the concern and "love" while another is ignored or subject to unreasoning prejudice (children in both these positions lose this game—the favored child has to struggle with the guilt, and the rejected child may fight eternally to gain the favor impossible to obtain, and feels murderous toward the sibling).

Henry Dicks (1967) was one of the first to translate Fairbairnian concepts into an interactional framework, focusing specifically on the marriage relationship. After recognizing the levels of social-cultural values and of personal norms, conscious judgments, and expectations in marriage, Dicks focuses on the unconscious, object-relational needs which flow between marriage partners. Discussing mate selection, Dicks states that:

> The partner attracts because he or she represents or promises a re-discovery of an important lost aspect of the subject's own personality, which, owing to earlier conditioning, had been recast as an object for attack or denial. At the height of the courting or mating phase, biological sexual urgency often obscures this potential source of future tension. The conscious aims and purposes are later invaded by hitherto latent dispositions to re-enact an intrapsychic pattern in the new setting of the marriage, which becomes to a varying extent a projection screen for such unresolved tensions *in* the individual. (pp. 30–31)

Dicks then brings in interactional concepts when he discusses the dovetailing of two inner worlds in the collusive marriage:

> This stressed the need for unconscious *complementariness,* a kind of division of function by which each partner supplied part of a set of qualities, the sum of which created a complete dyadic unit. This joint personality or integrate enabled each half to rediscover lost aspects of their primary object relations, which they had split off or repressed, and which they were in their involvement with their spouse, re-experiencing by projective identification. The sense of belonging can be understood on the hypothesis that at deeper levels there are perceptions of the partner and consequent attitudes towards him or her *as if* the other was part of oneself. The partner is then treated according to how this aspect of oneself was valued: spoilt and cherished, or denigrated and persecuted. (p. 69)

The partners in the disturbed marriage mutually use scapegoating, projection, and representation by the opposite in their unconscious attempts to force the spouse to fit or repudiate the split-off internal objects, even when the partner's real personality drastically contradicts the projection. Idealization is postulated by Dicks as being the link between all of the defense mechanisms in the marital field, whereby spouses attribute to the partner those bad feelings they must not own themselves or else make the partner all good while themselves taking on the badness. Dicks (1967) believes that warring couples have a deep, unconscious commitment to each other and need to protect their investment in the spouse. He states, "By protecting the image of the partner (for example as a 'drunk' or as 'sexually inadequate' or 'slovenly,' and so forth) they are in the other secretly cherishing the rejected, bad libidinal ego with its resentments and demands while *within* the dyadic system they can persecute it in an interpersonal framework." (pp. 122–123)

In previous publications (Framo, 1965a, 1965b, 1971) the present writer has attempted to widen Fairbairn's object-relations theory beyond marital interaction to include the several generations of the family. Without going into family-*system* theory at this point, the present focus is on "irrational role assignment" and "projective transference distortion" involving the children, who are also dynamic agents in the field. The writer has previously stated, "The various children in the family come to represent valued or feared expectations of the parents, based on parental introjects; sometimes the roles of the children are chosen for them even before they are born (such as in the case of the child who is conceived to 'save the marriage'). . . . In every family of multiple siblings there is 'the spoiled one,' 'the conscience of the family,' and 'the wild one'; the assigned roles are infinite." (Framo, 1965a). Boszormenyi-Nagy (1965c) has also discussed role assignment in the larger-than-dyadic system and, speaking of the "captivity of object-role assignment," stated that:

> The unconscious fantasy through which the parent assigns his own parents' role to his children may result in bizarre, inappropriate actions. The connection between acting-out patterns and their underlying needs, such as the one for the assignment of parental roles, may be completely unconscious. Such regressive fantasies of the parents may result in demands for premature responsibility on the part of the children, who may comply with the parents' wish through precocious development. Feelings of hatred and wish for revenge originally connected with a parental introject can be acted out toward the child in unconscious transference, as illustrated by the tragic cases of severe child beatings and murder. (p. 95)

Although not explicitly within a Fairbairnian framework, the work of the family therapists Bowen (1965) and Brodey (1959) is congruent with this thinking. Bowen's conclusions are described in chapter 1 (Bowen, p. 4). Brodey utilizes the mechanism of externalization (defined as projection plus the selective use of reality for verification of the projection) to describe the narcissistic relationships (defined as a relationship with a projected part of the self as mirrored in the behavior of another) which obtain in the more undifferentiated family. He notes that "the inner world is transferred to the outside with little modification, and the part of the outer world attended to is selected *only* as it validates the projections, *other impinging realities being omitted*" (Brodey, 1959; p. 385). Brodey (1959) further describes the disturbed family in the following formulation:

> A network of narcissistic relationships, in which ego-dystonic aspects of the self are externalized by each family member and regrouped into allegorical roles, each epitomizing a part of the major conflict which was acted out in the original marriage. . . . The constellation of roles allows the internal conflict of each member to be acted out within the family, rather than within the self, and each family member attempts to deal with his own conflicts by changing the other. (p. 392)

Speaking of the very young children in such a family, Brodey states, "The infant perhaps would learn that survival within this relationship depended on expressing his own needs in a way and at a time conforming with the mother's projected expectation. The long-term reinforcement of the needs which happened to match the mother's, and the frustration of the needs omitted by the mother, would then alter the child's behavior in the direction of validating the mother's projection. (p. 385)

When the projection process operates in more extreme fashion, every aspect of the child—his appearance, the way he crawls, walks, talks, cries, laughs, burps, and so forth is interpreted within the framework of the assigned traits or role, as proof that the trait is indeed present.[9] Aspects of the child which refute the assignment are blocked out, denied, or rationalized away. (Psychotherapists to whom parents have brought a child for treatment are often struck by the discrepancy between the parents' over-alertness to one behavior of the child, such as lying or stealing, and their indifference to another aspect of the child, such as being withdrawn or friendless.) In accordance with these views, Laing (1962) has stated, "we are denoting something other than the psychoanalytic term 'projection.' The one person does not wish merely to have the other as a hook on which to hang his projections. He strives to find in the other, or to induce the other to become, the very *embodiment* of that other whose cooperation is required as 'complement' of the particular identity he feels impelled to sustain." (p. 101)

One can ask the question: Since the parent's projections are his and his alone, why not treat him on an individual basis? The answer is that these kind of people,

---

[9]I am indebted to Carl Whitaker for the following incident. A father came to a family therapy session with Dr. Whitaker with the conviction that his son was a "Mongolian Idiot" because he had read in the *Ladies' Home Journal* that such children have a wide space between the large toe and the next toe. Dr. Whitaker skillfully handled the situation by requesting that everyone in the room take off their shoes and socks, and after examining everyone's toes the group concluded that the psychiatric resident who was present was the "Mongolian Idiot."

even though they have a great impact on their intimates, bring others to therapy and never seek it for themselves; family therapy is probably the only way to involve them in a therapeutic setting.

A number of family therapists and theoreticians have independently corroborated the phenomenon of "irrational role assignment" or "projective transference distortion" which occurs in families. Although the phenomenon has been hinted at in the individual framework, it was not until the advent of family therapy that it was observed in full force, and its implications realized. Prior to family therapy, it was not "seen" because psychotherapists, due to cultural and professional taboos, had never observed families interacting together in a diagnostic or therapeutic setting. One can ask what functions the projection process serves for the individual family members and the family system, aside from avoidance of inner anxiety and the maintenance of psychological equilibrium. Projective transferences, externalization, vindictive fantasies, vicarious participations all serve the function of recapturing the symbolically retained old love-objects who have their representation in current real family members, thus delaying the pain of loss and mourning. Object possession, perhaps the chief underlying motive behind irrational role assignment, helps prevent individuation, which can result in the catastrophe of separation, the old dread of abandonment, and facing of the fact that one has irretrievably lost one's mother or father. In many of the families treated, the parents have, in fact, lost one or both parents at an early age, and one can observe the desperate efforts to keep the children tied to them, notwithstanding impassioned statements to the contrary or the family seemingly flying apart with hostility. In the more undifferentiated families there is no opportunity for the children to experiment with a wide range of flexible roles necessary for functioning outside the restrictive, limited family culture, and if one of the purposes of family life is to prepare the young for life outside the family, these families fail. On this point Boszormenyi-Nagy (1965c) has stated:

> If the nuclear family remains ideally adjusted to self-perpetuation after the offspring have grown to biological maturity, one can assume that certain dynamic facets of the family's life support stagnation. Perhaps the parents cannot let the grown-up children go, despite their best conscious intentions; or the children may have grown up to be frightful of true individuation and of genuine extra-familial involvement. Naturally, the period in which the offspring attain separation age (launching stage) is stressful for any family. We have found, especially, that many families comprising schizophrenic members are closed social systems which tend to discourage such intruders as boyfriends, girlfriends, potential marriage mates, and so forth. Of the many possible criteria of family health or maturity, we can emphasize the one which, by flexible preparedness for giving up the family's togetherness, itself allows individuation and separation through formation of new relationships on the growing offspring's part. (p. 307)

The present author believes that the phenomena being described occur in some measure in all families, as a basic fact of human existence. It should not be necessary to emphasize that the projection processes resulting in role allocation, like any other family-system phenomena, are not the result of intent on the part of the family members. Even labeling the processes unconscious does not communicate how they have a life and rhythmic, gyroscopic force of their own, outside the plan or control of anyone involved, as in any group process that takes over as a regulatory mechanism beyond what anyone desires or expects. The "family way" of seeing and doing things becomes automatic and unquestioned, like the air one breathes. It is very difficult for anyone, no matter how grown-up or mature, to avoid the family role assignment when he is in the presence of his family. Whether his role is that of "the quiet one," "the smart one," "the slick one," "the trouble-maker," "father's protector," or any one of countless assignments, he will find himself behaving accordingly despite himself. The family role can appear incomprehensible, strange, or even ludicrous when viewed by outsiders—"the fighter of the family" may be the smallest, weakest looking member, or "the crazy one" may be the only family member who makes sense. Years of "training" went into the designation, considered as an absolute given and "ex cathedra" in some families; the assignment is further reinforced by family myths and rules and is ritualized into the family structure. The most powerful family persuasion to bring someone into line who has strayed from his role is to impute disloyalty to the errant one and, in some families, veiled threats of emotional or even legal disowning are used on those who resist the symmetrical role. Still, everyone needs a family, and those who cut themselves off from their family pay a costly price, as the statistics on high rates of psychiatric disorder and suicide for isolates will testify. One risks a great deal in going against the projections. Those who renounce their family of origin and have nothing to do with their parents or siblings tend to repeat with others the old conflicts; others spend a lifetime trying unsuccessfully to get back into the old system. Many people never really leave home when they marry, by living in the same neighborhood as the parents and marrying the kind of people who, perhaps because they need a family for themselves, will allow frequent contact with the family of origin. Still others deceive themselves into believing that individual psychotherapy or analysis will unstick them from the family emotional system. A universal dilemma consists of the question: how can one keep relating to his family and yet stay free of the irrational aspects of the emotional system and be a person in his own right?

What does all of this have to do with symptoms? It should be obvious that the entire range of symptomatology can come into play concomitant with being boxed in by a "transference fix"—all the way from the psychotic disorders to learning disabilities, tics, stuttering, overactivity, anxiety attacks, sleepwalking, withdrawal, rage reactions, obstructionism, and all the other symptoms usually viewed as properties of "the patient" alone. Laing (1962) has said, "There are many reactions, so far relatively unexplored by interpersonal psychology, to being seen not as one takes oneself to be, but as the other sees one." (p.100) The present author has previously stated, "To be on the receiving end of a projection of someone else's internal image can be a particularly frustrating and perplexing experience if that someone else is a vitally needed person; you must be seen as malevolent, spoiled, prematurely grown-up, deceitful, or what have you, and nothing can be said or done to change this view." (Boszormenyi-Nagy, 1965c, p. 153) If a father, say, zeroes in on his son as the cause of his misery, one can empathize with the hurt, bewilderment, and futility of this child who cannot get father to like him even if he sacrifices his life. Projections of those who do not matter can be easily brushed aside. We do not understand the complicated factors which determine whether a given child accepts the designated role, fights it, internalizes it, pretends to accept it, flees from it, is conflicted about it, or reacts to it in some other way.[10] In general, it would seem that some symptoms are developed as a function of efforts to escape the role assignment, and others as reflections of the designation. Some symptoms are manifested only within the family culture, as bargaining positions or as stakes in the intrafamilial relationship struggles, while others come into play only outside the family. (Family members often say, "But when I'm not with my family I'm an entirely different person.")

Children whose family role is limited to the reciprocation of the projection and who, in order to maintain a shaky identity, *become* the role set for them, whole and undigested, are likely to have the family role as the foundation of their personality, and consequently are high risks for psychosis. Ryckoff et al. (1959) have explored how stereotyped roles are maintained in the families of schizophrenics, and the disastrous consequences which can follow attempts to change the roles. The psychotic outbreak may come when attempts to establish the role (as with "the baby of the family") are inappropriate outside the family culture; for this person, being outside the family is like being a fish out of water. Because everyone has *some* autonomous strivings, there may be periodic attempts to establish relationships outside the family in the form of "proxy" family relationships; but these kinds of outside relationships are fraught with instability, since the kinds of people who lend themselves to such an arrangement have their own irrational demands to make. When such outside relationships fail, the individual may renounce all extrafamilial relationships and settle for the family role, feeling that the family system, however crazy, is at least predictable and seems more real. Another reaction to wholesale incorporation of the role assignment is to break away violently from the family, to cop out and become a drifter, with life being based on

[10]Not under discussion in this paper are some identifiable factors which can affect how irrational role assignments are handled by the child—such as basic personality differences in children, whether one fixed role is assigned with the collusion of the whole family or whether various roles are ascribed, the effect of the sibling subsystem or extended family on diluting or reinforcing the process, fortuitous factors such as opportunities that the child has for extrafamilial relationships, the capacity of the child to gain distance from the role or to select from, change, or integrate the projected roles, and so forth.

a refutation of the parents; this kind of individual will often suffer from the kinds of symptoms described by the existentialists, that of alienation, lack of meaning or connectedness with life. Some of the rebellious ones unconsciously arrange their lives in a way which guarantees their being pulled back into the old system (such as by forming a disastrous marriage from which the parents have to rescue, or getting in trouble with the law, thus inviting parental intervention.) Just as there are symptoms which insure one staying in the family system, preventing true individuation, so there are symptoms which are "designed" to help one get out of the family. For example, a child finds the home situation so unbearable that he behaves in such extreme fashion that institutionalization is required. Being removed from the family in this way cannot be interpreted as really wanting to leave, which carries implications of being disloyal. One adolescent seen at the juvenile court had been setting a series of fires, and at one of the fires he left his wallet containing his name and address. This boy's father had deserted the family, and mother began drinking heavily. He often had to undress his mother to put her to bed. Once, when she remonstrated with him about his getting in trouble, he said, "Mom, I'll make a deal with you; if you stop drinking, I promise I'll behave."

Some children, in response to irrational projection, develop a negative identity and exaggerate, with a vengeance, what they are led to believe they are; accordingly, they may act out at home, in school, or in the community with a variety of behavior problems (destructiveness, truancy, stealing, unmanageableness, and others). Still others may play-act at the role while they are with their family, always feeling phony, as if they have a false self; this kind of child may be "good" at home and a holy terror at school, or vice versa. Such children often develop character disturbances of the "as if" variety, going through life as if it were a charade, and their neurotic symptoms feel ego-alien; they may state in treatment, "I don't know why I do or feel these things—it isn't me." These individuals do not really know who they are. Those children who struggle internally with their part-identities and their ambivalence about the role assignment and their parents, are more likely to develop the kind of intrapsychic conflict which leads to the classical neurotic symptoms pf phobias, obsessions and compulsions, or depressions. Some children unconsciously accept the appellation and consciously assail it. Many adolescent suicides are aborted resolutions of these conflicts, resulting in punishing the parents from the grave. The victimization which occurs within poor ghetto families, documented by Rainwater (1967), Pavenstedt (1965), and Minuchin et al. (1967), has devastating effects on the identity development of children. Intense feelings of rage are often heir to real and projective exploitation, and since the fury often cannot be vented in the family, it is frequently displaced outside in the form of crimes of violence, riots, and even assassination of public figures.

In the case illustration which follows, the irrational role projection or intrafamilial transference distortion process is obvious and massive. Usually, the process operates in much more subtle fashion.

Case-in-Point.   Mr. and Mrs. Baker, in their determination to prove that their son Joe, age 17, was "schizophrenic," would go to any length to find corroboration of this diagnosis by professionals, and to greater lengths to demonstrate that they were good parents, as witness the fact that they never argued with each other and that their other son George, age 14, and their daughter Grace, were so "normal." The parents said they "sensed something different" about Joe from the time he was born. The parents believed, moreover, that Joe was a reincarnation of Father's mother, who had been in and out of mental hospitals as a schizophrenic most of her life. Father felt that Joe was not "all-boy," and decided to turn his upbringing over to his wife and mother-in-law, who lived in an adjoining house with an interconnecting passageway between the two homes. He had nothing to do with his first son, and when George was born he felt he got a second chance to have a "real boy," subsequently investing his aspirations in his second son. Joe, symbiotically close with mother and grandmother, was teased and beaten up at school for being a sissy, and in response to his father's withdrawal, the suffocation of mother, and being without friends, he became desperately unhappy and occasionally had screaming temper tantrums. On one occasion, in order to control Joe's tantrums, the parents managed to sneak him into a psychiatric ward of a hospital and there they showed Joe the mental patients, warning him that if he didn't behave he would end up like these patients. The parents, convinced that the tantrums were symptomatic of schizophrenia, then went from one clinic and psychiatrist to another to get him hospitalized. The clinics, after doing thorough workups, and the private psychiatrists, after examining Joe and the situation, refused to hospitalize, saying that his condition did not warrant institutionalization. The parents, on one occasion, hid a tape recorder in Joe's bedroom, provoked a tantrum (they said they knew how to trigger one), and then proudly took the tape to a psychiatrist to show how Joe had fooled him. (Fortunately, in this instance, the psychiatrist refused to listen to the tape.) After numerous work-ups and psychological testings, the parents were finally able to find a psychiatrist who did, indeed, hospitalize Joe, but he was discharged in two days because hospital personnel could see no reason to keep him. Subsequently, the parents initiated a lawsuit against the hospital for releasing a mentally ill person. The parents on their own gave huge doses of Thorazine® to Joe to "control him," often forcing the liquid down his throat. At a family evaluation session Joe, on cue, presented one of his temper tantrums, and after he calmed down he dared go against the system by disagreeing with his parents that they never argued. Father and mother indicated that he must be crazy to say such a thing, and they both turned to the 14-year-old son as the responsible parent of the family to render the final decision. George made his pronouncement that the parents never argued, and then, after being excluded from the family, Joe spent the rest of the session trying to take back what he had said and attempting to get back into the family again. The family chose not to undertake family therapy, and at last reports were continuing to search for some doctor or agency who would hospitalize Joe.

The following symptom-producing family situations will, because of space limitations, be described in much briefer fashion.

Blurring of Generational Boundaries

Considerable clinical evidence has accumulated, from family therapy observations, to demonstrate the symptomatic consequences of parentification of children and crossing of generational boundaries. Cultural factors are intertwined with psychodynamic ones in accounting for the frequency of violation of appropriate age roles in the contemporary American family. Emotional overburdening of the modern urban family has increased as a function of loosening of extended kinship ties, increased mobility, child-oriented trends, all occurring in an age of cultural revolution and rapidly changing values. With all relational needs expected to be filled through each other, parents over-involve children in matters which should only concern elders. Schmideberg, in her article "Parents as Children" (1948), predated the family therapy findings when she gave numerous clinical examples of how chronological adults are dependent on their children (for example, a woman could not buy a dress without consulting with her 9-year-old daughter; a father was unable to discipline because of fear that his child would not love him or might retaliate in kind, and so forth). Parentification of the child is one of the most enduring findings derived from family therapy; seen in vivo, these phenomena are often shocking. Parentification may be direct and obvious, as when one of the parents is explicitly allied with one of the children against the mate (making real the child's fantasies of dividing the parents and violating the incest barrier), or when the parents turn to the children to settle their arguments, setting the stage for intrapsychic conflict in the child over divided loyalties. The alliance between parent and child may be more disguised, as when mother secretly goes to her son to complain about her husband; the excluded father often becomes rivalrous with his son, and family wars may result, sometimes ending up in murder. (Murder, by the way, statistically, occurs much more frequently between family members than between strangers.) When the child is parentified, the real parent loses his parental authority and limit-setting function, feeling he has no right to require compliance. Parental abdication is often rationalized as an attempt to establish togetherness or democracy in the family, where "the dignity and rights of the children are being respected." Parents who are unable to establish the kind of benevolent dictatorship required for effective family life, and who are impotent with their children, are frankly bewidered when the children respond with rage reactions and other symptoms of the behavior disorder type. The consequences of crossing of generations and of the inability of the parents to exercise their parental role are felt in all the psychiatric and other societal institutions who have to deal with the products of these disordered family lives.

Case-in-Point. The Steinbergs requested family therapy because they felt they had ruined their other childrens' lives and wanted to make sure they did not destroy the last child remaining at home, 13-year-old Stanley. The other children refused to be involved in the family sessions, maintaining that the only way they could keep their sanity was to have nothing to do with their parents. One older son, contacted by telephone, told of having to intervene constantly in violent battles between his parents—fights which often threatened to result in someone's death; he also said that he had had to raise Stanley—for example, giving him his bottle feedings during the night. When family therapy started, Stanley had been having numerous somatic problems for which there was no medical basis, and, in addition, suffered from a mixture of anxiety and depression. In the family sessions, Stanley's role as the mediator of his parents' marriage was immediately evident. Whenever his parents fought they each used him to express hostility to each other; Mr. S., feeling helpless in dealing with his wife, used Stanley as a front-man, sometimes literally putting the boy in front of him while he fed Stanley the complaints to say for him. Stanley said he was not able to do his school lessons because, when he went to his room, one or both parents would pop in every few minutes. The parents never went out together; on the one occasion that the therapist was able to get them to go to a movie together without Stanley, father had to leave in the middle of the show to telephone Stanley. Mother had frequent tumultuous emotional outbursts, described by Stanley as "being like a wild woman"; Stanley was expected to control these episodes for her, a particularly embarrassing task when she would scream out on the street, in view of the neighbors. The most extraordinary overinvolvement of Stanley had to do with how he got pulled into their sexual life. Mrs. S. said her husband was "sexually obsessed," and that if she wanted to buy something she had to bribe her husband with sex. Further, whenever she took a bath her husband would come into the bathroom and make a pass at her, knowing Stanley was downstairs and would hear her protests against "this disgusting behavior." Mrs. S. found her husband's advances so unbearable that in order to get him to stop she made her husband sit down with Stanley and write out in detail everything he did to her sexually.

Symptoms Related to Changes in the Family Relationship System

Unusual events of family life, such as the death of one of the parents or a child, hospitalization or imprisonment of a parent, marital separation or divorce, accidents and physical handicaps, economic reverses and so forth can, of course, produce catastrophic strain and disruption in a family. An epigenetic view of the family, however, centers on the crises which arise as a function of developmental events which occur as a natural part of the family life cycle. Every family has to adjust to the changes and stresses which accompany each natural, successive stage of family development—all the way from the transition to marriage from a state of singleness, parenthood, the children going to school and later leaving for college or getting married, sequential marital stages, retirement, advancing age, and death. Symptomatic eruptions may be precipitated by the unusual family events, but may also occur in one or other family member at developmental junctures—such as when someone enters or leaves the family system. Grunebaum and Bryant (1966) have described a program of family diagnostic interviews which are oriented around family developmental crises, and they stress the importance of the family's style of feelings which are aroused by the life crises.

Sometimes the outbreak of symptoms is more subtly associated with some change in the family system—the flareup in the child may be timed to some breakdown in relationship between a parent and grandparent. In the more undifferentiated families, biological maturation of the children is often perceived as a threat, with the children getting the feeling that by growing up they are rejecting their parents. Levenson, Stockhamer, and Feiner (1967), in describing the family transactions in the etiology of college dropouts, found that the failure of the student played an important homeostatic role for the family in that successful individuation threatened the family integrity. They stated, "We have seen previously bland marriages explode and break up when the students go away. Parents often come shockingly into contact with the aridity and disappointment of their lives when the child leaves home. Students are often cued in by telephone calls and letters to come home." (p. 144)

Case-in-Point. Mr. and Mrs. Brownfain, both of whom had lost their parents at an early age, married on the basis of an explicit contract that Mr. B. was to be his wife's "father." They did not have romantic feelings about each other, did not even kiss during the courtship, and Mr. B. told his wife openly that he had run around enough and wanted to settle down with his pipe, TV, and a newspaper. This arrangement was initially acceptable to Mrs. B., who said she was so glad to at last have a father. But she became increasingly dissatisfied with the lack of affection and the fact that they never went anywhere together. Despite this arrangement, two daughters were born, Louise, the older one, and Jane, each of whom was fitted to provide for gaps in the "marriage." Mr. B., unable to discuss anything with his wife, turned to Louise for relationship; the week she got married he had to be hospitalized for depression. Mrs. B., terrified of losing her children, started with Jane when she was a small child, always finding something wrong with every friend the child had and repeating to her that people were not to be trusted. Mrs. B. always suspected that her daughters were up to no good and would constantly accuse them of doing bad things which they had not done. Despite her apprehension that Jane would get in trouble, she left Jane in Louise's care for weeks at a time. After Louise got married, Jane began to act out by becoming truant, taking drugs, and getting an abortion for a pregnancy. She and mother had violent daily arguments, in the midst of which they would telephone Louise to decide who was right. In family therapy sessions Mrs. B. spoke tearfully of how she was dying from lack of affection, that she had lost Louise, and that Jane, who used to be so loving toward her, was now drifting away, and, furthermore, was doing all the awful things she had always been afraid that Jane might do. Mrs. B.

was especially frightened of being alone with her husband, whose only words to her when he was home was to ask what they were having for dinner. Now she was afraid that if Jane ever got married, she would only have the family dog to love and kiss.

Symptoms as an Essential Part of the
Dynamic Economy of a Relationship System

There are many intimate relationship systems where the symptoms of one member, although regarded on one level as noxious by all concerned, are a necessary ingredient for the maintenance and even survival of the relationship. It is not uncommon for a marriage, for example, to be structured on the basis of one partner being the functioning, "independent" one, and the other partner being the "dependent" helpless one; the nonfunctioning person may be continually ill physically, always tired, have frequent, vague pains, or frank psychiatric symptoms, be unable to hold down a job or take care of the house. The words "independent" and "dependent" are put in quotes because these roles can shift, so that when one partner is up the other is down. On the other hand, there are marital situations which are relatively stable in this respect, where the husband, say an executive or doctor, is married to an alcoholic, chronically ill, or childlike wife whom he has to take care of. The nurtured one insures the continuity of the relationship and helps the parental one to conceal his own dependency by displaying it for him. If the weak one changes, by psychotherapy or other ways, or if they separate, there can be a rapid reversal of roles, revealing the basic picture of mutual dependency. Scheflen (1960) has described the "gruesome-twosomes"—regressive, infantile, one-to-one relationships (of a husband and wife, homosexual partners, parent and child) characterized by limitations of relatedness outside the dyad, decreasing gratification within the relationship, and the maintenance of the attachment by mutual exploitation of the partner's anxieties. Abandonment is the ultimate danger, and "symptoms" are used as gambits or blackmail to create guilt or anxiety in the partner; if one partner gets interested in a third party the other gets jealous, sulks, or develops a "headache" or "asthma attack" to pull back the offender. Since one partner gets hurt if the other gets involved in anything which takes away from the relationship, there will be restrictions in job advancement, interests, and hobbies, often resulting in what the analysts call "inhibition symptoms." In the psychoanalytic or individual therapy situation, the mutual role that the symptoms play in the maintenance of needed relationships is often missed. One wonders in this connection how many unnecessary divorces there will be because a husband and wife, seeing two therapists separately, never had an opportunity to examine the intermeshing of their dyadic operations and the nature of their marital bond. Symptomatic functioning in one member of a relationship system usually has its reciprocal in the overfunctioning of another (as with the all-powerful mother and schizophrenic offspring, or the overadequate woman and nonfunctioning husband). Family therapy observations have revealed how the symptoms of one member often serve useful and necessary functions for the others, how the underlying system reciprocity is revealed by symptoms appearing in the asymptomatic member when the symptomatic one improves, and how a marriage may rupture when the symptoms which had been built into the relationship are no longer present. During the course of family therapy, as the role of the symptoms in the dynamic balance of the family is exposed, there can be dramatic spontaneous "cures" in the designated patient, but often someone else develops symptoms. Symptomatic behavior in one or several members may express a displaced family conflict in symbolic form (such as a brother or sister always fighting with each other as a representation for parents who never get openly angry with each other. In this situation it is easy to see how the children may stop their squabbling as the hidden resentments of the parents come forth).

The realization that symptoms can equilibrate family as well as intrapsychic forces has momentous theoretical and practical implications. Multi-person systems, whereby one person carries part of the motivations and psychology of another person, are only beginning to be understood; the close other can become a structural part of the self. *Whenever two or more persons are in close relationship they collusively carry psychic functions for each other.* The collusiveness can be in the benign form we see in all our relationships, such as when something frightening happens when we are with someone, if they are scared, they carry out fear for us and we can be brave, or if they are responsible we can be irresponsible, or if our wives take the soft line with the children we can take the hard line. The deal can be more unconscious: "I will be your slave or your bad self if you will never leave me." The referent point of a feeling or behavior is always an "other" who will have some predictable reaction. One can always detect the interlocking of motivations when it is noticed that the individual will not take a personal stand on some issue, and instead claims he is not free because of the other person. Such an individual will not take a clear position in the form of "I want this" or "I don't like that"; instead he or she will say, "*You* won't let me do this," or "*You* should not do that because it's not nice." The relational environment is manipulated such that others are maneuvered into being chastising parents, monitors, or expressors of one's sexual or hostile impulses, faithful servants, oppressors, or what have you, in order that more primitive conflicts will not come to the surface. People are constantly "acting out" old conflicts, and they seek through marriage, children, friends, enemies, psychotherapists, the supporting responses which will enable the relationship with the internal role models to continue, and prevent the anxieties and fears associated with those internal relationships from emerging. That is to say, they avoid painful symptoms by interpersonal choice. The reciprocal roles are found with exquisite accuracy: George and Martha of "Virginia Woolf" fame found in each other the desired lover-persecutor; Hansel and Gretel found their witch; the King Lears will find their Cordelias to reject; the hurt lover his unrequited love object; the flirtatious woman her jealous husband; and the Little Red Hen will find her selfish associates, and triumph over them. Character defenses—the habitual, ingrained styles of warding off anxiety—only fail when the reciprocating others will not or cannot cooperate; it is at this point that the more standard symptoms are likely to develop (such as the depression which follows divorce of a couple who fervently anticipated how well off they would be without each other). This phenomenon has its parallel in the way an agoraphobic will never have symptoms so long as he is living in a monastery. Psychopathology in one member of an intimate relationship system, then, can be very protective of its other members.

Case-in-Point.   Mrs. Stennis had seven episodes of depression and "paranoid" emotional outbursts, on each occasion being hospitalized briefly and given electroshock treatments. The psychiatrist who referred the patient and her husband for couple therapy finally noted a pattern in Mrs. S.'s "illnesses"—that whenever the couple had an argument, Mr. S. would take his wife to the hospital for EST, and she would dutifully comply. When she was not on courses of EST Mrs. S. was kept heavily tranquilized. In the first marital therapy session, when the couple entered the office, Mr. S., a successful businessman, took his wife's coat, folded it carefully, took his coat, folded it carefully, went back to the coats three times to check if all the wrinkles were out of them, then sat down, picked lint off his suit, stooped and picked some lint off the rug, and then made his first statement: "Doctor Framo, our big problem is my wife's compulsiveness." In subsequent sessions, after Mrs. S. came out of her lethargy (due to medication being stopped), she became extremely bitter and hostile to her husband, who reacted, sequentially, with shock that his wife was angry at him, amusement, smiles, and finally ceremonious and overpolite behavior. Her chief complaint, that he responded like a mechanical robot, was not real, and wiped her out as a person by not acknowledging her feelings, added further to her fury. Following some therapeutic work, Mr. S. began recognizing her wrath and began getting angry himself, and there then ensued a phase of ritualistic aggression between the two of them of such intensity that the pictures on the wall were shaken; occasionally they had fist fights outside the sessions. During this phase it was learned that neither one had any friends, that they never had people over at their house and never went out, that whenever one tried to buy something without the other being present, or tried to make a friend or join an organization, the other would react by hurt withdrawal, threats to separate, have an affair, or kill himself or herself. The couple would conduct "experiments" with each other: Mr. S. once fell to the floor and feigned death to test whether his wife cared (She did: she became panicky and told him she loved him). Mrs. S. once made up a story that she had a job, predicting correctly that her husband wouldn't speak to her for a few days. Their symptoms played into each other in various ways—Mr. S. was afraid to walk on the streets alone, but he said he had to accompany his wife on the street because she had this "street phobia." After the ritualistic aggression was redirected, in line with George Bach's (1969) and Lorenz's (1966) work on aggression, they began to deal with the real issues between them. It was learned that Mr. S. had been raised by a psychotic mother who, when she was not in the hospital, was involutional and frequently could not respond to questions. Mr. S. had always been frightened of going crazy, so he married someone who, while "a nice, sweet girl, so I thought" had a "crazy look in her eyes which intrigued me." In effect, Mr. S. dealt with his own irrationality by obsessively handling it in his wife, which is why he was most solicitous about getting her in treatment—so his own illness would be taken care of. Mrs. S., on the other hand, played the role of patient for years because she was guilt-ridden by strict religious training and her fantasies of promiscuity, and, in addition, felt that her husband would love her and she would be doing her wifely duty by acceding to his wishes that she get shocked out of her strong emotions. As the sessions progressed, various symptoms shifted back and forth between the marital partners until they were able to achieve some differentiation from each other.

Symptom Choice

What determines the specific content of a symptom? There has been little investigation of this extremely important and complicated question. From the point of view of individual psychology, the kinds of symptomatic pathways selected can be understood on the basis of the idiosyncratic history of the individual. Prior to the family-system approach, family influence on the choice of symptoms was considered in terms of such factors as the child identifying with the symptoms of a parent (for instance, the offspring of an alcoholic will usually have problems around drinking) or the effect of a neurotic parent's fixation (thus, a mother who is preoccupied with anal functions may give her child numerous enemas, so it is no surprise when the child develops symptoms around elimination). More sophisticated knowledge of family dynamics has increased understanding of differential responses of several children to the same deleterious situation. For instance, if the marriage of the parents is characterized by immutable turmoil, demeaning of each other, and noisy battles, although all the children may share common feelings of fear, shame, disgust, being torn apart, yet wanting to save their parents' marriage, each child may incorporate separate aspects of the marital relationship: one child may identify with the aggressive role, going through life victimizing others; another child may incorporate the victim role and always get in situations which provoke abuse; another child may incorporate both aspects as an intrapsychic conflict; and still another child may block it all out and become silent and withdrawn, inwardly feeling, "Things are bad enough; I cannot make demands because it might make matters worse." To be sure, there are many factors which will affect such outcomes: the extent to which the children are pulled into the marriage difficulties, which child is selected as the marriage counselor, the birth order, sex, and ages of the children, the stage of the marriage into which each child was born, how much support the siblings were able to give each other, and so forth.

In addition to intrapsychic and family dynamics, wider cultural influences certainly play a part in the manner in which symptoms are manifested, such as the ethos of various societies, historical changes, value conflicts within societies, ethnic, religious, and social class distinctions. An outstanding example of the way cultural change affects fads in symptoms is that since the passing of Victorian repressiveness, the conversion hysterics of Freud's day are almost never seen. Everyone recognizes that behavior which is regarded in one culture as pathological or anathema may not only not be so regarded in another culture, but may be rewarded. Every society has its own defined ways of patterning human needs and giving approved expression to distress, and each culture regards its ways as normal and right. So, too, each family culture has its own standards, criteria, and precepts regarding what is and is not deviance.

The dimension of the family-relationship system, unknown before the introduction of family therapy experience, has increased understanding of the process whereby a family member's behavior is interpreted as abnormal by the family intimates, as well as the process of choice of symptoms. Behavioral scientists have long been puzzled by the phenomenon that some behaviors are defined by family members as mental illness, which to outsiders, including professionals, are patently not abnormal, and other behaviors which are clearly seen as disordered or perilous from a psychiatric or social adjustment point of view are denied, blocked out, minimized, or explained away by one or more family members. It seems that sickness, like love or beauty, is in the eyes of the beholder. Different investigators have offered various explanatory concepts to account for the interpretation of "sick" behavior on the part of another family member: tolerance of deviance (Freeman and Simmons, 1963); the type of relationship between the definer and the symptomatic one (Schwartz, 1957); whether or not the referring family member was a target of the behavior (Clausen, 1959); and the degree of satisfaction with the relationship (Safilos-Rothschild, 1968). Psychodiagnosticians and therapists often get their data for diagnosis or treatment of a patient, particularly a child, by interviewing the relatives *about* the patient. Who else but parents should know their own child? Yet, in another sense, the last person in the world able to evaluate or interpret accurately the behavior or degree of pathology in another's behavior is a member of the family. The lack of congruence in systematic investigations of this problem can perhaps be made intelligible by an elusive variable which rests on knowledge of how family systems work: The informant's psychology is intimately tied up with and even a constituent of the psychology of the "patient," and together they are part of a regulatory system which, quite out of awareness, has built-in biases and falsifications, sometimes of massive proportions, which stem from the vital relationship needs which are at stake. If a wife needs a husband for her psychic survival she may state about his severe delusions that "everybody gets peculiar ideas now and then." On the other hand, if the system requires that someone in the family have particular symptoms, no amount of outside evidence to the contrary would be convincing. (For example, two brothers had been stealing cars and were finally caught and sent to juvenile court. The parents insisted that one son be punished and detained because he was "bad clear through," and they dismissed the antisocial behavior of the other son, characterizing his actions as "childish pranks.") Sometimes the family's overconcern with one symptom and ignoring of others can have disastrous consequences—for example, the parents of an adolescent boy focused on his reading disability by requiring constant tutoring, and they were oblivious of an obvious depression and frequent threats of the suicide which was eventually carried out.

In general, the recognition and specificity of the symptom depends on what the family system does or does not allow; families usually only seek help when the system is hurting—when someone in the family is expressing anti-system symptoms. In a system, no one element is more important than another. When the nature of the "deviant" behavior threatens the integrity of the homeostatic balance of the family system (constitutes a true change in a role which demands modification of a reciprocating role) there can be intense family anxiety. No matter how bizarre or dangerous a symptom is, on the other hand, if it does not have a system function it is simply not acknowledged (thus, neighbors, school, or the police may force the family to do something).

Case-in-Point. The Rosa-Giordano family was in an acute crisis when referred for family therapy. Carmella Rosa, a 29-year-old housewife with two young children, was overtly psychotic and because of her delusions she was housebound and would not eat, was growing progressively weaker, and could not function as wife or mother. Several brief attempts at individual psychotherapy had ended in failure. Her mother, Mrs. Giordano, had quit her job a year ago to take care of Carmella's children and house. The family was terrified that Carmella would take her own life and felt she needed hospitalization. The designated patient's husband had emigrated from Italy 7 years previously and hardly spoke English. The patient's father was retired and on pension, and her older brother, John, was the only sibling still living in the city. All of these family members attended the family therapy sessions. In the early part of the treatment there was considerable preoccupation with the patient's failing health and depression; her paranoid delusions did not seem so strange to the family. Carmella was convinced that some "system" had organized a plot against her, was tormenting her in a variety of ways, and would not let her live. She had written down all the details of the plot in a large document and wanted the therapists to read it, feeling that after they understood the "system" they would take steps to put a stop to it. She had thought that the plot was centered in this country, but when she went to Italy a few years ago to meet her husband's family, she discovered it was international in scope. She then tearfully requested that the therapists intervene with the Secretary of the United Nations or, at the very least, the President of the United States, to get "them" to stop torturing her. The rest of her family looked hopefully at the therapists, confirming the urgency of the situation, and waiting for the therapists to take some action with a high official. When asked how she knew about "them," Carmella said that they got messages to her in various ways: by forcing others around her to make noises and gestures which were most upsetting—e.g., when her husband tapped his feet or her children yelled, or when her mother banged the dishes when she washed them, or when men jingled coins in their pockets or made smacking noises with their lips, and so forth. It soon became obvious, especially upon reading her document, that the most innocuous events and sounds around her were perceived as sexual provocations and suggestions. In order to placate her, the entire family had walked on eggs, tiptoed whenever they were in her presence, and had conducted their lives so as not to upset her—thereby giving validity to her delusions. This behavior had gone on for some time, but the family did not seek help until she threatened suicide and stopped eating. Subsequent developments in the family therapy demonstrated that our initial formulation of secondary gain was of limited value (that Carmella was punishing the family for past hurts, she was controlling everyone, and at the same time was getting them to take care of her). In the ensuing weeks the patient lost 50 pounds and the cotherapists were becoming quite alarmed; she was beginning to look like a concentration camp victim, and we realized we were engaged in a life-and-death struggle. The situation did not become understandable and begin to change until it was revealed that her father, Mr. Giordano, had undergone a religious conversion experience before the patient's birth which had changed the whole course of his life and subsequently that of his family. In the early part of his marriage there had been considerable marital discord because he had been, in his own words, "a sinner who got in with the wrong crowd and was a wolf with the girls." Marital separation was imminent until he had dreams and "visions" of Christ threatening him with the fires of Hell. After several of these terrifying experiences he decided to "surrender to the Lord Jesus Christ," and he then devoted the rest of his life to religious work. On the basis of his study of the Bible he left the Roman Catholic Church and experimented with several different religions (Baptist, Pentecostal) before finally becoming a Presbyterian. In later sessions the spreading and powerful effects of Mr. Giordano's religious struggles on the rest of the family were disclosed. He had indeed devoted his life to church work, with a zeal that went beyond any church teachings. John, who was much older than Carmella, related how his sister never knew his father before he got religion, when he was more human and real. The children were always confused because of the frequent changes in religion, and they were not only required to change with him, but had to follow the precepts of each religion. We also learned that Mr. Rosa, the patient's husband, had not been allowed to marry Carmella until he became a Presbyterian. The Giordano children were all required to go to church daily, could only listen to religious music or read religious stories, were not allowed to go to movies or dances, or to participate in other "worldly pleasures." Carmella had been conceived as an offering to God, fulfilling father's pledge. She had not been allowed to wear lipstick or to ride a bicycle because her legs might be revealed. Mr. G. described his daughter as "an innocent flower waiting to be plucked." John stated that all the children, unable to tolerate the restrictions, had left the home at an early age, and only Carmella had remained behind.

Omitting many other details from this account, it became more clear that the patient's psychosis was a kind of one-upmanship on father's ideas, which were more socially acceptable. He saw sex everywhere and so did the patient. Father's view of the world was that it was a pretty frightening place, where no one could be trusted, and this fear was related to the patient's paranoid fears in that everything was seen by her as a threat. The interpretation was made: "The 'system' is everything your father taught you." As an offering to God, as an angel and saint, Carmella was not entitled to be real or even to live; death was preferred to violating father's promise to God. It was better for her to be mad than to be bad. Another important part of the system was mother's role in the situation, in that father could not have done what he did without at least her passive approval. At any rate, following establishment of these connections, and painful working through, Carmella began to eat and rapidly improved. Follow-up several years later revealed that the patient was functioning much better. The symptoms which were alien to the system (depression and anorexia) were gone, but those which were syntonic with the system, her paranoid beliefs which the family tolerated and fostered, were still somewhat present.

Symptom Maintenance and Symptom Reduction

Whatever dynamic family process is involved in the formation of symptoms and giving them shape is also a part of what determines whether symptoms are short-lived, episodic, become unnecessary, or become chronic. Generally speaking, symptoms are maintained or reduced to the extent that they serve relationship-system functions and are an integral component of and bonding force in the relationships. Symptoms which sustain relationships and are embedded in stagnant contexts are likely to be the ones most intractable to change, as some individual therapists ruefully recognize when they find that, after lengthy psychotherapy, many of the original symptoms in their patients are still present. According to psychoanalytic views of therapeutic change (Luborsky and Schimek, 1964), the ego, when it gets stronger in its control and synthetic functions, can better deal with the demands of the id, superego, and external reality, including the family pathology. There is, however, a relentless stickiness in the quality of dyadic or triadic close relationships which has a force of its own, and individual treatment is likely to have a greater effect on the patient's nonintimate relationships than on those relationships which carry transference meaning and rely on repetitive, characteristic feedback. It is true, as Luborsky and Schimek say, that "favorable changes in patients (in analysis) do not always imply that all symptoms are gone. Symptoms may sometimes be present after treatment, even though the patient may have accomplished much change." (p. 88) One wonders, however, how many therapeutic failures are the result of lack of appreciation of the symptom-in-its-context; it could well be that the only symptoms which change in individual therapy or analysis are those which do not have family-system functions. Of course, changes occur in people and in symptoms in circumstances other than formal psychotherapy, most often when the context changes—when the symptoms no longer have meaning in a given relationship system in time.

Experienced family therapists are no longer excited by the striking "spontaneous cures," even of long-standing symptoms, which can occur early in family therapy. They know the power of an approach which, by moving the system just a small notch, can unfurl a process of change which can spread to all the relationships in the family; small system changes, in other words, can make a great difference in total family functioning. Indeed, the very fact that some families came to a session at all and discussed important matters with each other for the first time can have lasting effects, even if the family never returns. Opening up of communication on real issues between the parents, for example, often leads to invigoration of the marriage, almost invariably followed by symptom reduction in the children. Or, when a family member is able to dispute an irrational role assignment, the process of change has begun. Visiting professionals observing family sessions for the first time have been very impressed with the early dramatic changes, not knowing how family systems work, and not recognizing that removal of symptoms represents a very limited goal of some schools of family therapy.

Among the countless ways that symptoms are maintained by the supporting surround, only two examples will be mentioned: (a) When one person in the family has fixed neurotic, characterologic, or psychotic symptoms, there are always consequences for the family system beyond what has been called secondary gain. To be sure, the symptomatic one unconsciously exploits his dysfunction in a variety of ways: Families do indeed suffer when a hypochondriac extracts his worry dues, a compulsive housewife tyrannizes with her nagging, a depressed parent makes everyone feel guilty, a paranoid family member snipes behind the privileged sanctuary of psychosis, and a firesetting child keeps everyone on edge. *Secondary gain, however, can only function in a cooperative medium;* when the system is resistant (when the symptoms truly do not meet the needs of the other family members), the symptomatic one must resort to other defenses, changing the character of the disorder. Usually one person in the family is permitted to have his symptom because this arrangement allows the trading bargain of an unwanted behavior, reward, or defensive protection for someone else. (Example: "My husband is so damn miserable to live with, I figure I have a right to play around.")

Some families require that one of its members be symptomatic, a fact which partially explains the revolving of symptoms around the various family members during the course of family therapy. Changes in the system which result in the family no longer needing a patient, while difficult to achieve, represent one major goal of family therapy.

(b) A common, tragic situation consists of the one where the family's having a hospitalized, psychotic member has become fixed and integrated into the system as a way of life for the family. One can witness the melancholy ritual every Sunday in all the state hospitals across the country: family members visiting the hospital-ized one year after year, bringing food, asking the same questions of the patient and staff, and not really expecting any change. Some of these families, feeling the illness of the patient as the cross they have to bear, do get some surplus advantages from this arrangement; for some, the only social life they have is involved with hospital visits and activities, and such situations can become so calcified that attempts to get the patient out of the hospital will be sabotaged by the family.

Case-in-Point. This case illustration, the Rosa-Giordano family, is the same as the one discussed under symptom choice, but with more pertinent details of one aspect of the treatment process which illustrates why some peope have to hold on to their symptoms. It will be recalled that the elder Mr. Giordano, the father of the designated patient Carmella, had imposed his extremist religious views on all his children, using a variety of pressures to compel them to live "pure" lives. His son John, along with his daughter Carmella, had described how careful and circum-spect they had had to be whenever they were in their father's presence, even after they were grown up. In addition, if father found out about some behavior of theirs which strayed from his standards, he threatened to disown them. If they were with father when the TV set was on and women appeared on the screen with few clothes on, they had to quickly turn off the set. If they knew he was coming to visit them they would have to hide all the liquor and wine and cigarettes. When John's son wanted to marry a Catholic woman Mr. Giordano expressed his condemnation. Carmella always felt uneasy wearing shorts or a bathing suit on the beach or even attending an opera. John said, "If you do what my father wants, he loves you; if you don't, he doesn't love you. He even said once that if we had to choose between him and living God's word, he would rather we gave him up. . . . So we tried to go along with him and adjust to it. I'd hate to get to a point where I say, 'You live your life and I'll live mine.'"

Some attempts were made by the therapists to work with Mr. Giordano, but his defensive system proved too impermeable. The therapists then attempted to achieve differentiation in the family such that each member could develop his own independent views on how life should be lived. One could feel the rising anxiety in the room during these efforts: everyone said that if they lived lives of their own which went against father's religious teachings, it would just about kill father, or at the very least he would go crazy. Although the rest of the family had ways of dealing with father which permitted some degree of autonomy for themselves, Carmella was the most fearful of what would happen to her father if she changed. (Her motives, needless to say, were not entirely unselfish.) It is suspected that a mechanism similar to this is involved in most cases of symptoms which are recalcitrant to treatment—to give up the symptoms has relationship consequences which are unacceptable. In some cases it may mean divorce, total estrangement, or even death. At any rate, the therapists disputed these assumptions of theirs that father would die or go crazy if they enjoyed life. The family, in effect, we pointed out, was treating father like he was crazy; by going along with his irrationality they did not treat him like a human being, and it would be an act of kindness toward him if they refused to adhere to his beliefs. We caught the family on their own petard by pointing out that a person cannot be a dictator unless he has slaves, and that by treating him as God they were doing him a disservice.

Pseudo-symptoms

The modifier "pseudo" is used hesitantly in this section to characterize those symptoms which are even less "genuine" than those mentioned in this paper thus far. Labeling them less genuine does not necessarily imply fakery or malingering or conscious intent to assume a symptom. Rather, under discussion here are those symptoms which come into being, either momentarily or over a long period of time, to meet the conditions of some family-system contingency. Some of these symptoms rapidly disappear when the contingency context changes, but others may develop into "real" symptoms or character traits, sometimes on the basis of functional autonomy. For instance, in the situation where a divorce is imminent between parents, it would be surprising if the children did not develop symptoms of some sort; the young children may wish to sleep with mother (further increasing the threat if followed through), may somatize, lose interest in things, become irritable and impatient, or may act out in order to forestall the dire threat. These symptoms, which began originally as conscious or unconscious attempts to force the parents together may quickly vanish or may become fixed and internalized. Some situations are so ominous that pretty much any symptom will do, so long as it diverts attention from the main threat. As a matter of fact, a large proportion of the symptoms which people initially present in psychotherapy, either on an individual or family basis, are diversionary, pseudo-symptoms. It is not infrequent, for example, for the parents in family therapy to start off talking about some problem in the child in the first session, and then to never mention it again during ensuing months; this finding has led some family therapists to call the child's symptoms a passport for the parents to get treatment. Symptoms may be nonspecific attempts to introduce variability or excitement into a congealed, dead family, or they may be distress signals, dilatory tactics, games, manipulations, bribes, attempts to achieve closeness or distance, or any combination of innumerable strategic inter-personal gambits.

The "purpose" of some symptoms may be to block changes in the system in order to maintain the status quo (e.g., a child can be given the power to divide the parents and turn them against each other, and his symptoms may add to the parental struggle.) It is not uncommon in family therapy for the symptomatic child, who presumably has the most to gain from changes in the family, to be the one who is most obstructionistic, although careful examination sometimes reveals that the child is a spokesman for one or both parents.

There are several symptom phenomena which have important theoretical and practical implications for evaluation of psychopathology. A person shows differ-ent sides of his personality to different people in different situations, and certain behaviors are manifested only in the actual, physical presence of particular people. The presence of family members introduces the greatest effect on an individual's behavior; it is very difficult, for instance, for the most mature adult to avoid feeling like a child when he is with his mother or father. Some symptoms, therefore, will be exhibited only in proximity of either the family members or others who have family transference meaning for the person (as in the case of the boy who whines or has a tic only when with his mother; or the girl who is always an angel when her therapist or father is around). Self-consistency, then, is a myth, but so is object constancy. The current, real mother of an adult is not the same, transactionally, as the historical introject of mother: the relational meaning is different. Everyone at times behaves toward present-day mother as if she were the mother of childhood (occasionally noticing with shock the grey hair), but the more undifferentiated the personality the more the individual responds not to mother as she is today, but to the early imago. The schizophrenic adult views mother almost exclusively in terms of the introjected mother, an observation which can be confirmed by witnessing the interaction between the two. This writer has had the experience of treating patients in individual psychotherapy and suggesting that they bring in one or both parents; the patients' near-panic which followed this suggestion is prob-ably due, at least in part, to the threat of confrontation of the discrepancy between the introjected and the current, real parent. (Most often the patients said they felt that great harm would befall their parents if they came to the sessions, but this altruistic concern overlaid protection of the fantasy introject. One patient, who had been describing how "impossible" her mother was, finally admitted she needed to see her mother as impossible, and felt her actual presence in the sessions might destroy the coveted image.) There are also *interactional* behaviors which make their appearance only under specified relational conditions: for example, the couple who fight only when the children are around or when there is an audience, such as at a party, and behave very differently when they are alone. Because particular combinations of people-in-a-particular-context exhibit some behaviors and not others, this crucial factor must be taken into account when the professional wants to generalize from the behavior observed before him—whether he/she is evaluating dynamics, selecting who should attend family therapy sessions, or determining the composition and design of a family interaction experiment.

Another important related symptom phenomenon has to do with the observation that some people are only able to be spontaneous, human, creative, real, questioning, when they are nonrational or symptomatic. Warkentin, et al. in their article, "The Usefulness of Craziness" (1961), highlighted the value of certain kinds of episodes of disorganization, provided the people close to the person can accept the behavior. Some people are only able to deal with the real issues with close others when they are drunk, psychotic, under drug influence, or in other ways "not themselves." (For example, a woman was hospitalized on many occasions over a period of 15 years, each time following a period of great upset during which she would despair over her husband's lack of affection and cruelty, and declare her intention to get a divorce. Each time after she returned home from the mental hospital, she would claim that she loved her husband and could not understand why she said those crazy things.) There are occasions, then, when giving up "symptoms" means returning to a stultifying, restrictive conformity to the system patterns. Families and, too often, professionals, are sometimes too quick to assess these occasional "therapeutic" symptoms as pathology.

Sharing and Exchange of Symptoms

Just as a phobia, in intrapsychic terms, is an attempt to localize anxiety within a single situation while saving the ego from recognizing the real problem, and just as an obsessional isolates his symptoms from the rest of his personality and does not feel them as his own—so will people isolate, localize, and place forbidden tendencies and anxieties onto their intimates, manipulating others into expressing and carrying their problems for them. Example: Mother is having one of her "attacks"; she screams that she is going blind and is going to die. Her young son gets all upset, frantic and worried, and starts crying. Then, once the shift has occurred, mother is no longer anxious, placates her son, and asks, "Why are you upset?", or she may even get angry at him for being worried. Later on, when the son learns to ignore the attacks and not get hooked or tied up in knots, he is accused of being uncaring. Irrational fears, thinking, and memory can be transmitted from one person to another through these double-binding means, often getting to the point where one's own senses, perceptions, recollections, and feelings are mistrusted.

As we have seen in previous sections, one person can express a symptom for some other close person, several family members can, overtly or covertly, jointly share symptoms, and family members can manifest interchangeable clinical depressive, paranoid, or aggressive symptoms in their interaction with each other, yet be symptom-free in their extrafamilial relationships. The following examples are some representative prototypes of the sharing and exchange of symptoms within family-relationship systems.

1. Secondary gain is usually discussed in terms of an individual "patient," but that which is gain for the patient may also be gain for the significant other; bilateral secondary gain in a marriage, for example, may be the critical ingredient which helps create, maintain, and determine the fate of symptoms in each or both partners. Mutual secondary gain represents an investment and safeguard in the relationship itself, and the motivational interlockings and misalignments can themselves be the very constituents and essence of the disorder. It is in this sense that family therapists speak of the marriage itself or the family as being the patient. One can speculate how often more observable symptoms in one person serve to conceal, protect, and mask symptoms in an intimate; indeed, symptoms in one person can bind and protect a whole family constellation.

A woman was in psychotherapy because she suffered unbearable anxiety about her husband's health, even going so far as to lay awake at night listening to him breathe and dreading the cessation of breath that signaled a heart attack. Her husband was usually tolerant of his wife's overconcern, sometimes amused, but occasionally annoyed because her concerns imposed restrictions on his freedom of movement (he had to stay near a telephone at work because if he did not answer the phone quickly she would become panicky). So long as she was carrying his fears he was unconcerned about his state of health. It was noted, however, that whenever her concern about his health abated, he would "develop" chest pains.

2. Symptoms never exist in a void, and even before family therapy it was recognized how symptomatic people usually need someone to monitor their symptoms—the monitoring one usually being considered by the therapists as a constant, however. Take, for example, a married couple where the wife is obese. She demonstrates that in order to indulge her wish for food she needs another who will forbid this activity. Her husband is disturbed by her need to gratify herself and her inability to exercise discipline, so he chastizes her. She assuages the hurt from the chastisement by eating more. Deeper exploration reveals that the husband cannot allow indulgence for himself, so he participates vicariously in her eating and in subtle ways encourages it, such as giving her a pie for her birthday. Reciprocal gain is seen in the mates of alcoholics, gamblers, and other addictions where both members of a pair have a problem, and one manifests it while the other protests. There is the husband who handles his anxiety about being a male by taking care of the children and house because his wife is always "sick," or the wife who claims that because of her husband's fear of driving she has to drive him places, thereby not having to face her own phobia or what she gets from assuming the parental role with him.

3. Some relationships are kept in dynamic balance by virtue of an openly shared symptom which can constitute the cementing "third party." This transactional

situation is apparent in an alcoholic couple who are both married to the bottle, or a marriage maintained by mutual fantasies of the mate's infidelity with a rival.

4. Systems are often maintained on the basis of containing a scapegoated member whose symptoms have sacrificial value for the others. For example, a child may be the continuing focal point of a marital dispute, with father saying to his wife, "You always spoil that damn kid," and mother countering with, "I wouldn't have to if you loved him enough." The parents argue incessantly about the child and threaten separation, at which point the boy starts underachieving at school, develops enuresis, or any of many symptoms. Whether or not the child's "symptoms" continue depends largely on what happens to the marriage relationship; what happens in the marital relationship may depend on what happens with the child's symptoms. The child may be taken for treatment, and he may be willing to go if he feels he could escape being the battleground for the marriage or if he feels his going to a therapist will help his parents get along better. The professional to whom the child is referred will then usually evaluate the child and treat him as *the* patient, with the handling of the marital problem either being ignored or treated on an ancillary basis.

5. Another common mechanism through which symptoms are shared is through vicarious participation and gratification. Example: Mrs. Everett was in show business from the time she was a teenager, and although she was tempted to be as promiscuous as the other girls in the nightclub where she worked, she controlled her behavior and warded off advances of many men. Another reason she did so, in addition to moral reasons, was that she had a sister who had been so promiscuous that she had had to be institutionalized in a home for wayward girls. Mrs. E. married a man who could not be demonstrative, and occasionally she went out with other men with her husband's knowledge and approval. She insisted, however, "I never did anything wrong because I respect my husband too much." But she felt cheated out of something important, so she began living through her daughter, who cooperated by living a free sexual life. She fought with her daughter constantly about her behavior, yet would listen in on her daughter's telephone conversations about boys, would open her daughter's mail, and would follow her on dates. On one occasion she told her daughter she was going out and wouldn't be back until late, and she placed herself outside a window of the house to peek at her daughter making love. The next week Mrs. E. convinced her husband that the daughter needed treatment, so they took her to a child-guidance clinic.

The first real bridge and juncture between the personal and the social exists in the development of family transactional theory whereby man is viewed not as a personality constellation with defined limits, but as being linked to, shaped by, and shaping the natural habitat within which he is involved, feels and behaves. Family transactional theory and family therapy, in the writer's judgment, represent a major breakthrough which compels reexamination of the fundamental nature of psychopathology. The view that psychiatric illness, craziness, odd, disordered behavior is a socially intelligible response orchestrated to an odd, crazy, or disordered system has a significance as momentous as the Freudian revolution in psychiatry. On the basis of the material presented in this paper, one can question whether psychopathology can ever be contained within the boundaries of one individual, even if one grants the precondition of intrapsychic conflict for neurotic symptoms. It is the writer's view that although all symptoms are not interpersonally determined, they always have interpersonal and relationship consequences which will determine their nature, course, preservation, or removal. That is to say, the substance of psychological disorder can consist of the reciprocal interlocking of a multi-person motivational system, not only in terms of etiology, maintenance and reduction of psychopathology *in* the individual members and *between* the members, but also characterizing the interacting unit itself. Symptoms, in other words, can be looked upon as disordered relationship events. Although intrapsychic psychology and inner experience were minimized in this paper, it should be recognized that neither the intrapsychic nor transactional levels can be replaced by the other or reduced to the other, and that both are necessary for the whole picture, even though the enormous complexity of the relationship between the two levels has only begun to be explored.

Psychodynamic theorists and practitioners have known for a long time of the close relationship between family dynamics and symptoms, but it was not until actual treatment of the family together that the how and why of the kinship between the two were forcefully brought home by the transactions. Any complete theory of symptom formation could not be limited to the construct that a symptom is a compromise between instinctual gratification and defense; this writer postulates the theory that the universal human conflict between autonomy and reality on the one hand and the need to be accepted by intimate others on the other hand would have to be included in any comprehensive explanation of the development of psychopathology. The power of life-sustaining family relationship ties is much greater than instinctual or autonomous strivings. Whereas life preservation for animals depends on instinctive regulation in unfolding sequence, the human being must depend much longer on parental care, and the feelings surrounding the early symbiosis persist as an aspiration throughout the life span. For the sake of approval by the parents, and because abandonment has such disastrous consequences, the child will sacrifice whatever ego integrity is called for in order to survive. If the price for acceptance is to absorb unrealities, accept an irrational identity or role assignment, be persecuted, be overindulged, be scapegoated, be parentified or what have you, this price will have to be paid; to be alone or pushed out of the family either physically or psychologically is too unthinkable.[11] Adults, too,

---

[11]The tone of this paper thus far might suggest that psychopathology is the inevitable fate of family process, and that the family is a closed system. Assuredly, the positive aspects of family living, although not under discussion in this paper, are many indeed; families provide the safest emotional refuge from outside stress. Moreover, fortuitous life circumstances over the course of an individual's or family's life can have more salutary effects than the changes brought about by formal therapy.

require specific reciprocal identities in their intimate others in order to maintain their own identities. Family members are most content when everyone behaves according to the others' expectations. Family members are extremely emotionally involved, but not so much with each other as with their imprinted inner role formulae which require confirmation in the others' behaviors. The consequences of someone not cooperating with their assigned role can be calamitous.. George Bach (1967), who studied intensively a sample of spouse murderers, found the following: "Actually, all the spouse killings we investigated, including the few suicide displacement murders, can be conceptualized as punishing a partner for not fitting into a *role, image* or *situation* as defined and wished for by the other partner." (p. 6) It is suspected that instances of murder of children by their parents involves a similar dynamic. At any rate, in order to adapt to the system the child will deny, repress, distort, or project as much as he has to; the resulting symptoms, however, are byproducts of the imperious, compelling importance of family dependence. The psychoanalytic investigator, Weigert (1967), has expressed in a similar vein: "The child needs, before all, the constancy of being accepted. In his emotional conflicts, he often sacrifices the (for him) inferior value of pleasure gain or pain avoidance for the (for him) high value of object constancy and ego identity. . . . Man in his existential anxiety has to make conscious decisions between being and nothingness, between his responsibility for personal self-preservation and his loyalty to family and larger units of solidarity." (pp. 226, 236) One wonders whether any child can self-actualize without having to depend on parental figures for acceptance. Weigert (1967) addresses herself to that extremely rare instance when "The child loves himself not only when he feels loved by his family; in growing independence he loves himself in spite of rejection by others. But such firmness of self-esteem is hard to reach, because of the power of human inter-dependence and solidarity." (p. 231)

Though most psychological symptoms are painful, and matter much to the person who suffers from them or who has to deal with those who have them, in another sense symptoms are relatively superficial manifestations, byproducts, and precipitates of complicated processes arising from the nature of relationship struggles among intimates. Indeed, in a literal sense the word *symptom* means a sign or token which stands for something else. It is difficult to see how those systems of psychotherapy which deal only and directly with symptoms can achieve lasting results without getting involved in the processes which bring them about. Insofar as the *therapy* aspect of the family approach is concerned, symptoms themselves are generally bypassed and are translated into the deeper dynamic relationship occurrences which produced them. The family therapist uses symptoms transactionally, as components of the system, and the symptoms themselves may provide the therapeutic leverage for producing change. Ackerman (1966) sees the goals of psychotherapy in general as: (1) symptom relief; (2) self-realization; and (3) integration of the individual into his group, and he suggests further that the health of the group will determine whether people will get well and stay well. In constructing a theory of treatment involving intrapsychic and family-system factors he stated,

> Conflict between the minds of family members and conflict within the mind of any one member stand in reciprocal relation to one another. The two levels constitute a circular feedback system. Interpersonal conflict affects intra-psychic conflict, and vice versa. Generally speaking, interpersonal conflict in the family group precedes the establishment of fixed patterns of intra-psychic conflict. Psychopathic distortion and symptom formation are late products of the processes of internalization of persistent and pathogenic forms of family conflict. Potentially, these disturbances are reversible if the intrapsychic and symptom-producing conflict can once more be externalized, that is to say, can be reprojected into the field of family interaction where a new solution can be found. (pp. 75–76)

Once one has had the experience of treating families and being part of the process of emotional face-to-face encounters and reciprocal influences on each other's experience and behavior, it is almost impossible to go back to the old way of describing psychopathology in such standard individual terms as "strong sadistic impulses," "oral–passive needs," "inappropriate affect," "unrealistic ideas," "poor judgment," "withdrawn," and so forth. These stereotyped state-ments, seen in every psychiatric or psychological report, have little meaning without knowledge of their place in the matrix in which they are displayed. *It is necessary to specify when these characteristics are expressed, toward whom, under what conditions, and the part they play in a given relationship system.*

The isolating, individual point of view has consequences in fields outside the behavioral sciences. The law, for example, judges behavior only as a function of the properties and responsibility of the individual, even though this legal ethos is tempered by defense efforts to show the situational and extenuating circumstances under which a crime was committed. Despite the movement of the helping professions toward social factors, clinical practice is still overwhelmingly oriented toward the principle that there is an individual patient with a focal disorder. The alternative being offered here is that most people's problems stem from the difficulties arising from the familiar social systems in which they presently live, and that when there is family distress the symptoms may appear in any form, in any member, as a function of what is going on in that system. The symptoms of one or more family members may involve many community agencies and members of the helping professions, *each dealing with a limited sector of the family process, leaving the system untouched.* A marital difficulty, for instance, may spill over into the children, presenting problems in school or in the community, may involve the police, or juvenile court, family social service agencies, psychiatric intervention, visiting nurses, Alcoholics Anonymous, religious organizations, institutions for the aged involving grandparents, medical hospitals, and so forth. Because of lack of awareness of the total family situation there is inefficient duplication of services, and sometimes the various agencies serving the family are working at cross-purposes. One family that came to our attention was simultaneously involved with 18 agencies. The psychiatrist who does a consultation, the clinical psychologist who administers tests, the social worker who sees a relative—none of them are in a position to understand the meaning of the presenting symptoms they are called upon to diagnose or treat. It is for these reasons that it is recommended that intake family diagnostic interviews be done on a routine basis, no matter what the symptoms are of any member of the family. This is not to say that everyone should do family therapy or that there is no place for other forms of psychotherapy; indeed, not all families can make use of conjoint therapy, although most families can profit from short-term family therapy when they are in the midst of an acute crisis. (One practical consequence of great import is the promising finding of a family unit in Colorado (Pittman et al., 1966), that family therapy can keep most patients out of mental hospitals.) Rather, it is believed that clinical practitioners, when they observe the family interacting with each other, can make superior diagnostic appraisals of what is really going on, and will see symptoms in an entirely new perspective. These insights will be of great value even if the professional continues to treat only on an individual basis. *The family approach lends itself, furthermore, as a central integrative process for the entire scope of clinical services of a community mental health center,* with referrals being made to the various services on the basis of diagnostic family interviews. Because psychiatrists, clinical psychologists, and social workers have not had the kind of training which equips them to view psychopathology transactionally, one of the first undertakings should be modification of training programs along the lines espoused in this paper. The family approach offers a meaningful supplanter to the medical model which, while supported financially and ideologically as a vested interest, is proving increasingly inappropriate for these times of sweeping cultural change.

There is much resistance to the family approach, and many professionals have developed scatomata when it comes to the family. Perhaps this state of affairs results from attitudes about the sanctity of the family which most cultures have; another factor is the charged, emotional aspects of family life—which family therapists themselves feel when their own past or present family life is moved by the treated family's transactions (Framo, 1968).

Dicks (1967) has said,

It is my contention that the treatment of individuals 'in vacuo' by whatever method of in-patient or out-patient handling, is an obsolescent concept.

Unless we are dealing with an isolate, the meaningful unit of therapeutic action is the presenting individual's primary group: parents and siblings, spouse and children, sometimes also the work group. If this be granted, then the approach to diagnosis and therapy in large areas of psychiatry demands appropriate new techniques for analyzing such interpersonal networks which all attending psychiatrists and psychotherapists (including analysts) should possess. I will go so far as to assert that they do not know what opportunities for rapid insight and critically decisive help they are missing daily in their work by not having this conceptual and operational equipment. (p. 325)

Part Two

Application to Families

"Rationale and Techniques of Intensive Family Therapy" was actually written during 1963–1964, even though published in 1965. The chapter was based on experiences at the Family Therapy Project of the Eastern Pennsylvania Psychiatric Institute (EPPI) in Philadelphia, directed by Ivan Boszormenyi-Nagy. This project began in 1957 as a program of investigation into the nature, course, and treatment of schizophrenia. Intensive individual psychotherapy of young adult, hard-core female schizophrenic patients was undertaken three times a week, and, in addition, patient-staff meetings were held daily, along the lines of a therapeutic community. Since the EPPI was a research and training institute we had the luxury of study and research rather than the pressure of service. We began getting involved with families because they got involved with us (phone calls hinting at dark family secrets, strange behaviors on the ward when the parents visited, and so forth). Since families were intruding so much we began to invite them to join our daily patient–staff group meetings. Certain phenomena began appearing which impelled us to begin seeing whole families together, outside the group meetings. The creative step here was taking what had been regarded as a noxious interference, the family, and using it. In the beginning, frankly, we viewed the family as helping us to bring about change in the schizophrenic patient; anyone who has done individual psychotherapy with schizophrenic patients knows that you will try anything. We saw families for some time before we began to apprehend the family as a transactional entity with a life of its own—*the family as the patient*. I say "saw" families because in truth we had no idea how to "treat" families; we observed each other through the one-way mirror and went over each other's tapes, but it was like the blind leading the blind. Along about this time we began to hear about others who were seeing families conjointly (Ackerman, Jackson, Satir, John Bell, Bowen, Wynne, and Lidz).

Observations that are trite today were revelations then: schizophrenic symptoms began to make sense and could be decoded when seen in their family context; someone else in the family developed symptoms when the designated patient improved; the special rules and myths that guide families could be discerned; the parentification of children, emotional fusion and contagion, and family-wide thinking disorders were seen in glaring reality. We worked with families in cotherapy teams, largely for self-protection; individual therapy continued concurrently with family sessions, but after a while we found that the therapist treating the patient individually could not maintain a family perspective. Eventually, when we saw the power of the new family paradigm, we stopped doing individual therapy altogether, and still later we began discharging all our schizophrenic patients as soon as they were relatively symptom-free. Finally, we began working exclusively on an outpatient basis with families having a wide range of manifest problems. We had reached the point at which we realized it did not so much matter what the symptom was in which member of the family.

Chapter 3 was written while we were in transition from an individual to a family orientation. Although its primary emphasis is on the insights gained from family therapy, the chapter does reflect some thinking about psychosis and its treatment on an individual basis. Some things I said in this chapter I no longer believe—such as the necessity for seeing the whole family at all times, or that long-term family therapy is usually preferable. These days I see subsystems of the family in all combinations (although I do not do individual therapy), and practically all of the family and marital therapy I do is short-term (about 3 to 4 months in length). Still, this was the first paper in the field that examined in depth such topics as the phases of family therapy (particularly the process that occurs in the middle phases), the kinds of obstacles and impasses unique to the therapy of closely related people, marital problems in family therapy, the "well" sibling, transference and countertransference, and cotherapy. And although this chapter is rather old now, I was, on rereading it, surprised to discover how many of the ideas and observations have held up over the years, especially when viewed from the standpoint of having seen hundreds more couples and families since it was written.

3

Rationale and Techniques of Intensive Family Therapy (1965)

Expository writings on psychotherapeutic techniques have traditionally possessed the virtue of daring and the hazardousness of exposure. Some very experienced therapists have questioned not only the advisability of publishing books and articles on technique but honestly believe that it is futile to attempt to put into organized language what a therapist does or should do. It is their legitimate belief that the attempts to convey and analyze the therapeutic process always suffer in interpretation, and that the vital communications in all forms of psychotherapy are intuitive, felt, unspoken, and unconscious. Much of what transpires between patients and therapists is expressed by tone, gestures, expression, sensory impressions, feelings, and a host of other almost incommunicable states. Only a small part of therapeutic commerce takes place via words. Therapy supervisors have long known, moreover, that a wide discrepancy frequently exists between what a therapist says he does and what he actually does do. For example, one therapist may believe he is dealing with very deep material, but its impact on the patient may be quite shallow; another therapist may believe he is only doing supportive psychotherapy by dealing exclusively with reality problems, yet discover to his astonishment that the patient has become thoroughly involved. A further argument against defining techniques is that all therapists vary widely in personality, style, amount of activity, quality of focusing, goals, and so forth, even within the same psychotherapeutic school. Moreover, no amount of reading on technique will make an effective psychotherapist. It has long been known, but

Reprinted with permission from I. Boszormenyi-Nagy and J. L. Framo (Eds.) *Intensive Family Therapy*. Hagerstown, Md.: Hoeber Medical Division, Harper & Row, Inc. Copyright © 1965, Harper & Row, Inc.

rarely stated, that meaningful psychotherapy demands from the therapist the necessary personality equipment (admittedly difficult to specify) capable of development under personal treatment and competent, detailed supervision. This supervision, in order to be effective, should take place in a free "therapeutic" atmosphere which permits exploration of the feelings of the student.

There is another line of reasoning that argues against technique-oriented writings, that is, the nature of psychotherapy itself. From the writer's viewpoint we still know very little, in a definitive sense, about what happens in psychotherapy, why it happens, how people are helped, and what really constitutes help. From the subjective standpoint of the patient, the critical, therapeutic ingredient in psychotherapy, whatever theory it is based upon and no matter what the therapist does or does not do, may simply be that the patient comes to feel that *someone cares,* however he interprets caring or "love." When the patient feels that someone cares he can begin to care for himself. Sometimes the patient can feel "loved" on the basis of a transference dream. From the viewpoint of the conceptualizer who is obliged to explain the therapeutic factor in psychotherapy as a dynamic, explanatory mechanism, love, it is said, is not enough. Other elements are presumed to be involved: the uniqueness of the therapeutic relationship, the uncovering, the well-timed interpretation, the careful working through. But it takes a very mature patient to realize that what the therapist *can* give—technical skill, reliability, relative objectivity, sense of trust, relatively unambivalent interest in the patient's growth—truly amount to love. What patient, in a moment of unguarded honesty, has not asked the therapist, either verbally or non-verbally, "Tell me, would you be interested in me if this were not your job or you were not being paid?" What patient has not watched, with superacute alertness, for signs that the therapist is doing something "extra" for him outside the structure of his usual giving, or for indications that the therapist is being a real person to him? Sensing these patient needs, throughout the entire range of psychopathology, every therapist, whatever his orientation, at each check-point (that is, how to present an interpretation, whether to reveal his feelings to the patient, which part of the patient's productions to respond to, and so on) has to make a choice along the dimension: should I gratify or should I frustrate? Will the patient benefit more from my giving or from my withholding? Is the therapist so sure that the effect of his activity or nonactivity can be as nonspecific as, for example, feeding or not feeding? If we take away the patient's distorted fantasy that he was "loved" as a child, do we replace it with something else, or do we encourage the acceptance of his loss? These questions go beyond considerations of technique.

Though criticisms of technique exposition are cogent and valid, it is nonetheless encumbent upon practitioners to open the door to the treatment room and attempt to convey to colleagues information on how they conduct treatment sessions. Otherwise, practice, theory, and research would proceed along separate paths, uncoordinated and unintegrated, without a systematic discipline of therapeutic structure ever evolving.

It is especially important to reveal procedures whenever a new area of therapeutic endeavor is introduced. For example, in family therapy a host of new variables peculiar to the family approach must be considered in addition to the already incredibly complex variables of individual and group psychotherapy. However, this chapter on techniques of family therapy is not intended as a how-to-do-it treatise. A list of instructional rules would not only be premature but presumptuous. Rather, a statement of principles derived from our own practice in family therapy and a description of the development of techniques found to be useful, promising, limited, or antitherapeutic will be communicated. The views expressed in this chapter are an extension of those previously describing our work (Framo, 1962). The present statements reflect our learning experiences, shifts in conceptions, and, it is hoped, a greater sophistication in the approach to families since the previous publication.

It must be emphasized at the outset that the rationale and techniques to be described were developed under certain conditions within a particular setting. This setting and the history of development of the unit are described in more detail in Boszormenyi-Nagy (1965c). Our unit is one of the few in the country where *long-term* family therapy is conducted. We believe that there are certain deep parameters of the family system which can be revealed only by extended work with the family.

Although many of our observations were originally based on work with families with a female schizophrenic member, several years ago we began treating families which included designated patients of both sexes and varying ages and whose symptoms covered the scope of psychopathology from character and personality disorders to neurotic, somatic, and psychotic reactions. More accurately, however, we are no longer diagnostically concerned with psychiatric categories or symptoms. Symptoms in the designated patient often change from week to week, and symptoms, as nonspecific responses to accommodations in the family system which is undergoing therapeutic review, can shift from one family member to another.

Our criteria for admission to therapy is applied to the family instead of the individual patient. There are certain concrete guidelines we have followed: families referred to the project are seen for several evaluation sessions, not only to obtain a preliminary estimate of family dynamics but also to determine the kind of motivation which is operating within the family. It is extremely rare for a family to unanimously express motivation (such as by saying, "We need help as a family"), and when this does occur we usually discover that other stratagems are at work. For instance, several families were referred by an expensive private institution which allowed patients to stay only a limited time, and the parents, upon learning that we could provide hospitalization if the families agreed to participate in the treatment, could then easily "see" the problem as a family problem. The initial motivation in such cases was to save money and find a hospital in which to place the designated patient.

In our early work we tended to accept families on the basis of whatever motivation existed (most typically oriented solely around getting help for the designated patient). Because of lack of knowledge, we tied our hands and went along with the variety of excuses which were given for the absence of an important family member: one of the children could not get out of school, or grandmother would be too upset by the meetings, or father's job prevented him from attending all the sessions, and so forth. Gradually, we learned from our mistakes and, more significantly, gained more confidence in what we were offering; we have come to demand more from families by asserting conditions for acceptance into the program early in the evaluation process, conditions which give us maximum maneuverability. At the first evaluation session, and sometimes even before that, all family members are requested to sign an application for evaluation, which introduces the family concept that the entire family participate regularly in the treatment; a fee was established for the family sessions (previously none had been required); during the evaluation sessions we determined, on the basis of the family dynamics, what was to constitute the "family" we would be working with (all those immediate and extended family members as well as extrafamilial persons who exert a demonstrable influence on the total family system); the designated family members had to agree to arrange their schedules so they could all be present for weekly sessions; and, finally, in response to exploratory questioning, the family had to give some indication during the evaluation sessions that they could give more than lip service to family problems *other* than those having to do with the designated patient. Even though it may not be possible to get the parents or "well" siblings to admit that they have problems, the question should be raised and discussed in order to put the family therapy on a more realistic therapeutic basis. The therapists should ask each family member, "What changes would you like to see in the family that would benefit you?" or "What changes would you like to see in yourself that would make your life better?" Questions posed in this fashion avoid blame or accusation of sickness with all its moral and value judgments.

Whether or not to hospitalize the designated patient came to depend on the family dynamics as well as on the psychiatric condition of the patient. (After a patient is hospitalized, the presence or absence of symptoms do not determine whether or not he stays in the hospital. We sometimes send patients home with active, psychotic symptoms if this procedure is more likely to provide leverage in dealing with the family system.) From this position of strength we not only had a basis for dealing with the "absent-member maneuver" (Sonne, Speck, and Jungreis, 1962) by retaining the option of having any family member on call, but later we were able to be more flexible by allowing certain members to stay away with legitimate excuses and also by preserving the freedom to work with family subsystems. We had learned earlier that the greater the family's resistance in bringing in a particular member of the family, the more that member's presence was necessary to understand the total system. Of course, our early dropout rate increased; families telephoned to say, "We decided we really don't need help," or "Everything is a lot better now," or "My husband can't take time off from work," or "You doctors didn't tell us how to handle our sick daughter," or "We decided to send our daughter to a psychiatrist, or to another hospital." Nonetheless, we have learned that the families who persevere in the evaluation process are not as likely to terminate once they perceive the full impact of what is really involved in family therapy. Inasmuch as family therapy requires more than ordinary commitment in personnel and time, a weeding-out process is necessary. These, then, are the methods we have developed for dealing with motivation problems in those asymptomatic family members who would ordinarily never have sought psychotherapy for themselves inasmuch as their intrapsychic conflicts are acted out intrafamilially. With the advent of family therapy, for the first time we are beginning to reach the people who bring other people in for treatment. It is a mixed blessing that family therapy brings in as patients these kinds of people who, while they have a great impact on others, are often beyond the reach of treatment.

Despite our built-in filtering system, however, it needs to be stressed that we are still in the early stages of estimating motivation for family therapy. We have treated families who, motivationally speaking, initially looked like very poor prospects and later profited a great deal from therapy; there are also those who looked very promising during the evaluation process and made little or no progress.

Initial evaluation sessions are observed by the entire staff of eight therapists. Using their global human reactions as a guide, two therapists who have chosen to work with each other will volunteer to treat a particular family. The distinctive basis for a family's capacity to evoke an encountering response in certain therapists, and the reasons we use two therapists who select each other are interesting topics which will be elaborated upon later in this chapter. We are unable to determine, of course, how a different setting and a different set of conditions would have led to other techniques and conclusions.

As a further caution to the literal interpretation of our techniques, it must be recognized that techniques develop out of an ongoing process and are always incomplete. Only a small part of what we actually do in day-to-day treatment is described in this chapter, which may partly explain the paucity of writing on technique of family therapy (Ackerman, 1960; Bell, 1961; Bowen, 1961; Jackson, 1961; Midelfort, 1957), despite the growing literature on family therapy itself.

This chapter is arbitrarily divided into the following sections: rationale; early phases of family therapy; middle phases of family therapy; resistance in family therapy; marriage problems in family therapy; the "well" sibling in family therapy; transference and countertransference; cotherapy team relationship; terminal phases of family therapy; and, finally, a subjective evaluation of family therapy. While organizing the chapter it was found that these subdivisions fell naturally into place as important dimensions of the family therapy process.

Rationale

It must be recognized that techniques are designs or contrivances which implement a rationale of therapy. We are in the earliest stages of developing a conceptual understanding of family disorders, and, of course, the techniques for dealing with these family disturbances lag behind the comprehension of them.[1] The rationale of our therapeutic approach to families is based upon subsequent observations, which represent a distillation of our learning. Since our early experience has been with families with a schizophrenic member one could question the generality of these findings to family dynamics in general. However, our more recent experience suggests that pathogenic system processes should be used to diagnose families, and that such processes cut across diagnostic categories. All families have system properties, whatever form the manifest symptoms of one of its members may assume. Some of the following statements may appear contradictory, but they apply to different levels of inference and are regarded as valid at those different levels.

1. Unless one has had the experience of seeing family members together over a period of time, it is difficult to grasp the full implications of the notion that the *substance* of psychiatric disorder can be a family manifestation, and that the designated "patient" is only the most obvious symptom through which the family system manifests its pathology. When one first sees the family of a schizophrenic, for example, it is difficult to conceive of schizophrenia as a family disorder, since the patient appears so different from the other family members. The interconnected quality of the family problems can often be dramatically confirmed by observing a family session after a period of treatment and trying to pick out the sick member.

Some of these ideas can perhaps be illustrated by contrasting the individual and family approaches to the same problem.

A patient was referred to our unit with the following symptoms: she was suspicious and felt persecuted at the office where she worked. She was a dispatch messenger and believed that she was relaying messages of ominous intent. Ordinarily, in a good psychiatric set-up she would be interviewed, perhaps hospitalized, undergo psychological testing, and be presented at a staff conference. There would be involved discussions of diagnosis as to whether or not she was schizophrenic, and if so, how malignant the process was; there would also be some speculation about her dynamics in intrapsychic terms. A social worker might report on interviews with the parents

---

[1]Although there is a long history of interest in family conflicts and methods for handling them, particularly on the part of the social work profession, the specific dynamic, *clinical* emphasis on the family, dealing with the interactions and transactions themselves, and treatment of members of the family conjointly, are largely phenomena of the last decade.

who were able to give detailed accounts of the patient's developmental history and background. Following a factual account of the parents' backgrounds, the social worker might make some incidental observations about the parents, perhaps commenting on their individual oddities or on how concerned and responsible they seemed. After such a staff conference, a program of individual psychotherapy might be instituted for the patient, with perhaps one or both parents being seen by the social worker.

Now, contrast this typical approach with what we learned after a few sessions with this girl and her family meeting together:

After resisting efforts of the parents *and* the patient to talk about the patient's symptoms and difficulties at work, we learned that the designated patient was caught in the middle of a family-wide paranoia, that her symptoms were but one component part of a network. Out of all the intricacies and levels involved, one set of facts clearly emerged: Several years ago the father became extremely jealous, suspecting that his wife was having affairs with every man she met, and he would constantly follow and check up on her every movement. The patient was sometimes employed as the father's emissary on these missions. His jealousy then abated and, more recently, the mother, basing her suspicions on the flimsiest of evidence, erupted into the same kind of irrational and violent jealousy which had occurred with her husband earlier. The patient was again called upon to act as mediator between her parents, a role which she ambivalently accepted, displacing her rage, suspiciousness, and excitement onto her work situation.

We learned from the transactions of this family, as with every other one we have seen, that a part of the problem resides in each family member, like separate aspects of a multi-layered riddle.

2. The system of the family has regulating mechanisms of its own which control the collective mechanisms of its individual members. More is involved than the unconscious dynamics of each person; the complicated processes of the ongoing system govern the individual motivations. Despite numerous plots and subplots, the family remains a unity. Each family member uses every other member to balance his own pathology. Still, it is not one person acting upon another person; it can be any one person who affects the whole transactional structure. Although an event such as psychosis or delinquency, *if it disturbs the family system,* can introduce great strain and upset the existing equilibrium, it can sometimes be quickly absorbed into the system and become a part of the family's way of life. Sudden psychosis in one member can occasionally create enormous family anxiety of the kind generated when a dangerous fantasy or game threatens to become real.

3. Each member of the family has to fit in with the rules of the family game (Haley, 1959). Deviation from this fitting-together on the part of any one member

leads to a graduated series of injunctions, the most extreme of which is threatened abandonment (a punishment which is almost never meted out in any permanent form because each part is necessary to the whole). The members of undifferentiated families have never learned that it is better to have the voluntary love of a free, separate human being than the "love" resulting from emotional enslavement. At times a family member tries to fight his way out of his role: the father usually goes through his sequence of futile protestations and then gives up; his needs are too great for him to stay away if he separates. Frequently what seems like a separation gesture by an adolescent is actually an effort to get the parents involved (such as the daughter's indirectly letting her parents know she is having an unhealthy love affair). On rare occasions someone, usually one of the so-called "well" siblings, does manage to break free to some extent, but the "break" is typically of a violent sort, and the old conflicts are carried over into the new relationships. Many people delude themselves into believing that if they physically move far from home and never see their family again for the rest of their lives, they are no longer involved with them.

In the large majority of the families seen (especially the tightest family systems, those with an only child), all the significant emotional exchanges are contained within the closed, complete social system of the family, and there is little or no contact with the outside world. A minority of the families we have seen constantly explode distress signals and overinvolve others in the community. Neighbors, police, social workers, psychiatrists, and other persons are frequently called to give outside control or supplementary "feedings" to these deficient "family egos."[2] Every community is familiar with these families, who are registered with nearly every social agency in town; some of the members of these families are known to many of the psychiatrists in the city, the family having consulted each of them at one time or other.

4. In the more poorly differentiated family, it is more likely that the parents cannot see or act toward their children or each other as they really are but, instead, as screens to project on or as imagos through whom they can work through past, unsatisfied longings and hurts which stem from their original experiences with their own families. Each family, then, has its own fossil remains which are preserved from past generations and largely determine what goes on in the present. Though a one-to-one representation is rare, there is some merit in trying to discover which key figure or fusion of figures in each of the parents' background the patient represents. Since they need to be seen as good parents, however, the mothers and fathers will frequently show obsessive concern about some aspect of

[2]The author recognizes that a number of technical terms ordinarily used in other theoretical frameworks (particularly psychoanalytic) are carried over into the area of family therapy (family ego, family resistance, and so forth). In going into a new area one naturally depends on familiar terms, even though they retain a specific, restricted meaning within a theoretical system. The creation of new technical words, however, would have less communication value at this time.

the patient—her physical health, I.Q., pimples, weight, speech, clothing, and so on.

5. The designated patient half-willingly accepts her role as the scapegoat and sacrifices her autonomy in order to fill in gaps and voids in the lives of her parents or in her parents' marriage relationship, to conform to some preconceived notion of the parents as to what she should be, or to preserve the stability of the parents. She cannot evade any of the assigned roles of wife, husband, friend, mother, father, grandparent, sexual substitute, sibling to parent, pal to parent, object of ambition, or object of revenge. The designated patient, moreover, has been subjected to what we call the "yo-yo" syndrome; she is pulled toward the parents when they need her and pushed away or ignored when her own needs come to the fore. Outright rejection is never expressed, and if it were it could be better handled than continually teasing the patient with promised love which is never quite delivered or sustained. (During the course of family therapy we have learned that the parents, too, had similar yo-yo experiences with their own parents.) The designated patient tries to ward off her allotted role at the same time that she is enticed by its exciting qualities; she is constantly asking through her behavior, "What do I have to do or be to be accepted?"

The family concept of therapy clarifies the process of reality impairment. Ordinarily children develop the capacity for abstract thinking along the natural lines of genetic intellectual endowment. However, when unrealities prevail in the minds of the parents themselves, the child has little choice but to conform to these unrealities. Powerful guilt pressures and implications of treason or disloyalty can be brought to bear upon the child if he persists in pursuing reality. These pressures can not only force the child to renounce reality, they can block off the higher levels of reasoning which are associated with abstract thinking. After a while the unreality of the parents becomes the unreality of the child. Gradually, through the years, the designated patient is "trained" to be the living embodiment of the projected image. To be on the receiving end of a projection of someone else's internal image can be, however, a particularly frustrating and perplexing experience if that someone else is a vitally needed person; you must be seen as malevolent, spoiled, prematurely grown-up, deceitful, or what have you, and nothing can be said or done to change this view. One of the most baffling and painful emotional states results from having one's decent or autonomous motive twisted into something evil or unhealthy.

One patient in individual and family therapy was beginning to become autonomous; she confided less in her mother and would no longer allow her mother to set her hair. The mother, perceiving the withdrawal and threatened by the loosening of the symbiotic tie, responded with, "You must be getting sick again; I'd better take you back to the hospital." The patient, already painfully vulnerable about being labeled "sick," then became bewildered and anxious, especially since she found it so tempting to confide in the mother or allow the mother to fix her hair.

On the basis of such data we can perhaps understand more fully the genesis of some of the classical symptoms of schizophrenia (perplexity, disharmony of affect, and so forth). Whereas the symptoms of the designated patient can sometimes be translated psychodynamically as an expression of some family phenomenon (such as the patient's expression in exaggerated or symbolic form of the subclinical symptoms of a parent or some oblique commentary on the nature of the marriage relationship), at other times the symptoms have little or no meaning in either family or intrapsychic terms, and eventually prove to be epiphenomena or nonspecific "noise." Often the designated patient gives the SOS signal by such misleading symptoms and actions as stomach pains, stealing a car, locking herself in a room, truancy, or hallucinations. It is unfortunate that so many years have been spent on developing accurate nosological categories for individuals with specific treatments for specific conditions. Even family therapists have gotten into the habit of characterizing families by the overt symptoms of the designated patient (such as schizophrenic families, acting out families, or something else). One of our tasks for the future, on which some preliminary efforts are now being made, is to try to develop more meaningful transactional diagnoses for families.

6. Ordinarily, those who have achieved a relatively clear distinction between self and non-self realize that awareness of a need does not guarantee satisfaction of the need, and also that willing an external behavior on the part of someone else cannot magically bring about the behavior in the same way as one wills one's hands to move. Yet, in families where the individual members' ego boundaries are diffuse and where they have great difficulty distinguishing among each other, there are indeed occasions when one family member has only to wish or will the satisfaction of a need and it is met. The mother who feeds her child when she herself is hungry may addict the child into responding to her unspoken needs, and this phenomenon may spread into a family-wide magic and omnipotence which can be exceedingly difficult to dislodge. Why should these deep gratifications be traded for reality? The perpetuation and "stickiness" of these pleasurable-painful, preverbal needs constitute the main resistance to change in the family. When attempts are made to modify or eliminate them, the alternative ways of relating are perceived by the family members in terms of the ultimate horror—the agonizing state of unrelatedness. They dread reaching the point where nothing they do or are or become matters to anyone. In some ways families who argue openly or relate to each other in hurtful or humiliating ways are better off than they would be in a state of futile nothingness.

7. Whenever there are disturbed children there is a disturbed marriage, although all disturbed marriages do not create disturbed children. In some poorly differentiated families the marriage exists largely on the basis of what the children provide. The parents have long since given up on each other and live side by side with little

or no sense of real relationship, except to serve each other as objects of projected hostility or as representatives of introjects. To avoid the intimacy–aloofness conflict, various arrangements may be worked out to maintain the emotional divorce: absorption in television viewing when they are together; the husband taking jobs which keep him away from home; the wife or husband getting overinvolved in causes, organizations, or clubs; the parents intensifying their relationship with members of their families of origin, and so forth. Some of these marriages would be quite workable if there were no children. There are occasions when the parents' relationship to one child, usually the designated patient, can be stronger and more meaningful than any other relationship. The patient, her own Oedipal feelings realized under these conditions, finds that anything offered by anyone outside the family can in no way compete with or match the stimulation promised by the primary love objects. By offering themselves, the parents can inculcate a lifelong, built-in persuader against the patient's ever finding a life outside the family. Since the parents' real sexual satisfaction with each other is limited or nonexistent, they may turn to the children for sexual love. The more children are involved in the marriage and used by the parents the greater the threat of incest and the greater the chance of development of psychosis in the child. The expression of sexual feeling toward the child may range from overt seductive behavior to a preconscious or unconscious sexual temptation against which the family members must defend themselves by threats or sudden withdrawal. Families in which actual incestuous sexual expression occurs are uncommon. Severe sexual inhibition in a permanent atmosphere of great temptation is more characteristic. The family members cannot allow even normal affectionate displays or playful sexuality; some never even dare to touch each other.

The patient is almost always enmeshed in the marriage, although in a few situations we have seen she has been excluded from the marriage twosome; under these circumstances she is regarded by her parents as a misfit, a poorly designed piece of machinery which does not work properly. Though the patient may have been a "victim" in her early years because of an immature ego, by the time she reaches adolescence she ceases to be a victim because she is certainly part of the family system by that time. For example, she does not feel she can make a life for herself unless her parents have a life of their own with some degree of satisfaction with each other; on the other hand, she is likely to become more anxious if her parents do achieve greater closeness.

8. Traditional psychoanalytic views have stressed the following intrapsychic phenomena as fundamental hypotheses in the etiology of schizophrenia: a disturbance in the relationship of the libido to objects; a defect in the ego as a problem-solving agent; a defect in the ego as an experience in relation to the object world—past, present, and future; the existence of a greater-than-usual destructive drive; an abnormally great degree of anxiety; and a failure of integration and synthesis of all of the foregoing factors. From the standpoint of a transpersonal family concept, schizophrenia, or any other kind of mental illness, despite its

protean manifestations, can be looked upon as the only logical, adaptive response to a deranged, illogical family system. Despite the tempting gratifications provided by the parents and despite a symbiotic orientation, the designated patient has the most life to lose; she therefore sometimes "develops" the pyschosis as a way of signaling for help and change, while at the same time offers herself in the sacrificial role and denies responsibility for wanting change in the family. In this connection it is interesting to speculate how often an act of juvenile delinquency can be looked upon as the only "safe" way of calling attention to an intolerable family situation. The patient feels too guilty to be disloyal to the parents, as every therapist learns when he tries to interpret the obvious discontent. Still, when the patient does try to identify reality in the family distortions, this effort is often labeled by the family as "sick," and when she is hospitalized the doctors (and society, in effect) reinforce and confirm the family's diagnosis. Such considerations have led us to avoid hospitalization unless absolutely necessary.

The symptoms of the designated patient, while restitutional and regressive, do create numerous other problems. It has long been known that certain kinds of symptoms provoke attitudes in other people which can affect the course of the disorder itself (thus, passive withdrawal often promotes mothering; obsessive dawdling forces others to urge and push; paranoid twisting or aggressive behavior can make others punish or reject; delusions can fascinate or repel; depression arouses mixtures of pity, helplessness, and anger; sexual acting out provokes envy and disgust; and so forth). Then, too, the intact portion of the psychotic patient's ego is painfully aware of the stigma of mental illness; some of the patient's motivations and behavior can be understood as various means of handling the intolerable burden of shame and feeling like an outcast.

Mental illness can also serve as the means of obtaining secondary gains for the designated patient, primarily as a strategem of gaining some intrafamilial advantage. All anti-family symptoms are regarded by the parents with horror; those which are not are looked upon as minor annoyances, tolerated, or even indirectly fostered. Generally speaking, if the patient is giving the parents what they need, she is not regarded as sick (one father said, "Doctor, this lovely girl *can't* be sick; she kisses me with such feeling!"). Characteristically, once the anti-family symptoms disappear in the designated patient the parents are demotivated to continue family therapy.

Because therapeutic efforts are usually directed toward the young life which is hurting so much and seems especially vulnerable, and because the designated patient seems to possess a greater capacity for change (although this is not always due to the flexibility associated with youth), it has become common practice to conduct individual treatment in conjunction with family therapy. There are family therapists who have a deep conviction, based on their prior individually-oriented experience, that resolution of conflicts with introjects can only take place through transference work on a one-to-one basis. They reason, too, that in individual treatment, hopefully, the therapist can meet some of the patient's needs, although long-term individual treatment alone with the psychotic frequently threatens to develop into a lifelong dependency attachment with the therapist (Hill, 1955). The prospect of this outcome may be the reason why so many therapists shy away from commitments to treat psychotic patients. Some therapists have come to believe that it is necessary to almost adopt the schizophrenic in order to teach him how to live (Szasz, 1957). Others, particularly the therapists at Chestnut Lodge, feel that the symbiotic attachment between patient and therapist is a necessary phase in long-term treatment and that any resulting complications are capable of resolution (Searles, 1958, 1959a, 1959b).

Many aspects of psychotic behavior have the quality of a 2-year-old's provocative testing of its mother. This behavior may be oriented toward testing a mother's or father's concern and a commitment to see them through and care for them, no matter what. This testing-out behavior may also occur in the hospital with nursing staff and ward personnel in the roles of parental substitutes of the patient (Boszormenyi-Nagy and Framo, 1961, 1962). If a therapist stands by the patient through a stormy psychosis and follows through afterwards, then the patient can begin to trust others and build up ego-constitutive goodness. From time to time, however, the therapist's true concern will have to be proven. If the therapist withstands the patient's tests, he gains a place in the patient's relational world and can assume at times more importance than the parents. Not many therapists can endure this testing, which can get very nasty at times, taking the form of direct physical assaults, escapes from the hospital, furious rages, gifts, seductive pleas, hunger strikes, and other actions.

Experience over the years has led us to deemphasize individual therapy for the designated patient in favor of working with the interdependent family system. The member of the therapy team which was seeing the designated patient in individual therapy, because of his special relationship with the patient, frequently found it more difficult to see and maintain the family-system point of view. We learned, further, that the individual therapy had a diluting effect on the family therapy and came to be used as a resistance to exploration of family dynamics. The parents were usually eager to have the doctors deal with their sick daughter, rationalizing that it is the doctor's responsibility to take care of the sick person. We have found it more realistic that the parents rather than the therapists assume the responsibility of raising the child. The termination of individual therapy is usually followed by an increase in the intensity of family therapy. There are, of course, still occasions when individual therapy is indicated for the designated patient as well as other family members.

9. Do people really do things to other people or do they do things to themselves? The extent to which psychopathology is purely an internal, intrapsychic affair and the extent to which it can come about, be attenuated or modified as a function of how people in close relationship affect each other has been and will continue to be one of the central theoretical and practical issues of our time. (The two polar positions on this issue are taken by traditional psychoanalysts on the one hand and

by family therapists on the other.) An ultimate theory of personality, it seems to us, will have to consider an intricate but appropriate combination of both the individual and transpersonal points of view.

People who do not successfully resolve problems that arise with each step of growth carry over to each successive developmental stage a series of conditions and handicaps which limit their capacity to relate to others except in the light of their own needs (see Chapter 8, Erikson, 1950). Narcissistic relating, however, is never total; people in a relationship of long duration (such as a husband and wife) also respond to each other on the basis of their accumulated experience of mutual accommodation, even though their relationship is intermingled with and framed within past transference relationships. That is, there are occasions, even in the most symbiotic relationships, when the persons concerned see and respond to each other as separate individuals. Nevertheless, in our experience we have seen that the family cannot undergo deep or meaningful change if the therapists deal only with current, immediate interaction among the members. The most powerful obstacle to successful treatment is the individual members' libidinal attachments to their parental introjects, no matter what the parents were like in real life (Guntrip, 1953); it is necessary for each individual to work through the struggle with the incorporated internal objects (Fairbairn, 1954) which are being acted out with the other family members. The unconscious clinging to the disturbing internal-object world is associated with the endless attempts to change real others into unconditionally loving parents. (The need to help parents become better integrated people is probably based on the belief that if the parents were better integrated they could give more.) One of the most pathetic situations arises from an individual's lifetime efforts to obtain something from a mother or father that can never be obtained.

There are also important parameters in the family concept which are only beginning to be realized—that introjects are not only based on a one-to-one relationship to the mother and father as individuals, but on the nature of the marriage relationship between the parents; on the *psychological* mother and father of the family; on the family itself, including the sibling system. In other words, a whole family system—its emotions, its codes, its style—is sometimes introjected. In introjection of family emotions, for example, at one extreme there are families where affect is open and explosive and at the other extreme where intense emotions are muted or never expressed; such methods of handling affect can have drastic consequences for the personalities of the children of such families. Further, people are strongly motivated to experience specific emotional states or combinations of emotions in specific sequences under specific conditions; the relevant motivational formulae always bear a lawful relationship to the emotional network within which the original family drama was enacted.

10. Professionals in the area of family treatment have discovered that because of the vital stakes involved for each family member, dealing with the family system

in any meaningful way is always much more threatening to the family than dealing with a single individual's defenses and conflicts. Therapists have long sensed that a patient in individual psychotherapy or analysis has not changed and has developed great resistance because the transactional elements of his family life (what analysts put under the category of "reality problems") have not been under direct observation or dealt with directly. The "resistance" of the patient often resides in part in someone else. The uncommunicativeness of adolescents in individual therapy is often mute testimony to their inner recognition that the wrong person is being treated. Therapeutic work with a child is often undermined at home, and work with an adult patient is often sabotaged by a spouse or parent or sibling with both the patient and the other member often conniving to maintain their bilateral and pathologic fantasy "game." How often have individual therapists heard their patients say explicitly or implicitly, "I will change if so-and-so also changes," or "What good would it do for me to change if so-and-so doesn't change too?" When the therapist counters with, "But we don't have so-and-so in this room; you are the one we have to work with," the patient may overtly agree but silently feel, "You can say what you like, but I have too much to lose from somebody important to me if I really do change." The purely intrapsychic approach has often failed for these reasons, and the therapist is often at a loss to explain why. When the silent but powerful outside influences are brought within one therapeutic setting more factors can be observed and controlled, but, of course, the therapeutic task is made none the easier. Techniques for dealing with these system defenses are next discussed.

Early Phases of Family Therapy

As stated earlier, in our recent work we have selected for family therapy only those families who met the minimal conditions of agreeing to meet weekly with all those immediate and extended family members specified by the therapists, and those families who could see problems in the family other than those having to do with the designated patient. Consequently, the accepted families are already a selected group, and presumably there would be some degree of uniformity among them in their approach to undertaking family therapy, but such is not the case. Anyone who anticipates that families will come to the treatment sessions and relate their difficulties in living as, for example, a well-motivated individual outpatient might do, will be considerably disappointed. All people, of course, have to present their problems in the only way they know how. Problems are usually set forth inferentially by the family—by their behavior, by nonverbal "acting out," by their family style. The dilemmas can be exhibited by a myriad of forms which are rarely meaningfully constructed with genuine affect, such as helpless silence, bickering, half-concealed smirks, a flood of words, the patient's "standing on her head," intellectualized abstractions, constant over-agreeing with the therapist to avoid listening to him, and so on. Most families cannot put into words their need for help.

Some families present their pathology in a striking way from the first contact. They over-reveal their dynamics. In other families it is much more difficult to see the pathology at first; everyone except the designated patient may seem reasonable, conventional, and psychiatrically well-balanced. The parents seem to have remarkable insight into their daughter's illness and to be able to accept easily their own share of responsibility and contribution. The marriage seems fairly healthy, and even when the therapists listen carefully they can detect nothing grossly unusual in the family's description of its past or current modes of relating. Everyone seems to say the right thing, and it all sounds like they've read the textbooks. It may take a long time to perceive the extremely subtle strains of pathology which are interwoven through the system; the "sweet" sacrifice of mother, suppression of autonomy in the child, competition of father, or a concealed alliance between two family members may all hide behind multiple covers or be only delicately apparent. It takes the proverbial "sixth sense" to detect the specific sources of pathology; one knows one is close to these sources when the family tries to avoid the topic or gets anxious as it is approached. Both the open and closed, or expressive and repressive, family systems present their own kinds of resistance to exploration.

The quality of near-public exposure is one of the most striking attributes of family treatment, in contrast to the privacy of individual treatment. Communication is naturally freer between a patient and his own doctor in the privacy of the office. The sanctity of the doctor–patient relationship in psychotherapy is unquestioned. To most therapists, treating a family together seems not only an unwieldy and chaotic prospect, but also one which would thwart any attempts to work with defenses and explore underlying motivations. It would seem to be impossible to keep track of all the factors involved. Therapists ask: "How can you deal with five people talking all at once?" "Do you really think people will open up in a situation like that? Everytime something is said, everybody hears it; how can you possibly expect to elicit anything but superficialities to work with?" Further complications arise from experience in family therapy; much of the family's defensiveness revolves around not only self-protection but also the "protection" of other family members. When people in close relationship are under therapeutic surveillance this interesting protection phenomenon always appears and seems to be related to the guarding and preservation of vested interests and vital needs which are fulfilled in the relationship. The protection may appear in a variety of ways, most often in the form of one member blocking therapeutic exploration of the other (interruptions, completing the other's sentences, diversionary tactics, and so forth). Resistance against change in oneself as well as disturbance over the possibility of change in the other—even a change which is desperately desired consciously—always elicits protection ploys as each member attempts to restore the previous balance in the relationship because the old gratifications, no matter how much pain goes along with them, are at least familiar. Not only will whole families conspire to keep family secrets and prevent revelation of the family plot, but because of the public nature of family therapy it is often difficult for one member to acknowledge even a consciously defended painful feeling. For example, when it is interpreted to a mother that she is jealous of her husband's preference of their daughter to her, how can she react, even when the implication is made explicit? In individual insight therapy she may come to admit it after defenses are softened, perhaps proceed to wonder why it bothers her so, and then trace its roots to the past. But does she want her husband and daughter to know she feels jealous? Her final response to the interpretation (denial, evasion, or some other) is determined not only by her resistances, but by the added factor in family therapy of having to make a public admission, sometimes in front of the very people she would least want to inform.

In the face of these almost insuperable difficulties, then, what can be done, what techniques promise to make the process one of actual therapy, rather than the recurrent actualization of repudiated and projected motives? As in all therapy, one has to be selective, depending, among other bases, on the current constellation of individual and system defenses and the possibility that the family is listening to and making use of therapeutic intervention. Naturally, many things are missed, but if they are important they will recur in some form.

We regard the entire family unit as a patient, usually structuring the treatment situation as an opportunity for the family members to explore problems with each other. When parents are told that we work with the entire family, they initially accept the idea with equanimity, saying, "Yes, doctor, we understand. We want you to know that we will do everything in our power to cooperate to get our daughter well. No sacrifice is too great." In our early years of operation we used to allow discussion about the designated patient to go on for a number of sessions; our rationale was that the sessions should begin with what most concerned the family, which obviously would be the illness of a member of the family. A typical exchange at that time was as follows: The parents would turn to the patient with the words, "Tell us what is wrong, dear. Why don't you talk to the doctor? Don't be afraid to say anything; we can take it. Would you like to tell us off or hit us? Will that make you feel better?" The majority of the time the patient, sensing the concealed injunction that she'd better say the right thing or at least avoid self-incrimination, would respond, "Nothing's bothering me," or she would behave in some irrational way to confirm the view of her as a demented or inept person. If the patient, particularly if she has undergone individual psychotherapy and feels the support of her therapist, actually reveals what is on her mind, for example in the form of "disloyally" commenting on the parents' unhappy marriage or angrily passing a judgment on mother (thus violating family dictum number one [Jackson, 1959; p. 138]) a series of events follows very quickly. Father quickly changes the subject, a sibling begins to laugh, and mother, after a dumbfounded look, hits her hand on her thigh, turns to the doctor, and says, "See, doctor, this is what I mean. She's getting sick again." We have repeatedly noticed in most families that the mother can never consider her daughter well until the patient no longer manifests anger or deep resentment toward her.[3]

As we gained more experience we felt more comfortable about probing into other family problems early in the therapy and deflecting discussion away from the problems of the designated patient. Families are usually unable to deal with the general question, "What are the problems in the family?" Such a question usually gives rise to embarrassed silence or clichés or the statement, "We don't have any family problems except for our sick daughter here." Instead, we sometimes approach indirectly by asking each of the family members in turn to talk about their experiences in this present family, their views about each of the other members, their ideas about the family life, in order to get the history of the family from the vantage point of each member. In the course of the recounting there may be frequent interruptions as other members may dispute a characterization of themselves or some event, or react with astonishment to some statement with: "John, I had no idea you've felt this way all these years." We also ask the parents to talk about their families of origin, significant losses and trauma, their own parents and their parents' relationship with each other, as well as a history of the present marriage. In the beginning only expurgated, well-defended, and distorted accounts of people and events are divulged, but that is not important at this early stage. The children are usually avidly interested in hearing about their parents' backgrounds and marriage, sometimes hearing some secrets for the first time. Our strategy in opening up all these areas consists not only in obtaining outlines of the parental introjects in order to understand problems in the present family, but also to uncover the underground psychological elements in the family. As these various views and opinions are discussed, new issues arise, the family members interact, and the patterns, divergencies, coalitions, forms of influence, cross-complicities, persuasive techniques, motivational struggles, status hierarchies all begin to emerge. A dawning realization of the real meaning of the family therapy procedure emerges out of this intensive mutual exploration, usually precipitating marked anxiety. The anxiety may be manifested in a variety of ways: there may be renewed, frantic efforts to bring the focus back to the patient ("Now, just a minute, doc, it's our daughter who's the sick one"); there may be an attempt to withdraw from family treatment, using a diversity of rationalizations; or the patient may

---

[3]An interesting counterpart to the parents' shock when the patient begins to open up after being pressured to talk is seen in the individual psychotherapy of schizophrenics. As Searles (1961) put it, "Not infrequently one hears from fellow therapists and ward personnel of how 'stunned' or even 'shocked' they were at seeing dramatic improvement in the long-ill patient, and I have felt this way many times myself . . . Noteworthy, also, even among the most technically capable of therapists, is the initial reacting with dismay and discouragement to a patient's new-found ability to express verbally the depths of his despair, loneliness, confusion, infantile needs, and so on."

become the spokesman for the family fear and say, "I don't think family therapy will help. My problems have nothing to do with my family," hoping all the while that she will not be taken seriously.

An unexpected occurrence at these times is when one of the parents edges his chair close to one of the therapists and begins to recite a detailed history of unfilled need and disappointment, thereby displaying himself as the hungriest and angriest one of the family. The patient is usually surprised by an occurrence of this type, which may confirm a dimly perceived, long-held suspicion that in some ways her parents are worse off than she. Sometimes, when the patient is acutely psychotic, she may be so intent on making the sacrificial gesture by rescuing her parents or calling attention to herself that she will attempt to block exploration of the family by such diversionary tactics as psychotic rambling, screaming, responding loudly to hallucinations, wandering around the room, or something else; it is necessary at times simply to shut the patient up, occasionally requesting that the parents control her. We have seen a few occasions where the psychotic patient, from the privileged sanctuary of her psychosis, would try to humiliate her parents, making them perform like trained seals, or try to force them to deny reality and go along with her delusions. The parents, embarrassed in front of the therapists and intent on showing them that they love their daughter, will, despite their helpless rage, often try to go along with the unreality because after all, "you can't get angry at someone who is sick." Their behavior is often explained as "humoring" the patient. On a deeper level, however, the patient is caricaturing the important role she has in her parents' life; parents and child have made a deal: "Let me possess you and I'll be your slave." The master–slave role alternates between the two. When the designated patient is loud and noisy, the therapists must skillfully follow both the primary process level of the patient and the mostly secondary process level of the rest of the family, especially since at these times the psychotic productions are frequently burlesques of some deep aspect of the family dynamics.

There are also problems in the handling of sessions when the designated patient is quietly psychotic. The less dramatic near-mute passivity which follows a period of overt disturbance in the psychotic patient always bothers the therapists more than the family; the parents are likely to be more diffident about the quietness than the "well" siblings, explaining their apparent unconcern with, "But she was always like this before she got sick." It is very difficult to prevent parents from settling for the premorbid nonperson status of the patient, and since it is at this point that families frequently want to terminate therapy, the necessity of the patient's role as an incompetent in maintaining the economy of the family system is confirmed. We have found it important at these times to try to bring the quiet one into the discussion and to create dissatisfaction in the parents about their child's condition. Such efforts, however, do not always succeed because they threaten one of the essential cogs of the family system. Many of these parents feel adequate only if their child is inadequate; therefore one of the tasks of the therapists is to help raise the parents' self-esteem so that the inadequate child becomes dystonic to the system. It is sometimes very difficult, however, to want more for people than they want for themselves.

When the therapists sense that the balanced family arrangement is too tenuous to be dealt with, it is sometimes useful to spend the early phases of the family therapy doing individual therapy with the member who is hurting the most or who is most accessible. It is surprising how often someone other than the designated patient, usually the mother or father, presents himself for this purpose. Although this "individual" therapy takes place in the presence of other family members, the latter frequently benefit from it even though they may seem not to participate in it. Sometimes it is necessary to eliminate the pressing problems of one person or an alliance from the treatment scene before one can deal with the whole transactional system. For example, a family could not begin to examine a mother's nonexistent relationship with her husband or her overinvolvement with her delinquent son until the mother was better able to understand that her real struggle was with her own mother.

Rather early in the treatment, the therapist may combine exploration with confrontation or low-level interpretation, setting the stage for future family therapy and commenting on the essence of the family dynamics, saying, in effect, "These are the things we have to work on." As the therapists give their impression of the dynamics, some of the following hidden coalitions and family myths are exposed: lack of commitment to the marriage relationship, the deep attachment of the parents to the families of origin, how the symptoms or acting out of the designated patient are related to what is going on in the family, and so forth. When reality is brought into these forbidden areas, the shock of disbelief, half-recognition, or fear appears on the faces of the various family members. Family secrets are often exposed, and it is interesting to note how often these secrets concern sex (illegitimate births, affairs, previous marriages, or something else). There may even be some work done with introjects during the early phases, but at this time the discussion is largely intellectual and only later are some of the emotional connections established. Much of the material uncovered in the early phases is repeated in the middle phases but with more detail and more emotional substance.

During the early phases especially, acting-out behavior outside the sessions and emergency problems are likely to appear, necessitating greater activity on the part of the therapists. The therapists frequently find it necessary to keep one foot in the reality problems and one in the fantasy system. There are times when flagrant misrepresentations, scapegoating, or exploitation of a victim need a controlling hand. For example, when one set of parents would argue vehemently and then turn to the two young children for the final decision as to who was right, the therapists stepped in to interpret their use of the children as parents and pointed out the consequences of their behavior. However, when one of the parents said to these same children. "We were all right until you kids came along," the therapists were angered at the gross unfairness of this statement. The handling of acting-out outside the sessions (such as sexual or delinquent behavior on the part of the adolescent who is intent on "saving" the family) is a broad topic which requires extended separate discussion.

It is difficult to generalize about the early phases of family therapy because of the wide differences among families, differences in the way problems are approached or presented, and variability in the styles of the therapists. But the preliminary stages of family therapy are largely characterized by the accommodations and adjustments which must be made between the family and the therapists, the harmonization of the cotherapy team, the jockeying for position as well as at least partial apprehension of the interlocking quality of the family pathology. There are many paths to these goals, and some families remain in these early phases for a long time without ever advancing into the real core of family therapy. Most succinctly, in the early phases the therapists are trying to break into the family system and the family is trying to keep them out. If the middle phases are reached, the therapists are *in* the family.

Middle Phases of Family Therapy

There are centers in the country who see a family for only several months, offering a family therapy program which does not go beyond what we would consider the preliminary phases of treatment. The real test and serious work of family therapy, in our judgment, resides in the laborious working through and building of trust in the therapists, a process which takes time. There are, to be sure, numerous difficulties which have to be overcome, some related to the nature of the family, some to the nature of the therapy team, and some to the unique quality of family therapy itself. What follows in this section is an attempt to deal with some of the problems which come up in these middle phases of family therapy, which comprise the heart of the process, as well as some of the techniques which have been developed for handling them.

The one overriding goal of these intensive middle phases, once the therapists are part of the family, consists in understanding and working through, often through transference to each other and to the therapists, the introjects of the parents so that the parents can see and experience how those difficulties manifested in the present family system have emerged from their unconscious attempts to perpetuate or master old conflicts arising from their families of origin. In general, the parents impose the same acts of unfairness and overburdening on their children that were once imposed on themselves. The parents in these families have each had their own grievous betrayals and shortchangings, and in order to make any real progress in family therapy they have to be led gently to remember and face them. It is a great deal to ask of any person to reopen old wounds and reexperience old guilts which have been shunted aside, discounted, ignored, or lived through with someone else.

In an atmosphere of trust and reliance toward the therapists, established over a long period of time, this sometimes anguished self-exploration can take place. The essence of the true work of family therapy is in the tracing of the vicissitudes of early object-relationships, the varieties of human experience, and the exceedingly intricate transformations which occur as a function of the intrapsychic and transactional blending of the old and the new family systems of the parents, as well as the contribution of the children. The process is long and arduous with many levels; intense feelings are aroused, and progress is by no means in a straight line. When one person moves ahead the whole family equilibrium is disturbed and many painful adjustments have to be made; there may be frantic efforts to resume the status quo and reestablish old patterns. For example, after the wife has faced some of her anger toward a parent, she may no longer need to use her husband as a bad object of transference rage, but the husband may continue to "ask for it," even after complaining about it for years. Not many families can achieve this level in therapy, but when it is reached it is very impressive, and, unless it happens, we believe there can be no real hope of resolution of conflicts or meaningful change in the individuals or the family.

Once the early stages of blaming are past and questions directed toward the therapists are deflected back to the family, the members do try to interact with each other, and, as a general rule, the therapists attempt to expose the hidden feelings underlying the manifest interactions. There are families, however, who find it almost paralyzingly difficult to talk to each other in the presence of the therapists. These sessions begin with the therapists asking, "How are things going with the family?" (focusing on the family as a unit). Father or mother reply, "Everything is all right." A long silence follows and one can sense the fear. Then one of the parents will turn to the designated patient with, "What have *you* got to say?" The patient, aware that any meaningful statement may incriminate her, will usually say, "Nothing." The therapists usually become more active at this point. Sometimes it isn't discovered until the end of the session that there has been a violent scene at home, or that between sessions a bitter, silent war was being waged at home. It usually takes a great deal of probing and pressure to find out what actually transpires at home between sessions. We have tried the technique of maintaining, along with the family, silences which last as long as half an hour, and everybody, including the therapists, finds these silences unbearable. We have occasionally fallen into the trap, through clever interpretations, of doing the thinking (and the "feeding") for the family by telling them what their problems are. In these middle phases of therapy the family members, because of the transference feelings which by then have been established, are usually less interested in exploring their difficulties than they are in sitting back and getting something from the therapists. This presents the therapists with the dilemma of whether to supply nourishment or to provide a free atmosphere of introspective inquiry. It is perhaps under these conditions of mixed therapeutic motivations that the therapists become more active and interpretive. It is now our conviction that those techniques which promote family interaction are the most productive in the long run.

A useful technique in therapy is to focus on the immediate situation, rather than get lost in abstract formulations, and specifically point out to the family those characteristic behaviors and mannerisms of which they are unaware (such as, "Have you noticed, Mrs. Jones, that you complain about your husband's not talking enough but every time he tries to speak here you stop him from talking or you finish his sentences?" or, "You both keep nodding your heads in agreement with what we say, but I don't really think you're listening to the words," or, "Don't you think Suzie handles her skirts poorly, exposing her legs?" or, "Have you all noticed how often you all exchange with each other those secret smiles?"). These behaviors, when brought to the attention of the family, almost always precipitate embarrassment, denial, evasion, and rationalization. But sometimes they make an impression and the family begins to wonder about them. It is especially useful to concentrate on here-and-now feelings; this method usually penetrates much deeper than dealing with feelings described in retrospect. The technique is particularly useful with intellectualizing families who isolate affect (as with the statement, "Mr. Jones, your daughter just told you to get out of the room, yet you smiled and ignored her statement and then got angry about something else").

Every family has its own unique practices, customs, and myths, which, because they have served the needs of the family system for a long time, seem logical, right, and comfortable to the family members, but to outside observers (in this case, the therapists) they may not only seem weird and incomprehensible but often bewildering and even outraging. Sometimes the family myth is some glaring injustice which has been isolated from everyone's awareness. For example, in one family the mother, instead of wearing her husband's wedding ring, wore the ring of a fiancé who had been dead for 30 years. One of the cotherapists, a female, astonished by this state of affairs, said, "This is crazy! Why do you stand for this, your wife wearing on her finger the ring of another man?" In another family it was revealed that the wife was the sole breadwinner, handled all the money, gave her husband an allowance, and had her husband sign the house over to her as sole owner because of his "incompetence." One of the male therapists turned to the husband and said, "For God's sake, why did you allow this to come about?" Sometimes the therapists are prompted to comment about some feeling which has been massively excluded from the family arena: "This whole family seems to be dead. Don't any of you ever have any fun?" The interjection of the therapists' feelings frequently helps as a powerful stimulant in opening up issues and areas which had long been closed and walled off by the family. There are other occasions when the therapists seem to step out of their roles as professionals and use themselves as real people. This maneuver occurs most often in response to the drastic violation of semantic meaning which some families present (Schaffer et al., 1962), although it must be remembered that every therapist will find strange and disturbing things in every family, depending on how different they are from his own family experience. At such times we have tried the technique of admitting ignorance or perplexity as to what is going on; one therapist adopted a "playing dumb" attitude and kept pleading to the family that he didn't understand, saying "I'm lost; find me." The cotherapists may even interrupt the interaction, turn to each other as islands of reality in the room, discuss their confusion, and speculate about the meanings. Sarcasm and impatience may be used to make the family defenses more pliable; also reassurance, physical touching, sympathy, empathizing with the family all have their place. The therapists may also openly admit to having personal taboo feelings, which the family cannot express; they may admit, for example, to having had sexual or hostile feelings toward their own parents, siblings, or children.

Rarely does one observe overt seductiveness or direct sadism, or full expression of socially undesirable feelings in the sessions, not only because no family ever fully relinquishes its loyalty to the family code, but also because the approval of the therapists is greatly desired. The same person who says of a family member during the session, "I admire her courage and perseverance and wonderful personality" or "He's kind and tender and sweet and like a rock for me," has been quoted as saying in the privacy of the home, "I'll knock your teeth down your throat, you stupid bastard!" or "You're just a piece of shit." Goffman (1956) has beautifully illustrated how people present themselves to outsiders, in contrast with their behavior at home. After several years, as the family begins to feel that the therapists are really with them, there is a deepening of confidence and an increase in spontaneous behavior, but, of course, the degree of openness can only be conjectured.

As we gained experience in working with families we became less hesitant about taking more forceful, active positions in order to help the family become unshackled from their rigid patterns. Sometimes these procedures are used in the early phases. At times, we would insist that loud, disorganized families who jumped from one topic to another focus on one issue and discuss it in minute detail. On other occasions, especially with the more regressed families, we have found it useful to make certain demands calculated to cause a shift in the intrafamilial dynamics. For example, in one family the father had lived away from home for a number of years and the therapists insisted that he move back into the house; with several families, we have suggested that the parents, who had not done so for years, sleep together in the same bed; in another family situation we referred a father, long unemployed, for vocational training so that he could gain self-respect by working. In one family the parents never made a joint decision; decisions had always been made by a steamroller of a mother who felt she had to handle everything. The designated patient, an only child, had exploited this situation by driving a wedge between her parents and manipulating them against each other. The father made his futile protests, often complaining that he had no authority, and was envious of his daughter's capacity to exact favors from his wife by constant demands. At a certain point in the family therapy, the patient had been discharged and was sitting around the house being waited on by the mother; we insisted that the parents, then and there, jointly discuss and decide what daily chores the daughter should carry out. It was interesting to watch the anxiety build as all three family members repeatedly misinterpreted these simple instructions; the parents avoided discussion between themselves and kept addressing their statements to either the daughter or the therapists. Without proper timing, these active moves by the therapists may result in meaningless, ritualistic conformance.

Some of the therapeutic procedures utilized have been frankly experimental and occasionally accidental. On several occasions when one of the cotherapists could not attend a session another member of the staff would sit in in his place. We were surprised to note that when this happened the family would often adapt to the change with extreme docility and passivity, continuing their discussion from the week before as if nothing was different, not raising any objections, and frequently not even asking about the missing therapist. This type of reaction has made us wonder about the extent to which therapy is perceived by some families as a nonspecific absorbing and feeding process wherein the therapists, whoever they may be, are faceless dispensers of nurturance. There have been instances when the therapist replacement, because he has not been so involved in the countertransference, has been able to "see" and deal with the family and cotherapist on new terms and with a new perspective, thereby helping to break up a long-standing logjam. The use of a visiting therapist has been a standard procedure at the Atlanta Psychiatric Clinic (Whitaker et al., 1956) where a member of the staff is routinely invited to sit in on problem therapy situations as a consultant.

One procedure which has proven its worth is temporary work with family subsystems. There are certain family systems with built-in sets of conditions which make it extremely difficult to work with the system as a whole. One such family situation is where divided loyalties are operating, for instance in a family where a man is torn between his wife and his mother and paralyzed in the presence of both. We have found it useful in situations of this type to approach the system at its weakest point by dealing with one segment of the total system. In the aforementioned family, after meeting for some time with the entire psychological system of father, mother, two children, and paternal grandmother, we learned that the father called his mother every day and confided in her, while at the same time his wife resented his lack of closeness to her but felt unable to verbalize her feelings because she, too, needed her husband's mother as a substitute for her own dead mother. When we met with just the father and his mother together we were able to make some inroads into the problem of their symbiotic relationship; for the first time in his life the father was able to get angry at his mother, especially when she uttered her familiar guilt-provoking statement, "Don't worry about me, I'm going off to an old ladies' home. Go back to that wife of yours." The work with subsystems, of lesser or greater duration depending on the nature of the dynamics, must sooner or later be tied in with the larger picture. There is the possible handicap of creating anxiety and suspicion in the family members who are transitorily excluded, but this newly created anxiety itself may also be an avenue for the opening up of new areas.

There are a number of typical family problems which appear repeatedly. One of the most common results from the parents being so overwhelmed with their introjects that there is essentially no marriage and the children, for their own survival, are engaged in attempts to save their parents' marriage. Another common problem is when the mother identifies with the child and obtains fathering through the child and the father identifies with the child and obtains mothering through the child; then their complaints about their mates as *the* mother or father relate to themselves. One usual pattern is for the mother to be overinvolved with her own mother and, from this hostile-dependent alliance, the two women use the men as scapegoats, so that when a child gets psychiatrically ill it's because father "was not a father to the children." In such a situation the father has derived vicarious satisfaction from his wife's involvement with her family and frequently seeks the projected, scapegoated role. Some of the complexity of scapegoating as a transpersonal, rather than intrapsychic, phenomenon is better understood when it is observed in its family context. In one family the mother had strong feelings of unrecognized hostility toward her daughter who to her represented a hated sister. The mother constantly reminded her husband of the daughter's misbehavior, and the husband would punish the daughter by whipping her. Then, after the beating, the mother would comfort the daughter and, in the daughter's presence, would accuse the father of being brutal and lacking in understanding. Family therapy sessions dealt with the theme of father's "brutality," and the father, confused by the double bind, could only sputter helplessly and defensively about how his daughter's bad behavior deserved punishment. Father and daughter argued and mother, skillfully scapegoating her husband, remained in the background, concealing her role in the transaction by quiet and righteous comments. These situations are further complicated by the fact that every family member scapegoats every other family member behind camouflaging maneuvers. Sometimes the scapegoating involves a network of collusion with a dyad against a larger number (as when both parents unconsciously allied against the children's autonomy, by, perhaps, trying to turn the children against each other.)

The dominating-aggressive mother and inadequate-passive father stereotypes have become part of the folklore of family psychiatry, and like all stereotypes there is a bit of substance to the oversimplifications. Our initial experiences with the mothers of this type led to considerable difficulty because we tried to meet them head-on. This type of woman projects all of her undesirable qualities onto the other members of the family or the therapists. She does not "hear" anything that does not agree with her own notions and she can be bafflingly infuriating. Interspersed between the servile flattery of the sycophant are belittling statements such as, "What psychiatric textbook did you get *that* out of?" and cutting, retaliatory enjoinders which raise the small hairs on the back of one's neck. These women have a vital need to engage in emotional in-fighting and a compelling talent for getting the therapists involved to the extent that much therapeutic time has been spent by the cotherapists in rescuing each other from the engulfment. In our early experience the cotherapists struggled to maintain tight control by working together, but in extended work with these women we learned to avoid noticing what they did and pay attention to what they missed in life. This procedure helped to slacken their defensiveness so that sooner or later there would emerge from behind the awesome pseudostrength the deprived, frightened little girl who had always felt worthless and unloveable. When this step was reached the rest of the family reverberated to the change, initially with fear of loss of the powerful parent and later by having to make necessary accommodations.

Despite the frustration in dealing with the aggressive mother, however, we soon learned that the passive father presented a more formidable challenge. First of all, some degree of humiliation and admission of failure on the part of the father is contingent in coming for family therapy. And although the therapists make every conscious effort to build him up during the sessions, some double-binding is inherently operative when either the "sick" child is taken over by a therapist in concurrent individual therapy or when the father observes the therapists dealing with his wife in a way which he has never been able to. Inasmuch as some of the built-in procedures may reinforce the father's inadequacy, we have wondered whether the therapists unconsciously subsidize the powerful forces from wife, children, and the father himself which synchronize to maintain the system. An additional obstacle the therapists have faced is that sometimes it just doesn't seem cricket to question such a nice, reasonable guy. A number of techniques have been tried in dealing with these predicaments: forcing more interaction between the husband and wife; assigning tasks (such as insisting that for a given period of time the father make the decisions at home, right or wrong, and that his wife give unquestioned support); having a female therapist give encouragement in a flattering way; occasional individual sessions with the father. Metaphorically speaking, we have not been as successful in giving the father a "penis" or getting him to use it as we have been in removing it from the mother. There are many dynamic bases for the adoption of passivity as a defense; in our experience one common one is that it serves the purpose of warding off murderous feelings. More accurately, however, we find greater success in dealing with the system aspects by focusing on the struggle for ego strength between the parents, how the mother and father represent dissociated aspects of each other, and how the children often help reinforce the internecine conflict.

In the exploration of the entire family system, the problems of the designated patient, the spark which precipitated the referral for family therapy, should not be ignored. It is necessary for the designated patient to accept her own share of responsibility for her behavior. One of the most instructive experiences for the family, however, occurs when they can recognize the connection between one of the designated patient's symptoms and a glossed-over family situation or long-avoided characteristic of one of the parents. One of the patients kept saying, "There's no sense in living when you can't talk to people." Her parents tried to reassure her that her ideas were foolish, that she *could* talk to people, and so on. Afterwards we learned that in this family nobody talked to each other at home; the parents, in particular, never meaningfully discussed anything with each other. One father had been complaining for months about his son's stealing, accusing him of being a "loner," and holding himself up as a paragon of virtue; he finally sheepishly admitted that he used to steal and had never had any close friends. In their ramblings, psychotic patients frequently use the words "phony" and "counterfeit," referring not only to themselves but also to their parents. We have had to spend much time dealing with duplicitous behavior. One can tell that the family is making progress when the members become more honest about their feelings about themselves. The motives of the parents can usually be hidden behind conventional views which no one could dispute. The father who complained about his daughter's aimless wandering through the streets at night stated his realistic fear that something sexually dangerous could occur; yet he revealed another motive besides fatherly concern when he said, "As long as she does this sort of thing, there can be no real intercourse between us. . . ." When their daughters date obviously undesirable men, parents feel justified in objecting and can safely conceal from themselves their wish to keep the daughter bound to the family and free from enduring heterosexual attachments. The patient, by going out with objectionable men, cooperates with the motives of her parents. Only when she begins to date eligible men in a realistic way can the reluctance of the parents to liberate her be unmasked.

Actually, when family therapy has really begun its effect, the problems of the designated patient, which used to be the exclusive preoccupation of the family, have long since receded into the background. Each of the parents has had the sobering experience of struggling with his own inner world, of having taken back some of his projections inside himself (a process usually followed by depression), of having had to reexamine his whole manner of existence and outlook on other people, and, especially, of having had to reevaluate his feelings about his own parents or siblings. There are always mixed feelings about the process of decathecting from introjects. One father who badly needed to sustain the illusion that he was loved as a child brought in a picture of himself as a baby, saying, "See me smiling there? I *must* have been happy then!" One mother burst forth with, "All right, my mother never gave me anything that counted and never appreciated anything I tried to do for her. What can I do about it now? What do you doctors want me to do, go to her grave and scream and curse at her?" The children are usually quite moved and sympathetic to their parents during these revelations; it is not uncommon to see them cluster around a mother or father and hug and kiss them as their parents cry over past hurts or disappointments. The designated patient or one of the "well" children may even develop symptoms or act out outside the sessions in order to save a parent from suffering. These later sessions are usually quiet, punctuated by sudden realizations, connections between the past and the present, and, occasionally, of turning to a mate or a child and really seeing him for the first time. Such revelations of the parents bring to them that curious combination often seen in those who have gained some true emotional insight: a new-found sense of relief, sometimes accompanied by omnipotent feelings as to their limitless possibilities as people, plus a sense of depression and regret over partial loss of the introjects and, in addition, some guilt over the way family members and other people have been "used." Sometimes the changes of the parents are evident in their increased interest in their appearance and in extrafamilial matters; we have even noticed marked changes in voice quality and other physical characteristics. The most important change which occurs, however, is the strengthening of the marital tie, a topic discussed in greater detail in the section on "Marriage Problems."

In family therapy as in all forms of therapy, there seems to be a great deal of wasted time, lost motion, and empty chit-chat before the few dramatic moments occur, when a meaningful connection is made, or an honest exchange of feeling is expressed. However, it is hard to tell when something internal is happening even though on the surface everything seems the same. The seemingly empty fill-ins may be necessary in order for the significant changes to take place. Personality change is very subtle. Sometimes even the therapists do not recognize the change in one of the family members or in the family patterns; occasionally it takes the observation of some outsider, like another member of the therapy staff, to direct the therapists' attention to the change. There are many levels on which change can take place. Frequent regression to old patterns occurs, sometimes precipitated by real change in one member, sometimes by separation anxiety when the therapists go on vacation or talk about future termination.

As the families begin to consider the idea that they *can* change their feelings about each other they will become more unguarded, and their behavior in the treatment setting will more closely approximate that which may occur at the dinner table when, for example, they have an argument. In fact, some families will unwittingly exaggerate their feelings in order to provoke more interest from the therapists. It must be remembered, though, that the motivation for change in most families is dissociated. At the deepest level they continue to attend sessions in order to get the therapists' assistance in restoring things back to how they used to be. During the course of the therapy they become more dependent on and involved with the therapists, and when positive change takes place it occurs almost despite themselves.

We have been describing thus far the kinds of families who make the most effective use of family therapy by achieving the ability to open up, to relate, to reflect, and to change. There are other families, of course, who are unable to use the structure of family therapy as a means of growth. These families frequently require constant transfusions in the form of more explicit parental-like roles taken on by the therapists, and even by bringing into the sessions extended family members or significant peripheral persons who could contribute added strength to the main family. These are the families who provoked some of the more active and experimental techniques described earlier; they seem to need concrete action rather than words. We have realized with some of these families that they cannot be forced to change; you sort of have to go along with them.

What has been called in this section the middle phases of family therapy may be a misnomer since there is insufficient knowledge of the therapy process to be able to delineate regular phases or whether a particular aspect belongs in one phase or another. Although the problems of resistance, marriage, the "well" sibling, transference/countertransference, and the cotherapy team relationship are here included as subsections of the middle phases, they will make their effect known at any stage in the therapy process.

Resistance in Family Therapy

Resistance, the opposition against attempts to expose unconscious motives, can assume many different guises in all forms of psychotherapy. Sometimes even professional therapists slip into thinking of resistance as contrariness or stubbornness because the blindness of people toward recognizing what they are doing may seem like obstinacy. Conscious resistance (the fear of rejection, shame, or distrust of the therapist) creates particular therapeutic problems, but unconscious resistance, which is dealt with most carefully in classical psychoanalysis and is at the root of all conscious resistances, is far more complicated, not only because the unconscious of the therapist can dovetail with that of the patient, but also because anything can be used in the service of unconscious resistance (for example, silence or too much talking, lack of affect or too much affect, acting out or inability to act, and so forth). These, then, are the intrapsychic resistances of individuals which operate within the relatively nonthreatening setting of one-to-one psychotherapy.

Different kinds of resistances come into play in traditional group therapy, largely as a function of the defenses of the individual in the group situation (Varon, 1958) as well as the nature of the group resistance itself (Redl, 1948). The individual in the group situation not only has to protect himself from knowing certain aspects of himself, but he has to conceal his deeper motives from others while at the same time he is attempting to adjust and accommodate to other members of the group. Here we have one of the key differences between group and family therapy (Handlon and Parloff, 1962). The family comes to therapy with a long history of fit, private understandings, highly predictable responses, and deep feeling for each other; group dissolution at the end of treatment is highly unlikely. In group therapy the culture is created de novo, and the members do not expect real satisfaction of needs from each other. Family therapy and group therapy both provide the opportunity for the members to master in a socially real situation the types of near-refractory experiences which produced the particular kinds of pathologic defenses in the first place—group therapy by providing sibling and parental surrogates and family therapy by the presence of the original figures. However, because of the unique quality of the family group and the special bonds of relationship and familiarity, both conscious and unconscious resistances have a distinctive quality and life all their own in family therapy and operate *in addition* to the familiar ones seen in individual and group therapy. It is selected aspects of these latter endemic transactional and system defenses which this section describes.

Once we felt in our early years of operation that we had made important discoveries about the validity of the transactional and shared psychopathology viewpoint in diagnosing what was going on in the family which eventuated in overt disturbance in one member, we optimistically believed that all we had to do was bring the members of the family together regularly, utilize our knowledge of psychotherapy, and we would then be in a position to alter the total structure in a therapeutic way. This kind of naïveté about the enormous complexity involved in bringing about change in people probably accompanies the development of every new psychotherapy approach. At any rate, our therapy teams not only ran into types of resistances which were unlike any previously encountered in prior experience with individual and group therapy, but occasionally the therapy teams were surprised and disappointed when they began to realize the formidability of the therapy task before them. For example, they learned that a massive resistance phase is encountered with every family once the preliminaries are out of the way; although this phase should have been expected, in our early experience it still came as a shock. One therapy team said at that time, "I can't understand it; the family was working so well, we were really getting somewhere, and now suddenly they don't want to come in anymore." We learned two lessons from this experience: (1) to be wary when things seem to be going too well in therapy; and (2) that families will manipulate when they sense that the therapists want them too much, just as they will respond by withdrawal when they feel that the therapists do not like them. Families can evoke feelings of jealousy and possessiveness in therapists much more powerfully than can individual patients.

There are some people who start family therapy with great enthusiasm because they have a strategy in mind, and when the therapists do not fit in with their strategy they are quickly demotivated. One mother, who had abandoned her children for many years after the break-up of her first marriage, remarried and then tried to make a home for her children. This second husband was seen by her and the children as a monster who was strict and arbitrary. The mother persuaded her reluctant husband to attend the initial evaluation session and was hoping to get her children and the therapists to see what a bad man he was. As the therapists saw the situation, however, this man was a better parent to her children than she was; his so-called strictness showed genuine care for the welfare of the children. Her strategy became more clear: to use her husband as scapegoat and convince everyone that she had not abandoned and rejected her children. By the end of the initial evaluation session, the mother did not want to continue family therapy and her initially reluctant husband was pushing for it.

The massive resistance phase usually follows when the immediate crisis presented by the designated patient is past and the family system is not hurting so much. There then ensues a "don't rock the boat" attitude. The resistance makes its appearance innocently enough when the family spokesman (usually the father, urged to speak by the mother) requests that they come in every other week instead of every week. Or there may be complaints from the children about missing school. In their early experience with families the family therapists used to meet the resistances head-on, engaged in controversy, and even attempted to persuade families to continue, citing reality reasons (such as, "Now which is really more important—that the family continue with this sick kind of living or that Johnny misses his class in English?"). There was something about the quality of family therapy and the anxiety aroused which subtly provoked therapists to bypass their usual precautions in working through resistances and making confrontations palatable. These early kinds of activities caused such narcissistic pains that the families often terminated the therapy. At any rate, by using the security of the cotherapy team relationship we learned to deal with the fears of loss and all the other unconscious reasons which lay behind the resistance. As in all matters of technique, more depends on *how* something is said rather than on *what* is said.

Resistances in family therapy can assume many different shapes and forms, and in the final analysis it may become a question of whether the therapists can tolerate them over a long period of time. One type of resistance that is particularly frustrating is a kind of passive mastery practiced by the family whereby they come in week after week, produce little or no material, and do not relate their feelings. After making valiant efforts to stimulate and get the family to move, the therapists frequently end up feeling useless and wiped out as people.

Another test of the therapists' tolerance occurs after many months of treatment when the families seem to go round and round, fixated in an immovable rut with each other, recognizing that much distress is created but being unable to do anything except repeat the same pattern over and over, even though they say they want something different. When it is interpreted that they must want it this way, that everything they do perpetuates the situation, and that essential needs are being filled through this manner of torturous relating, they always deny it. We have speculated that perhaps, given the inner and outer circumstances, this is the best that the family can do, that perhaps they are settling for what they have rather than what they really want because they view the alternative as an even greater danger (such as abandonment). Many problems are encountered in the process of resolving such massive resistances. Occasionally, interruptions or hiatuses in treatment, whether planned or accidental, have often helped a family to surmount these seemingly endless repetition compulsions.

Whether or not treatment sessions should be held without all specified family members being present is one issue on which there seems to be some division among family therapists. Sonne, Speck, and Jungreis (1962) first pointed out the absent member maneuver as a major resistance in family therapy. They suggested that one member of the family would absent himself from the therapy sessions in order to preserve fixed paired relationship patterns in the family, and that this maneuver, entailing the cooperation of the whole family, occurs in order to avoid the anxiety of a triangular heterosexual growth experience. The maneuver is generally handled by insisting on the presence of the absent member. Another point of view, set forth primarily by Bowen is that the family approach can still be utilized by seeing the family members in any combination. Bowen maintains that there are occasions when the therapist can, at certain stages in the treatment process, see one family member in family therapy and that this procedure is not individual psychotherapy because the raising of the level of differentiation of one member is oriented toward serving a therapeutic need for the entire family. The contradictions between these two viewpoints may be only superficial since they both stem from increasing recognition of the way family-system resistances operate. When it is the therapists, rather than the family, who control the situation and decide who should be included, many resistances can be anticipated and managed. Further understanding will be needed before family therapists can decide with a particular family when to approach the family system through one member or a pair, or when to insist that all members be present at all times.

Several other controversial issues have confronted family therapists: whether or not children should be present when parents discuss their sexual relationship; or how old children should be before they are to be included in the treatment sessions. These decisions should be decided on the basis of a particular family's level of integration and dynamics. In general, in families where the children have already been overexposed to sexual talk or behavior between parents, we have tended to have children present, largely in order to help clear up distortions in their minds. Some therapists are more reluctant to follow this procedure and are more convinced that children should be protected from this aspect of the adult world. Also, some family therapists can work comfortably with preschool children present during the sessions, whereas most would prefer including only children of at least 6 or 7.

Resistance in essence revolves around the question of change, inasmuch as the unavoidable, powerful forces which protest and try to maintain the pathologic arrangements are most operative when the therapy begins to deal with conflictual areas which, if fully faced and resolved, could result in growth and change. Searles, in a very penetrating report (1961), has written about some of the reasons why individual schizophrenic patients are so afraid and unable to change (many of his concepts could be applied also to neurotic patients and character disorders in psychotherapy and analysis). Families, too, conceive of change in terms of deprivation rather than enhancement, and, at the deepest level, they fear change in the family system which will result in loss of some vitally needed form of relationship, even if the relationship has its hurting aspects. Family members are threatened to the core of their beings by the prospect of having to abandon infantile needs provided by or hoped for from other family members, and they will jointly resist efforts to reveal these motivations, much less give them up. It is the theory of psychoanalytic treatment that when infantile needs are frustrated (unconditional love, sympathy, indulgence, total acceptance, comfort, fondling, nursing, and so forth), the analytic patient reaches the turning point of renouncing them in their literal, infantile form and can seek gratification of these needs in more mature and realistic ways (Menninger, 1958). The much-deprived members of the families we have seen, however, seem to need to pursue gratification of their infantile needs in a very real sense and have great difficulty renouncing any of them, despite the fact that they are chronically frustrated. Each family member participates in the resistance, moreover, for each member has an investment in a role which serves a system function and maintains family homeostatic balance. Efforts made by dissatisfied members to change the system have had the paradoxical effect of perpetuating the system.

There are, of course, many other reasons for resistance to change other than the inability to abandon infantile needs, which we consider the most fundamental. Although on one level each member of the family recognizes the necessity for changes in someone else in the family, rather than in himself, on another level each member unconsciously suggests that he would feel a burden of guilt if he himself changed. For example, the designated patient signals trouble in the family by developing symptoms or acting out; then, once family therapy is undertaken and the parents get upset, the designated patient begins to feel guilty over disturbing the parents and then makes efforts to terminate the therapy. (One wonders, in this connection, how many individual psychotherapies and analyses have failed because the patient would rather keep his particular symptoms than to feel guilty over maturing and making someone else suffer in the process.) When we see parents blocking each other's therapeutic explorations we know that they fear that if their mate matures they themselves will be seen as they feel they really are (unlovable, childish, hateful, and so forth) and, therefore, they will lose them. It is very difficult for people to realize that ultimately they can only change for themselves.

Sources of resistance are complex and varied: parents' use of the sessions to report on the designated patient's crazy behavior; avoidance of discussion of the marriage relationship; exaggeration of the therapists' comments to the point of absurdity; motivation for family therapy expressed in order to screen and deflect from intrapsychic exploration; particularly strong injunctions against family disloyalty; family members' "protection" of each other; intense feelings of family honor and position; reciprocal scapegoating. Other sources of resistance are based on countertransference factors such as fathers who are important members of the community; "well" siblings who have managed to free themselves to some extent from the family embroilments; social standards about the sanctity of the family; sweet, grey-haired mothers; the fragility of some families (such as those in which there has been a great deal of trauma); wide cultural differences between the family and the therapists. These are all examples of resistance factors which can operate, sometimes very subtly, to thwart exploration and change. There are occasions when the therapists learn relatively late in the therapy process about some very significant peripheral person (friend, neighbor, extended relative, lawyer, doctor, religious advisor) who exerts a great influence on the family but whose existence is concealed. This special relationship can act as a strong resistance and it is advisable to invite such a person to the sessions. Resistances are always a function of an intricate interplay between variables in the family and variables in the therapists (such as conflicts in a single therapist or between the cotherapists). As Carl Whitaker once remarked, is there really resistance or is there something in the therapist which prevents exploration?

Marriage Problems in Family Therapy

As we acquired experience working with families, one functional goal of family therapy gradually evolved: to separate the generational differences which had been breached extravagantly and to emphasize that parents are parents and children are children. We soon discovered that this goal cannot be approached until the parents begin to meet each other's needs. Our implicit set of values may, as anthropologists have pointed out, be an anomaly of Western society; apparently, there are parts of the world where parents are not expected to raise children alone or to fill all their important needs in each other. We would agree with Bell (1962), moreover, that the family should not be viewed as a "self-contained unit existing in a social and cultural vacuum," and that one should not neglect the extended family and surrounding society network as the framework within which the family develops. From a practical clinical viewpoint, however, our approach of strengthening the marriage has paid off the greatest dividend in terms of freeing the children to have lives of their own. The impact of extended family relations and the wider community, in terms of what they mean to a particular family and how they are used, is an inherent part of our daily therapeutic work.

Attempting to create a marital bond where there has never been a husband–wife arrangement, however, is no small task. Before recounting our experiences in handling marriage problems in family therapy, some theoretical considerations about marriage will be discussed. It has been said, with some justification, that the greatest happiness which can be achieved in life emerges as a by-product of a "good" marriage and, conversely, that an incredibly varied range of human misery can result from a "bad" marriage, ranging from legal divorce, emotional divorce, perpetual bickering, destructive acting out, psychosomatic and psychological disorders and their pernicious effects on children, society, and the human spirit. Another truism is that the greatest gift which parents can bestow on children is to give them the security of two parents who love each other.

It is very difficult to determine, nonetheless, what constitutes a happy or even a workable marriage. The writer, while preparing this chapter, looked over a number of books on marriage and was surprised to discover the number of contradictory statements made by equally experienced professionals in this area. It has been said by some that no one ever cured himself of a neurosis by marrying and that the neurotic problems of the two marriage partners are cumulative; on the other hand, others say that a marriage by virtue of its being unhappy can mask or prevent the emergence of a neurosis, or that the marriage relationship may embody compensatory mechanisms for seriously disturbed partners. One group of investigators maintains that the personality is fairly well fixed by the time a person marries, and that marriage partners are doomed to disappointment in their eternal efforts to change the personalities of their mates; other practitioners say that marriage partners can help each other to grow and mature.

These contradictions are probably not as incongruous as one may suppose when some of the intricate complexities involved in the marriage relationship are examined more deeply. One could start with Kubie's chapter in what is probably one of the best publications in the marriage field, *Neurotic Interaction in Marriage* (1956; chapter 2). After stating his initial point that there are neurotic ingredients in every human personality, and, consequently, in every marriage, Kubie goes on to present his major thesis that the main source of unhappiness between husband and wife is found in the discrepancies between their conscious and unconscious demands on each other and on the marriage, as expressed first in the choice of a mate and then in the subsequent evolution of their relationship. Congruent with this thesis, Kubie describes how unconscious forces derived from the family of origin and based on the need to "wipe out old pains or pay off an old score," can create profound marital discord and estrangement, particularly when the partners can be so misled by the illusory romantic tradition. One finds, then, that individuals unconsciously seek parents instead of spouses, that they marry those with whom they can prove or correct something about themselves, those with whom they can duplicate or master an old conflictual relationship, and so on. Since the unconscious demands cannot be met without conflicting with reality and conscious considerations, lack of marital integration is the rule rather than the exception. The foregoing helps explain why marital prediction studies, which rely on conscious report, are so limited, why the pre-marriage courtship relationship is no predictor of marital happiness, why agents which may help one marriage relationship may serve to destroy another, why hasty marriages can be as successful as those made with serious foresight, why reading marriage manuals or books on sex instruction can make matters worse, and that, as Kubie says, a happy marriage may be a happy accident.

The preceding considerations represent insights into the dynamic aspects of marriage difficulties which orthodox psychoanalytic thinking has given us. Although this thinking does stress the importance of unconscious motivation and there is some recognition of complementary patterns, it remains essentially an individually oriented emphasis. What is not taken into account is the interlocking collusion which occurs on an unconscious level, a bilateral reciprocity which has only been discerned through exploration of the transactional operations between people. When the interacting relationship of a couple has been studied as the partners were treated together as a dyadic unit (Whitaker, 1958; Haley, 1963), the fit of the contours of their internal object relationships was observed for the first time, no matter how other factors served to obscure the unconscious mutuality. In order to clarify the implications of this finding, it is necessary to discuss some of the dynamics of mate selection.

Whenever professionals in the marriage field have wanted to point to one factor as being responsible for marital difficulties, romantic love has been cited as the culprit. Kubie (1956), for example, defines "being in love" as "an obsessional state driven in part by anger." Still, romantic love as a psychic reality must be reckoned with since, in our culture at least, it is a powerful tradition reinforced by advertising, popular songs, movies, plays, and novels. (One can cite such fine British films as *Brief Encounter* and *Room at the Top* and such contemporary American plays as Chayevsky's *Middle of the Night* and *Marty,* which portray how profound the effects of sentimental love can be for even the unlikeliest matches. As one character put it, "Why should I give this up? When I feel like this there aren't enough hours in the day!") The process whereby a woman and man become attracted to each other and fall in love is an intricate almost magical one. In order to achieve that subjective, inspirational, pleasurable–painful state of "being in love," an extremely complex and subtle blending of conscious and unconscious conditions must be met: the loved one must have a certain combination of physical characteristics associated with sexual appeal, and certain mannerisms, style of relating, quality of affect, and so forth, which will stimulate the re-creation of the childhood, idealized family romance with all its promise of unconditional love; at the same time the prospective mate must be enough like the bad inner object to allow for eventual penetration of old hatreds. The ego may say: "I want to marry a man who will be strong but gentle, who can make me feel like a woman, who will be dependable, who will be successful, who will be faithful, who will control but not dominate me, who will make a good father for my children, who will be easygoing." The unconscious may seek "a man who can *almost* love, who lies or cheats or drinks, who is undependable, who will make a good father for *me,* who will keep me guessing, who will be unsuccessful, who will be weak and helpless, whom *I* can control, who will be difficult to get along with, who will be detached." The forthcoming marriage promises to make everything right that has always been wrong, and part of the function of the romantic ritual of courtship is to deny recognition of the bad object in the partner which will provide confirmation for the inner role model. The unconscious confirmation and dovetailing, moreover, is a two-way process; each partner has had his signal from his emotional radar system which recognizes the other as closely fitting the internal object needs. During the courtship and honeymoon period each partner, for the first time in his life, accepts the other and feels accepted for what he is, with all his different selves, all the residual part objects; the two merge into a satisfying oneness; the couple are "in love." It is no wonder that at times of stress during a long-lasting marriage the partners will try to recapture the feelings of the courtship and honeymoon period, the time when they felt united and fulfilled, each by the other.

Gradually, however, a spouse begins to feel that rather than having his real personality confirmed he is being trained to conform to and behave like the mate's projected internal image; at the same time he is unwittingly doing this to his partner. Each spouse begins to maneuver the other, unconsciously, into fitting the mold of the despised, exciting inner imago. The more the partners behave like the anticipated bad internal object, which is compounded of real, sometimes partially disowned traits of one's own plus the unreal projections of the mate, the greater the likelihood that a new kind of confirmation will take place, one that has been unconsciously sought and consciously dreaded. Each partner will begin to sense vaguely that some old ghost has risen to haunt him. This is the reason why spouses' complaints of each other, while containing some irrational elements, may be quite justified; the mate can give numerous instances of their validity ("She is not affectionate," "He nags," "I can't count on her," "He runs around with other women," "She doesn't really know me," "He is no longer passionate," "She is too jealous," "He is untidy," "She puts everyone before me," "He never listens to me," "She can't love," "He doesn't really care for me," "She's too bossy"). What is not recognized by the complainers is that this is what they "asked for." When disillusionment sets in, as it does in all marriages in some form ("You're not what I thought you were") the individual "remembers" the faults disregarded during courtship, feels betrayed, and then transfers to the spouse the reactivated hatred originally felt toward the split-off bad object of childhood. The disappointment occurs most frequently in the early part of marriage as the partners test each other out with their infantile ambivalences, which is why so many divorces occur in the early years of marriage. (The problems of legal divorce, multiple marriages, and inability to separate are probably different aspects of the same dynamic.) The crises of disconfirmation may occur later, however, during crucial check-points and stages of the marriage: the arrival of children, economic insecurity, involvements with in-laws, acting out by one or both partners, the separation of the children from the parents, retirement, or some other event. The greatest test of emotional maturity is the ability to make the exceedingly complex adjustment to another person in marriage, to tolerate in each other the working through of hated, ambivalent internal objects, and to permit each other's regression, in all of which infantile strivings are embedded in the context of bonds of affection, the process of give and get, the acceptance of adult responsibility, and the overflow of love to the children. Feelings of outrage and frustration will be greatest in those couples whose own parents could not resolve the universal marriage struggle and who were themselves subject to deprivation, resulting in low self-esteem, a weak sense of identity, and a polarization of their love–hate conflict. These partners have even higher expectations of marriage, and they feel even more keenly a sense of treachery and having been cheated.

In the more chronic, prolonged kind of marital disharmony situation that we see in family therapy, the "can't-live-with, can't-live-without" syndrome is the most common. Dicks (1964), some of whose thought is represented in the prior statements and whose concept of the "shared internal object" as a bond between marriage partners is very intriguing, has made the following incisive statement on the question as to why unhappy couples stay together: "social values and duty to the children apart, there is a need in each partner to wring out of the other the response that signifies to the unconscious the typical interaction model with the internal object or objects which have come to be vested in the marital relationship." (p. 269). When these kinds of marriages persist through many years the mates are caught up in a relentless open or silent warfare, obtaining their gratification by using each other or the children almost purely as bad internal-object representations. The real personalities of the family members have long ceased to exist, and we witness a marriage characterized by the absence of sexual relations and the partners' almost exclusive use of each other as child or parent, far beyond the occasional alternation of roles seen in all marriages. One system aspect of the marriage problem is that the roles of each of the children can reflect the partners' ambivalence about their marriage, one child often representing the good and one the evil. Or, the children may be ignored, punished, or become the battleground of an unhappy marriage.

Clinical counterparts of the previous theoretical notions are seen in our work with couples during the course of family therapy. With the goal of "remarrying" the parents, we attempt to explore the relevant motivational formulae in each partner, help them come to terms with their introjects, and explicate the interlocking nature of the meaning of their marital bond. There is considerable diversity in the capacity of couples to work along these lines, as well as variability as to the stage of family therapy in which the marriage relationship can be approached. Many couples are very fearful of having their marriage relationship explored and use the problems of the children as dilatory tactics to ward off exploration of themselves. Sometimes we have found it useful in these situations to make a direct confrontation of the unspoken horror: "How long have you both felt that this marriage hasn't really existed?" After exploration we usually find that these couples have long ago abandoned honesty in their relationship. Early in the marriage attempts had been made to relate real feelings to each other, but these talk sessions ended in great frustration because neither could get the other to see his point of view. Communication had become impossible because each was using the language of his own background where words of love, closeness, jealousy, intimacy, and aggression had different meanings. The partners then arrived at a modus vivendi whereby they wrote each other off and played a role by not letting the other know their real feelings. By mutual unspoken consent their problems with each other no longer existed, although they could be quite concerned about problems in the children. As these marriages are probed by the therapists, their implicit contract of "I won't tell on you if you won't tell on me" (Carroll, 1960) can be violently ruptured. The mate who breaches the contract and begins to "tell" can expect a vitriolic counterattack, such as, "Okay, brother, if that's how you're going to play, now watch me!"

Other couples' marriage difficulties are in the open from the first session, as each partner pours forth upon the other a welter of grievances and bitter recrimina-tions. They turn to each other with accusations and counter-accusations as they recount obsolete injuries, blame each other's families and ancestors, using the therapy sessions to gain allies for their cause. Curiously, though, a dispute of this sort may suddenly cease and the parents will point toward the designated patient as the real problem in the family; their controversies with each other appear to them to be extrinsic and isolated from the problems presented by the designated patient. At times they give the impression that they're relieved to have their child's illness to contend with so that they won't have to face fully their despairing, terrifying, and potentially murderous feelings toward each other.

Although in both types of marital discord problems—the silent and the open—there are threats of divorce, the real possibility of separation or divorce is almost nonexistent; in the unconscious, separation means psychic death. When the therapists wonder, in view of so much obvious discontent, whether they have thought of leaving each other, a partner may say, "He does this and that cruel thing to me, but deep down I know he loves me." The variety of meanings given to the word "love" is legion. Note the universality of the statement: "I love you so much I wish I liked you." Or take the following interchange: He: "I wish you could be as kind to me as you are to strangers." She: "But I'm not in love with *them!*" For some people, sad to say, it is true that, in the words of the popular song, "You always hurt the one you love." Of course, the children *must* feel their parents love each other because if they don't there is no love in this world and what hope would exist for them? While it can be said that love which is never demonstrated becomes an abstraction with no content, on another level deep attachment can be revealed during extreme emergencies or loss, for example through death, as witness the depression in a sadomasochistic partner when his mate dies. A man and woman who have touched each other, had sexual intercourse and children together, argued, smelled each other, and shared experiences and reminiscences together do become a part of each other. When there has been intense emotional investment in each other, people can only separate savagely. Note, for example, the vituperation and acrimony which surrounds divorce proceedings; the bitter quality of the exchanges shocks even experienced lawyers (Nizer, 1961, chapter 2).

In many marriage situations one of the partners acts out in some gross fashion (such as through alcoholism or unfaithfulness), and we often learn how the objecting partner's needs are being served by the acting out. Very frequently, the partner who brings the erring mate to treatment ends up being the more seriously disturbed member. There is an old saying, "Be careful about what you say you want very much; you may get it," or, in converse form, "Be careful about what you say you don't want; you may lose it." We have seen spouses begin to change in the direction demanded by their mates, only to find the fulfillment of their wishes followed by severe disturbance. And we have seen "objectionable" behavior cease in one mate, followed by acute anxiety in the other over its absence.

As we work with the parents' past life, their deprivations and confusions, how they misused and were misused by their own parents, how they have misused their marriage partners, and how their pathology interlocks, they frequently develop a more empathic understanding of each other and thereby increase their capacities of giving to each other. There is a level of communication between husband and wife which is unobservable even by trained therapists; the medium of exchange is subliminal and may not be detected during the sessions because it occurs when they are alone with each other. In other words, improvement in the marriage may be seen only by its side-effects; for example, the parents may still argue, but the children are less involved in the arguments.

Does family therapy, however, end up being couple psychotherapy conducted in the presence of the children? Why have the children present at all? Is it possible that the therapists are subsidizing the family pathology by implicitly or explicitly calling on the assistance of the children in "marrying" their parents, thereby again parentifying the children? We have found the presence of the children helpful because when the therapists assume the responsibility for bringing the parents together, the children can be children again. If the therapists do not bring this union about, the children feel that they have to; the children have been trying unsuccessfully for years and the therapists help free them from the healing task. As my colleague Oscar Weiner says, what the therapists are doing, essentially, is kicking the children out of the parents' bed. Sometimes the designated patient or one of the other children will develop symptoms during this process because they are losing the familiar, cherished but ego-disruptive role. Children also get upset when they see their parents suffer over past hurts, but in the long run it is comforting; they have always sensed unhappiness in their parents, but they didn't know why. As the uncertainty becomes more understandable, the parents seem more real; the ultimate in the relationship with parents, as Oscar Wilde put it, is when you come to forgive them.

The "Well" Sibling
in Family Therapy

The chief questions, raised by both professionals *and* the family, against the concept of interrelated pathology in the family and against the view of parental contribution to the illness of the designated patient are: "If the parents are to blame and it's the family atmosphere that is responsible, why aren't the other children in the family sick? How can children from the same family be so different?"

Several investigators have attempted to answer these questions by interviewing patients, siblings, and parents, but unfortunately these studies were restricted to the one syndrome of schizophrenia and were, with one exception, based on separate interviews rather than observation of family interaction. Yi-Chuang Lu (1961) found that schizophrenic patients had concentrated all emotional invest-ments in their parents, especially in mothers, whereas the normal siblings had wider emotional investments and avoided either a strong attachment or repulsion toward the mother. Prout and White (1956), utilizing separate interviews with schizophrenic patients, their siblings, and their mothers, concluded that the schizophrenic patient had been different from his siblings since infancy; they maintained, *on the basis of reported recollections*, that the patients had been more sensitive, unhappy, and less social than their healthier siblings. They further suggested that since the pre-schizophrenic child was so dependent and needed such an unusual degree of support and attention, the mother's overprotection was invited; the mother was merely meeting the needs of a weak child. The shortcomings of these studies are fairly obvious; they accept the statements of family members at face value, exclude fathers, and are oblivious to family interaction and system factors. A far more sophisticated approach was undertaken by Lidz et al. (1963) who utilized repeated intensive interviewing, home visits, projective testing, the reports of friends and teachers, and observation of family interaction of 16 families. The problem of the differential effects of the family on siblings was examined by these comprehensive methods, with the following considerations: the effects of changing family circumstances, the mother's capacity to provide nurturing care during the patient's infancy, the child's role in the family dynamics, the sibling's gender, idiosyncratic problems in the parents' relationship to the schizophrenic offspring, and the interaction between siblings. They found, first of all, that the so-called "well" siblings were not so well when studied carefully. As many siblings were psychotic as were reasonably well integrated, and all except 5 or 6 of the 24 siblings had serious personality disorders. Those siblings who had made a good adjustment did so by the defensive maneuvers of constriction and flight from the family. They found that in half of the families the patient was raised under conditions quite different from those under which the siblings were brought up; the family circumstances were so deviant in several cases that the patient seemed to have been born into a different family than the one into which the siblings were born. Moreover, a child of one sex may be more vulnerable within a given family than a child of the opposite sex. They found, further, that the child who becomes schizophrenic often lessens the impact of the parental pathology upon the siblings by serving as a target of the parents' intrusiveness, as a scapegoat, or as an example for the siblings to avoid. By identifying some of the dynamic elements which are involved in the differentiative forces which operate on children in the same family, Lidz et al. have advanced knowledge considerably in this area. However, although it involved some observation of family interaction, their work could not explicate the deeper levels of learning which can be revealed in extended family therapy.

Before relating our experiences with "well" siblings in family therapy, a few thoughts about the relatively neglected area of the sibling world are appropriate. Important learning and emotional experiences take place among children in the same family. Siblings learn to test strong love and hate feelings toward each other which are too dangerous to express toward parents because of the stakes involved and because a brother and sister cannot do much to you in any lasting way; the siblings know who stands where with what parent and they learn how to win, lose, or draw. When children play together they learn how to have fun; they see each other receive punishment or favorite treatment and have to deal with the resultant guilt or envy; when siblings quarrel they learn how to deal with their conflicts, and when parents quarrel the children can vent their frustrations on someone only slightly weaker or stronger. The siblings protect each other against parents or any extrafamilial threat; they can find an ally of like size in times of crisis; they master the skill of getting along with someone they don't always like; they struggle with the conflict between sharing and wanting everything. The sibling world, in brief, is a powerful family subsystem with a culture all its own. Excluding this sector of the family from treatment would result in an incomplete picture.

Inherited random variation of the genes has always been assumed to be the basis of personality differences among siblings, and it was not until the advent of the family concept that other factors began to be more fully appreciated. For example, role inculcation can contribute diversified personalities in the children which serve family system needs. Wynne et al. (1957) have reported on a set of monozygotic quadruplets whose roles within the family social organization accounted for differences in personality development and variability in the forms which their schizophrenic illnesses took. The various children in the family come to represent valued or feared expectations of the parents, based on the parental introjects; sometimes roles of the children are chosen for them even before they are born (such as the child who is conceived to "save the marriage"). Sometimes one child can represent the superego of the family and one the id. In every family of multiple siblings there is "the spoiled one," "the studious one," "the conscience of the family," and "the wild one;" the assigned roles are infinite. The "well" siblings frequently fill in gaps in the family and act as more successful interpreters between the parents than does the designated patient and are often highly valued for this purpose. Certain kinds of impulses (for example, sexual or hostile) are considered to be peculiar to particular children in the family; these children are sometimes seen in these fixed ways even when their basic nature presents evidence to the contrary. Every therapist is familiar with the mother or father who continually anticipates that the girl is going to "get in trouble with boys," so much so that daughter finally "cooperates" by getting in trouble with boys. Roles can be so fixed in a family that when role exchange takes place between two siblings the family may perceive the change as tantamount to psychosis in one or both children; Ryckoff et al. (1959) have illustrated how "good" and "bad" daughters acted out conscious and unconscious pressures from their parents by exchanging roles, an exchange which precipitated violent upheavals in the family. It is not uncommon to see in the family of the schizophrenic one rebellious child who acts out a destructive role complementary to the patient's overconformity; the same core conflict can exist in both patient and sibling but may be handled oppositely.

The aforementioned considerations partially account for several striking phenomena which we have observed during the course of family therapy. Those "well" siblings who managed to adjust by not dealing with the crazy contradictions of their family and who utilized the defenses of isolation, constriction, repression, and amnesia in order to survive, did become more disturbed as past trauma and the family ways unfolded in therapy. These siblings frequently began to display some of the same symptoms exhibited by the designated patient. Even the superadequate, successful sibling shows deep pathology when the surface is scratched. For years one mother had been blackmailing her family into giving in to her by constantly threatening to leave the house and go back to her mother. The only way this dire event could be thwarted was for one of the children to get sick. When the designated patient began to improve, the mother stated her threats again and one of the children, who had previously been considered the most outgoing and healthy one in the family, began having some of the same symptoms which the designated patient had shown earlier. This kind of experience is the basis for the statement of family therapists that the symptoms which shift from one family member to another represent relatively nonspecific accommodations to stresses in the total family complex and have a system value.

As a general rule, although some "well" siblings reflect the family system during therapy sessions, conceal it, or go along with it, most of them almost act as assistant therapists or observing egos because of their willingness to expose the system, reveal family secrets, comment on the pathologic communications, and expose the duplicities (one child said, "Now, mother, you know darn well you hate these meetings and you don't like what the doctors say to you, yet when the doctors ask you you say you like them"). Because they are usually willing to expose the family system, the "well" siblings are particularly directed toward the "absent member" role. It is more rare for the designated patient to risk being considered the family traitor. Some of the siblings, while they bear the imprint of some of the family pathology, are sufficiently sturdy to offer rescue to their ill brother or sister. We have seen siblings manage the psychotic one in a far more reasonable way than do the parents, thereby providing a bridge away from the family entanglements.

There is one possible drawback in utilizing the openness of the "well" siblings in family therapy sessions. Sometimes it may seem that the therapists are allied with the children against the parents. Great conflict of loyalty can develop in the children when they perceive that the therapists can have more realistic concern for them than do their own parents. And the parents may indirectly encourage the children to oppose the therapists or may even take retaliatory measures against the children. It is very necessary for the therapists to convey the message that they are interested in helping all the members of the family, even though they may temporarily seem to favor the view of a particular one. Sooner or later the parents have to be helped to take over the role which the therapists have transitorily adopted.

Initially we were hesitant to include in family sessions the "well" sibling who managed to escape the pathologic family, but since we began to insist that the siblings do attend we found that progress increased. Besides, we learned that in the long run the siblings benefited themselves and felt deprived and excluded when they were left out. The whole question of the "well" sibling is an intricate one which needs to be elaborated as further experience in family therapy is accumulated.

Transference and Countertransference

Any attempt to cover the multitudinous aspects of transference and countertransference in family therapy in several pages is destined to be incomplete. Since the transference distortions in these complicated family therapy situations become extremely involved, only a few components which seem important to us can be identified. The topic of countertransference is presented in greater depth in Whitaker, Felder, and Warkentin (1965).

Freud discovered the phenomenon of transference as an ubiquitous human quality whereby people displace feelings, thoughts, and fantasies which are applicable to significant others from the past onto others in the present; the psychoanalytic treatment situation creates the conditions for this process to occur with greater intensity and specificity. The very nature of any therapeutic situation has regression built into it. It is almost impossible for any person not to feel childlike and not to have certain unique and deep transference expectations vis à vis the therapist, no matter what the therapist is like and what he does or does not do. The affects which are transferred are most commonly complex mixtures of fear, hope, hatred, admiration, contempt, wonder, humiliation, love, shame, and so forth. These transference anticipations are so compelling that the actual personality of the therapist often does not begin to make a difference until fairly late in the therapy process; the feelings are so powerful that they can override personality differences between cotherapists. In general, transference interpretations tend to be made relatively late in family therapy, not only because transferences have become more fixed and the therapists are differentially responded to, but also because it is more difficult for the family members to utilize the interpretations when they are only peripherally engaged in the therapy in the early phases.

Transference certainly does not occur in the same form in individual or family psychotherapy as it does in orthodox psychoanalytic therapy. The family therapy situation is complicated by the simultaneous presence of two or three generations plus the therapists. When emotional attitudes are repeated from the past and roles are assigned to each other and to the therapists, one has to distinguish between the real family member being responded to and the introject of that person. In other words, the transference distortions of the family members not only are manifested toward therapists but toward each other. While the therapists are reacted to as grandparents, mother, father, siblings, or others, by each of the family members, additional complexity arises from the fact that the transference paradigms are perceived and apprehended by each other, resulting in feedback effects. Moreover, the transference distortions all occur within the context of the conventional social role expectations of patients and doctors, as well as other reality considerations. The therapists, of course, introduce their own transference and counter-transference misconstructions. It is, therefore, an understatement to call the subject of transference in family therapy complex. Its intricacy may account for the absence of literature on transference in family therapy, but does not lessen its importance. Indeed, as in all forms of therapy, transference phenomena are crucial, and techniques for dealing with them are indispensable if one is going to do the kind of intensive, protracted family therapy espoused here.

Family therapy has also revealed a new kind of transference, that of the family system as a whole, which is more than a collection of the individual distortions. The "sicker" the family the more obvious the family transference; more integrated families can play their "normal" role much better. As mentioned in the beginning of this chapter, two therapists who select each other choose a particular family to work with; the initial evaluators of the family may or may not end up as the therapists. The basis on which the therapists choose a family undoubtedly has its roots in the early family life experiences of the therapists as individuals, as well as in the nature of the cotherapy team relationship. While this instinctive response to a patient occurs in individual psychotherapy, when it happens with a family it has an an entirely different quality. The following are some aspects of the family which may attract or repel therapists: the family's physical appearance, their manner of dress and bearing; how they come to grips with their feelings, their style of relating to each other, how disorganized or tight they are, how the parents handle the children and each other; whether they seem insatiable or whether they are capable of being filled; whether they make the therapists feel that they can give them nothing or whether they are hungry for too much; the depressed or the paranoid family; whether the hostility is too naked or whether the therapists sense murder in the family; how they respond when someone cries; how drastically they violate meaning. Further, we have all had the experience of initially disliking a family and then growing to like them, and vice versa. When certain aspects of the family appeal to particular trends in the therapists, which are derived from the therapists' own internal imagos, the therapists are able to make an encounter and thereby select the family for therapy. These transference elements of the therapists are often unrecognized, but they are certainly part of the process which determines how the therapy will proceed. The subjective, often unconscious attitudes of the therapy team probably have more to do with the outcome of the therapy than the nature of the family problems. The one source of transference or countertransfer-ence that is the most loaded emotionally, and about which little is written, with the notable exception of the group at the Atlanta Psychiatric Clinic (Whitaker and Malone, 1953), has to do with the needs of the therapists and how their own personal family relationships, both current and past, affect the therapy process.

The fact that countertransference is an unconscious phenomenon is often overlooked; when therapists react with their own irrational biases and preconcep-tions, *at the time* they do not know it. They may recognize the exaggerated feeling or response later, when it is pointed out to them by a cotherapist or by the observing group of therapists. Family therapy is particularly disposed toward eliciting inappropriate responses because of the charged quality of the interactions. One cannot remain as detached with a family as one can with an individual patient; it is almost impossible not to get caught up in the drama of the family interaction. There is also something about working with a family as opposed to working with individuals which tempts one to pass judgment under the guise of being objective. When a child is being cruelly exploited or when someone is helplessly squirming under the impact of a devastating "damned if they do and damned if they don't" bind, the therapists find it difficult to maintain clinical detachment. With a family there is a great temptation to circumvent defenses, to get to the heart of the matter, to do less structuring and less preparation for an interpretation, to disregard all the do's and don't's which had been learned while training to be psychotherapists. This does not mean that this reactive procedure is wrong; however, with a family a different set of rules of therapy seems to apply, and this attitude seems to be a natural outgrowth of seeing an entire family together and having to deal with the raw materials of life, so to speak. Family therapy can be heady stuff for therapists; there is a magnetic compulsion to refashion our own parents and make a better mother and father out of the parents under observation. What an ideal opportunity to reconstruct one's own family struggles so that in *this* family they can be worked through and mastered!

The safeguard usually recommended for minimizing countertransference distortions is one's own personal analysis or psychotherapy, but no amount of analysis really frees anyone from all neurotic proclivities, and besides, psychoanalysis cannot directly deal with transactional family elements. In our organizational set-up, through direct observation of sessions by the entire therapy group and by tape recordings, there does exist the opportunity for staff members who are not involved in the therapy to comment on countertransference falsifications as well as sticky reality problems. (For example, one therapy team needed considerable help from the staff in handling their feelings about overt, consummated incest which occurred in one family.) Continuous discussion of dynamics, goals, techniques, transference, and countertransference phenomena between cotherapists, between therapy sessions, has been found to be essential. These goals can be much better accomplished in staff conferences where independent observers can lend their impressions and help clarify team differences. Introduction of a third therapist in the therapy sessions as temporary consultant has been particularly useful when the therapists were in danger of being absorbed into the family system and of following only certain grooves and channels, losing their freedom of action.

Family therapy is emotionally demanding work which creates intense feelings in therapists which must be contained during sessions, or at least given therapeutic expression. Behind the observation mirror, however, the staff of therapists frequently vent their frustrations by becoming childish with each other, making snide remarks or hostile interpretations about a family, joking and taunting—all from the position of this privileged sanctuary. We have found this sort of release necessary and have even wondered whether family therapy can ever be done in isolation from one's colleagues.

Cotherapy Team Relationship

Ever since we first began treating families it has been routine for us to use therapy teams of two rather than a single therapist, but we do acknowledge the fact that some therapists in other family therapy centers are willing to face a family alone and, by their accounts, are able to work effectively in that manner. We frankly admit, moreover, that the team approach was probably originally created more for the security of the therapists than for the family, for if therapists cannot be secure they will diminish their usefulness to patients. The security of the team relationship is a necessary resource, in our judgment, because family therapy, especially on a long-term basis, can create strong and alien feelings which can be profoundly disturbing. The system of the family is much more powerful and practiced than that of any therapy team.

As we amassed experience through our modus operandi, we learned that working as a team, in spite of disadvantages, introduced another dimension which had its own therapeutic value—giving a family a set of parents. The total therapy process, then, has come to include not only the intrafamilial dynamics, but the dynamics of the team relationship and the impact of the team and the family on each other. The entire process is all one, although for purposes of discussion in this chapter each factor has been artificially abstracted from the interconnected aggregate. A more elaborate report on cotherapy team relationship in our unit is given in a paper by Rubinstein and Weiner (1967).

The dynamics of the relationship between cotherapists is involved and exists on a number of levels. The therapists choose to work with each other partly on the basis of extremely subtle, unconscious cues which are probably related to having had, in their own families of origin, similar experiences, style of expression, quality of affect, and so forth—all of which draw them to each other and enable them to work out their differences in relatively congruent manner. The cotherapists may seem to be quite different kinds of people working in a complementary fashion, yet they probably share similar introject experiences. Their basic personality affinity supersedes differences in sex, profession, culture, religion, or theoretical orientation and, in all likelihood, accounts for the fulfillment of deep needs in the relationship as well as for transference distortions. The trust, confidence, and sensitivity which the therapists have toward each other is a prerequisite in their ability to work with families; this primary concordance can tolerate divergence between them as well as allow them to handle family anxiety. As in a marriage, a team relationship has its own evolution and phases, and the ambivalences between therapists, often exploited by the family, have to be worked through. If the foundation of the relationship is solid enough, the two therapists can alternate being child and parent for each other, even while being two parents or husband and wife for the family. If there is not a good team relationship, good family therapy cannot be done.

We have learned that when the family therapy has bogged down or is floundering, the first effort to diagnose the difficulty should be directed toward the team relationship rather than the family. If one therapist gets disturbed by something going on in the family he should first look for some difficulty in the team relationship. In our unit, if the team is unable to resolve the problems on its own, the entire staff observes a family session or listens to tape recordings of the sessions. When the team members can overcome their individual and collective defensiveness they can examine the source of their difficulties with each other. For example, one therapist may feel excluded because the other therapist has established proprietary rights over a family member; when a therapist gets more from a family member than he does from his teammate, he is behaving like the parent in the schizophrenic family who turns more to his child than to his mate. Part of the process which occurs between the cotherapists is a function of the group process of the entire staff; the total family of therapists, of course, has its own system, rules, and myths. Sometimes the behavior of the therapists is monitored more by the impression they are trying to make on their colleagues behind the one-way mirror than it is by the team strategy or the needs of the family.

The bond of the team relationship enables the therapists to tolerate wide deviance in style as well as tests which the family will make upon the relationship. One therapist may deal with primary-process material and one with secondary-process material. One therapist can stay relatively free of the family entanglement and rescue his cotherapist when the latter loses objectivity. Even a smoothly functioning team with long experience in working with each other can be ruffled by certain family maneuvers. One of the severest tests occurs when the family attempts to split the therapists into good and bad objects, isolating the bad one. This omnipresent human phenomenon has a variety of motives behind it: it may be seen as a remnant of former attempts to divide and conquer between parents, the testing out of parents; it may serve resistance purposes, or may lead to the arousal of jealousy or competition between therapists. The maneuver can be especially effective if there are latent rivalries between the therapists or if it fits in with the unconscious need of one therapist to be seen as the giving, over-responsible one, or the unconscious need of the other therapist to be seen as the "baddy." If one therapist has a strong need to be liked by a family, the other team member can be regarded as being in the way, or perhaps even be used as an avenue to gratification from the family. There is a sibling paradigm in this team problem: it feels better to outdo a sibling for parental love than to be an only child with no one to compete with. Another problem arises when one team member is regarded as the senior therapist and the other as the junior therapist. Frequently the family will impose their structure on the therapy team (thus, a Jewish doctor regarded as the senior therapist by a Jewish family, or, if one of the therapists has been the individual therapist for the designated patient he will be regarded as "the doctor" by the family). The preferred therapist cannot help but respond to the family's view of himself. Some of these problems should be brought out into the open and discussed with the family; if the therapists do not communicate with each other, the family will not. The emergencies and trials which the family goes through in therapy frequently bring the team members closer together, and thereby unite the team and the family.

There are some families who will not allow the therapists to enter their system because they utilize passive techniques of noninvolvement. These kinds of families, which usually contain an acting-out member, are shallow and superficial once the immediate crisis is past (as when the police arrest the child). They come to the sessions, but their silent behavior says, "Do me," as if to say, "Okay, we're here; now do something for us, without our having to ask for it." The security in the team relationship is very important on these occasions because of the anger and anxiety aroused in the therapists. The cotherapists, after making efforts to provoke feelings and interaction between family members, frequently have to rely on each other for contact, or have to learn to use each other to maintain silence. The families who let the therapists into the system too quickly can be deceptive, and it is occasionally necessary for the therapists to save each other from engulfment.

In conclusion, we have found that there is a quality about the relationship of a good therapy team which helps allay family anxiety so that the members can more freely explore the depths of their relationships. The team relationship itself helps create hope for the family that something better can come out of their misery.

Terminal Phases of Family Therapy

Among the vast unexplored areas of family therapy lies the question of the dynamics and handling of the final stages of treatment and its termination. There is not a great deal of information on this area, not only because there are so few places in the country where long-term family therapy is done, but also because there are not many families who reach the phase of natural termination (a termination mutually agreed upon by the therapists and the family with the unanimous conviction that growth has taken place). We have not been operating long enough to see enough families reach the final phases; also, the dynamics of the termination process are difficult to understand.

Family resistance of all types characterizes the final as well as the middle phases of family therapy, but they assume a somewhat different form. For a long time there is much monotony as each member of the family reports the same material over and over again, eternally adding two and two and getting five. There is certainly no undeviating progression; a new connection is made here, a bit of backsliding there; several members are ready to move ahead to new definitions of relationships, but one member keeps obstructing the process; or a combination of two retards a third. The same old family patterns and habits constantly pull the family backwards at the same time that these desperate people are looking for a way out of their wretchedness. Interpretations that had been repeated many times are reacted to as if heard for the first time.

When the family system begins to crack, intense turmoil is precipitated; there may be threats of suicide, murder, and divorce. Rupture of the system also creates anxiety in the therapists, who may react by going in one of two directions: by offering more support, more frequent sessions, or offers of individual therapy. Or, the therapists may begin to withdraw from the family; later reflection may make them realize that they have been giving clues that the family should terminate—by coming late to sessions, getting more impatient, increasing the amount of inter-pretations, insisting on conditions they know the family will not meet, or attending to the manifest, negative side of the family's ambivalence about coming to the sessions.

We have found the threat of termination to be a powerful mobilizer for inducing motivation for change and loosening things up. When we ask some families why they come week after week without essentially changing, they rarely can verbalize their goals except to reply, "We want our daughter or son to get well," or "We need a happier family." When we point out the futility of continuing without some evidence of a desire for change, great apprehension arises, even in parents who have never accepted the idea that they are patients or have paid only lip service to the idea. One mother hinted darkly that if we dropped them she'd make her child sick again. The family members are in great conflict between the overpowering urge to maintain the status quo, the previous homeostatic balance on the one hand, and the dependent desire to please the therapists, to be liked and accepted by them on the other hand. Yet they are often honestly confused as to what "change" means. One of the mothers, who had controlled all the family money and had the house in her name, interpreted change as doing more, rather than less, of what she was already doing; she said, "I've already done enough; I can't possibly do more!" Her husband started off one of the meetings saying, "Well, I suppose it's required that I be a stronger, more dominant man," and then he checked with his wife and asked, "Don't you think so, dear?"

The family then enters a frozen state of suspended animation where the old ways are no longer effective and the new ways are not yet available. This state may last a considerable time, and families may be fixated there and never move ahead. It is a painful period for everyone. Ever so slowly, with the families who do make progress, the family members begin really to listen to each other and to the therapists. Gradually they find that the old gratifications no longer seem to work. There just doesn't seem to be much point, somehow, in continuing the relentless alienation or ruthless accusations. They are the same people, and yet there is something different in the family atmosphere; perhaps that nameless dread no longer seems to be hovering over the family. The parents may be able to be less fearful that their daughter will be raped if she goes out on a date, and the children may be less concerned with what goes on in that bedroom which has come to be òccupied by both parents. The husband may see the essential unhappiness behind his wife's shrewish ways and may use her less as a censuring mother. The wife may be able to feel more like a woman since she doesn't feel so compelled to see the husband as a tormentor or serf. Unlike other forms of psychotherapy, there is not much verbalized insight; the family members seem to get along better, but have great difficulty understanding why they do. One could draw a parallel with some forms of child therapy, where a child may benefit by the experience without even knowing he was undergoing treatment.

The dynamics involved in terminations which occur precipitously, either in the early, middle, or later phases, can be most instructive. One of the major reasons why families terminate suddenly is based on an awareness of what the therapists are doing to the system, as well as on an unwillingness to change. Counterpoint to this theme is the transference–countertransference gambit whereby the family's needs and the therapists' needs are tested out against each other. That is, a struggle ensues between therapists and families as to "who wants who." When the family senses that they are going to be abandoned, they want to quit, giving the message, "I'll reject you before you can reject me." Although families feel libidinally rejected when therapists threaten termination, they often learn, too, that they can hurt the therapists by rejecting them. If the therapists have greater need for the family than the family has for them, then the family is stronger, and vice versa. We have learned from this realization and the fact that the families' involvement with the therapists often increases when the therapists become less interested in changing them that therapy teams often need help from the rest of the staff to "play it cool" or to let a family go. Greater experience has led our therapists not to show eagerness to possess or retain families; when the families sense this, they put more serious effort into their therapy work. The relationship with the team member, we have learned, will remain long after the family has departed.

Hiatuses in family therapy have their usefulness, as they do in individual therapy. Some families have interrupted treatment and returned as new families, with new attitudes and motivations. For some of these families, we later realized, the rejection of the therapists represented a step toward individuation and growth; the separation was a trial action. When they rebuffed the therapists they did not truly look upon the therapists as the bad parents; in the unconscious the only really bad parents are those who get sick, leave, or die. These families needed to test whether the therapists would be available when needed, would be *there*. During the course of therapy this testing out may assume the form of missing appointments or behaving irresponsibly, to see whether the therapists would go after them or rescue them, to see how much the therapist wanted them.

One of the most important observations we have made on the question of termination is how dependent these families become on the whole treatment process. The new, artificial family created by the treatment situation acts as a crutch for the family, and its withdrawal is frightening to the family members.

Implicit in many of the statements during the sessions is the plea that the therapists accept an enduring consignment to take care of them. As a matter of fact, when the family members are asked to define their own goals of treatment they behave as though they cannot commit themselves to treatment unless they feel that the therapists are making the first commitment to them; they seem much more concerned with whether *we want them* (to continue with the treatment) than they are with their own personal aspirations.

The dynamics of termination are central and are suffused throughout all other problems of family therapy. As more experience is gained in the area of termination we may come to understand more about how to anticipate and handle resistances in all phases.

A Subjective Evaluation of Family Therapy

The question we have seriously asked ourselves is: If family therapy "works," how could it? Though it may not be fair to compare family therapy to individual psychoanalysis, the "major surgery" of psychotherapy, one must consider what is involved in changing the human personality. Even under the ideal conditions of analysis, five times a week, the patient must go through the long, painstaking process of enervation of defenses, surmounting resistances, deep regression, transference neurosis, working-through, and finally, if analysis is relatively successful, there is abandonment of fixations, diminishing of primary-process phenomena; the patient ends up doing things for himself rather than for the analyst and seeks gratification of needs through the reality principle. Analysts can state with conviction that in order to effect really meaningful change and achieve resolution of deep-seated personality problems, no part of this process can be skipped or aborted, and even under these ideal conditions the clinical outcome is uncertain. Then, it might legitimately be asked, how can you possibly hope to bring about real change under the unmanageable conditions of seeing four or five people together once a week? In the analytic situation, when an interpretation is made, the patient usually responds with self-justifying statements and a variety of resistance maneuvers while the analyst patiently listens; at a certain point there is a long pause, and then the patient usually considers the interpretation, sometimes grabs hold of it, and then begins to speculate on its implications in his life and possibly goes back to its earlier antecedents. In family therapy, where the lines of inquiry cannot be pursued without interruption, where each person, in the early phases at least, stops at the point of blaming the other and is intent on saving face in front of the family, is it possible even to approximate the working-through of resistances? Are not the most heavily charged events and fantasies of a person's life deeply buried under so many layers that they require special techniques of individual therapy to be revealed? Are not very early conflicts in each person too far removed from the immediate situation for them to be traced back from derivatives to their past connections? How can a severely regressed family possibly abandon infantile needs?

Despite every theoretical reason why family therapy should not work, we who have been doing it have developed an inner conviction that it does work for most families and that it has even greater potential for becoming more effective as more is learned. But what do we mean by the treatment "working"? First, it is necessary to use criteria of change different from those applied to individual therapy. The criteria of interpersonal and transactional processes are pertinent, even though our conceptual standards for evaluating these kinds of changes are in a primitive stage. On what level should we look for change? Do we seek changes in attitudes, in behavior, on the level of deep needs, homeostatic balance, shifts in alliances? Do we seek freedom from symptoms for the designated patient? Do we find, instead, exchange of symptoms among family members? Do we look for differentiation from each other in the family members, less family distress, more togetherness, less togetherness, more unqualified communication messages in the family? Do we try to help the family members get more meaning out of life, or, in the last analysis, as in all forms of therapy, do the patients set their own goals? This criterion, too, is not dependable, inasmuch as the goals, based on accumulated insight as the treatment progresses, are often quite different at the end of treatment than they were at the beginning. Besides, are not estimates of health needed from therapists and society? But what constitutes a healthy family? What right do the therapists have to decide what the good family life is? Should family therapists not avoid being agents of society in making families conform to some idealistic standard? And so on.

Rather than attempting to deal with the foregoing questions, we can specify some concrete, operational ways of estimating family improvement. Intrapsychic changes lead to interpersonal ones, but interpersonal changes in turn lead to intrapsychic alterations, especially when the changes are shared jointly within the most basic living unit, the family. We know families have improved when we notice continuity in the sessions and when the family is able to resolve conflicts at home instead of bringing them to the therapists to solve. We know there is growth when the family members use each other less as transference figures and seem more like real people to the therapists and to each other. When the family pathology is lessened the family members can enjoy each other and life better. Without attempting to specify precisely what is meant by our language, we do find that greater individuation occurs, so that the shared ego of the family slackens and separation of the members from the system can be tolerated. Each individual becomes more free to explore an individual definition of self, which may be quite different from his role as formerly viewed by the family. The affect which was discharged into the family arena becomes more dispersed and less primitive gratification value is attached to it; the old "kick" out of the family craziness is gone. Emotional forces tend to become less family-adhering so that, for example, the sexual energies of the children can begin to turn toward extrafamilial figures. Communication tends to open up between parents and, despite the initial confusion, futility, and disappointment when they really open their eyes to each other, the marriage partners usually end up with more sympathetic views of each other and, consequently, increase their chance of a meaningful relationship. Improvement in the marriage, as we have said, is almost invariably followed by emotional growth in the children. As the parents were "fed" by the therapists they came to feed less on their children. Perhaps most important of all, the families discover that there are other ways of behaving toward each other and still remain a family.

Family therapists are hopeful about their work because they have seen improvement in families where a great deal of prior individual therapy for the various members did not materially change anything.

The family as an institution has survived many thousands of years as the most workable living unit for human beings because, as the mediator of the culture in preparing the young for the next generation, it has served to digest social change as well as act as a flexible bulwark against upheavals which have occurred through time. It is perhaps not accidental that, despite a century of enlightened psychiatric endeavor, it has taken so long to get around to treating the family unit as the patient. Most people rather instinctively regard the family as sacrosanct, as perhaps the last bastion of freedom left to man. (Note, for example, the recent protests against psychological tests in schools which inquire into personal aspects of family life.) Where else but in his own castle, with his own family, can a person pick his nose, flatulate, lose his temper with impunity, whine, let the child in him emerge—in short, regress and "be himself"? Although the reader may have gained the impression that we have focused heretofore only on the pathologic and the bizarre in family life, we fully recognize the emotional refuge and deep satisfactions in family living. Even in the most alienated families the blood ties and continued associations create loyalty and a kind of caring—the family jokes, holiday celebrations, the smell of cooking, and so forth. Nonetheless, family gratifications can sometimes paradoxically provide the background for human tragedy and emotional disturbance of endless variety—the cruel rejections, the discriminations, the child unloved as a person, the humiliations, the parentification of the child, the lack of intimacy, the overindulged, the unrealized fulfillments and thwarted potentials, and the outrages against the human spirit.

People are often misled about the degree of pathology in those they think they know well because most people, in customary social relationships, manage to conceal not only their fantasy life but many aspects of their overt infantile behavior which is acted out only with certain special people (such as a mate, child, sibling, parent, or friend). The individual psychotherapist or analyst does become acquainted with the fantasy life, but even they can misjudge the full impact of a person's pathology because they get only second-hand reports about the quality of the social interaction and, except for transference, rarely see it unfold before them. The distorted behavior may not even appear in full force in the transference if it is being acted out in especially intense fashion with someone outside the sessions. Family therapy is the only kind of therapy which can witness the "sick" behavior with the key figures as it actually occurs in vivo. Therefore, no matter how mature some people seem to be in ordinary social relationships, certain childish features of their personality emerge only when they are in the presence of members of their family. The layman knows this when he says, "You have to live with a person to know what he's really like." As one woman put it, "In the outside world my husband is the essence of goodness. He is capable and admired; he goes out of his way to do things for everyone. Everywhere I go people tell me what a lucky person I am to be married to him. Yet the minute he walks in the front door something happens, because to his family he can give nothing and he acts like a little boy!" The private "back-room" of the family is rarely exposed to outsiders, in contradistinction to the "front-room" exhibited to the public (Goffman, 1956). Even close friends can "know" a family for years and not be aware of not only the family skeletons and scandals consciously concealed, but of the sometimes weird underground of the family.[4] The footnotes in the biographies of famous people only hint at the deeply personal but extravagant and strange practices which occur in every family in some form and degree, even in those families known to the community as ideal.

To expose the subterranean currents of family life occasionally makes the therapists uneasy. Some of the disclosures in the family meetings have the disturbing and embarrassing quality of an obscenity uttered in church. In individual therapy we have become used to the patient's relating intimate events with great guilt or shame, reliving with acute suffering the death of a child or a parent, reexperiencing the feelings that a brother or sister was preferred, describing masturbation fantasies, and other events. One sees in the privacy of the office all the beauty and ugliness of the human character. But it is quite another sort of discomfort when these things are disclosed semi-publicly, such as when the son comes increasingly to have poorly disguised contempt for his soft, ineffectual father who always abdicates on making decisions, or when the simmering, spiteful battle between mother and grandmother culminates in the scathing denunciation, "You should never have had children!" or to witness the horror in the mother who has become aware of how she has hurt her child, or to hear a "well" sibling say to her sanctimonious mother, "You know, mother, you really do rotten little things."

---

[4]Perhaps this is what the author of the play *Five Finger Exercise* (Shaffer, 1959) was getting at when the tutor comes to live with the family and the son tells him upon their meeting, "Well, let me give you a warning. This isn't a family. It's a tribe of cannibals. Between us we eat everything we can. . . . You think I'm joking?" The tutor, feeling uncomfortable, replies, "I think you're lucky to have a family." And the son says, "And I think you're lucky to be without one. . . . I'm sorry. I'm making tasteless jokes. Actually we're very choosey in our victims. We only eat other members of the family."

Though the children are used to seeing their parents' childish behavior in the home, to see it openly displayed in front of outsiders, the doctors, is humiliating for them.

It must be remembered that we often see these families at their worst; the father whom we see as a "passive-dependent character with depressive features" may be, to his children, a warm, lovable person with other sides to his personality. The alcoholic mother is sometimes more affectionate with her children than other, more proper mothers. No matter how bad, unsuccessful, or unlovable a parent may seem to others, the children may "love" him or her unreservedly and fiercely, and it's difficult for parents to give this up. Every therapist has seen that no matter how repugnant or peculiar a patient or family may seem on first contact, after they have been worked with for a while they seem more like persons and one can understand a little more why they do what they do, that given their particular background and present circumstances, they do what they *have* to do. On the subjective side, the therapists have a mélange of feelings as they sit with these families: empathy, hate, bafflement, isolation, love, disgust, sympathy, and so forth. Cognitively, they evaluate, judge, sense, combine strategy with the co-therapist, maneuver, or self-observe.

We have occasionally wondered about how families were being disturbed by the therapy. It is not unusual to hear patients in individual therapy complain that they're worse off than when treatment started. Families, too, often report that they are more disrupted; there are threats of divorce and murder (none of which have actually been carried out), complaints that we are "ruining" the family, reports of more contention in the home, and the like. As we have examined this question more closely, however, we ask: What was the state of affairs with the family before we came into the picture? Was their relative serenity achieved by sacrificing one member of the family as the patient? Had there not been deep but unrecognized dissatisfaction for years? Any investigative procedure is bound to disturb rigid patterns, cause more distress, frustrate intrafamilial vested interests, and make things temporarily appear much worse. It is interesting that as we have become more experienced in family therapy we have heard fewer complaints of this sort. As in all forms of psychotherapy, family therapy undoubtedly has its spreading side-effects. Families occasionally overanalyze at home and interpret to each other; they may even use therapists' statements made during sessions to bolster an argument at home (such as, "See, the doctor said you have hostile feelings toward your mother and you take it out on me"). Extended-family members may find changes in the family members most upsetting.

It is interesting to speculate why Freud, with all his genius for apprehending so many fundamental truths about the nature of man, stopped short of fully recognizing and therapeutically handling the interpersonal, interlocking pathology *among* people intimately involved with one another. Though, in one sense, no one understood intrafamilial struggles better than Freud, his emphasis on the reconstruction and elaboration of the family dynamics within one mind, and his discouragement of involvement of family members in the treatment process of individuals, established the practice of the exclusion of the family in most forms of psychotherapy. Heretofore science has always had to rely on information *about* the family second-hand, from reports given by patients, from questionnaires, or from individual members of the family seen separately. By observing the family interacting together, phenomena began to be discovered which had never before been known to exist because the special conditions for their disclosure had never been present. It is likely that this generation of family therapists have made their contribution by identifying the family concept and recognizing some of its profound implications; perhaps it will take another generation of clinician-theoreticians to further integrate the intrapsychic and transactional spheres before family therapy will be a refined, specific form of treatment with known limits. Practical considerations of the treatment aspect aside, in the long run the significance of the family transactional approach is that it represents a major conceptual challenge to contemporary psychopathology and personality theory as a whole.

We are only now beginning to realize some of the wider connotations and consequences of the family approach. Family therapy, which originally focused on schizophrenic patients and their families, has come to be applied to a wide variety of clinical conditions in the designated patient, including the neuroses, acting out character disorders, resistant psychosomatic conditions, learning problems, problems of ego-restriction and inhibition, alcoholism, problems of the aged, sexual deviation, and others. Suicide prevention centers are learning that suicides have a better chance of being thwarted when the whole family is seen and the meaning of the suicide attempt or threat can be better discerned. The traditional child-guidance approach is gradually giving way to the family approach in a number of states, and the community mental health centers of the future may well become family mental health centers. Even in those clinic situations where family therapy cannot be undertaken, clinicians are beginning to discover the value of the intake family diagnostic interview as a routine work-up since it has been realized that this approach represents the best method of ascertaining the meaning of the illness and what went on in the family to help create it. Family therapy is here to stay, but because there are so few trained family therapists, because it is such a time-consuming endeavor, and because knowledge in the field is still in its prodromal stages, family therapy will remain a highly selective, limited procedure for some time to come, although adaptations of some of its tenets may someday be applied to some of the social ills of our day. The ultimate value of family therapy probably lies in the area of prevention; the children in the treated family who will marry and form families of their own will have a greater capacity to create healthy family living.

The writer is indebted to Dr. Ivan Boszormenyi-Nagy, not only for being an innovator in leading the Family Therapy Project toward the insights of family therapy, but for providing the organizational machinery and overall inspiration which helped to promulgate many of the ideas in this chapter. Cross fertilization of concepts and opinions which have occurred in ongoing conferences are also reflected in this chapter. Special thanks are owed Dr. Oscar R. Weiner for participating with me in many discussions which resulted in ideas borrowed consciously and unconsciously. Drs. Boszormenyi-Nagy and Weiner have both read the chapter and offered useful suggestions. The author acknowledges those mentors and friends who influenced his personal and professional development: Drs. James R. Frakes of Lehigh University, Joseph J. Rubin of Pennsylvania State University, Wayne H. Holtzman of the University of Texas, Leslie Phillips of the Worchester State Hospital, Sylvan S. Tomkins of Princeton University, and Morris D. Galinsky of Philadelphia.

Part Three

Application to Marriage and Divorce

Even though the paper "Marriage and Marital Therapy: Issues and Initial Interview Techniques" was published in 1980, it was based on notes from lectures I had been giving in classes for a number of years. In 1971, while giving a workshop in Rome, I met Maurizio Andolfi, a psychiatrist with a burning interest in family therapy, who later came to the United States to study, and has since achieved some prominence. In 1978, Maurizio invited me to participate in an international conference on family therapy in Florence. How could I turn down an invitation to Florence, a place with wartime memories for me? Later, when Maurizio and Iz Zwerling decided to publish some of the papers from that conference, I converted my notes on marriage and marital therapy into a chapter for their edited book *Dimensions of Family Therapy* (1980). In this chapter I present some theoretical notions about marriage, a classification of marital problems, and my method of conducting initial interviews with couples.

The genesis of my work with couples groups evolved from my experience doing multiple family therapy with families of schizophrenics at the Eastern Pennsylvania Psychiatric Institute. At that time I observed the therapeutic efficacy of the group process, particularly that which occurs between one family unit and another (as contrasted with the group process between unrelated individuals, as in conventional peer group therapy). Later, in private practice, I began seeing couples in groups as a clinically expedient way of dealing with formidable couples, and it was only subsequently that I recognized couples group therapy as a powerful, synergistic form of treatment in its own right. Don Bloch, who was editing a book on family therapy (*Techniques of Family Psychotherapy: A Primer*, 1973), requested a paper from me and I chose to write about my experiences with the couples group method. In the course of time I have come to see couples group therapy as the treatment of choice for couples living together, and for premarital, marital, separation, and divorce problems. Couples groups have been incorporated into my present sequence of treatment methods (described in chapter 9, "The Integration of Marital Therapy With Sessions With Family of Origin"). I have found that seeing couples in groups is the most productive way of preparing the partners to bring in their families of origin.

The chapter entitled "Husbands' Reactions to Wives' Infidelity" is a clinical vignette describing the range of reactions of husbands whose wives, during marital therapy, disclosed their extramarital affairs. This paper contains neither theoretical breakthroughs nor clinical innovations, but does describe an interesting phenomenon that is occurring more frequently these days.

Following a presentation I gave on divorce at an orthopsychiatric convention, I was invited by *Psychology Today* to write an article on the treatment of couples going through a divorce. The article was published in the February, 1978, issue of the magazine, but unbeknownst to me, the magazine changed the title I had submitted ("Divorce Therapy") to "The Friendly Divorce," a title that somehow missed the point. In any event, I describe in that (now) chapter, from a family-system viewpoint, some principles and techniques that have been developed to deal with the breakup of a marriage and family. Divorce therapy came into being because it had to, adapting to the hard reality that divorces are occurring more frequently, and aimed at making more humane and constructive what is usually a bitter, painful experience.

Although I still do conventional family therapy (parents and children together from beginning to end), I have, over time, moved more in the direction of working with couples. Most couples enter therapy explicitly for marital problems and either do not have children or do not present their children as the focus of concern. Less frequently, the couple enters marital therapy after a period of family therapy, during which time the symptomatic children have been defocused as the problem. In my judgment, with rare exceptions, a viable relationship between still-married parents is basic to family health, as is a workable relationship between divorced parents. I emphasize the centrality of the marital relationship because of the severe and sometimes tragic consequences of marital suffering and of poorly managed separations and divorces. The spreading effects of divorce and marital distress will not only suffuse outward to the family network, but forward in time, through the children, to succeeding generations. The damage can be personal and devastating, as in suicide or the murder of a spouse, child, or parent, as well as social, as in drugs or crime, or the general deterioration of society. These are among the reasons that the couple (and the partners' relationship with their family of origin) has become the target of decisive change in my treatment methods.

4

Marriage and Marital Therapy: Issues and Initial Interview Techniques (1980)

In this paper, I attempt to describe some of the things I have learned about marriage and marital therapy, based on over 20 years of working with couples and families. The focus is largely on the earliest, engagement phase of treatment, when, by the kinds of questions I ask, I prepare the couple for what lies ahead. The real work of marital therapy comes later. I do not presume that I could begin to describe in words the later *process* of therapy and change; I don't think anyone's written accounts have ever accomplished that.

Some Theoretical Propositions About Marriage

The following theoretical notions about marriage are not presented in any systematic order; they represent, in random fashion, some of the varied conceptual ideas, including my own, put forth by professionals about marriage. Since no observations can be addressed to all the multiple levels of intimate relationships, they may appear contradictory, and some of them may even seem downright absurd. One of the things that makes the subject of marriage so fascinating is that whatever you want to say about marriage is true and not true. Everyone knows everything about marriage, and no one really knows very much. Marriage experts are as subject to distortion about marriage as anyone else.

Reprinted with permission from M. Andolfi and I. Zwerling (Eds.) *Dimensions of Family Therapy*. New York: The Guilford Press, 1980. Copyright © 1980 The Guilford Press.

1. It has been postulated that people select mates on the basis of need complementarity; that, for example, the logical man will choose an emotional wife (Winch, 1958). On the other hand, it has been proposed that those who marry tend to have similar needs (Murstein, 1961). Both statements are probably true, depending on the depth and level of inference.

2. Social learning theory, translated into clinical practice by the behavior therapists, views marriage in terms of sequences of rewarding and negative behaviors between partners. Therapy from this point of view consists of establishing quid pro quo negotiations that can increase mutual positive reinforcements (Patterson, Weiss, and Hops, 1976). (Husband to wife: "I will listen to you more if you will not spend so much time on the telephone.")

3. Conventional psychoanalytic views on marriage stress that the discrepancy between conscious and unconscious demands creates marital problems, expressed first in the choice of a mate and then in the subsequent evolution of the relationship. Kubie (1956) described how conflicts stemming from the family of origin and based on the need to "wipe out old pains or pay off an old score" can create profound marital conflict and estrangement, particularly when the partners are misled by romantic feelings.

4. Dicks (1967) extended traditional psychoanalytic theory, using object relations theory to deal with the interlocking collusion and bilateral reciprocity that go on between married partners (or in any intimate relationship). He stressed the unconscious complementariness of marriage—a kind of division of function by which each partner supplies part of a set of qualities. The partners' joint personality enables each half to rediscover lost aspects of the primary object relations that they had split off and that in their involvement with the spouse they reexperience by projective identification.

5. The definition of what is appropriate and normal is based on the way one's original family viewed and did things. When people marry, there occurs a mixture of two "normal" family systems, each of which was "right," giving rise to profound bewilderment and misunderstanding. Yet the very differences between spouses are what attracted them to each other in the first place, since a way was opened, through the spouse, for conflicts from that old family to be worked out and lived through. I have postulated that mate selections are made with profound accuracy and, collusively, in two-way fashion. The partners carry psychic functions for each other, and they make unconscious deals: "I will be your conscience if you will act out my impulses." The relationship between the intrapsychic and the transactional constitutes the core of my own approach (Framo, 1970).

6. People tend to marry those who are at the same basic level of personality differentiation, however different their social functioning may appear to be; the spouses, moreover, have opposite patterns of defensive organization (Bowen, 1966).

7. The secret agendas of marriage partners defy reality. People make impossible demands on marriage, based on the idea that one's spouse should make one happy.

No one can make this work. It is not possible to go through life, with or without a partner, without experiencing some pain and loneliness. Yet people act as if their spouse *owes* them happiness as an inalienable right. You can't make anyone love you, and no one can make you happy. People do not marry people, not real ones anyway: they marry what they *think* the person is; they marry illusions and images. Many end their marriages because the spouse does not match the internal image. Jourard (1975) said that a real marriage can begin at just the point where the marriage appears to be finished. The exciting adventure of marriage is finding out who the partner really is.

8. Marriage is more than the sum of its parts; it is a system within other systems, kept in balance by such universals as how dependency flows back and forth, the power struggles, who is one down and who is one up, who pursues and who distances, who fights and who withdraws, who approaches whom sexually, who does what jobs around the house, how the kids are handled, who deals with the in-laws, who is the day person and who is the night person, who is going to take care of whom, and who determines the values about what the good life should be. Spouses, over time, often switch positions along these dimensions.

9. All lasting marriages go through stages, or what Warkentin and Whitaker (1966) have called "serial impasses" (starting with the honeymoon, through the first pregnancy and subsequent children, through the "ten-year syndrome," and so on). These authors stated that the bilateral transference on which the marriage was originally based has become exhausted by the 10-year impasse, and the couple have "fallen out of love." They already know how to hurt each other; in marital therapy, they may learn how to love each other. It is only after they have fallen "out of love" that they learn to behave lovingly. People are quite different at various stages of their marriage; Jourard (1975) has stated that he has had many marriages over time, all with the same person. Uneven growth spurts can make spouses feel like strangers to each other.

Warkentin and Whitaker (1967) also believe that the usual rules of social behavior do not apply to intimate relationships, that fairness is not appropriate, consistency is impossible, and factual honesty is not relevant: "All is fair in love and war, and marriage is both."

10. Societal and cultural factors, of course, all affect marriage. No one can deny that governmental policies, a developing ethos of individualism, the women's movement, the high divorce rate, changing population trends, world events, and inflation have an impact on family and marital life. It is also true that differences in race, age, religion, or social class are influences on marital outcomes. But there is a sector of the marriage relationship that is impervious to external conditions and events, a kind of private world that is unique to the couple alone. This is the part of the marriage that is usually not open even to the view of the marital therapist, for it is underground, sometimes not known to the partners themselves. But the force of this private experience (his marriage, her marriage, and their marriage) can have powerful effects on feelings and behavior. Marriage can be the greatest or the most

humiliating experience of one's life. Whitaker and Keith (1977, p. 70) said that marriage is "an experience which threatens one's being and wrenches one down to the roots. Like hypnosis, marriage is an altered state of consciousness. . . . The deeper one goes the more possible it is for things to happen." Marriage can be like a sterile field, where you can't catch anything but nothing will grow in it. Marriage can be like a beech tree, beautiful to admire from afar but cold and dark underneath. Or marriage can make you feel like a million bucks.

11. One intriguing hypothesis about marriage developed by Napier (1978), one that tends to scare almost everyone, is that people tend to marry their worst nightmare. More precisely, this author suggests that partners who feared rejection or abandonment in their families of origin are likely to marry those who felt engulfed by their parents. The former partner is seeking greater closeness in the relationship, whereas the latter partner pushes for more separateness. The partners, who selected each other on the basis of their deepest fears, also selected the one person who offers the opportunity for mastery of those fears. When you marry, you don't just marry a person; you marry a family. Sometimes people try to improve on their original family when they marry (Napier, 1971). One client said, "I married her because her family seemed so warm and accepting—something I never had in my own family."

12. Family problems tend to repeat themselves from one generation to the next. The greatest gift that parents can give their children is a viable marriage relationship and a sense of self. Strengthening marriages, in my judgment, is the best way for the children to be free to live their own lives. After all, the primary function of family life, when all is said, is preparation of the young for the next generation.

A Preliminary Classification of Marital Problems

The following categories of kinds of problems and couples that come for help are based on my own private practice experience and are frankly impressionistic. The couples I have seen are largely upper middle class, educationally and economically, and they tend to be more motivated and sophisticated about therapy than most people seen in public clinics. I must mention, however, that even in private practice, the dropout rate for conjoint marital therapy is high; about one-fifth of the couples I see do not return for a second session. There are various reasons that couples have not stayed in treatment: some couples could not afford the fee and were too embarrassed to tell me; one partner wanted the therapy and the other did not (perceiving the marital therapy as a commitment to the marriage); some couples did not "connect" with me or sensed that I was reluctant to work with them; some couples with a very tenuous relationship were afraid that if the therapy continued, they would end up divorced; some people had no concept of how therapy worked and were disappointed that their problems were not solved in the first session; and there were various other reasons for dropping out that I could not figure out.

Not all the couples I see are married; the partners "living together," however, are deeply involved in a relationship that they either want to make better or need help to terminate. In this paper, I discuss all these relationship problems as "marital problems."

The following classification of marital problems is presented in order of the treatment outcomes I am able to effect operationally. That is to say, I personally find those categories in the early part of the list less difficult to treat than those toward the latter part. This scale of difficulty is very crude, and, to be sure, there have been couples in the last few categories who have had good treatment outcomes, as well as those who initially looked very promising but got nowhere in therapy. The more experience I have, the more respectful I am of the enormous complexity of marriage relationships and the difficulty of changing them.

I do not believe that this classification scheme is precise enough to be called *marital diagnosis*. Diagnosis would imply that specific treatment strategies have been devised for each category, which is certainly not the case.

1. There are couples, recently married or married a long time, whose marriages are basically sound and whose problems are relatively superficial. Although most couples who come to marital therapy state as their chief complaint, "We do not communicate," these couples' problems really can be handled as communication ones. By clarifying misunderstandings and utilizing the sessions to really listen to the other, this kind of couple essentially rehabilitate their own marriage and leave therapy after a few sessions. I find it best largely to stay out of the way and not do anything stupid, such as trying to make patients out of them. Some of these couples, by the way, come to therapy at the urging of friends who had had a good marital therapy experience; it was "the thing to do."

2. The kind of marriage I feel I can best help is the kind in which each partner is committed to the relationship and each says in some form, "I basically love my spouse and know he/she loves me, but for some reason we can't get along. Will you help us make this marriage work?" Some of these couples are reeling from the impact of their first child ("Why didn't someone tell us what it would be like?"), whereas others are "fight phobic" and afraid to deal with conflict. Some premarital couples, trying to determine whether to marry, fit into this category, whereas other premarital couples belong in the more difficult classifications. Although most professionals agree that premarital therapy is the best way to cut down on the divorce rate, few couples at this stage will come for therapy because they are in love and do not want to examine the relationship too closely.

3. Some partners come in saying that they basically care for each other a great deal but that the zing has gone out of their relationship. They report that there is no excitement, that sex is routine, and that everything is too damned predictable

between them. They will state that their spouse is their "best friend," "like a member of the family," and neither one wants to be married to anyone else. These "brother–sister" marriages have mixed outcomes: some of them do manage to enrich their relationship; others come to accept the status quo; and still others keep searching for ways to recapture the romantic excitement they once had. Therapy techniques for bringing excitement into dull or empty rather than conflictual relationships are not very well developed, at least by me. This category is probably a mixed one with masked depression or blocked hostility possibly in the background.

4. Next comes the garden-variety type of marital problem where the partners have considerable conflict about a variety of issues. One partner may be having an affair and the couple are fighting over that person's giving up the other relationship. Both partners may be struggling over the issue of having an open sexual arrangement. Couples in conflict almost always have a sexual problem, either an outright sexual dysfunction or, what is more common nowadays, loss of interest in sex in one or both partners. The conflicts may be over in-laws, money, control, children, or, in the case of dual-career couples, whose job should take precedence in determining where they live. In recent years, feminist issues have come up more frequently in marital therapy, ranging all the way from women retaining their maiden name to conflicts over more even sharing of parental responsibilities and household tasks. In many of these conflictual marriages, the partners may state, "Either this marriage is going to work or let's end it." One client said, in that universal statement about marriage, "When I needed her she wasn't there, and when she needed me, I wasn't there." Some of the divorces that occur in this group seem to be necessary, whereas others are unnecessary.

5. Marriages in which one partner is symptomatic require unique treatment strategies. In these kinds of marriage, there has typically been marked imbalance, with one partner being more overtly dominant, or one partner (usually the wife) wanting more emotional responsiveness from the other, or one partner being the patient and the other the caretaker. Usually the asymptomatic spouse either does not want to come in with the partner or is willing to come in to help you treat the disabled one. Most of the time, it is the wife who has the symptoms and the husband who sees no problem in the marriage. If the wife is depressed, this depression frequently lifts quickly as she begins to express her dissatisfactions with the relationship. When the husband becomes involved in the treatment, as usually happens, the couple move up into the "conflict" category. Some marriages, however, stay stuck in this position.

6. There are marriages whose problems stem largely from incomplete marital maturation. These spouses never really left home; their primary allegiance is to their families of origin, and there are many complaints about interference from in-laws. The parents are so much in the marriage that it is necessary to involve

them in the treatment. Some of these couples do manage to give up their credit cards and make it on their own, whereas others remain bound to their original family. A case description of the treatment of this type of couple is in Framo (1978b).

7. Mental health professionals present special kinds of difficulties and challenges. These partners have usually had oceans of psychotherapy; they have been in analysis or individual therapy or encounter groups, have been to EST and have been Rolfed, and have made pilgrimages to see Milton Erikson. Each partner has profound understanding of the mate's dynamics, and each is trying to change the other—which never, never works. The partners have talked over their problems ad nauseum, and their use of technical language and interpretations further befuddles the situation. Often these couples are quite frightened of being on the other side of the therapy fence. The chief therapeutic task is to stop the therapy they are doing badly with each other and to help each to focus on self.

8. Remarriage problems are usually complicated because of the ghosts of the former family and the rearrangements of loyalties. The sequelae of divorce are, in general, more entangled than those following the death of a spouse (thus, the second wife resents part of the paycheck going to the former family). Not only does the former marriage create problems in the marital relationship, but there are often problems around step-parenting and children's allegiances to biological parents. I am not reluctant, by the way, to bring both former and present families together for sessions.

9. There are couples who have come too late for marital therapy. These are usually older couples whose relationship problems have calcified and whose options are limited. Sometimes it is the woman experiencing the loneliness of the last child's having left home. Other times it is the man whose career is closing down at a time when his wife's world is opening up. Efforts to help the partners get some satisfaction out of outside jobs or activities are occasionally successful in warming up the relationship. Some of these couples are tired and beyond fighting, and if you can create some conflict between them, there is hope.

10. One of the most difficult categories to treat is the marriage that is in extremis. In these situations, one spouse may have someone else and wants out, and the couple come to therapy as a last resort before seeing lawyers. Often the partner who is finished with the marriage would like to exit from the therapy and leave the partner with the therapist. Some of these couples can be engaged in divorce therapy (Framo, 1978a).

11. Finally, there is the kind of long-term, chronically unhappy marriage where the partners "can't live with and can't live without." These are the couples who have had many unsuccessful marital therapy experiences; they should have divorced but could not. These marriages have alternated in the past between "agony and ecstasy," but now they are past all that, and some of these spouses are waiting

for the other to die. Occasionally couples' group therapy helps these people to separate or come to terms with what they have. Sometimes sessions with their grown children can be useful.

Individual versus Conjoint Therapy

Sager, Gundlach, and Kremer (1968) have reported that half of all people requesting psychotherapy do so largely because of marital difficulties and that another 25% have problems related to their marriage. Despite these facts, the overwhelming treatment method used for marital problems in the past has been individual psychotherapy. Part of the reason is that most therapists have been trained in understanding intrapsychic psychology and the treatment of inner conflict is the one-to-one doctor–patient relationship. There must have been some recognition of the shortcomings of the individual approach to marital problems, as evidenced by the variety of experimentations with many different methods, described by Sager (1959), Greene (1966), Grunebaum, Christ, and Neiberg (1969), Hollander (1971), and Berman and Lief (1975). The following are some of the methods that have been used: therapy or analysis of husband and wife in succession by the same therapist; therapy conducted by two therapists, each of whom sees one spouse, with the therapists periodically conferring about their clients (Martin, 1976); four-way sessions in which each spouse has a separate therapist and at regular periods the two therapists and two clients have joint sessions; simultaneous treatment of both spouses by the same therapist but in separate sessions; conjoint therapy wherein both spouses are seen together by one therapist or by cotherapists; combined individual and conjoint sessions by the same therapist(s); couples' group therapy (Framo, 1973); spouses in separate groups; and therapy with spouses and their family of origin (Framo, 1976a).

The foregoing methods of treatment for marital problems reflect, as I see it, the conceptual confusion between the intrapsychic and the transactional models of marriage. As the findings from family therapy began to appear in the literature, there occurred a mixture of models whereby traditional practitioners tried to incorporate systems thinking into their treatment of marital problems, sometimes inappropriately. At the present time, marital therapy seems to be in a transitional phase between the medical model, which focuses on illness and the neurotic features in the individual spouses, and the systems model, which examines the unity of the marital dyad, the interaction between the partners, and the system of the marriage as a part of larger systems. Adding to the complexity are the theoretical differences within the family therapy field, polarizing into dynamically oriented work with families and couples as contrasted with dealing with observable interactions and shifting of sequences of behaviors (often labeled structural or strategic marital and family therapy.)

Without going into the merits or disadvantages of either approach, I should lay my own theoretical cards on the table. My experience has led me to believe that it is just as important to know what goes on inside people as to know what goes on between them—that neither dimension can be reduced to the other and that both are important. This is one of the reasons that I agree with Whitaker that when you treat a couple you have three patients—the husband, the wife, and the relationship—and that therapy may focus on any one of those three at any given time. Furthermore, as I stated previously, I think that it is the relationship between the intrapsychic and the interpersonal that will provide the greatest understanding and therapeutic leverage, that is, how internalized conflicts from past family relationships are being lived through the spouse and the children in the present. I see a deeper exploration of this relationship by the mental health professions as the number-one task over the next century. I predict, further, that conceptual extensions along these lines will result in more sophisticated marital and family diagnostic systems and treatment approaches. In addition to theoretical advances, we need many more hard data, which will come from the systematic variation of approaches and conditions. Then we might be able to answer such questions as: What kinds of therapy for what kinds of people in what kinds of combinations for what kinds of problems with what kinds of therapists?

In our society, whenever there are problems in a marriage, the one who typically accepts the patient role and goes for psychotherapy is the wife. (In most recent years, since more wives are leaving husbands, it is the male who sometimes becomes the patient.) When there is an argument between the spouses, the husband may say, "Get off my back and go talk to your doctor"—which explains why many women cynically refer to their therapists as "My paid friend." In an important and influential paper, Whitaker and Miller (1969) have described how the wife, under these circumstances, learns how to communicate beautifully with her therapist; she forms a more intimate relationship with her therapist than with her spouse. These authors stated that treating a married person alone and hoping that the result will generalize into the marriage usually does not work. Furthermore they state, and I agree, that individual therapy with one spouse when the marriage is weak increases the likelihood of divorce (recognizing, of course, that some divorces are healthy steps). I myself only see partners together and I no longer do individual therapy, nor do I see spouses separately for individual sessions. I have found that the advantages of individual sessions (learning about secrets, for instance) are not worth the suspicions of the absent spouse and the conflicts of loyalty and confidentiality in the therapist that such sessions give rise to. Besides, each married person exists in the context of an intimate relationship, and breaking the couple into private sessions negates the context and obscures the collusiveness that goes on between married partners. I have learned that when spouses work on their intrapsychic conflicts in the presence of their partners, the latter develop a more empathic view of the spouse, especially when they come to recognize what their partners have had to struggle with during their lives. The dilution of the transference to the therapist I see as a plus in marital therapy; in more recent years,

I have found it more productive to deal with the transferences of spouses to each other.

I recognize that many marital and family therapists do not work as I do; they claim many benefits from having individual sessions concurrently with conjoint therapy. The one time some clients seem most insistent on having individual sessions is during the latter stages of divorce therapy, when some people seem to need the separate sessions to reinforce the reality of the divorce. I do not mean to imply that individual therapy is not useful; indeed there will always be a need for that special, one-to-one confidential relationship. I have referred clients for individual therapy at the conclusion of marital or family therapy, especially when they were motivated to work on inner problems in a more intensive way.

Grunebaum et al. (1969) have postulated that individual therapy should be done when the marriage does not appear to be the problem of greatest priority (you can't tell that from the initial contact), when one partner has severe psychopathology (I see symptomatic spouses who are seriously disturbed at the beginning of therapy), and when the couple appears to be uncommitted to the marriage (you can't always tell at first who is really committed to whom and whether the couple wants to keep the marriage). These authors' thesis, that one does marital therapy only when the problems arise primarily from the marriage, is not consistent with my own experience. I have successfully treated many couples whose problems initially did not seem related to the marriage (such as the depressed woman who says, "My problems have nothing to do with my husband; they're all in me"). Admittedly, however, there really are not any reliable guidelines on indications or contraindications for individual or conjoint therapy for marital problems.

Marital Therapy Goals and My Philosophy of Therapeutic Change

The average length of time I see couples is about 15 sessions. Approximately three-fourths of the couples I see improve in therapy, defined as mutually agreed-upon termination with agreement that the major goals have been achieved. (Some divorces are regarded as improvement, whereas others are seen as therapy failures.) More technically, from my theoretical viewpoint, I regard as improvement that the partners are more personally differentiated, they have come to terms with the roots of their irrational expectations of marriage and of the spouse derived from their families of origin, they have developed a more empathic understanding of their mate, they can meet each other's realistic needs in the face of their differentness, they can communicate more clearly and openly, they like each other more, they have learned to deal with the issues between them, and they each can enjoy life more. For a more complete account of my conceptual view of family and marital dynamics, the reader is referred to Boszormenyi-Nagy and Framo (1965), and Framo (1972, 1973, 1975(b), 1976a, 1978b, 1980).

I once wrote, "Each married person secretly believes that his or her mate is seriously disturbed and cannot love." The majority of people who enter marital therapy do so in order to change their mate. They believe that while they may have some minor adjustments to make in their own personality, it is the mate who needs to make deep, fundamental changes. Some partners have been waiting a long time to have their day in court, where at last they can prove to an objective professional how strange, peculiar, sick, thoughtless, and unloving the spouse really is. One of the first disappointments may occur in marital therapy when the therapist not only does not instantly leap to one's side and begin forthwith to berate, correct, and treat the spouse but has the temerity to suggest that one is expected to take responsibility for change in oneself. (To be sure, there are spouses who take upon themselves all the wrong and badness, but this stance is usually short-lived and, in time, is revealed as an accusation in disguise.)

I believe it is very difficult to change oneself despite the lip service that people give to wanting to change themselves. Some people spend almost their entire lives trying to change someone else (a parent, a child, a spouse), and I communicate to these clients that that is never going to work. The only way I know to change someone else is to change oneself, because when you are different, the intimate other has to change in response to your changed behavior or attitude. That is to say, the other person can no longer rely on your predictable responses. (When I say "change oneself," I do not mean that one can play-act at it, role-play the change, pretend or "play games"; the change must be genuine.) But people not only fear change in themselves, they fear change in their intimate other. For instance, spouses are usually quite threatened when their partner goes for individual therapy; they feel that if the spouse gets his or her head together, that person won't want them anymore. This is one of the reasons I insist on seeing spouses together, so they can participate in the process together and their interlocking collusion can be dealt with. (In this connection, a woman once called me to say, "Doctor, I'm having terrible marital problems. Can you see me?" When I told her to bring her husband with her, she said, "Oh, but I don't want him to know we're having problems!") Anxiety about change in the other can be manifested during therapy sessions in many ways, such as protectiveness toward the spouse when the therapist tries to work with that person or anxiety when the other begins to change in the direction originally demanded (such as when the formerly sexually cold wife begins to warm up, or when the husband who never talked or expressed feelings begins to do so). There is an old song that goes "I can't adjust to the you that has adjusted to me."

When I first started doing psychotherapy many years ago, I used to spend a lot of time worrying about my clients—losing sleep over whether that lonely, depressed woman was going to commit suicide, whether that teenaged boy was going to run away from home. In those days, I encouraged clients to call me at any time, and I gave the message that I would give of myself ceaselessly. Virginia Satir once told me that when she got out of social work school, she felt she was covered with breasts. (There seems to be something about social work training that communicates that social workers must be self-sacrificing, all-giving.) As the years have gone by, I think I have become more appropriately selfish. Carl Whitaker claims that one of the differences between an amateur and a professional is that a professional learns to cut off at the end of a session. Although there are occasions when emotional transactions in treatment sessions truly move me and carry over after the session is over, I have generally learned to keep separate my professional work and my private life. Once I wrote a paper on the difficulties I had handling this dilemma because the ghosts of my own family came into the treatment room (Framo, 1968). In any event, I do not do therapy over the telephone; by my manner, I discourage phone calls, communicating thereby, "Let's take it up in the next session." During treatment sessions, I give my all. I am so hyperalert to what is going on that I will hear things being said that no one else hears; when everyone in the room denies it was said and I play the tape back, sure enough there it is. Needless to say, my "third-ear" listening does not work in dealing with my own close relationships; I'm lucky there if I hear with one ear.

Finally, on this question of my philosophy of treatment, I expect a great deal of the people I work with; I push them to their limits, and when they achieve that, I push for more. I want them to get their money's worth. The people who come to see me professionally either change or leave. A family therapist friend, Oscar Weiner, once said, "You can't want more for people than they want for themselves." Believe me, it's true. Some people cannot tolerate prosperity or good things in their lives. One client once said, "I can't stand it. My wife has been nice to me all week, and even my car is working!"

The Initial Interview

In this section, I attempt to describe in concrete terms what I actually do, from the first contact with a couple to the end of the first interview.

Most couples are referred to me by ex-clients, in which case it is the wife or husband who calls me directly. Some couples call who have seen my name in a magazine article; others are referred by family therapists in other cities; and occasionally referrals are made by mental health professionals in my own area of Philadelphia. When a professional is making the referral, I suggest that the client call me directly. I prefer not getting a long history about the couple, not only because about half of the time I never hear from the referred clients but also because I do not want to be biased by the referring source. I never accept a school's, court's, family's, or mental health professional's definition of the problem, unless I know that the referring, uninvolved person thinks in systems terms. Besides, I prefer meeting people where they are now rather than on the basis of their past experience with someone else. As John Rosen once put it, "No one is as sick as his case history."

When the husband or wife calls me, I keep the conversation very short because I do not want a relationship to start with one person; one can be triangled very fast. I don't even go into the problem much except to ask whether the problem is primarily marital or one concerning the kids. If the problem is child-focused, I next ask who is in the family and state that the way I can best help is to see the whole family. If the problem is presented as marital, I state that both partners must come in together. The great majority of clients know I work this way and prefer conjoint therapy, but when the caller insists that he/she or the spouse be seen alone, I will refer that person elsewhere. In the past, when I was asked about my fee, I used to give the standard answer of "We'll discuss that in the first session." Now I simply state my fee. I conclude the call by making an appointment and giving directions to my office. I have been asked by prospective clients about my theoretical orientation and my philosophy of life, and I have been asked to state what kind of person I am, whether I am married or divorced, where I got my training, and how long the treatment lasts. Some of these requests are legitimate ones that consumers have a right to know, but others are strange or frustrating, or make me angry.

I work both as a solo therapist and as a cotherapist with couples; over the years, I have worked with many different cotherapists. My wife and I have worked together for some years, a unique combination that brings a special dimension to the therapy. The great majority of clients are pleasantly surprised that they will be seen by a man and a woman. The topic of cotherapy is complex and beyond the scope of this paper.

I can usually tell something about a couple on the basis of their behavior in the waiting room. Spouses who are talking to each other or laughing seem to do better in therapy than those who do not talk to each other, bury their heads in magazines, or sit there in frozen silence, waiting for the "doctor." I notice how they enter the treatment room, note their appearance, age, the way they are dressed, and the dominant affects. They are, of course, sizing up the same things about me (or us). (Sometimes there is an immediate positive or negative reaction between me and the clients, based on unknown nonverbal cues or on looks. The first statement out of one woman's mouth was "You have one helluva nerve making me walk up those steps to your office." After that, our relationship went downhill). I bring to their attention immediately the microphone on the table, which is in the middle of a circle of swivel chairs, and I state that I tape all sessions, primarily because I like to lend the tapes to couples so they can listen to the sessions at home.

I then start off with the question "What seems to be the problem?" Usually the partners turn to each other and say, "Would you like to go first?" I have always been curious about the process that goes on between husband and wife that determines who will first state the problem. After one person gives his or her view, I ask the other partner to state the problems as he or she sees them. Following these brief statements of the problems, I get such identifying data as ages, occupations, the length of the marriage, and the ages and sexes of the children. Even if the problem is presented as marital, I ask whether there are any problems in the children. Later I may have family sessions with the couple and their kids. Bringing in the children for sessions, even when the focus is on the marriage, can add much to understanding what goes on between the parents. Children have a way of cutting through adult obfuscations and telling the truth. Furthermore the kids get to be relieved of the burden of being marriage counselors; I tell the children, in effect, that they do not have the training for it and that I am going to take over that job. Children are usually glad their parents are getting help, and besides, the parents do not have to lie about where they go every week. Sessions with the children toward the end of marital therapy can give a reading on how things have settled down at home.

These initial interviews vary considerably in content, activity, coverage, pace, and intensity. I have a general sequence of questions in my head that I tend to follow, but sometimes the interviews go off in unexpected directions, particularly if the emotions are explosive and the crises acute. Some couples talk so freely and rapidly that I can't get a word in, whereas getting others to talk is like pulling teeth. Most of the time, couples start off with cover stories, rehearsed speeches, or stiff, overintellectualized, stilted language. I have learned to ride with those preliminaries, which stem from anxiety about the therapy situation. In the first interview, I try to get maximum information without affecting the flow and process; that is to say, I rarely make therapeutic interventions in a first session. Whenever a spouse says, "We feel," I suggest that things go better if each person speaks only for himself or herself. The partners are acutely aware of my responses to them, I am sure—my facial expressions, degree of interest, my grasp of what they are saying, and so forth. Most people are unnerved by silent therapists who sit there, staring at them, not giving feedback. It is part of my natural style to be active, open, and direct.

Most couples are fearful when they come to therapy; they feel unusual and different and wonder how "sick" they are. Without necessarily being explicit about it, I think it helps to convey in some form that the therapist has had some life experience, that he or she is no stranger to pain and disappointment, and that marital difficulties are well-nigh universal. In my attempts to decrease the distance between us, I will at times make social comments and even relate something personal about myself when relevant. (This latter can be overdone; some people are offended if the therapist is too disclosing about his or her personal or marital problems.) Sometimes remarks between cotherapists and humor can help ease the tension. It should be remembered, however, that the therapy situation is a professional rather than a social situation.

I try to cover a range of topics in the initial interview: history of previous therapies, previous marriages, what stages of marriage they have gone through, whether they were in love when they got married, whether they ever had a good relationship, what their expectations of marriage were, how the arrival of children affected the relationship, what their fight styles are or how they deal with conflict, and a description of the courtship from each vantage point. I try to evaluate how much the partners seem to care for each other (I always ask the direct question, "Do you love your spouse?"), whether the basic bonding is strong enough to tolerate the pain of change in oneself and in the mate, how motivated each is to do the work of therapy, whether each blames the other or each can take responsibility for himself or herself, whether one partner wants to stay in the marriage more than the other, whether they came too late, what kinds of secondary gains are operating, whether there are factors external to the marriage that would handicap the therapy, and so forth. As I said in a previous paper, however, (Framo, 1975b), it is difficult to predict which couples are going to "make it" in therapy. I have had couples who I was sure would have a successful outcome who got nowhere in therapy, and I have had others whose marriages looked hopeless who profited a great deal. The science of predicting marital therapy outcomes is in its primitive stages. All the while, I am trying to put together pieces of the puzzle that will explain the nature of the hidden agendas in the marriage contract, that is, how they came to select each other as spouses. (Many people have said, "I loved her because she loved me.")

I regard the sexual relationship as a diagnostic indicator in the sense that when the sex is good, other problems can be tolerated, and when it's bad or nonexistent, all other problems get exaggerated. I have learned that you often cannot accept at face value in the first session the partners' characterization of their sexual relationship; couples who initially tell you that sex is "great" or "no problem" later tell you the truth. Since the sexual relationship is uniquely sensitive to feelings of hurt, anger, rejection, disappointment, and so forth, it is not surprising to discover that almost all couples who come for marital therapy have either sexual dysfunctions or diminished interest in sex. Most couples' sexual difficulties disappear as a function of working on other problems. For those sexual problems that persist beyond successful marital therapy, I refer the couple to a sex therapist. The couples who report that the only thing they have going for them in their marriage is exciting sex, are rare. I do not pussyfoot about affairs and usually ask directly whether there is a third-party involvement on either side. Although I do not expect that I will always get honest answers to this question, I can usually surmise the existence of an extramarital relationship by the way the replies are given. Long hesitations, reddening of the face, or a quick "no" and an abrupt change of the topic leads me to expect a private phone call the next day. From my practice, I judge that women are having more affairs than they used to (Framo, 1975a).

It frequently happens that one partner, most often the husband, has come to marital therapy unwillingly or is willing to come only as a cotherapist in treating the spouse. These kinds of clients are always a challenge to me, and over the years, I have developed some techniques for "hooking" them into therapy: if a husband brings in a wife with symptoms, I frequently spend most of the session talking with the husband about his own life (particularly his family history). If the questions are not pathology-oriented, these men usually respond to the interest shown in them as persons. Another technique I have used after getting noncommittal or hostile replies to questions is to ignore these men to the point where they feel left out and want to be included. In these circumstances, when I am asked, "How come you always focus on me and not my spouse; am I the sick one?", I use a therapeutic double bind by saying, "On the contrary, you are healthier because I find you more receptive and open to change." The most effective method in dealing with reluctant spouses, I have found, is to put them into a couples' group. Almost no one can resist getting involved in that group process.

To couples who are on the edge of divorce, yet torn up about ending their marriage, I say something like "Let's postpone a decision about the fate of the marriage until later in the therapy. Let's meet for a while, and when each of you knows yourself better and how the two of you interlock, you'll have more information on which to make a decision about the fate of your marriage." Most couples are very frightened of ending even a bad marriage, so this statement relieves most people.

Unless the couple is in a state of crisis that requires immediate attention, I usually get a brief history of each spouse's family of origin. I have found questions like the following to be pertinent: How many were in your family? What was your birth position? What kind of work did your dad do? What kind of person was he as you were growing up? What was your mother like? How would you characterize their marriage? What was the atmosphere in your home or what kind of a family did you come from? Which parent did you feel closer to? How was your relationship with your brothers and sisters? Were there any unusual circumstances in your family (serious illnesses, deaths, grandparent in the home, or something else)? I ask the circumstances under which the person left home, how the parents reacted to his or her getting married and to the prospective mate. After finding out whether the parents are still alive, I inquire into the client's *current* relationship with parents and sibs: how often they see each other, whether the relationship with the parents is fused, superficial, distant, close, or alienated and cut-off. In my experience, unless you directly ask clients about their current relationships with parents and siblings or about problems with the in-laws, that sort of information is not volunteered. Many couples are surprised that the therapist, by this line of questioning, believes that there is a connection between their marital problems and their previous or ongoing relationship with the original family. While relating a family history, some people become upset or tearful. For instance, a man may choke up describing the distant relationship with his father, and I may comment, "That's something we'll have to go into further later on." I always ask about deaths in the family and have found that the old, muted affects can be revived by questioning in minute detail about the actual circumstances of the death (such as, "Who told you your father was dead? What did you do next? Did you cry? Who picked out his clothes for the viewing? What happened at the funeral? What was left unsaid when your dad died?"). Following each person's account of his or her family history, I always ask the spouse to give his or her reaction to that account and also to give his or her own views of the in-laws. Occasionally the mate corrects severe distortions, such as the wife who said, "I'm sitting here amazed. My husband just told you what a normal, average family he came from, and I remember his telling me how he and his sister were always afraid that his parents were going to kill each other. And the police were always called to his home!" Most couples are involved in a web of complex interrelationships with both extended families. A fairly common situation is that, say, the husband works for his father or works in his wife's family business; this arrangement creates all sorts of interesting problems. I tell all couples in the first interview that at some point toward the end of therapy, I would like each spouse to bring in his or her family of origin for a session. My paper on this topic demonstrates the great power of such sessions and also describes how I overcome the strong resistances of clients to this suggestion (Framo, 1976a). I may have sessions with the spouses and extended families or in-laws early in the therapy if there are immediate problems in those relationships, but I consider such sessions different from family-of-origin work, for which adults are prepared to confront and deal with the hard issues with their parents and brothers and sisters.

Simply making the decision to come to therapy starts bringing about changes in the relationship of most partners. For instance, they start talking about topics that could not be talked about previously without much anxiety. Some couples, however, are in a state of euphoria in that first session, not only because they have hope after such long despair but also because, often unrealistically, they expect that they will be made over and achieve ecstasy in their marriage. Everything that has always been wrong will now be made right. When I sense this kind of magical expectation, I tell the couple that after the honeymoon phase of therapy, some disappointment is inevitable once they get to see what's really involved in change. I state that the relationship may get worse before it gets better, and I do not minimize how difficult and painful marital therapy can be.

By the end of the initial interview, I can tell whether the couple will want to continue with the therapy. When they are uncertain, I suggest that they talk it over with each other and let me know; this is analagous to the situation where a couple is making an expensive purchase and the salesman leaves them alone so they can tell each other what they really think. As I stated previously, one-fifth of the couples do not continue with therapy; about half of those who do not return state their reasons during the first session, whereas the others telephone later. I do not try to convince couples or try to change their minds; therapy is difficult enough with motivated people.

Diagnostic interviews usually precipitate strong emotions, not only in the couple but in the therapist(s) as well. Although emotions can serve defensive purposes, I see powerful affects as providing the fuel for change, and I have learned not to be afraid of them. I agree with the statement made by Bryant and Grunebaum (1966) in discussing the emotions generated by family diagnostic interviews: "A well run family diagnostic is almost always painful for the leader. It is when we have felt too little that there has been only an evaluation of the surface." (p. 154).

The purpose of this paper was to focus on the beginnings of marital therapy. I have not discussed ongoing techniques in the later phases. I should mention that practically all the couples I see come into a couples' group. I have come to regard couples' group therapy as the treatment of choice for premarital, marital, separation, and divorce problems (Framo, 1973). To be sure, I have been discussing the easiest part of therapy, which is why these early phases are written about more frequently (Franklin and Prosky, 1973; Haley and Hoffman, 1967; Napier and Whitaker, 1973; Skynner, 1976). One of these days, I'm going to try to describe the part of the therapy process where change takes place, the part that has been called "the dirty middle" of therapy. But for the present, that story will have to wait.

5

Marriage Therapy in a Couples Group (1973)

There is little question that marriage as a social institution is in a severe crisis at this time. It has been estimated that, when the statistics are examined carefully, about half of all current marriages are ending in divorce; in some parts of the country the divorce rate exceeds the marriage rate. Taking into account the number of married people who stay together unhappily, we can understand that some people question the viability and workability of the marriage state and experiment with "living together" and forming group and multi-person marriages.

A more balanced view of marriage is not as pessimistic as the foregoing suggests. There are many positive sides to a marriage relationship that are not observable to outsiders, even to marriage therapists. One certainly cannot tell how a marriage is doing by how the husband and wife behave with each other in social situations; unless one knows otherwise, one assumes that other people's marriages are working. It is true, in a sense, that the public reports given out about one's marriage are like the communiqués issued by heads of state after an international meeting: Neither one tells you very much about what is really going on.

A realistic view of marriage, based on intimate knowledge of a couple, has to recognize not only the cliché that "all marriages have problems," but that in the course of a marriage over time *every* marriage has serious problems to the point where divorce or separation is at least considered.

In examining some of the dynamics involved in mate selection and the relationship between marriage partners, we note that people are usually unaware of their own secret agendas when they marry, partially because these unconscious

Reprinted with permission from D. A. Bloch (Ed.) *Techniques of Family Therapy: A Primer*. New York: Grune & Stratton, 1973. Copyright © 1973, Grune & Stratton, Inc.

designs are clouded by their conscious goals: romantic love and sexual attraction (which, by the way, have an essential validity in their own right and should not be discounted) (Kubie, 1956). Because of conflicts hanging over from the family of origin, people often marry those with whom they can prove or correct something, or those who will fill gaps in their own personality; they marry those who will punish them or whom they can punish, or those who will enable them to continue or master old conflictual relationships. There is some evidence, too, that people marry those who will help them to replicate or improve on their family of origin (Napier, 1971). Many people believe that marriage should provide a solution to their personal problems, or at least provide an escape from an intolerable situation in their family of origin. The discrepancy between the conscious and unconscious demands placed on marriage, then, helps to explain why untroubled marital integration is the exception rather than the rule.

After the initial euphoria of togetherness in the early months of the new marriage, some disappointment is inevitable. Each partner unconsciously attempts to maneuver the other into some earlier relationship pattern in the family of origin; each has the disquieting feeling that some old, tormenting ghost has risen to haunt him. The marriage, seriously entered into with such dreams, hopes, and expectations for happiness, often begins to sound like a broken record from the past, even to the point where some of the same lines from the script will be repeated. A wife, for example, may hear herself repeating the same words she heard her mother use with her father during an argument, or the husband may use his father's coping methods of bitter silence or leaving the house to get drunk.

Many people are unable to make a genuine emotional commitment to the mate, other than to have fantasies of romantic fusion. The married person's primary loyalties and commitments may be to the family or origin rather than the mate. Sometimes the overriding loyalty to the original family is direct and obvious, as seen in complaints that in any showdown the spouse always sides with his own parents, brothers, or sisters. Sometimes the criticism is that the mate must see or talk to a parent or sibling every day on the telephone, or must live with or near a parent, or must give time, work, or money to his family of origin. Primacy of devotion to the family of origin over the current family or marriage can be present even when the person has little or no contact with his parents and considers himself liberated from them. Those adults who have cut themselves off from their family of origin are even more likely to act out with their mate and children the irrational hangovers from the past. In any event, out of the despair and outrage that the mate has not fulfilled a promise (to love, honor, obey, take care of, overlook, tolerate, care unconditionally, and so forth) and out of the disappointment that the marriage did not make right what has always been wrong, spouses often turn to third parties to assuage their hurts. The third party, often triangulated to reduce tension in the marital twosome, can be a child, mistress or lover, liquor, hobbies, organizations, relatives, sports addictions, drugs, beauty parlors, or a psychotherapist.

Rationale for Marriage Therapy

Marital partners should be treated together, partly because, when a marriage is in serious trouble, the likelihood of divorce is greater if the partners go to two therapists separately, or if only one goes for treatment (Whitaker and Miller, 1969). In treating a couple one must consider that there are three patients: the husband, the wife, and the relationship. Sometimes the relationship cannot be saved, in which event "divorce therapy" is done for partners who are truly allergic to each other (more about this later). Although marriage counseling has a long and respectable tradition, it should be distinguished from marriage therapy: a form of depth treatment, which not only deals with the intrapsychic dynamics of each spouse but also examines the interlocking nature of the marital bond. The motivational feedback system between husband and wife, moreover, occurs in the context of the whole family, including the children, as well as the extended family. It is not surprising, therefore, that many marriage therapists are basically family therapists who view human relationships in systems terms.

Experience with family therapy has indicated that the marriage relationship is the core of the family (Framo, 1965a). The greatest gift parents can give children is two adults with a secure sense of self who enjoy life and who have a viable relationship with each other characterized by love, sexual satisfaction, open communication, and mutual respect. Although most of the professional literature emphasizes the parent–child relationship in dealing with children's problems, family therapy experience has shown that the husband–wife axis is more critical to the welfare of the children. In many ways, it is much more difficult to be a mate than to be a parent. Whenever there is a disturbed child there is a disturbed marriage, although not all marriages in difficulty entangle or involve the children. Because of the interrelationship of parenting and marriage, most of the couples we have seen in marital therapy have come from family therapy that has progressed to the point where the originally symptomatic children no longer need treatment. Some couples, both with and without children, however, have started therapy explicitly because of marriage problems, in some instances because of open conflict, whereas other couples are estranged by silent warfare or by sexual dysfunctions. A few couples entered therapy to revitalize their "empty" relationships. Couples who have had successful marital therapy experiences often report that as their marriages improved, so did their children's problems, even in cases where the children were never seen in therapy.

A Method of Running a Couples Group

Married couples were originally put together into a treatment group for my own benefit—that is, in order to allow myself more therapeutic freedom to effect change. Although many couples utilized the conjoint marriage therapy setting most effectively and rehabilitated their relationship in a short period of time, other couples boxed me in by their triangulating efforts—such as by insisting that I be judge or referee and decide who was right and who was wrong. Some couples moved for a while and bogged down; others developed such strong transference feelings that I was expected to be a super-parent and adopt them; and some couples were unable to stop fighting and listen to each other or the therapist. The idea of putting several of these difficult couples together in a group came from finding my own freedom of action blocked by my feelings of frustration, anger, and boredom. Although this step was originally taken for practical reasons of clinical expedience, it has had the serendipitous effect of demonstrating that couples group therapy is a powerful form of treatment in its own right. Based on experience with this method with over 200 couples, my belief is that couples group therapy is the treatment of choice for marital problems. (Incidentally, not all of the couples in treatment are married, but all have an ongoing relationship that the partners either want to make better, or feel they need help to terminate.)

Some of the reasons for the usefulness of couples group therapy are fairly obvious: Couples come to realize that their marital difficulties are not unique, and some marital relationships improve simply from recognizing how general marriage conflicts really are. (It is not uncommon for a couple leaving the first session to say, "My God, did you see *those* two! And I thought our marriage was bad.") In our culture, people do not get much opportunity to examine other people's marriages in depth. In the permissive, frank atmosphere of the group sessions, they can discover that every marriage has to work out accommodations in the universal areas of the handling of children, sex, money, and in-laws, and they learn that people are essentially more alike than different. They learn to use other marriage struggles as models of what to avoid or how things can be worked out. In this setting, spouses have a forum where the unrealistic expectations of marriage and of their mates can be exposed to the reality testing of the group. In a group context, transference and counter-transference feelings are diluted, the therapist is less viewed as the rescuer, judge, persecutor, or all-loving parent, and the group process can be used for therapeutic leverage. Spouses can be stimulated to reconsider their own behavior by being exposed to contrasting patterns in other couples.

Often the individuals listen more to others in the group than they would to the therapist; people in the group, who do not have to take a therapist's stance, can confront someone in street language in such a way that the words have greater impact than a clinical interpretation. (For example, one woman in the group did not modify her bitter, attacking behavior toward her husband until another man in the group told her, "You're really a ball-breaking bitch. I sure would hate to be married to you.") In many ways, the group serves the supportive and confronting function for marriages that used to be served by extended family.

Couples group therapy as conducted by the present method does not bear much relationship to conventional peer group therapy, even though there is a similarity in the sense that a group of people are being treated together. Group therapy is based on an assemblage of strangers who have no past history with each other or likelihood of a future together. In couples groups, the marital unit has had a past history and is likely to have a future long after the group is disbanded (although, of course, the couples are strangers to each other initially). Consequently, in order of priority, we consider the individuals' first obligaton to be to themselves, then to their mates, and only peripherally to the group. In my particular method of conducting these groups, I deemphasize the group process as such, although I am continually aware of it and use it to help bring about change. What is meant by this is that *there is not much focus on the relationships and distortions between individuals across couples*. For instance, the transference of a husband to someone else's wife who reminds him of his sister would not be worked with, whereas the transference distortions that occur between marital partners would be of paramount importance. However, the group process is used in various ways—by drawing contrasts between couples, by managing the time allotted to each couple, by dealing with group feelings when a couple is especially hostile to each other, or regresses, or has made much progress and is ready to terminate.

Usually, there are three couples in a group and sessions last for about an hour and a half; the focus is on one couple at a time, while the other two couples are instructed to attend carefully. The target couple is engaged rather actively; at the end of approximately 25 minutes, each other person in the room is asked to give his or her reactions to what was observed. Although each couple usually gets about a half hour of time, there are occasions, such as when a particular couple is in an acute crisis, that the allotted times are made more flexible. This particular procedure of running couples groups owes a theoretical debt to the work of M. Bowen, which emphasizes differentiation from the marital symbiosis as a primary goal of therapy. Bowen also pays much attention to the use of the self of the therapist in helping to bring about the development of a sense of self in each person in the group (Anonymous, 1972).

The only criterion used for selection of couples for a particular group is age and stage of the life cycle. Couples who have recently married or have young children seem to do better with couples near their own age, whereas older married couples with adolescents or grown children tend to relate better to couples who are roughly in the same phase of the family. Couples are *not* selected on the basis of individual or marital psychopathology, social class, intellectual level, or any of the other conventional criteria. When dealing with intimate relationships people are reduced to the same level, whether the husbands and wives are Ph.D.s or housewives and plumbers. Often the lesser educated members of the group can zero in on an emotional level in a way that cuts right through the intellectualization of the more sophisticated members. Although some individuals have had a history of "mental illness" or hospitalization, this factor has not been a determining one in the progress they will make in this form of psychotherapy.

Most couples, who had been initially seen in either family therapy or conjoint marital therapy, are reluctant to enter a couples group. Sometimes there are valid secrets or skeletons in the closet that the partners do not want to reveal to others. Other times an individual will say, "I can't talk in front of other people," or "I'm not interested in other people's problems." Sometimes couples have been placed in groups after extensive periods of prior work; in other instances they have started with the group after only one initial interview as a single couple. More recently, having been impressed with the fairly rapid progress made with explicit marital problems in couples group therapy, we have put spouses in groups after only several therapy sessions as a couple alone. Those partners who are reluctant to join a group are encouraged to attend several sessions on a trial basis, with the option of going back to single couple therapy if it is felt that the group method is not productive. It is extremely rare for a couple to drop out of the group once having tried the experience. One husband, who entered the group unwillingly, with the warning, "OK, doc, I'll come, but I won't say a word when I get there," became the one member of the group whom we could not get to stop talking.

When I start a new group of three couples who are all meeting each other for the first time, I structure the beginning of the session with a few simple ground-rules: (1) that a premium is placed on openness and honesty and the members are free to reveal themselves, their thoughts and feelings, but no physical violence is permitted; (2) that spouses are free to discuss the sessions afterwards, but should refrain from talking about the other couples in social situations where there might be other people present who know one of the other couples; and (3) that the members should try to make all criticisms of others in the group in a constructive fashion. My aim is to develop a safe, trusting atmosphere in this small society that does not operate with the social facades, and according to the rules of ordinary social behavior.

Once a group is started, it becomes open-ended—as couples terminate, new couples are added to the group. When one person cannot come to a session the partner is encouraged to come alone, to work on self. If a husband or wife drops out of treatment altogether, the mate is allowed to continue with the group if he or she is so motivated; this happens rarely. This procedure emphasizes the focus on autonomy and differentiation of self within the context of a relationship. Occasionally, the couples are seen with their children in family sessions, outside the couples group situation. This is done not only to get a reading on how the children are doing but also to evaluate how the whole family system is operating and to gauge the children's reactions to changes in their parents.

Most people enter marital therapy in order to change their mate; they are convinced that they are in the right, as any "reasonable" outsider would "plainly see" when the full story about the spouse is told, documented with specific examples. They believe that while there may be some petty quirks in their own personality, they would have no real difficulty becoming a good marriage partner if their mate would undergo some fundamental changes. Each married person secretly believes that his or her mate is seriously disturbed and cannot love.

Individuals, as members of a marital unit, then, enter therapy with different hidden agendas as well as varying levels of motivation to change self, the mate, or to preserve the marriage. The couples who have the best prognosis, and who will make it with each other, are the ones who state, in essence, "We basically love each other and want to stay married, but for some reason we can't get along. Will you help us make this relationship work?" Some couples are on the verge of divorce and come to treatment as a last resort before consulting lawyers. It is rare, however, for couples to present their problems in joint fashion in these two ways—*both* wanting to continue or terminate the marriage. What is more common is that one partner is more explicitly discontented with the relationship. At the initial evaluation session, I suggest a period of exploratory therapy, with major decisions about the fate of the marriage being postponed until the partners can make more realistic and honest choices, based on the new knowledge and freedom that therapy can bring. When the negative emotional intensity is very high, I may suggest that a couple live apart from each other for a specified period, but that they continue to attend therapy sessions. These planned trial separations, suggested at various stages of the treatment according to the circumstances and the amount of mutual destructiveness, often help partners grow through the separation process and eliminate "if it weren't for you" games (Toomim, 1972).

One of the saddest and most difficult situations to deal with in marital therapy is when one partner wants out of the marriage and the other desperately tries to hold on to the mate and grasps at any straw of hope to maintain the marriage. This circumstance is not always obvious in the beginning. Some people come to therapy with their mates as a token gesture; they may have someone else they want to marry but feel guilty about abandoning the mate. They agree to come to therapy so that later they can say they tried everything to "save" the marriage, and, besides, it would ease the conscience if the mate were left in the hands of the therapist. As soon as I become aware of this ploy and of the lip service being given to commitment to treatment, I expose it and suggest that honesty would be kinder in the long run. More commonly one partner is disturbed about the marriage relationship and the other, usually the husband, who came reluctantly in the first instance, does not feel their problems are unusual in kind or degree. He cannot understand what the fuss is all about. Men of this sort are uncomfortable when questioned and are loath to reveal feelings or anything "personal." Often this kind of man is difficult to involve in treatment until the therapist or the group provokes or challenges him. Not uncommonly, the wife discloses that because of his emotional neglect or indifference she has had an affair, a disclosure often followed by his becoming seriously upset. The differences in levels of awareness of a need for change of self, or the mate, or the desire to continue the marriage, provide the kind of heterogeneity that is useful for couples group therapy.

One of the reasons couples group therapy works rests on the truism that people can be much more objective about other people's problems than they can be about their own. It is not unusual during a session to witness an individual be active, perceptive, and right on target in his observations about someone in the group; as soon as he starts talking about himself, or his partner, there is a dramatic shift in tone of voice, his manner becomes hesitant, he blocks, and seems to be reduced to the functioning level of a mental defective. It is a sign of real progress when an individual gets to the point where he can get outside his own emotional field and view himself with objectivity.

When people start with a group, they are usually so preoccupied with their own distress that it is very difficult for them to attend to the problems of other couples, and it is an indication of movement when they can begin to be concerned about others. Members of the couples group are not always objective about others, however. Occasionally someone makes a very distorted observation about someone else, and it becomes necessary to modify this comment, or to check it out with the other members of the group. The therapist must be aware of this phenomenon of one forceful person projecting his or her own problem onto others under the guise of helpfulness. More difficult to detect and handle is the phenomenon of group irrationality. It is possible that an entire group can share a myth. (For example, if all three husbands are passive men who have lived by the formula of "peace at any price," they may be unanimous in the view that it is not necessary for men to take stands on issues. It is generally wise to have at least one vigorous male in a group.)

The mutually reinforcing defense systems or "games" that go on between married partners (as when one attacks and one defends, one overfunctions and one underfunctions, or one is jealous and the other provokes jealousy) are quickly exposed in these groups. Each couple has its own style of interactional behavior, which is picked up rapidly by the other couples; these game-like patterns are repeated again and again until therapeutic change takes place. In this connection, a recurring event that takes the inexperienced therapist by surprise occurs when the spouse begins to change in the direction originally demanded by the partner and the partner not only seems indifferent to the change but even uncomfortable with it. This paradoxical reaction can occur, for example, when a formerly sexually unresponsive wife becomes more sexual, or when a silent husband begins to state his thoughts and feelings. Interestingly, partners often switch in their behavior, exchange symptoms, or shift positions on issues; a couple may start therapy with the husband wanting to rehabilitate the marriage and the wife wanting out, and the group is astonished when they reverse positions about the continuance of the marriage.

In general, most couples go through a predictable sequence as their repetitive interchanges undergo review by the reality testing of the group. Because of the premium placed on openness, early in the treatment the partners are apt to learn things about their mates that they never knew before; marital partners can be in the dark about what their mate really thinks even though they may have lived together for many years. Some of these disclosures can be shocking and painful, and one can sense the group discomfort when, for instance, a wife tells her spouse that she does not really love him or that he is not the real father of their daughter. Group anxiety can also rise when the hostility between partners becomes especially hurting and ugly. However, marital fighting can have a salutary effect on other couples, particularly those who had never had an open disagreement. "Pseudo-mutual" couples, that is, those who need to deny all differences, find it very difficult to maintain their illusion of compatibility when they are exposed to openly combative couples. One couple, who had never had an open argument with each other in 15 years of marriage, had their first fight about another couple in the group while they were driving home from a couples group session. Interestingly, the 15-year-old son of this couple, who had never had an open argument, had been arrested for fighting in school. This particular couple reported their joint fear that their first fight would lead to divorce. An important part of marital therapy consists of teaching couples who have never argued the value of learning how to confront and deal with issues between them. Bach's principles of "constructive fighting" are more useful for those fight-phobic partners than for the Virginia Woolf couples for whom insult-exchange is a ritualistic way of life (Bach and Wyden, 1969).

Most couples have an immediate and temporary positive response to the group and report after a few sessions that their marriage is much improved. However, another predictable stage of treatment, with some exceptions, is that, as they begin the work of therapy and as change threatens the system, there is usually some regression before they pull up again. One sign of improvement, even though it is accompanied by suffering and confusion, is when each partner becomes more individuated and there are more "I" position statements and fewer "we feel" or "we think" statements. The use of "we" is customary early in therapy because the expression conceals differences between the partners which might be frightening if revealed. A sense of personal identity, and respect for the partner's separate identity, is a critical ingredient in successful marital therapy; separateness of this order paradoxically brings about increased intimacy between the spouses.

Those couples who make considerable progress in the group often report that they feel really married for the first time; it is not unusual for older married couples to act like adolescents in love. Even though the other couples express their pleasure at seeing another couple "make it," and some are even spurred on to achieve the same state, there is also usually some envy and minor resentment as well as mourning when a couple leaves the group under these circumstances.

It should be mentioned that I do not discourage the couples in the group from having social contact outside the sessions. Indeed, some isolated couples made their first friends in the group. Often, the couples go to a restaurant together after meetings, rehash the sessions and gossip about the therapist and each other. Many couples have maintained friendships with each other long after the group has disbanded. However, in the many groups that I've seen there has never been an instance of extramarital sexual acting out between group members, although several couples in groups were involved in mate-swapping activities *outside* the group. (A few couples, on being invited to join the group, did have the fantasy that they were being invited into a sex swinging group. One husband angrily said, "I want you to know that I don't go for that sort of thing.")

An atmosphere of discouragement can pervade sessions when one or more of the couples have a sense of hopelessness about their relationship; in this sense there can be group contagion. A shock-wave of fear also runs through the group when a couple decide to divorce. When there has been intense emotional investment in each other, most partners cannot separate without bitterness, and a need for revenge. Divorce therapy is a relatively new therapeutic approach designed to help partners disengage from their relationship with a minimum of destructiveness to self, the mate, and the children, and with the freedom to form new relationships. The emotional turmoil surrounding such issues as child custody, visitation rights, and division of property are better handled in this therapeutic rather than legal atmosphere. The group can be of much help during this process of mutual recrimination and also in dealing with those situations where one partner is already out of the marriage and the other cannot let go until fault and blame has been dissipated as an issue. One couples group consisted of one couple in divorce therapy, one premarital couple trying to decide whether or not to marry, and one couple struggling to rehabilitate their marriage. In that particular group, the wife of the couple in divorce therapy dropped out of treatment, finished with the marriage, but her husband stayed on, and, with the help of the group, was finally able to achieve an "inner emotional balance," as he put it, before he was ready to give his wife an uncontested divorce.

Occasionally, "sibling rivalry" occurs between couples in the group. Until the group gets used to the format described in this paper, they are frustrated by the time limitations, and one person may state, "They got five minutes more than we did." It is true that if one couple is in an acute crisis they do get more time, but over a period of weeks the time allotted to each couple evens out. Besides, the couples soon learn that they can often get more out of observing the work being done with another couple than the time spent with them. The rivalry, furthermore, can be used to provide therapeutic leverage. For instance, if a couple is resistant and does not want to talk, I may say, "Well, I better move on to someone else. I can see you're not ready to deal with this." Couples handled in this manner are much more likely to be productive the next time their turn comes around.

At times, the therapist is accused of favoring or not liking men or women; as one may imagine, this creates lively discussions and smokes out hidden marital issues. Social movements such as women's rights or changes in sexual attitudes are interwoven with marital conflicts—a common example is the woman who wants to change her traditional housewife role and have an open marriage, or start a career. Because of these factors, as well as others, I have found that a heterosexual therapy team can run these couples groups more effectively than a solo therapist of either sex.

Since the relationship problems adults have with their mates and children are reconstructions and elaborations of earlier conflicts with the family of origin, I try to have at least one session with each adult and his family of origin, whether I am doing family, marital, or couples group therapy. Of all the treatment methods used, I find this the most powerful in terms of having an effect on the problems originally presented. The majority of adults are most reluctant to bring in their parents and siblings, often with the words, "Look, doc, you don't know how *impossible* my mother (or father) is." Some fear their parents will go crazy or die of a heart attack in the treatment session. Most of those who initially react negatively to the idea gradually come to see its value, especially when they see other individuals in the couples group do it and they hear about what was accomplished. These sessions with adults and their families of origin reveal important diagnostic information on how past family problems are being acted out in the present. More to the point, however, in these sessions opportunities are available for genuine corrective experiences and the clarification of old misunderstandings, providing a chance for adults and their parents to get to know each other as people. Many adults who have been cut off or alienated from their parents, sometimes for many years, find that when they have established more adult-to-adult relationships with their own parents and siblings they are able to relate to their spouses and children in a more adult manner.

Couples group therapy is not a new procedure, even though former publications on the topic have stressed quite different rationales and methods of running the groups (Blinder and Kirschenbaum, 1967; Gottlieb and Pattison, 1966; Hastings and Runkle, 1963; Leichter, 1962; Neubeck, 1954; Perelman, 1960; Von Emde Boas, 1962). This writer believes that there is great potential in this therapeutic method, and, as stated previously, that couples group therapy is probably the treatment of choice in dealing with marital problems. The consequences of marital stress, on children and society, are important enough to warrant further experimentation with this method and its techniques.

6

Husbands' Reactions to Wives' Infidelity (1975)

Extramarital affairs are only one aspect of the complexity of marital dynamics and are woven into the fabric of other problems. It is difficult to make generalizations about affairs because they have different meanings and determinants in each situation. Exploration can reveal that the affair was an act of desperation, that it had little to do with the mate at all, that it was consciously designed to arouse the mate's interest, that it was based on revenge for real or fancied wrongs, that it was destructive in intent (aimed at getting rid of the mate), that the third party was a way-station on a route back to the mate (and in this sense the affair revived an empty marriage and was therapeutic), that the affair was set up by the marriage partner, and so forth—the individual and interactional motives are infinite.

The wife having the affair is more frequent in my practice, which is contrary to the popularly assumed trend and the findings of Kinsey where twice as many men as women have extramarital experiences. Although my sample is small, of the 31 couples I have seen where extramarital affairs had occurred, in 27 it was the woman who had the affair. This would seem to be some support for the observation that women are becoming more free sexually; one hears more complaints from wives that their husbands are not too sexually interested in them, whereas in previous years it used to be the other way around. So something seems to be happening.

It is possible, however, that my data are an artifact of the conditions under which they were obtained. I see husbands and wives together in conjoint marital therapy. Men may not be as likely as women to regard an affair as something for

Reprinted with permission from *Medical Aspects of Human Sexuality*, May, 1975. Copyright © 1975 Hospital Publications, Inc.

which marital therapy is needed. What I mean by this is that some of the women have telephoned for appointments, asking either to be seen alone for the first session so they can discuss whether their husband should know about the affair, or they set up the therapy session so as to tell the husband in a safe situation. Men seem less likely to handle affairs in this way. One typical syndrome in couples who have been married for just a few years is that the wife feels neglected. She says things like, "The romance is gone out of our marriage; I get my weekly ration of sex on Sunday night. Sex is mechanical, and I feel like I'm being used as a receptacle; he treats me like a piece of furniture and never talks to me." The husband is usually a student, or wrapped up in his work, or absorbed with watching sports on television.

He is usually quite reluctant to come to therapy, in some cases being dragged or tricked into coming to the office. When questioned, the husband doesn't feel they have more problems than any other married couple, and he can't understand what the fuss is all about. These husbands speak laconically to the point of inarticulateness; they are most uncomfortable and loath to reveal feelings or discuss anything "personal." At a certain point in the interview, following the wife's tearful complaints and the husband's minimization of their problems, the wife asks tentatively, "How would you feel if you found out I've had an affair?" Some husbands have no visible reaction to this initial question and continue the conversation with a smile on their face, as if the question had never been asked. I have been impressed with the capacity for denial that some people have. Some of these husbands ignore the most blatant clues and hints that their wives are having affairs, and a few refuse to believe the overt disclosure of an affair even when they are given graphic details.

The denial, of course, serves many functions: in some cases they do not want to hear it because then they would have to do something about it. Some husbands adopt a nonchalant attitude about the matter as long as they feel they are talking about a theoretical possibility. Still other husbands react to the provisional question with surprise as if the possibility had never occurred to them, and they proceed to ask what she means by the question. I can feel the tension begin to rise in the room. The wife's toying with the idea of an affair sometimes leads the husband to ask, finally, "What are you trying to tell me?" or "We're not talking about what we're talking about, are we?"

The distinction between dealing with an abstract possibility and dealing with a reality is not a subtle one. Some of the husbands who accepted the abstraction with equanimity later developed most severe reactions when they had to deal with the hard actuality. The range of reactions of husbands, when they know for sure that their wives definitely had an affair, is very wide. At one extreme is the husband who said, "Great! I didn't think you had it in you," to the other extreme where the man is truly devastated, deeply hurt, and rocked to the very foundations of his personality. Psychotic reactions, suicide, and murder in response to infidelity appear in the newspaper every day, but when the situation is handled in conjoint marital therapy by a competent, well-trained marital or family therapist, and the meaning of the "infidelity" is explored, these dangers are minimized.

There is no question that for some people sexual unfaithfulness of the mate is the worst thing that can happen to them, and the most primitive passions of jealousy, revenge, depression, rage, and urges to murder are aroused. Those wives who set up the therapy to tell their husbands in that safe situation knew what they, were about because they knew their husbands. One can often detect in these people who react so extremely a kind of mourning and grieving, tied in with the theme of lost love. These extreme reactions are usually a function of earlier, unconscious rejections being stirred up.

In the middle range of reactions, the husbands on first hearing about the affair usually react, observably, with mild upset and curiosity, and the impact does not hit them until the ride home in the car or the next day. Often after learning of the wife's affair the couple argue or talk into the night, do not get much sleep, and the husband cannot go to work the next day. I can usually predict when I will get a call for an extra session. The husband wants to start dealing with these crucial questions: Who did you have the affair with? What did it mean to you? How did you do it? When? Where? And then the wife yells back, "Aren't you interested in *why?*" It is important for the husband to know who the lover is or was, particularly whether it was someone he knew, perhaps his best friend. Some men press for all the explicit details, and others do not want to know any of the particulars.

Those who want to know everything are often fed all the details, sometimes in graphic fashion, by their wives, who sense it "turns on" their husbands. It is necessary to emphasize the multiple levels of the reactions in a given husband—on the one hand being excited and titillated at the image of the wife locked in sexual embrace with another man, and on another level being horrified and sickened. Some wives report that after the husband found out about the affair they had the best sex with each other that they had ever had; one man with prior impotence became potent after knowledge of his wife's affair. The whore versus virtuous woman dichotomy that most men have about women often finds its expression in intense sexual relations, alternating with hurt, anger, accusations, and the kind of denial one has on hearing about the death of a loved one—"No! It can't be true!"

There are certain stages the couple go through around the affair. For varying periods of time the husband, needing to overcome what he perceives to be castration, feels that he is in competition with the lover and has to prove he is better. Threatened by the implication that his own sexual appeal must be inferior, he also feels that the lover has set a standard he cannot meet. During sexual relations he asks the wife, "Am I as good?" "I'll bet he never gave you a charge like that." This period is a very painful one for both parties, for the husband is largely dealing with his own fantasies about the lover, which are often discrepant from the wife's knowledge of what the affair was actually like. If she is kind she reassures the husband about his sexual prowess and minimizes the pleasure of the affair; in some cases, if the affair was not all that satisfactory, she does not have to lie.

Some of these husbands develop a close identification with the lover, who can become a fantasied superman who has stolen away his wife, or the lover can become a dissociated bad aspect of the self. Indeed, many of these men (and women, too, when they are in this position) seem to maintain an interest in the lover long after the one who has had the affair has lost interest. (One woman whose husband had told her of an affair followed her rival everywhere, saying bitterly, "That slut is everything I struggled all my life *not* to be.") Some of the husbands imagine during intercourse that they are the lover, and this fantasy usually creates a kind of bittersweet torture. In most cases the men are far more furious at the lover than at the wife, probably because it's safer that way; the feelings toward the wife are very mixed, because she is still needed, whereas the feelings toward the lover can be experienced as pure hatred.

Still others are angry at their mate, partly because they feel that the confession has forced them to share in the guilt and the responsibility. What is especially difficult for these people is the developing recognition that they did, in the majority of cases, play a part in the unfaithfulness of their mate. An additional complication is the concern the couple have about who knows about the affair—whether her family, or his family, or their friends know. And the wife, who never experienced guilt about the affair at the time it was going on, is more likely to feel guilt now because somebody besides herself knows about it. The projection of the superego is an interesting phenomenon; many people do not feel bad about what they have done until it becomes public knowledge.

There were a few husbands in my sample who reacted with encouragement or apparent indifference to the disclosure of their wives' affairs, and several who did not have even a delayed reaction. The wives tended to perceive these as the most hostile reactions of all, since it meant to them that their husbands didn't even care enough to get angry. One husband smiled through the whole thing until his wife hit him. Some of the men were overforgiving and blamed themselves, and still others took a "scientific" attitude about the affair, handling it like a research problem.

One of the saddest situations seen in marital therapy is when one partner wants to get out of the marriage and the other desperately tries to hold on to the mate, grasping at any straw of hope that develops in the therapy for saving the marriage. Often, in these cases, the affair was one more method used to terminate the relationship, and the one who had the affair hopes that the therapist will give professional confirmation that there should be a divorce. The trouble is that often the "betrayed" mate does not want to break up the marriage and lose the partner. He is definitely in the one-down position and feels he can't make demands or go too far in honest leveling or objecting lest the last tenuous tie be broken.

Some of these wives continued the affair after the disclosure, and their husbands did not feel they had enough of a bargaining position to insist that they stop. The poignant suffering of these husbands is like those under a death sentence waiting for a reprieve; as the wife breaks the marital ties bit by bit (such as, by confiding only in others, or by taking the wedding ring off) one can see the man's heart break with each step away that she takes. He feels humiliated and helpless and hates himself for "not being a man," but he can no more control these feelings than he can control his breathing. Sometimes he tries to become the kind of person his wife says she wants, but if her complaint, for example, is that he is not exciting enough, he finds it impossible to be exciting or glamorous while he is depressed and full of suppressed anger. This is the kind of untenable position that gives rise to frank psychiatric symptoms or suicide.

The mate who is in the one-up position may exploit the one who cares more, yet she also suffers from guilt. These women may feel pity for their rejected, begging husband, but they also feel contempt and are frightened by the husband's helplessness. Deeper exploration can reveal, moreover, that having a man in this humbled position represents to the woman a neurotic payoff and triumph over, say, a father who had once rejected her. The man, too, may be reenacting some earlier situation in his life; one man reported that he found himself in the same weak, subservient position his father had been in with his mother. It is particularly difficult for a male therapist to handle his feelings when he witnesses a man on his knees, pleading for his wife not to leave him.

In the population I have seen it was not difficult for the women to end their affairs because there had not been that much emotional involvement with the lover. One woman said she didn't miss the lover so much as she missed the feeling of love that the affair gave her. The primary motive for the affairs discussed in my practice was to create the husband's interest, and once this happened, as it usually did, the lover became superfluous. Usually, the women say that they would not have married their lovers; the husband may have been looked upon as dull, but he is regarded as more substantial, responsible, and really caring. Husbands hate to hear their wives say: "I want to stay married to him for sensible reasons" or "because he's the father of my children." The husband who has had an affair may say he wants to stay married to his wife because she's a better homemaker and mother for his children than his girlfriend would be.

What are the consequences of affairs on the course of the marriage and the therapy? In my special population it is rare for the affair to break up the marriage; when a marriage terminates, the causes are much more complex and deeper than unfaithfulness. In most cases the couples move beyond this crisis and begin doing the real work of therapy. Sometimes the affair helped create a wholly new and reinvigorated relationship for the couple. In other couples who stay together unhappily, the earlier bond and trust are very difficult to reestablish; the marital partner may become extra suspicious when the mate is late or has to go to an evening meeting, and a process of checking up may begin. Sometimes the distrust can lead to binding and artificial behavior: one husband kept watching his wife's eyes at parties to see if they rested too long on another man; one husband had to keep his eyes straight ahead when he walked with his wife down the street so that he wouldn't upset her by looking at pretty girls; some people have had to call their mates periodically during the day in order to prove that they were where they were supposed to be.

Some individuals are unable to get their spouse's affair out of their thoughts: they are obsessed by it, keep making connections and remember and reinterpret past events that at the time seemed innocent. Some feel they were duped and say, "What a fool I was to be so trusting," or "There I was, carrying on a one-sided love affair with my wife, and she was screwing some other guy." With some couples unfaithfulness gets incorporated into longstanding sadomasochism, always being dredged up in arguments. The act of infidelity itself sometimes reveals previously hidden neurotic trends, and the one who feels he has been betrayed may use the affair to continue punishing the errant mate in many conscious or unconscious ways. Unconscious vindictive behavior can take the form of constant berating, putting the mate down in public, flirting with others, becoming nonsexual with the mate, being uncommitted, putting the welfare of others before the mate, or becoming slovenly, forgetful, thoughtless, and neglecting. The unkind behavior is often rationalized as an attempt to protect oneself from being hurt again, and there is usually an underlying formula of emotional blackmail: "I can get away with anything now; my faults are inconsequential compared to that awful thing my mate did to me." Although some of these behaviors are understandable for a period after finding out about the affair, when they continue as a vendetta for years it is apparent that the affair is being used for neurotic purposes, especially when there is some evidence that the mate was unconsciously maneuvered into having the affair.

An affair, then, can serve as a vehicle for the exacerbation or resolution of preexisting internal problems for both individuals. When the turmoil and feelings get especially intense and the couple find living together too destructive, in order to tone down the feelings I may suggest the partners have a period of trial separation and that they either meet together just for the therapy sessions, or they are seen separately for a while in order to explore their intrapsychic conflicts, especially focused around the family of origin.

There are many widely accepted beliefs which now and then are questioned. A doctrine I question at this time is whether honesty is always the best policy. At issue here—especially propagated by the encounter movement—is whether complete openness and frankness is always wise or therapeutic. I am aware of the tremendous beneficial changes that can occur in relationships when people level with each other, and for some marriages disclosure of the affair was the best thing that could have happened. Some people, however, simply cannot handle that kind of information, and I believe that there are some secrets which should always remain secrets (one woman I saw had a son who was the child of another man, but neither her husband nor son knew about it; this was one secret I respected). Each situation has to be decided on its own, with all the relevant consequences taken into account.

Despite its frequency, societies throughout the world almost universally condemn unfaithfulness; the only legal ground for divorce that all 50 states have in common is adultery. In most states the divorce laws require that there be an innocent and a guilty party before a divorce is granted. Yet every judge and lawyer, and certainly every professional marriage therapist, if they know enough about the history of a deteriorated marriage, are quite aware that one cannot blame one partner or another. In a marriage that did not work out both parties were participants in a relationship that failed. The overt act of adultery is usually the chance byproduct of chronic marital unhappiness to which both parties contributed, yet the law judges only on the basis of the overt act. A few states recognize this psychological truth by having no-fault divorce, but in the majority of states the marital partners and the children suffer long-term tragic consequences from the law's insistence on labeling a guilty offender. For instance, one husband I saw persuaded a friend to seduce his wife so he could divorce his wife for adultery; others I have seen have consciously and unconsciously pushed their mates into having affairs.

There are instances of extramarital sex which occur because of marked differences in sexual needs between the two partners, and there are some individuals who compulsively seek sexual relations with others even when they are quite satisfied with their sexual relationship with their mate. This unfaithfulness which occurs relatively independent of the relationship with the mate, even though there may be drastic consequences for the fate of the marriage, is sometimes based on deep-seated internal problems of the individual. Some of these individuals feel alive only during sexual contact or during its pursuit, or they ward off depression by sex and their encounters are usually followed by remorse and self-punishment.

Although infidelity does often create emotional pain and has other deleterious side effects, in some situations extramarital affairs seem to be the best possible compromise or even a necessity in a given marital predicament. I am not discussing here those situations in which a spouse is physically incapable of participating sexually, is institutionalized, or is unavailable for some other realistic reason. In some marital situations affairs have occurred as acts of desperation arising out of a miserable relationship that could not otherwise be changed. Many people have made numerous attempts to better a marriage relationship, including seeking professional help, but the efforts have failed, sometimes because only one of the spouses is interested in change, but even when both partners want change and are unable, for various and complicated reasons, to improve their relationship. In these marital circumstances the partners are unable or unwilling to get a divorce, for both realistic and unrealistic reasons.

Although children are often used as an excuse when spouses stay together unhappily, the children are an important consideration. The husband, for example, may truly love his children, may enjoy the day-to-day contact with them as they grow up, may not want to be a weekend father, and would miss that important family feeling.

Both partners may be afraid that they could not make it with someone else if they got divorced; to love is to risk rejection, and the partners may settle for physical proximity with each other because they are terrified of the vulnerability that loving another would bring. In addition, they may be afraid of living alone, or of joining that sad world of the nightclub circuit or of singles groups where the forlorn frantically try to make human contact with other lonely people. Sometimes the partners are older and recognize how difficult it is to find eligible marriage material; the eligibles are likely to be those who have had divorces themselves, or, having never married, are likely to be living with their mothers.

People can be deeply attached to each other even though they do not get along; in addition to fears of abandonment there may exist the anxiety of losing the partner to someone else. Mutual jealousy may keep a couple locked into each other; the spouses may have largely negative feelings toward each other yet be unable to let the other go because they would be tormented at the thought of the partner being sexual with someone else. So these couples continue to live together with emptiness, punctuated by quarreling, hurting, or ignoring of each other, with rare moments of empathic touching when they try to recapture the love they once had for each other. I have heard people say in these situations where they can't live with and can't live without each other, "Surely there ought to be more to life than this," or "I've learned the bitter lesson of how to be married but alone," or "In the years I have left I want something more than what I've had."

Extramarital relationships have a high probability of occurring in the foregoing circumstances as a solution or accommodation to the situation. These people feel that, free from the routine of home responsibilities and the marital void, they can bring the best part of themselves to another relationship and get some enjoyment out of life. Some even maintain that they can feed back into their family life the pleasure obtained from the outside liaison; that they are not as irritable or frustrated. Some partners who have affairs deliberately maintain them on a sexual basis only, for to form an emotional attachment to another would be perceived as real disloyalty to the mate. Numerous marriages are maintained on the basis of one or both partners having extramarital sex; the partners under these conditions usually uphold their responsibilities as parents, and the effect on the children may not be damaging if the affairs are handled discreetly. Those partners who have only casual sexual encounters sometimes do become emotionally involved with someone else; if this happens the person often unconsciously manages to get discovered, and it is at this point that the partner goes to a lawyer or seeks professional marital therapy.

In this paper I have not discussed the treatment methods I have used in working with married couples. These methods include working with the couple as a unit, helping the partners to develop clearer and more honest communication with each other, and coaching the couple in their efforts to deal with the real issues between them. Deeper methods involve bringing in the family of origin of each of these adult spouses, couples group therapy where several couples together learn to develop more realistic expectations of marriage, and finally "divorce therapy" for partners who are truly allergic to each other. In divorce therapy the partners are helped to disengage from their relationship with dignity and with a minimum of destructiveness to themselves, each other, and the children, resulting finally in the freedom to form new relationships.

I do not want to end this paper with the subject of divorce, even though divorce can be looked upon as an opportunity. Because the stakes are so high for the family and society, life's greatest challenge is the ability to make the exceedingly complex adjustment to another person in marriage. In order to be able to accomplish this it is necessary that the partners tolerate in each other the working through of ambivalent feelings about past figures, permit each other's regression at times to infantile strivings which are still operative in the adult, bonds of affection, commitment, efforts to give and get, acceptance of adult responsibility, and the overflow of love to the children.

7

The Friendly Divorce (1978)

The decision to divorce is not made lightly by couples who have strong invest-ments in their marriage. But when a man and woman have thoroughly explored the possibilities of saving their marriage in therapy together, they sometimes discover that they are truly allergic to each other and that a break is inevitable. When both partners accept it, most marital therapists will turn them over to the lawyers; marital therapists have been trained to bring couples back together, not to help them come apart. Yet, at this crucial point, the couple—and their children—have never been more in need of help.

A couple going into a marriage gets all the ceremonial and institutional support that society can offer, but little assistance is offered to those who are ending a marriage. The hidden emotional scars of divorce may be untouched by traditional forms of individual therapy and may last for generations. It is only in the last few years that the literature has begun to recognize a separate form of treatment at this phase, with its own goals and techniques, known as divorce therapy (although certainly many therapists have done much the same thing in the past without calling it that).

The goal of divorce therapy is to help a couple disengage from a marriage with a minimum of destructiveness to themselves and their children, and with the personal freedom to form new relationships. In the emotional climate of the disengagement, it is usually difficult to convince them that this is even possible. One man who came to me was having detectives take secret photos of his wife dating other men. When I tried to stop him, he pulled me up short, remarking,

"Look, there's a half million dollars at stake if I can get the goods on my wife. Now, do you really think I should listen to you?" Another couple's fights were so horrendous that they once started tearing apart my office. I told them, "If you two don't negotiate and come to terms between yourselves, the lawyers are going to end up with all your money, and a judge, on the basis of a few minutes' testimony, will decide for you the future course of your lives." The husband replied, "I would rather the lawyers, instead of her, get all the money." Then the wife said something very interesting: "Dr. Framo, there's something you don't understand about divorce. You are trying to be logical, and divorce is neither a civilized nor a logical matter." I gave them my blessing and said, "Far be it from me to interfere with your fun and games." Divorce therapy can be frustrating for the therapist, partly because it is without immediate rewards. The process can also, at times, elicit irrational responses from the therapist that may reflect his own life at the time.

As a family therapist, I treat divorce as a system problem that involves not only the immediate family but also the extended family and the rest of the couple's social network. The offices of therapists have been filled with men, women, and children who are experiencing the pain of separation and divorce. But their problems have usually been handled piecemeal. Most therapists are not comfortable with the concerted unpleasantness of seeing several distraught family members together. I prefer to see the spouses together, and bring in the children and even the couple's parents and siblings at appropriate stages.

Most of the couples who have come to me were seeking marital therapy at first. About three-fourths of them have improved their marriages in therapy; the rest have been unable to resolve their problems and some have divorced. My observations in this article, however, are based on work with 55 couples who were eventually divorced. I saw 35 couples in private practice who were largely upper-middle class; the rest were middle and lower-middle class and came to be treated at an urban community mental-health center.

A gradual process of emotional estrangement starts long before the actual legal event, and the emotional involvement often continues long after the decree. Before a couple decides on marital therapy—as a last resort before seeing lawyers—they have already been through despair, frustration, loneliness, depression, and anger. They have made frantic efforts to recapture old sexual feelings, had countless talk sessions, made repeated efforts at reconciliation, gotten advice from family and friends, and perhaps tried individual therapy. When they come to me, I begin by telling them that we should have an exploratory period of treatment before any decisions are made about divorce. Only after the spouses better understand themselves and each other—and how they interact—will they have reliable information on which to decide the future of the marriage.

I usually treat them in groups of three couples, not all of whom are divorcing; some are in marital or premarital therapy. In such a situation, the spouses can get intimate views of other marriages as well as their own, along with support, understanding, and constructive confrontation from other group members. The group helps to temper powerful and often intense emotions. A man and woman working as cotherapists with the three couples are much more effective than a single therapist, and my wife, Mary D. Framo, a clinical social worker, and I have worked together for 5 years.

Sometimes one partner in a marriage will request individual sessions in order to deal with material he or she does not want the other to know about. A few have said that after the decision to divorce, they are uncomfortable in sessions with their spouses. I have mixed feelings about seeing them alone. A client who cannot be in the same room with his or her partner has not emotionally divorced that person. Private sessions may be necessary at a late stage of therapy to reinforce the separation, but they often give rise to suspicions, secrets, and even conflicts of loyalty for the therapist.

In the early stages of couples' group therapy, I employ conventional marital therapy techniques. I encourage couples to really listen to each other and to learn to deal with the issues between them; I play tapes of their sessions back to them. When there are sexual problems, and there usually are, I may use some sex-therapy techniques. I attempt to negotiate differences and reach quid pro quo compromises.

One of my most useful techniques is to ask each spouse to meet with us along with his or her parents and siblings. Most people resist the idea. There is a strong tendency for people to repeat the marital patterns of their parents. Although some people do have better marriages than their parents, the best predictor of success is the quality of the parents' relationship. The sessions help to reveal how past family problems are being acted out in the present. In some cases, people have to find out *whom* they are really getting divorced *from*. One woman who had a poor relationship with her mother took out her problems on her husband. Once she dealt with her anger toward her mother, she realized that a divorce was unnecessary.

Marriages that end in divorce do not differ very much from other marriages. Whether or not an unhappy relationship ends depends on many things, among them how the rest of the family looks on divorce and whether there have been any previous divorces (it is difficult to be the first one in a family to divorce).

Most couples, even when they recognize at some level that the marriage is over, go through periods of agonizing indecision, ambivalence, and vacillation. One way of helping them come to a decision is to explore the consequences of the divorce. I ask each mate to think of the future and attempt to imagine what life will be like after the divorce. How will each of the children react? How will the separate partners deal with the loneliness? Do they have fears that they will never find someone else who will love them? How will they handle sex, parents, friends, colleagues, the legal aspects, and so forth? Can each person face responsibility for his or her contribution to the breakup? A critical clinical decision to be made is whether divorce represents a healthy step away from an earlier neurotic choice of mate or an illusory means of solving an internal problem. In the second case, I confront the person and attempt to work it out in therapy with the mate. If that fails, I refer the person to individual therapy.

The crucial step in the dissolution of a marriage occurs when the intention to divorce becomes public. When everybody knows about the breakup, the process somehow changes and begins to accelerate. The husband or wife may try to gain allies, may run to lawyers, get the money out of the joint account, destroy the partner's personal possessions, or force the other out of the house and change the locks. Friends become important since they are needed for support, but they can also complicate, and aggravate, the struggle. Symptoms in the children at this stage are highly predictable.

The worst effects of the break can be mitigated by therapy. First, I try to keep lawyers out of the situation as long as possible, because as soon as they come in, the hostilities escalate—even for those couples who are determined to have a "friendly" divorce. The legal maneuvering goes much more smoothly when preliminary negotiations have been worked out in therapy. I tell my clients that they can be in control of events, rather than vice versa, and I encourage them to negotiate in therapy on such practical matters as child custody, division of property, support, visitation rights, and so on.

When feelings are especially intense, I may suggest a period of structured separation, in which the couple agrees to live apart for a limited period of time, to avoid contacting lawyers, and to continue in therapy together. It is at this stage that sessions with both sets of parents can help disentangle the in-law complications of divorce. (A divorce causes marked repercussions in the couple's relationships with their parents, who are usually chiefly concerned about seeing the grandchildren.) At this point also, videotape playback usually helps the partners develop some control over the explosiveness.

When the intensity of feeling has died down somewhat, I bring the children in for treatment. I urge the parents to tell them about the divorce as soon as they decide on it for certain. Some, however, postpone it until the family sessions, which are very painful for everyone, including, at times, the therapists. Sometimes the children, especially the older ones, encourage their parents to divorce. (One teenager said, "That ridiculous façade you two put up all these years never fooled us kids; you should have left each other long ago.") The great majority of the children I have seen, however, have difficulty accepting the reality of the breakup.

Some parents are so preoccupied with their own problems that they are oblivious to the children's suffering. I impress upon them that while they are divorcing each other, they are not divorcing their children and have responsibilities to them. One man, furious that his wife was leaving him, claimed that he loved his children so much that he would move far away after the divorce because it would pain him too much to see his kids. Needless to say, that was a problem we had to work through in the therapy. Only after a member of his couples' group, himself the child of divorced parents, explained how much the man would hurt his children by running away, did he realize the implications of his threat.

How deep is the impact of divorce on children? While I believe that divorce is the best solution for all concerned in certain unhappy marriages, I also agree with the assessment of child psychiatrist Richard Gardner, who has written, "I believe that divorce per se does not necessarily produce psychopathology in the child. However, I also believe that the child of divorce is more likely to develop such reactions than the child who grows up in an intact, relatively secure home."

One of the saddest and most difficult situations occurs when one partner wants out of the marriage and the other tries to prevent the divorce. One woman, who had someone else she was planning to marry, agreed to come for six therapy sessions if her husband would give her a divorce. He was still in love with her and hoped she would, as a result of therapy, change her mind.

After they began fighting violently at home, I suggested a structured separation. The husband moved to an apartment, but would stand outside his wife's house every evening until he saw her bedroom light go out. One night, he watched her bring her lover home. At the end of the six sessions, the wife left therapy, and he gave her the divorce.

This man and his wife had joined a couples' group after their first two sessions, and the husband continued to meet with the other couples and get support from them in dealing with his personal problems (although ordinarily I do not permit a person to take part in such groups without the spouse). At other sessions with his parents and siblings, he was able to deal with his former attachment to and dependency on his mother. He realized that he had transferred the same unhealthy dependence to his wife during their marriage.

When only one partner wants a divorce, the spouse who wants it may regard the therapy a great success. The aggrieved party, on the other hand, may see the treatment as a failure; some may even refuse to pay. There have been lawsuits against therapists charging them with "ruining" a marriage.

Like the woman in the case described above, some people come to therapy as a token gesture. They already have someone else they want to marry but feel guilty about abandoning the spouse. Therefore, they agree to treatment, so they can say they tried everything to save the marriage. It also eases their conscience if they can leave their spouse in the hands of a therapist. As soon as I become aware of this ploy, however, I refuse to see the mate alone, and suggest that honesty would be kinder in the long run.

A spouse's inability to accept the divorce often leads to frank psychiatric symptoms, illnesses, accidents, or suicide attempts. After the couple separates, demands to see the children may really be excuses to see the spouse. Lawyers are familiar with cases in which the rejected mate pushes for legal action just to be able to glimpse the loved one in the courtroom.

A woman who wants out of her marriage may feel pity for her begging husband, but she also feels contempt and is frightened by his helplessness. Deeper exploration may reveal that humbling the husband represents a neurotic triumph to the woman, who may have been rejected by her father. The man, too, may be reenacting an earlier trauma. It was very difficult to handle my own feelings at one session while listening to a man on his knees for one hour, whining and crying and pleading with his wife not to leave him.

Sometimes the person pushing for the divorce suddenly announces he is not so sure. Maybe, he suggests, they should try again. On the other hand, sometimes the person who had opposed the divorce may decide he wants it after all—or may confess later on that he really wanted it but felt he ought to put up a fight. In situations like these, I explain to the couple that the collusive aspects of their "flipflops" have to be dealt with in therapy, and perhaps neither one really wants the divorce.

Some clients, as a means of dealing with feelings of low self-esteem, may regress and compensate with narcissistic and omnipotent feelings. A 40-year-old woman may be convinced she will have a great love affair, become a model, live life to its fullest; her euphoria knows no bounds. A man may make plans to go to the South Seas, become a great artist, and settle down with some native beauty; he may talk of climbing Mount Everest or becoming the president of his company. When the parents are still alive, they sometimes encourage these grandiose notions. One mother told her son, "I always knew that bitch you were married to stood in the way of your success." Some therapists mistake the client's new expansiveness for a pathological condition, not realizing that people going through divorce are simply not themselves.

Attorneys are usually not familiar with the mourning process in divorce. They are often shocked, for example, to discover that in the midst of the fiercest legal contest, the couple is having sex or fighting over who's going to get the stereo or the cat.

Often the lawyer is forced to serve as a kind of therapist himself. Sometimes, when a couple reunites, they may turn on him suddenly and blame him for their problems. This and other bizarre behavior sometimes bewilders attorneys and may make them withdraw from a case with the attitude of "a plague on both your houses."

Divorce therapy can be stalemated or sabotaged when the therapist is unaware of the secret power plays and paranoid maneuvering going on outside the sessions in the lawyers' offices. One might ask, "Should not the lawyer and therapist get together and cooperate?" Except for a few notable instances, I have not found attempts at lawyer-therapist teamwork too productive, and not because the lawyers were not well intentioned. We were simply operating from different premises. The adversary system of the law runs directly counter to the therapist's goals.

Some lawyers have raised the question of whether the adversary system should be involved at all in a private matter like divorce. Perhaps, some experts suggest, divorce should be treated as an administrative matter that is worked out by an arbiter or magistrate. For now, however, I firmly believe that both therapists and lawyers should have at least some training in each other's specialties.

While most couples who come to me seek marital counseling, a few ask for "divorce therapy" specifically. Most of them want just one or two sessions to deal with a specific problem, such as how to tell the children, or deal with disagreements over a property settlement. Sometimes they want to negotiate a trade-off of some kind without bringing in a lawyer. For instance, one divorced woman who had helped put her husband through law school when they were married thought she was entitled to get financial aid from him to study for a master's degree of her own. I supported her claim, and the ex-husband agreed.

Occasionally, there are women who do not want their husbands to see the children, and I have to persuade them that they are not thinking of the children's best interests. Although therapists claim to be impartial, we are often forced to side with one spouse or the other on specific points. We consider some outcomes better, or healthier, than others.

After the divorce, few couples come for therapy together. When they do, it is usually because of a problem with the children. Unlike some therapists, I do not hesitate to bring divorced parents together for sessions; in fact, I insist that both come in with their children. I am often forced to persuade unwilling mothers or fathers by reminding them that the children's problems are likely to worsen without their cooperation.

Usually the problems with children grow out of unresolved conflicts between the parents. The children may be used as messengers, weapons, or spies by one parent or the other. In post-divorce therapy, it is sometimes necessary to bring the children into discussions of such matters as money, parental visits, relationships with grandparents, dating by the parents, and lingering resentments over custody decisions. Children, after all, have a stake in these decisions. If they are not included, they can sabotage the efforts of therapy.

When divorced couples want therapy to deal with the residual problems between them, they are usually depressed, coping with revived adolescent sexual problems, or perhaps wondering whether the divorce was a mistake. A man finds out that the swinging bachelor pad filled with beautiful blondes never materializes; a woman discovers that attractive men are not fighting each other to get to her door. One wife asked, "How come I miss so terribly someone I couldn't stand?"

Some people frankly admit that they are repeating the behavior patterns of their marriages in their new relationships. I have treated people in second marriages who cannot deal with their problems without having their former mate present. These sessions, which include the previous and present spouses, are not particularly awkward and are surprisingly productive.

Then there are the couples who, although legally divorced for many years, have never separated emotionally. Many of the problems seen by therapists, I am convinced, are the consequences of incomplete emotional divorces. As long as one's ex-mate is considered the enemy, one is not free, because hate is a relationship. The fact of the matter is that marriages and families never end. Knowing this helps husbands and wives understand and deal with the emotional shocks that follow divorce.

Part Four

Application to Intergenerational Processes

The paper with the long title of "Family of Origin as a Therapeutic Resource for Adults in Marital and Family Therapy: You Can and Should Go Home Again," is the first report of the most consequential of my works. My kind of family-of-origin therapy is the clinical application of the conceptual formulations contained in "Symptoms from a Family Transactional Viewpoint" (chapter 2). Whatever other therapies I conduct—family, marital, couples groups, or divorce—is directed toward the final goal of having the adults have sessions with their parents and brothers and sisters so that all can deal with the hard issues among them that must be dealt with. Anxiety about the potential for confrontation with family members—something people may spend a lifetime avoiding—often creates an intense, primitive dread of having these sessions. Those clients who work through the survival issues that are at the basis of that anxiety, and who come to terms with parents before they die, can usually relate better to the people who matter to them.

The foregoing paper on my work with families of origin communicated some of my early experiences with this method of therapy. Since that time I have conducted many more family-of-origin sessions and have fine-tuned the technical problems associated with running them: I have learned more about how to deal with clients' fears of these sessions, how to prepare individuals for them, how to conduct the sessions, and how to maximize their potential; I know more about the side-effects and aftereffects, and I have a more sober appreciation of the impasses encountered as well as of the limitations of the method. Nonetheless, more experience with family-of-origin work has reinforced my conviction of its power and usefulness in most situations. In my judgment, one session with an adult and his or her family of origin, conducted in this special kind of way, can be more productive than an entire course in one of the other therapies. Whenever I give workshops I have been asked, "What data do you have to support your clinical impressions about your family-of-origin work?" Well, I can now report that an independent, data-based investigation is presently underway, consisting of follow-ups of couples who have had family-of-origin sessions over the past 7 years. What has been especially gratifying to me are the letters I have received from family therapists who write that my family-of-origin contribution has not only been useful to them professionally, but that it has helped them reappraise their relationship with their own family, in some cases leading to contact with parents or siblings from whom they had been cut off.

More recent developments in my method of working with family of origin, and how the procedure involved is integrated with marital and couples group therapy, is presented in the chapter entitled "The Integration of Marital Therapy With Sessions With Family of Origin," a chapter written expressly for Al Gurman's and Dave Kniskern's *Handbook of Family Therapy* (1981). In this lengthy work I was required to respond, in detail, to substantive questions about my theory and treatment methods. The editors of this monumental volume requested that the contributors answer a series of standardized questions about their work so that the various approaches could be compared. Accordingly, I was forced to examine my premises and views on such issues as my concept of the healthy marriage or family, my view of dysfunction, my methods of assessment, goal-setting, for whom my methods are applicable, the structure of the therapy process, my role as a therapist, techniques, curative factors, effectiveness of the approach, and training. I did not like being pushed to respond to all these parameters of family therapy, but being obliged to address those issues did help me clarify my thinking, and also made me aware of gaps in my theory.

Peggy Papp, editor of *Family Therapy: Full-Length Case Studies* (Framo, 1978b), gave explicit instructions to her contributors. She requested that we write up the entire course of a family or marital therapy case from beginning to end. We were specifically asked to give a step-by-step personal account of the thinking and feeling process that takes place in the therapist over the course of treatment. I selected one of my cases, a couple who had been in marital therapy, in a couples group, and who had also had sessions with their families of origin. I recounted the cotherapists' and couples' experience over the course of therapy in the paper, "In-laws and Out-laws: A Marital Case of Kinship Confusion." This case description shows how theory is put into practice with real, live people, and also attempts to describe therapy the way in which this actualization really happens—the mistakes, the doubts, the frustrations, the backsliding, and, at those occasional times when therapeutic change takes place, the events that make it all worthwhile.

8

Family of Origin as a Therapeutic Resource for Adults in Marital and Family Therapy: You Can and Should Go Home Again (1976)

Theoretical Introduction

The treatment method described in this paper is fundamental to all therapies I engage in—family, marital, couples' groups, and divorce therapy. The procedure is a practical, clinical application of my theoretical paper "Symptoms From a Family Transactional Viewpoint" (Framo, 1970). This theory of symptoms, based partially on the object-relations concepts of Fairbairn (1954) and Dicks (1967), attempted to explore further the extraordinarily intricate relationship between individual and transpersonal psychology. A simplified recapitulation follows:

1. When parents' behavior is interpreted as rejection, desertion, or persecution, the young child, unable to give up the external object or change it in outer reality, handles the frustration by internalizing aspects of the loved-hated parents in order to control the objects in the inner psychic world. The internal object is repressed and retained as an introject, a psychological representative. These internal objects, according to Fairbairn, undergo various splits and become part of the structure of the personality.
2. During the course of development of the individual, external, real figures are assimilated in successive strata or by fusion into the inner bad-object introjects. Other people, especially intimates, are perceived largely in terms of the individual's own needs, or as carrying for him his own guilt-laden, denied, split-off traits. Life situations in outer reality are not only uncon-

Reprinted with permission from *Family Process*, 1976, *15*, 193–210. Copyright © 1976 Family Process, Inc.

ciously interpreted in the light of the inner-object world, resulting in distorted expectations of other people, but active, unconscious attempts are made to force and change close relations into fitting the internal role models. Mate selections are made with exquisite accuracy, and unconscious deals are made—"I will be your conscience if you will act out my impulses."

3. The foregoing is the basis for numerous human dilemmas, such as people struggling against their identifications with their parents (Greenson, 1954). The interpersonal resolution and projection of inner conflict is the source of the irrational demands and expectations of spouses and children that bring families and couples so much distress and for which treatment is sought. Since people in close relationship collusively carry psychic functions for each other and there is mutual projection and transference of internal objects among family members, we find the basis for dealing with the interlocking system in marital and family therapy.

4. The client, by having sessions with his or her family of origin, takes the problems back to where they began, thereby making available a direct route to etiological factors. Dealing with the real, external parental figures is designed to loosen the grip of the internal representatives of these figures and expose them to reality considerations and their live derivatives. Having gone backward in time, the individual can then move forward in dealing with the spouse and children in more appropriate fashion, since their transference meaning has changed. This view of the relationship between the intrapsychic and transactional spheres constitutes the core of this theoretical orientation.

Involvement With Family of Origin in the Adult Years

How do most people handle relationships with their family of origin after they are grown up and are married? It is curious that while there has been intensive investigation of the areas of infant, child, and adolescent development, there has been very little work done on stages of adult development. Most theorists (Erik Erikson is a notable exception) seem to have the attitude that development stops after age 19.

Relationships with family of origin tend to fall into four categories. One may be over-involved with family of origin—for example, live with the parents or down the street from them, take vacations together, or have to talk every day to a parent on the telephone. Such people have no social life other than with the family. Mates of such persons may welcome or resent the closeness of the spouse with his or her parents, depending on that person's own needs for the in-laws. If, for example, a man lost a father at an early age, the opportunity to get another father through a father-in-law is almost irresistible. On the other hand, a wife may feel that her husband puts his parents before her, and in any competition for money, time, labor, or loyalty, she can only lose. The systematic investigation of in-law relationships is long overdue.

Another pattern, the most commonly found (and probably true of most of the readers of this paper), consists of superficial, nonpersonal contact. Family of origin is seen for duty visits several times a year and at weddings and funerals. People following this course usually consider themselves as having resolved their problems with their family of origin in a mature way.

The next pattern, least frequent but with the most serious consequences, is typified by those who proudly proclaim that they are truly independent because they have cut themselves off completely from their families of origin. Such people never see their mothers, or fathers, or brothers, or sisters, or extended families at all. Some wistfully regret this situation but claim it is necessary, saying the only way they can keep their sanity is to stay away from their crazy families. Others are extremely bitter toward a parent or sibling and may even go so far as to forbid their mates or children to mention the name of the offending relative. For these adults, that family member is dead. These people have the greatest likelihood of repeating with their mates and children, or any intimate relationship, the irrational patterns of the past.

Finally, there is an appropriate pattern of relationship to parents in adulthood, stemming from having established a self within the family of origin before separating from it. These people did not have a desperate need to stay with, or get away from, their parents; there is presently neither overattachment nor angry distancing. They relate less to parents as their children (although no one completely accomplishes this); there is more of an adult-to-adult, personal relationship with parents. Affection and a sense of obligation are still present, but not at the expense of one's present family or one's integrity of self. In Boszormenyi-Nagy's and Spark's terms (1973), there is balance in the ledger of relational justice, the debits and credits in the emotional accounts, and in the loyalties.

Comparison With Bowen's Work With Family of Origin

The relationship problems that adults have with their spouses and children are reconstructions and elaborations of earlier conflict paradigms from the family of origin. It seems almost naive to state this truism, but when one searches the professional literature for those who have a systematic theory for utilizing family of origin as a therapeutic resource, there are few to add to Murray Bowen, the pioneer in this area (1978). This present work with family of origin must be distinguished from regular family therapy in which the therapist works conjointly with parents, grandparents, and index, symptomatic child; in a sense, that more conventional procedure is also work with family of origin. However, the methods and therapeutic goals of both this author and Bowen are distinctively different from the latter since they involve preparing *adults* to deal actively with members of their original families in special kinds of ways.

Bowen is a singular figure in family therapy who has developed quite sophisticated concepts about the universal question of how to deal with irrationality in one's family without giving the family up. In the book *Family Interaction* (1972), there is a courageous account of Bowen's attempts to differentiate himself in his own family.

My method of involving adult clients with their family of origin differs from Bowen's. Murray Bowen, after starting consultations with the adults individually or in marital or family therapy, sends his motivated adult clients home on timed visits to their family of origin and supervises them in their differentiating efforts. A client is coached to gain control over his emotional reactivity to his family and to become a more objective observer of himself and his family. Since these individuals will inevitably run into nearly overwhelming emotional roadblocks from the family, Bowen, often over periods of years, helps them develop strategies for detriangulating themselves and taking "I"-position stands with their parents, siblings, and other relatives. He uses the same method in training family therapists, supervising his trainees to conduct genealogical family voyages and research their families in the quest for self. Whereas Bowen rarely has the adult bring in his or her family of origin for sessions with him, I do just that since I am working toward somewhat different goals and use different methods.

Bowen does not usually encourage the actual presence of the family of origin in sessions with him because this technique would militate against the goal of the client personally taking responsibility for his own differentiating efforts. However, the greater number of people seen in clinical practice can be motivated to take only the most preliminary steps in reconnecting with a family from which they are alienated or in rebalancing their priorities when they are overinvolved with family of origin. Since most family and marital therapy is of the short-term crisis variety, the majority of clients simply do not give themselves the time to follow through on work with family of origin of the sort that Bowen espouses. Bowen recognizes this when he writes: "There is much clinical experience to support the thesis that people are not motivated to work on the past when they are involved in a process that offers a solution in the present generation" (Bowen, 1974; p. 93). Another way of putting it would be: "When the house is burning down you can't pay attention to your influenza." As I understand his views, moreover, only a minority of those who are even well-motivated to make an extended family effort can significantly change their basic level of differentiation. He wrote:

> It is difficult to communicate the notion that the basic degree of differentiation of self is a rather fixed quantity that is usually determined early in childhood by the degree of differentiation of the parents, and by the prevailing emotional climate in the family of origin. The degree of differentiation

determines the life style of the person and thereafter change is difficult. One's own level of differentiation is replicated in marriage following which one's self is emotionally interlocked with parents in the past generation, the spouse in the present generation, and children in the future generation. Any change in this is difficult and accomplished only by change in the others (1974, p. 82).

My own method and goals in involving family of origin are different.

A Treatment Method for Adults and Their Family of Origin

In order to better understand this method, it is incumbent upon me to provide some context by briefly outlining the evolution of my work with families and couples. My rationale and techniques for family therapy were originally presented in *Intensive Family Therapy* (Framo, 1965b). With the passage of time, my work has undergone a number of modifications. Although there are some families that should, in my view, continue with family therapy (including the children) throughout the course of treatment, most of the family therapy I do these days is converted into marital therapy when the originally symptomatic children have been defocused (Framo, 1975b). In addition, there are those couples who enter treatment explicitly for marital problems or who do not have children or do not present their children as the primary focus of concern. Since marital therapy seems to be more effective and briefer in the couples' group format, I try to put couples into a couples' group as soon as possible, usually after the first few diagnostic sessions (Framo, 1973). (Special circumstances, however, require that some couples be seen on the basis of single marital therapy.) Within a given couples' group containing three couples, I may have unmarried couples with ongoing relationships, couples with varying degrees of marital conflict, couples who had originally presented their children as the problem, couples who wish to revitalize an empty relationship, separated couples, and couples in divorce therapy (Framo, 1978a).

During the course of the first diagnostic interview with a family or couple that have come for help, while getting information about their presenting problems, what they are like, and how they relate to each other, I ask each adult to give me a brief sketch of his and her family of origin. Toward the end of the session I discuss with them what treatment opportunities I have to offer, and I mention casually that most people I have seen have found it helpful to bring in their family of origin at some point during the course of treatment, usually toward the end. Most couples are hesitant and reluctant to enter a couples' group, but this apprehension is trivial and easily overcome compared with the reaction to the idea of bringing in the parents and siblings. As a matter of fact, several couples did not return for a second session, stating on the telephone that they would prefer going to a doctor who did not "do that sort of thing." Those couples and families who do return often mention in the second session that the only thing they remember from the first session is their anxiety about the prospect of dealing with their mother, father, brother, or sister.

It is difficult to communicate in words the almost instinctive, aversive response of people to this idea.[1] Over the years, I believe I have heard about every reason for not bringing in one's family; the reactions have become quite predictable. When the idea is initially presented, it is reacted to with shock by most people: "Wow, that's heavy," or "You have to be kidding!" or "That's out of the question because they live too far away," or "My parents are too old and I don't want to upset them," or "Look, you don't know how impossible my mother (or father) is." (It is interesting that everyone thinks his or her own parents are uniquely impossible.) Another consideration that is expressed is that their parents would have to know they were in therapy and they do not want them to know that their child or their marriage is in trouble. There are a few adults who have seized the idea and welcomed it as an opportunity; this happens so rarely that I am unable yet to draw any conclusions as to what it means. Initial eagerness to bring in one's family of origin makes me suspicious and does not seem to be related to outcome.

I do not bring up again, for a while, the matter of involvement of family of origin, as the spouses, usually in a group, deal with current issues between them. These issues, which range over the spectrum of conflicts and miseries that can occur between husband and wife, are dealt with by conventional marital therapy and couples' group techniques—developing clearer communication, feedback techniques to encourage listening in the interaction, fight training (teaching the couple how to deal with issues between them), quid pro quo negotiations, confrontations by therapists or group members, utilizing the group process, structured separation, work on differentiation, audiotape playback, and so forth. The therapy usually gets to the point where the issues between the partners have been fully explored, where they are stuck with their "irreconcilable differences" as to what each wants out of the partner, and their differing conceptions as to what marriage should be. The couples are in what has been called "the dirty middle" of therapy where someone has to change. The issues have been drawn, and they are unable to conciliate fundamental expectations.

Some marital expectations seriously conflict with reality considerations as the mates use each other as screens on which to project unacceptable aspects of the self. However, during the course of treatment even insatiable, "bottomless pit"

---

[1]People in treatment are not the only ones who find the idea anxiety-arousing. When I talk informally with therapists, including family therapists, about this work, I am met with the same kind of reactions: "You mean you *actually* bring the parents in? There's no way I'd bring mine in. Isn't there danger in doing this?" These statements remind me of the responses made by individual therapists when the idea of bringing in the family of children was first mentioned in those early years of family therapy.

people, who demand that their spouses relieve all their anxieties, fill all their needs, and make them happy, develop a growing awareness of the irrationality of their demands. Some of these clients go through a phase of depression as their perception of the source of all their discontent shifts from outside of themselves to inside. Furthermore, since people are really in love with, or hate, the fantasized image or concept of the partner, as they become more aware of what the real partner is like, there often occurs a period of healthy confusion and questioning of their perceptions and beliefs. For instance, a wife may say, "I realize now that I can't look to my husband to take care of all my wants and fears, but why do I still feel so needy and unfulfilled? Where does that come from?"

This whole area of distorted perceptions and expectations, of being unable to commit oneself to the present relationship because of obsolete injuries, provides the context for me to bring up the relationship of these problems to the family of origin. Past relationships with parents and siblings had been referred to during this period of time, but the individuals had been talking *about* those relationships, which is safer. At this time I get more detailed family-of-origin histories and try to discover, among other things, the bilateral, hidden agendas of the marriage contract—such as what, from the previous family, were they trying to work out in their choice of this particular person as a mate? After an individual relates his or her family history, I ask both spouses for reactions to their mate's account; the spouse often provides a more accurate picture of the partner's relationship with his or her family. For instance, a wife once said, "I'm astonished. My husband is telling you what a normal, average family he came from, and for years he's told me how all the kids in his family lived in fear that his parents would murder each other."

It is at this stage that I reintroduce the idea of each person bringing in his or her parents and siblings for a family conference. The resistances assume a different form at this time, because now the possibility is real. Most often there is an expressed fear that parents might either die of a heart attack or go crazy if they were to be brought in. Such comments are even made by people who had been expressing much hostility toward their parents, which confirms my notion that one of the deepest motives of people is to rescue or save parents. Some people reject the idea even more vigorously with the words, "Let's get one thing straight; *that* is never going to happen." Sometimes people are willing to bring in parents but refuse to ask a brother or sister. I have been surprised to discover that some adults are much more frightened of confronting siblings than parents. These fears occasionally develop into panic proportions; several people have had to go to family physicians for tranquilizers, and others developed somatic disorders. One fellow said, "Ask me to climb Mount Everest, ask me to swim across the Atlantic Ocean, but please don't ask me to bring in my mother!"

Earlier, such objections were accepted at face value. Not knowing how to deal with the resistances, only about 10% of my clients would actually bring their families in. Now, because I really believe in this method and have seen its benefits, I am able to get about 60% to follow through. Because of my own convictions about what the process can do, I stick to the idea tenaciously, bringing it up at every opportunity as a goal that will contribute to growth more than any other thing they can do. Every time clients get frustrated with their progress in therapy or about their life and don't know how to proceed, I set up the session as a benchmark. I have used persuasion, sarcasm, and even taunting: "If you don't want to move beyond where you are, that's OK with me." Although I tell them they should do it for themselves and not for me, in all honesty, when clients are deeply engaged in treatment, my words and attitude do have an effect.[2] When people say their parents or siblings would refuse to come in, I tell them that when they themselves really want them in, they will find a way. Most people are very surprised when their family readily agrees to come in. Those who are not yet committed to the undertaking sabotage the prospective session by presenting the idea to their family members in such a way as to elicit a refusal. For example, one woman said to her father, "The doctor wants to see you to talk about your drinking and its effect on our family." Later, when she was ready, she was able to get her father in with the words, "Dad, I want you to come in because I need you and because there are some things we have to deal with about our relationship."

My heavy artillery consists of having them imagine that their mother or father has just died and they are standing by the grave. What would they regret never having said to the dead parent? I tell them, "But they are still alive; now you have the chance."[3] The group process in the couples' group helps, inasmuch as a kind of contest often develops as to who will be the first one to bring in his or her family. Besides, the group members usually urge the others to do it, even if they rule it out for themselves. Later, when some individuals have had their sessions with their family of origin and report back to the group what it did for them, others are influenced to find the courage to do it.

Gradually, most people come to see the value of meeting with their family of origin; some of those who were most resistant earlier eagerly pursue the matter, making arrangements for their parents and siblings to visit them in Philadelphia. At this point they are doing it for themselves, and I have the client take the responsibility for bringing the family in. Logistical, travel arrangements, and work and school schedules usually do not present that much of a problem; when people are motivated, they write and phone and gather together their parents and siblings, even from long distances. Also, families usually get together for special

[2]More technically, a split transference may be operating here. That is to say, the positive transference to the therapist may enable the clients to deal with the negative transference to the parents.

[3]Some adults become motivated to do something about or with their family of origin even though their parents are dead, and in these cases I suggest they bring in siblings, aunts, uncles, or any close friend of their parents. These relatives and friends can help give the parents back to them. Virginia Satir uses a technique she calls Family Reconstruction in which members of a group role-play an individual's family members; people who have participated in this simulated procedure describe it as a profoundly integrative experience.

occasions, which is the reason I work a lot during holidays. It should be mentioned that when I first started doing this work I did not think the timing of the sessions mattered; with experience I have found that sessions held in the early part of treatment tend to be more superficial and social. They are more productive toward the end of treatment, when the individuals have already undergone some changes and are ready to deal in a meaningful way with their families.

I have found it necessary to spend time structuring the purposes of such a session. Since the focus is on a given adult's past and present relationship with parents and siblings, I do not have the mate present in the session. The mate's presence would be an invitation for parents or siblings to talk about the couple's marital or parenting difficulties, a method of triangling which would divert from the main purpose.[4] The purpose is not, I tell them, to bring their parents in for me to see how sick they are and straighten them out; the purpose is not for me to tell them off, or have the client, necessarily, tell them off; the goal is not for me to be the advocate or explain the client to the family or act as spokesman for him or her. *I put the burden of responsibility on the individuals to think about and take up with their family the issues about the family relationships that have concerned them throughout the years.* Some clients state that there is nothing to talk about with their family, or there is too much. When individuals respond that they have no issues with their family, I ask them to go over their history again and, of course, during the recounting, hundreds of issues come up.

As the session approaches, the anxiety can build up and spread from the client to the rest of the family. This is manifested by a great increase in phone calls and letter writing to each other, and even surreptitious phone calls to me from family members about who should, or should not, attend or what should, or should not, be discussed in the session.

In the family-of-origin conferences the interest is centered on what went on during the life cycle of that family; what were the key events, traumas, happy memories, tragedies, atmosphere; how were the roles distributed, what were the alliances? In these sessions important diagnostic information is obtained on how past family problems are being lived through in the present. More to the point, however, opportunities are available for genuine corrective experiences, the discovery of information about the family not heretofore known, the clarifying of old misunderstandings and misinterpretations based on childhood perceptions, and the clearing away of the magical meanings that the family members have for each other. This kind of experience also gives people the chance to get to know their parents as real people rather than as fantasy figures who have to be idealized or denigrated. Further, the way is opened up for the possibility of establishing an adult-to-adult relationship with one's parents.

---

[4]It is recognized that other family therapists work differently, such as including the mate in the family-of-origin session. Under special circumstances I have done this also, but in general I find the sessions more free and productive without the mate being present.

Description of Family-of-Origin Conferences

When the foregoing kind of preparation has been done, and when the clients are ready, we have our sessions. How do they tend to go? The sequence to follow is fairly typical, but it must be kept in mind that each of these family meetings is unique and does not follow a fixed pattern.

First of all, these meetings are more difficult, in a way, for the family coming in than for the client with whom you have been working. The parents don't know what to expect, except that in some way they anticipate being blamed for the troubles of their offspring. Brothers and sisters may be resentful at having to come in, and besides, they often have the same apprehension as the clients about the sessions possibly hurting their parents. Furthermore, many parents had been described by the clients in such extreme terms (as overpowering, as psychotic, as defenseless, feeble, and at death's door, as a mystery, and as monsters) that we never know who will be walking through the office door. Although a few parents turned out to be as described, the great majority were much more interested in, and concerned about, the client than we had been led to believe. To be sure, the visiting family members initially exhibit polite "office behavior," but as the session progresses, more characteristic family interactions are revealed. Nonetheless, we have learned that the incoming family needs considerable support. I would agree with Boszormenyi-Nagy and Spark (1973; p. 374) that "It is never advisable to encourage devaluation of the *parent's position* within the family. Furthermore, it is axiomatic that no one wins where the outcome leads to shame or hate of the parents." (Italics in the original.)

When the family is all together, I usually start off the session with several sentences that go something like this:

> "As you know, we've been seeing So-and-So for a while, and I find that it's helpful to bring in the family of the people we work with. You all spent many years together before So-and-So got married, and you had many life experiences together. Unfortunately, many families don't get together to talk about really important and meaningful things. Although it can be painful or embarrassing, in the long run most family members find this experience beneficial. Our purpose here is to help all of you to get to know each other better and deal with some of the issues you've all had with each other. And remember, all families have problems."

Since most families are fearful in this new situation, we try to establish some rapport with the visiting family, making small talk about their trip, asking them how they felt about coming in, and asking each parent and sibling about their work or school or other life circumstances. Following this brief interchange, the session is usually turned over to the client. Despite their preparation, some clients freeze at this point, and their minds may go blank. We may assist the client in getting started. The clients then state some issues with their family, usually mild ones in the beginning and usually starting with the family member who is easiest to deal with, often the father. After the client has raised a few issues, the family members respond, and they are off. Usually there is so much that has been pent up and there is so much overtalking, that we become kind of traffic managers—clarifying feelings, redirecting questions, asking others to listen when someone says something meaningful, or when a dyad interchanges. These sessions are usually quite active, and, of course, intense feelings are aroused as the old family ways and conflicts are revealed. There is often shock on hearing an expressed feeling for the first time ("I had no idea you felt that way"; or "I can't *believe* what you are saying now.") Sometimes we have to soothe hurt feelings as a mother cries or a father sulks. The client sometimes needs to face the occasional counterattack: "You were a pretty rotten kid yourself sometimes." Or the client is made to face his or her contributions to the misunderstandings or emotional injuries; parents can feel rejected by their children too. Some clients have been displeased that we did not give them unconditional support but later say they are glad we did not. Sometimes a parent will say to the client, "If you felt that way I didn't know it; why didn't you tell me then?" Why not, indeed? It reminds me of the scene in the play *I Never Sang for My Father* when the angry adult son asks his father, "Did you really think your door was always open to me?" and the father replies, "It was not my fault if you never came in." The family transactions often spontaneously move the parents to talk about their own family backgrounds in order to explain their behavior in this family. Occasionally, their adult children hear facts and secrets about their parents' families for the first time.

The family-of-origin sessions vary considerably in focus, style, pace, content, and issues. Some sessions are largely run by the client, whereas in others the therapists are more active. Some families spend considerable time on their distant past as a family, while others need to deal with current issues. At times the parents recede in importance as the sibling relationships become salient. The therapists must adapt to the particular rhythm and dynamic circumstances of a given family.

So much happens so fast in these sessions, it is advisable to have a cotherapist, particularly a heterosexual team. My wife and I have been working together for the past few years. Being a woman and a parent gives her a special position that helps ease the gap between sexes and generations. Frequently, the parents turn to Mary for understanding and she can resonate with their feelings that it's damn tough raising children. Often the incoming families have expressed their relief and pleasure that a man and woman were seeing them. There is something about this arrangement that makes the session not seem like psychiatry or "mental illness," about which most people are fearful and distrustful.

Almost all families go through a phase of hostility and mutual recrimination during which there are usually corrections of distorted childhood fantasies or an emotional redefinition of memories. For example, a client will say to parents: "I always thought that the bad times you two had in your marriage had to do with me.

It's such a relief to find out they had nothing to do with me." Toward the end of the session we start a healing, reentry process by pointing out the essential caring behind the anger (it's always there) and by stating our belief that the family members should keep relating to each other but perhaps in a different way than they had done before. Parents, who had originally thought that our strategy was to create a total break between them and their children, are always relieved to discover that they're not going to lose them after all. A process of negotiation usually begins then around the frequency of contacts and the new rules for the nature of the relationship they will have with each other in the future. Those who have been alienated from each other often make their peace, and it's not unusual for these adults and parents to cry and hug each other. When we suggest that all the family members contribute toward the fee, most are glad to do so.

The majority of these sessions, lasting for several hours, are usually one-shot deals, largely because of geography. We consider, and tell them before they leave, that obviously many problems remain unresolved but that a process has been started in the office that they should continue on their own. These sessions certainly do jar and loosen a family system, and sometimes several sessions are needed to deal with the aftershocks. The sessions are always audiotaped, and we lend the tape to the client to make cassette copies to send to the family as well as to members who could not come to the session; repeated listening to this tape often helps them develop a more objective view of the family relationships since they are not as caught up in the emotional system as they were during the session itself. Also, we suggest that the mate of the client listen to the session as well, since he or she has a stake in the matter. It is important that the mate not feel left out. We have been impressed with the high degree of cooperation of mates during this procedure; they had all along suspected that their spouses had been projecting stuff onto them that did not belong to them.

Some Preliminary Results

This procedure can only be evaluated clinically and impressionistically at this stage of its development; systematic research is badly needed.

One of the reasons family members have such great difficulty honestly stating their wishes, hurts, and concerns to each other is that, between intimates, expectations are high and feelings are potentially explosive. Once they are in a safe atmosphere that places a premium on openness, feelings are revealed that previously lay dormant or were disguised or were expressed through symptoms. They may say things to each other in the session that were said many times before, but in this setting, for the first time, they are heard.

There have been some individuals who struggled with bringing in their families who, for one reason or another, were unwilling or unable to do so. However, most of these clients did start talking to siblings or parents about heretofore avoided topics, and this effort had spreading effects throughout the network as the messages got transmitted from one member to the other. These communications often led to families having their own conferences, or dyads having their own meaningful confrontations. Occasionally, important things happened without the family having come in. I still prefer to have them in the office, however. When outside, objective observers are present with a family—those who have no real stake in the outcome and those who can more easily view the parents as real people, without the bonds and historical filters—their presence has a calming effect on the built-in anxiety in the situation. For instance, clients often report an interesting phenomenon following the sessions. They say that some nameless dread or anxiety that had always been present in their family seems to have been removed by the session. As one client put it: "Nobody died." I have yet to find out exactly what this nameless anxiety means.

The clients' working through their internal struggle about bringing their family in, as well as dealing with the external realities of family members reluctant to come in, constitutes a process that can be more significant than the events of the session itself. Sometimes, as a result of my having introduced the idea of working things out with family of origin, there has been so much preliminary work on the relationships that the session itself is anticlimactic.

I have come up with the following rough categories, which will have to be refined with further experience, of the effects of these sessions:

1. Sometimes the effect on the original problems in the family or couple or individuals is direct and obviously helpful. One woman who was married on a grossly distorted basis to a much older man whom she'd been supporting for years was not able to leave him until she had a session with her mother. Some clients reflect that following the session their mate or children are being "seen" for the first time. Others, who were hell-bent on getting a divorce, find out in the family-of-origin sessions who they are really getting divorced *from*—making the divorce unnecessary. Others are grateful that they got their alienated parents back, or the overly involved ones are not as attached to their parents and feel more committed to their present family.

Some clients report they discovered in the session that their lifelong beliefs about a family member turned out to be a myth. For instance, one man always had felt that his brother was so much better off than he—successful, having no hangups, and so on—and he learned in the session that his brother had many problems he had never talked about. This disclosure made this man feel much better about himself. Another example is the split ambivalence by which one parent had been seen as perfect and the other as malevolent; this illusion usually gives way, following these sessions, to the reality that both parents have human imperfections and worthwhile traits. Usually a more sympathetic view of both parents is developed when the clients understand what their mother and father had gone through with their own parents. Some people report improvement in their marriage or their work performance following the session, and others say their relationship with their children improved.

There have been some clients who have an initial negative response to the session and report later that with the passage of time the benefits were realized. For example, one woman, an only child, who felt smothered by her parents, told them that she actually envied a man in the couples' group whose parents were in a mental hospital and had neglected him. She said to her parents during the session, "Please, please don't love me so much." The parents, deeply hurt, refused to see her for several months afterward, but then, when they reestablished contact, they did so at a higher level, giving their daughter the emotional freedom to marry a non-Jewish man. Another woman client, whose role in her family of origin had always been that of the strong one on whom others in the family leaned, told them in her session of her vulnerabilities and asked for help for herself. Ryckoff, Day, and Wynne (1959) have documented how shifts in roles that served the family system can create much anxiety in the family. In this case, following their initial disorientation, the family members were able to give her support, which in turn enabled her to stop treating her husband like a helpless child.

2. A few individuals felt an initial high right after the session and then a letdown. One man said, "I guess I expected too much; I thought it would cure me." There are those who reported more turmoil with their family of origin following the session; they told of mothers who now hated the therapists because they (the grandparents) did not get to see their children or grandchildren so often. One parent threatened suicide if things didn't go back to the way they used to be. Follow-up sessions have often helped these older parents, who had been living through their children, to find some gratification in their own marriage and in other life satisfactions, especially when the clients stuck to their autonomous positions. A few of these parents have been referred to therapists in their home towns, and some have gone into marital or individual or peer-group therapy.

I have not yet seen long-term negative effects, but one cannot be certain about this. For instance, one woman said that following the session between her husband and his family, when the father found out the couple were getting a divorce, he began to drink more. She felt that parents should not be burdened with the pain in their children's lives. Although she felt the session accomplished some things, she wondered if it had been worthwhile.

3. There is a final category in which there does not seem to be any apparent effect on the client or the problems with which the couple or family are struggling. In some instances it is not the client but a parent or brother or sister who get the most out of the session. We are dealing with such extraordinarily complex matters here that it is difficult to tease out the truly relevant variables. I can say, however, that in the long run I have not yet had a client who regretted having the session; there always exists some sense of accomplishment at having overcome a vital, heretofore impenetrable, barrier and having at least tried to work out something

with parents before they died. I do find, further, that following the family-of-origin sessions the family relationships in the original family can never again be the same.

Case example 1. This example illustrates a number of points about family work. When this couple came for their first session, I assumed that the husband was the identified patient because he looked very depressed. But I learned the following story. Mrs. A., age 40, had been in individual therapy for 8 years, at the end of which time she was hospitalized for a disabling depression. When she was in the hospital, she was placed in group therapy where she kept saying, "My problems have nothing to do with my husband; they're all in me." Another woman in the group told her, "That's what I used to think, but you'll learn better." Then a social worker in the hospital began working with her and her husband in conjoint marital therapy. As Mrs. A. became less depressed, her husband became more depressed—a not uncommon sequence with fused couples. When she got out of the hospital, she went back to her individual therapist and told him of her helpful experience with marital therapy; he told her she had an obsessional neurosis and needed many more years of individual therapy. Then the husband went to see her therapist and told him how depressed he was, and the therapist told him that he would be fine as soon as his wife was cured of her obsessional neurosis.

As we began working with this couple in a couples' group, they insisted on presenting themselves as patients, and we refused to respond to them as patients. We soon learned that one basis for the husband's depression was that his wife was so preoccupied with her relationship with her mother that she couldn't relate to him or the children. We began working, then, on getting Mrs. A. to bring in her mother and brother. She was one of those people who went into a panic at the prospect. She cried every time the subject came up, went through alternating depression and anxiety states, saying that everywhere she looked she saw her mother. She indicated that discussing her mother for 8 years in therapy had not diminished this uncanny experience. As far as she was concerned, her mother was 25 feet tall and had the power to reduce her to nothing.

It took a whole year for Mrs. A. to get her mother and brother in; the father was dead. We tried many strategies, including role-playing rehearsals, the encouragement of the group, her husband bringing in his family first. Finally, Mrs. A. worked through her brother to get the mother in. The session itself did not seem that remarkable but for the fact that, symbolically, the session was held at all. We had known that another brother had committed suicide, but the mother had always said it was an accident, claiming that he had fallen out of the window. During the session, Mrs. A. and her brother forced their mother to face the fact that the son had killed himself. The whole family mourned his death together for the first time. Mrs. A. also dealt directly with her mother about the effect her mother had on her.

Mrs. A. reported in the next couples' group session that she had had a striking perceptual experience during the family-of-origin session; that, as the session had progressed, her mother kept getting smaller and smaller in size. She said, "You know, she's just a little, old, unhappy woman; what in hell have I been afraid of all these years?" In later sessions she said that she no longer saw the haze of her mother between her and everything she looked at. Her husband and children appeared very different to her, as persons in their own right. These changes lasted, and when the couple left therapy neither one was symptomatic, and they were enjoying sex for the first time in years. One could compare these results, after only one session with the real mother, with several hundred sessions talking *about* her mother in individual therapy.

Case example 2.   A couple was referred by the wife's mother, who said on the telephone that her daughter was having marital problems and asked if I would see her daughter, Mrs. E. I told her to have her daughter call me and that, further, I only worked with husband and wife together. She said she was sure her daughter's husband would not come in. When Mrs. E. called, I told her to bring her husband in. When the couple came, I told Mr. E. his mother-in-law's prediction; he said, "That fits. The truth is, I've been dying to come in." The couple—bright, likable, and nondefensive—indicated that their chief problem was sexual, that they had not had relations for 6 months, and only sporadically before that. Mr. E. was 36, Mrs. E. 32; they had two children, ages 2 and 4. Mr. E. had been a successful commercial artist but said he had been fired from four jobs because of the spillover of his anger and frustration about his marriage onto his work, and he was presently unemployed. Mr. E. described their marriage as the "bitch-nice guy" syndrome, and Mrs. E. described it as a "mother-irresponsible son" marriage. She felt he approached her nonromantically for sex, and he felt that no matter how he tried to approach her she pushed him away. He said at one point, "My wife is like Lucy in the cartoon who promises she'll hold the football and always pulls it away; and I'm like Charlie Brown who keeps trusting and gets disappointed each time." The couple were caught up in a pattern of mutual rejection and longing for each other, and, despite their conflicts, there appeared to be a basic caring for each other, although Mr. E. felt he loved her more than she loved him.

Later in therapy Mr. E. revealed that he often felt like a sex object with his wife because she had many sex manuals, and, following relations, she would critique his performance and, further, would suggest they try different sex exercises described in the books. Mrs. E. had a large collection of sex manuals piled beside the bed; they had been sent regularly to her for years by her mother. My comment that her mother seemed to be in bed with them caught hold, and I suggested they get rid of the sex books. Mr. E. had been very critical of his mother-in-law's interference in their marriage, which I indicated was not in his best interest, because when he criticized her mother, his wife, of course, had to defend her and did not thus have to face her own anger toward her mother. Mr. E. described his wife as "The Manchurian Candidate" who had been programmed by her mother to hate men.

Although Mrs. E.'s parents had been divorced 20 years previously, she was willing, after some resistance, to bring them both in for a session. During the family-of-origin session she worked on her distant relationship with her father, whom she felt she hardly knew. For the first time, also, she confronted her mother with her feeling that she had been used by her as a peer confidante (the mother, during the divorce, had told her of father's problem with premature ejaculation), and that she had been expected, as the only child, to take care of mother through the years. At her request, the parents finally told her of the reasons they divorced. It was interesting to observe that, despite the divorce of 20 years ago, the conflicts between the parents were still alive, neither one had remarried, and they had maintained frequent contact with each other. Mrs. E.'s knowledge of her father had come only through mother's bitter denunciations of him, and in this session Mrs. E. was able to begin forming her own relationship with him, independent of her mother's critical evaluation of him. Fortunately, father was receptive to his daughter's efforts. At one point she requested that her father show more love to her children, and she suddenly realized she was saying, "Love me." Father and daughter made plans to continue these personal talks. Mrs. E. told her mother she needed to have more distance from her, and she asked her not to send her any more sex books. Her mother was hurt by this request, and following the session she sent her daughter an astrological chart that warned her to "beware of people who break family ties." After a period of hurt withdrawal, however, Mrs. E. and her mother were able to establish a new relationship, one founded more on a mother-daughter basis.

Subsequent to the family-of-origin session, Mrs. E. went through a period of confusion as to whether she wanted to stay married to her husband; she said she did not see stars or hear violins when they made love. The situation did not change until Mr. E. took a stand that he was leaving her. After a few more sessions in the couples' group, Mrs. E. announced she suddenly realized how much she loved her husband, that somehow the impact of dealing with her parents and coming to terms with their divorce made her appreciate her husband more. She did not want to lose him. Interestingly, the couple indicated they could not make a commitment to each other until they were committed to themselves. Although Mr. E. had not brought his family of origin in (the parents were dead, and he, too, had been an only child), he did work through many of his own problems. Following the improvement in marriage, Mr. E. started having successes in his new job.

Theoretical Discussion

In addition to the baffling question of the complex interchange between internal and external objects, another level of theory is hereby proposed. In the "Symptom" paper referred to earlier (Framo, 1970), I stated:

This writer postulates the theory that the universal human conflict between autonomy and reality on the one hand and the need to be accepted by intimate others on the other hand would have to be included in any comprehensive explanation of the development of psychopathology. The power of life-sustaining family relationship ties is much greater than instinctual or autonomous strivings. Whereas life preservation for animals depends on instinctive regulation in unfolding sequence, the human being must depend much longer on parental care, and the feelings surrounding the early symbiosis persist as an inspiration throughout the life span. For the sake of approval by the parents and because abandonment has such disastrous consequences, the child will sacrifice whatever ego integrity is called for in order to survive. If the price for acceptance is to absorb unrealities, accept an irrational identity or role assignment, be persecuted, be overindulged, be scapegoated, be parentified, or what have you, this price will have to be paid; to be alone or pushed out of the family either physically or psychologically is too unthinkable. . . . Adults, too, require specific reciprocal identities in their intimate others in order to maintain their own identities. (p. 163)

Children, and adults as well, will forego their own nature in order to save a parent from going crazy or in order to become the kind of person a parent (or parent representative) can love. No one ever really gives up the yearning for the love and acceptance of parents; this motive underlies the search for all other loves and is probably the basis of the ecstasy promised by romantic love and the devastation following rejection. One does not count the costs of the kinds of sacrifices family members will make for each other, for they are measureless. However, the drive for autonomy cannot be denied. How much does one owe oneself, and how much does one owe others?

A number of theoreticians have dealt with this fundamental dimension of human existence—the need for independence, on the one hand, and the need to belong to a larger whole, on the other. Bowen's concept of fusion versus differentiation is pertinent (1978), as is the work of Angyaz (1973) who postulates the two basic motives as self-assertion or autonomy versus affiliation or homonomy. Bowlby (1969) posits attachment versus separation, and Horney and others deal with a similar dual organization as the basic quandary of man. One outcome of this universal dilemma is a human conflict that all have to some extent: longing for merger with those one loves so they are part of each other (reflected in almost every popular song or love poem ever written)—but then feeling possessed, tied, trapped, and losing one's personality (which is at the basis of fear of commitment to an intimate relationship); having to break away for independence, resulting in feeling lost, lonely, isolated, futile, or depressed; then moving toward merger again, and so on.

The price paid for the robbing of self during the growing years exacts a toll and leaves a legacy, giving rise to the ambivalence that all people feel about their close relationships. Since old scores have to be settled and reservoirs of hatred cannot be contained, someone has to pay. Those someones are usually the current inti-mates—the mate and the children; the demons of today are punished by the internal ghosts of yesteryear. The belief that one was loved by parents must be clung to, even as an illusion, else one is a nothing. The old loyalties to parents must be retained, and parents must be absolved, even at other people's expense. As Boszormenyi-Nagy and Spark (1973) put it:

It is probable that one's comparative lack of guilt about the unjustness of such projective exploitation of others is due to an internal sense of relief from guilt over disloyalty to the projector's parent. As he attributes the 'badness' again and again to current partners in his relationships, the person in effect tempor-arily exonerates his parents from the responsibility of having caused his long-pent-up resentment over injustice. (p. 372)

The linch-pin of the treatment approach discussed in this paper is the achieve-ment of balance between the old and the new family systems, the inner and the outer worlds. Coming to terms with one's inner furies and devotions, originally compounded and shaped in the relationship with the parents of childhood, and completing the mourning over losses, can free one from invisible shackles and help one to enjoy personal liberation, as well as the fulfillments of deep rela-tionship. This process can sometimes be accomplished by intensive individual analysis or psychotherapy, but my belief[5] is that if adults can get the courage to face and deal with their parents—who are simultaneously both the symbolic and the real parents—they have a greater chance of achieving their goals. Under either therapeutic approach, it is a frightening enterprise indeed. Fairbairn (1954), speaking of psychoanalytic treatment, gave a partial explanation of this fear when he said:

. . . the deepest source of resistance is fear of release of bad objects from the unconscious; for when such bad objects are released, the world around the patient becomes peopled with devils which are too terrifying for him to face. It is largely owing to this fact that the patient undergoing analysis is so sensitive, and that his reactions are so extreme. (p. 69)

Although Fairbairn's observation refers to intrapsychic processes, his description appears relevant to the great anxiety that people have about confronting their

---

[5]A personal note. Usually when a theoretician or clinician has a heavy investment in a particular point of view, there is a personal element in the interest. As might be guessed, my strong belief in the value of this work came from certain events in my own family of origin. I wrote a paper once, my favorite paper, in which I tried to show that a critical but unnoticed ingredient in all family and marital therapies is the presence of the ghosts of the therapist's own family (Framo, 1968).

parents and siblings. One aspect of this anxiety is that when adults relate to their parents of today they are, in part, still viewing the parents as they did when they were children, when they were small and more vulnerable and when their feelings were experienced in gross categories. When it comes to dealing with parents, the residuals of those early affects of love, hate, shame, and awe almost never disappear.

Despite the anxiety that most people have about raking up old coals, there is, nonetheless, a universal human need, pushed to some extent by nostalgic memories, to reconnect with one's estranged family. This phenomenon can happen with teenagers who, having felt exploited and having run away from home with the thought, "I can't save them, so I must save myself," later reconsider whether total alienation works for them. Sometimes this process occurs at the opposite end of the life spectrum, in old people who want to reach out to siblings or their children before they die. The current interest that adults who were adopted or raised in foster homes have in finding their biological parents testifies to the longing in people to find lost pieces of themselves in roots of the past. Colon (1973), for example, gives a poignant account of his search for his mother. As is widely known, for several generations in this culture, people have become less and less involved with their extended families; perhaps a part of the appeal of family-of-origin work rests on dissatisfaction with this trend. Americans have paid a heavy price for their ethos of individualism.

The politics of family life require that family members live with each other for many years and never tell each other how they really feel; through a lifetime they do not meet or touch. One of the things we try to accomplish in family therapy and in family-of-origin sessions is to help the members to really see each other, to tell each other frankly their warm, positive feelings as well as angry ones, and to allow happiness to become something to be experienced, rather than something to be remembered. In short, you can, and, indeed, should go home again.

9

The Integration of Marital Therapy With Sessions With Family of Origin (1980)

Anyone who treats families and couples knows of the deep satisfactions and measureless sacrifices of family life, and also of the hurts and emotional injuries that closely related people can inflict on one another. In most families children are treasured and cared for, yet in some families children are neglected, overindulged, discriminated against, exploited, seduced, persecuted, and occasionally killed. Some marriages are growthful and enrich peoples' lives, yet husbands and wives are also capable of creating a whole range of miseries for each other, ranging from loneliness in marriage, bitter frustration, cruelty, degrading conflicts, to spouse murder or waiting for each other to die. Whitaker has said, ". . . marriages end up driving some people mad, pushing others into homicidal and suicidal acts, producing hateful demons out of perfectly nice people, and inducing alcoholism in others" (Whitaker and Keith, 1977; p. 69). Professional therapists have developed many theories and techniques for understanding and treating such problems, most of which are quite resistant to change. When one considers the billions of pieces of input that have gone into individuals over many years, and the fact that therapy effects can occur only during a relatively fleeting moment of time, inducing change is a formidable task indeed. I believe it is very difficult to alter attitudes and behavior in individuals, much less change systems. Of all the forces that impinge on people (culture, society, work, neighborhood, friends, and others) the family by far has the greatest imprinting influence. And as every family therapist knows, a family or marital system is a well-oiled machine that often musters all its resources to neutralize and impede change while yearning for something better.

Reprinted with permission from A. S. Gurman and D. P. Kniskern (Eds.) *Handbook of Family Therapy*. New York: Brunner/Mazel, 1980. Copyright © 1980 Brunner/Mazel, Inc.

I started seeing families and couples in 1958, and since the publication of *Intensive Family Therapy* (Boszormenyi-Nagy and Framo, 1965), my work has undergone various changes as I refined and modified my conceptual thinking and techniques in order to get the most favorable results. The treatment methods to be described therein represent the culmination and direction toward which those 21 years of experience have led me. I have streamlined my approach from the early days of long-term family therapy to a more efficient short-term treatment progression.

This chapter will describe a treatment sequence (starting with conventional family or marital therapy, utilizing the couples group format, and aiming toward the adults having sessions with their parents and siblings) which can have powerful effects on the original problems for which the families or couples entered treatment. Although these methods do not always work and are not easy to use, I have found them, through trial and error, to be the most effective in producing lasting change. These procedures are the clinical application of my depth theoretical orientation, which postulates that current family and marital difficulties largely stem from attempts to master earlier conflicts from the original family; these conflicts and transference distortions from the past are being lived anachronistically through the spouse and children (Framo, 1965a, 1970). When these adults are able to go back to deal directly with their parents and brothers and sisters about the previously avoided hard issues that have existed between them, an opportunity exists for reconstructive changes to come about in their marital relationship and in the relationship between these adults and *their* children. The great resistances of adult clients toward bringing in family of origin testifies to the great power of this approach. Because of my conviction that even one session with original family can accomplish more than many regular individual, family, or marital therapy sessions, I have developed techniques for dealing with client resistances and for preparing clients in special kinds of ways for these sessions. This procedure has general applicability and serves diagnostic as well as therapeutic purposes. Not only can clients discover what from the original family is being worked out through the spouse and children, but these adults are being given the chance to come to terms with parents before the parents die.

The methods to be described in this chapter will be largely oriented toward marital theory and conjoint marital therapy rather than the two-generational situation of family therapy. Although I still do see whole families, including the children, from the beginning of therapy to the end, most of the family therapy I do these days is converted to conjoint marital therapy when the originally symptomatic children have been defocused. Those couples who enter therapy specifically for marital problems either do not have children or do not present their children as the primary focus of concern. The major reason for this strategy is that, in my judgment, most children's problems are metaphors about the quality of the relationship between the parents. In a previous publication I wrote, "Whenever there are disturbed children there is a disturbed marriage, although all disturbed marriages do not create disturbed children" (Framo, 1965a; p. 154). Consequently, it is suggested that the best way to help children is to help their parents. The greatest gift parents can give their children is a viable marriage relationship based on each parent's having a strong sense of self. My treatment sequence does not consist only of orienting clients toward working things out with the previous generation. Much of the therapy that goes on with the couple alone or in the couples group consists of dealing with the current marital issues. Consequently, I will be describing my marital assessment methods as well as marital treatment techniques, in both the early as well as later phases of therapy.

In the rest of this chapter I will attempt to follow the guidelines offered by the Editors of this *Handbook* (see Preface), but will not be able to adhere to them strictly. For instance, my treatment model involves different settings and interventions at different stages of treatment, and since therapy goals may change accordingly, it is not possible to comply strictly with the guidelines on goal-setting.

Background of the Approach

Those who write textbooks on family therapy have had difficulty classifying my work as a readily identifiable "Framo" theory, in the way that there is Bowen Theory or Minuchin's Structural Family Therapy. Every family therapy student knows that there are a number of family therapy "schools," classified variously as communication, systems, brief/strategic, structural, psychodynamic, experiential, gestalt, behavioral, intergenerational, problem-solving, and so forth. The history of various movements reveals a repetitive pattern of initial unity and then separation into various factions, sometimes resulting in denunciations between the "true believers" and the revisionists. The bitterness between Freud, Jung, Adler, and other factions within the psychoanalytic movement is well known. The family therapy movement is no exception to this historical sequence of events, except that the rivalries are more or less friendly ones. The early workers in the family therapy field are like a family; they are sometimes jealous of each other and they compete for preeminence, but they also care for each other. It is always difficult to separate ideological, theoretical differences from issues of territoriality, however. The family therapy pioneers were highly creative, charismatic individuals who, being mavericks within their own profession, needed to establish their unique professional identity and stake out their domain. One unfortunate consequence has been the politicization of the field, which sometimes resulted in one or other of the family therapy schools using pejorative labels about the other schools. I wince, for example, when I see myself categorized in the textbooks as a "psychoanalytic family therapist," not only because the word "psychoanalytic" has fallen into disrepute, but also because that characterization is largely inaccurate. I would like to take this opportunity, as a family therapist, to briefly state my views on psychoanalytic theory.

In recent years it has become fashionable to attack psychoanalysis, both as a theory and as a method of treatment. It is difficult today to take a long perspective and appreciate the truly profound nature of Freud's discoveries. For the first time in human history, explanatory concepts were applied to disorders of behavior, experience, and feeling. He brought the *person* into the study of emotional disorder by tying in mental phenomena with the substance of human existence. With Freud, mental processes began to make sense and become lawful: an emotional disorder was not just something that happened, or the result of satanic influence or a diseased body organ, but came to be understood as part and parcel of being biological and human, of being aggressive, of needing, hoping, fearing, loving, and hating in a world which required socialization in order to survive. Freud's concept of the unconscious and the principle of psychological determinism aroused intense fear and hostility, however. Even today there are mental health professionals who disavow or give lip service to the unconscious and cannot emotionally accept the idea, partially because the unconscious, by definition, is not acceptable. The phenomenon of ready aversion to the unconscious is similar, I have found, to the automatic repulsion and denial to which the family-system approach is subject, by professionals as well as families. (In one family I evaluated, referred by the court, in which consummated incest had occurred between father and daughter, the fear of family exploration was so intense—especially mother's role in the incest—that the father and his wife preferred for the father to accept the possibility of a 30-year prison sentence rather than to continue with the family sessions.)

Psychoanalytic theory in its comprehensiveness deals with a staggering range of phenomena. If we wiped out all knowledge which psychoanalysis has given us, how much would be left to explain human motivation and why people feel and behave as they do? Although some psychoanalytic constructs have not stood the test of time, and others are so mystical that they are untestable, few seriously question the validity of such concepts as defense mechanisms, narcissism, the repetition compulsion, mourning, and the like. Insofar as therapy is concerned, it must be kept in mind that psychoanalysis was never intended as a treatment for the masses; its real value lies in the insights that its depth, long-term, clinical-laboratory work can give to basic knowledge of human psychology. Psychoanalysis is not suitable for reality problems; it is not a good idea, for example, to be in analysis when one's marriage is falling apart.

I have my own criticisms of psychoanalysis. One gets the curious feeling in reading the psychoanalytic literature that the patient lives in a vacuum, that the intrapsychic world is almost a closed system, that life stops when one is in analysis, and that the environment is largely treated as a constant. With characteristic perceptive genius Freud identified the fundamental extrinsic determinants of human distress when he classified the external dangers as loss of the object, loss of the penis (castration), loss of the object's love, and loss of the superego's love. There are also occasional references to such exogenous factors as the primal scene, or the effects of poor mothering upon ego development, or some unusual circumstance in the patient's life, and there is even recognition that neurotic parents bring up neurotic children. Most psychoanalysts, however, operationally function from the assumption that it is not the environment that makes people sick (even though Freud in his philosophical writings on applied psychoanalysis does discuss the deleterious effects of society on human adjustment), but that *people do it to themselves* via fantasy and intrapsychic work and elaboration of what goes on outside.

Experience in family therapy has indicated that symptoms or disordered behavior can be viewed as adaptive, nay, necessary responses to the intimate social contexts of a person's life. The most powerful social influence is, perforce, the family, yet psychoanalytic theory has been ambiguous and contradictory about the role of the family in the etiology and maintenance of emotional disturbance. Freud, admittedly, was the first person to recognize in a systematic way the part that love, hate, jealousy, rivalry, ambivalence, and generational differences which arise from the inherent nature of family relationships, play in the development of psychopathology. He was certainly not oblivious to the actual reality of the family environment. In his case histories, he described his involvement with the families of his patients, such as in the cases of Dora and Little Hans.[1] Despite all this understanding, however, Freud set the model that psychotherapy should consist of a one-to-one confidential relationship between patient and therapist, and that the family should be kept out because the transference field would be contaminated. Psychoanalytic theory, which utilizes a family dynamic in its nuclear concept of the Oedipus complex, deals either with the intrapsychic struggle over the Oedipal wishes, or leaps to its wider social aspects in the culture at large. In *Totem and Taboo, Civilization and its Discontents,* and *Group Psychology* Freud proposed that the function of the Oedipus complex was to protect the family from disruption—for only if incest and patricide are outlawed can the family and thus society survive. Yet though in one sense psychoanalytic thought sees the survival of man as dependent on the preservation of the family, the lack of focus on the transactional dynamics of the family itself represents a real gap in the theory.

Over the years since the heyday of psychoanalysis a series of developments in many different fields (ego psychology, group dynamics, child development, sociology of the family, communication theory, general systems theory, and others) have blended into a family transactional approach. Jackson (1967) gave explicit recognition to this movement when he stated, "We are on the edge of a new era in psychiatry, and the related disciplines of psychology, social work,

---

[1]Even in Freud's case histories there were some notable omissions. For example, he did not mention that during the course of Little Hans's treatment Hans's parents were in the process of getting a divorce and indeed did divorce when the treatment was over. For a reexamination of the case of Little Hans from the standpoint of family dynamics see Strean (1967).

anthropology and sociology. In this new era we will come to look at human nature in a much more complex way than ever before. From this threshold the view is not of the individual *in vitro* but of the small or larger group within which any particular individual's behavior is adaptive. We will move from individual assessment to analysis of contexts, or more precisely, the *system* from which individual conduct is inseparable" (p. 139). To be sure, as Zilboorg and Henry (1941) have pointed out, for each stage of history emotional disturbances have been defined in a manner which is congruent with the spirit and ethos of the age. It may well be that the family movement reflects, in part, an American emphasis on environmental reform, as Spiegel and Bell (1959) have noted.

There is a major theoretical controversy within the family field. There are the so-called family-systems "purists" like Haley (1975), who polarize the intrapsychic and the interactional, claiming that family theory and therapy should only concern itself with what goes on *between* people. For these family therapists, intrapsychic phenomena and the past are irrelevant for producing change. My own point of view is that while I believe that psychoanalytic theory cannot explain family-system phenomena, I do not agree that in understanding and treating family relationships we should discard everything we have known about dynamic psychology. My position is that what goes on inside people's heads is just as important as what goes on between them, in their interpersonal relationships. *Neither level can be reduced to the other; one does not have to make a choice as to which is more important.*

More technically, the core of my theoretical approach is the *relationship* between the intrapsychic and the transactional. That is to say, I see insoluble intrapsychic conflicts, derived from the original family, being acted out, replicated, mastered, or defended against with the current intimates, via some very complicated processes that are poorly understood. Not only do spouses have transference distortions of each other, giving rise sometimes to outlandish expectations of marriage and of their partners, but the children can also be caught up in bizarre "transference fixes" that are impervious to reality considerations (such as that the small child should mother the parent, or that the child is inherently a "bad seed" that needs to be repaired or exterminated). Indeed, the interpersonal resolution of inner conflict is what creates the kind of profound human distress that we see clinically in troubled families and couples. Whenever a group of people are closely related to each other, as in a family, they reciprocally carry part of each other's psychology and form a feedback system which in turn patterns and regulates their individual behaviors. The creative leap of this family-system theory was recognition of this interlocking, multi-person motivational system whereby family members collusively carry psychic functions for each other. Exploration of this phenomenon, in which dynamic and systems concepts are amalgamated, can provide a conceptual bridge from the personal to the social. The foregoing perhaps explains why Foley (1974), in his classificaion of family theorists, refers to me as an "integrationist."

A summary of the main tenets of the theory of intergenerational transmission of beliefs, attitudes, and symptoms, expanded from Fairbairn's (1954) object-relations theory, and elaborated by Framo (1970, 1976a), follows:

1. Fairbairn (1954) has postulated that Man's need for a satisfactory object relationship constitutes the fundamental motive of life. His object-relationship approach is contrasted with Freud's theory of instinctual gratification as being primary in Man.

2. Since they are unable to give up the maternal object or change it in outer reality, infants incorporate the frustrating aspects of their relational world. These internalized objects are retained as introjects, psychological representatives of the external objects.

3. These introjects form part of the structure of the personality and undergo various splits. During the course of development of the individual, external real figures may be assimilated in successive strata or by fusion into the existing bad-object situations.

4. Intrapsychic conflicts arise from experiences in the original family, and reparative efforts to deal with these conflicts impel the individual to force close relations into fitting the internal role models.

5. One's mate or children are perceived largely in terms of the individual's own needs, or as carrying for him his own denied, split-off traits. Mates select each other on the basis of rediscovering lost aspects of their primary object relations which they had split off and which, in their involvement with the spouse, they reexperience by projective identification (Dicks, 1967). A main source of marital disharmony is that spouses project disowned aspects of themselves onto the mate and then fight them in the mate.

6. Children are especially prone to these projections; some children cannot get their parents to love them even if they sacrificed their life. One's current intimates, one's spouse and children, are shadowy stand-ins for old ghosts, the embodiments of old introjects.

7. The adult, by having sessions with his or her family of origin, takes the problems back to their original sources, thereby making available a direct route to etiological factors. These sessions serve diagnostic as well as therapeutic purposes in that both the old and new families can be cross-referenced for similar patterns.

8. Dealing with the real, external figures loosens the grip of the internalized representatives of these figures and exposes them to current realities. The parents and siblings of today are not the parents and siblings of the past; indeed, they never were. The original transference figures can also be the objects of transference today; few adults ever get to see their parents as real people.

9. Having gone backward in time, the individual can then move forward in

behaving toward the spouse and children in more appropriate fashion, as persons in their own right, since their transference meaning has changed.

10. Family-of-origin sessions not only can help resolve problems in the current family, but coming to terms with parents and siblings before they die can be a profoundly liberating experience.

In addition to my work being based on the intrapsychic object-relations theory of Fairbairn and the marital interaction theory of Dicks, I have been influenced by theories of family therapists as well. A theoretical debt is owed to Bowen (1978), who was the first to relate present family difficulties to multigenerational processes. The professional world is still reverberating to the account of his study of his own family, reported at a family conference under the title of "Toward the Differentiation of a Self in One's Own Family" (Anonymous, 1972). Boszormenyi-Nagy and Spark (1973), Whitaker (1976), Haas (1968), Paul and Paul (1975), and Headley (1977) have dealt with related concepts in work with the family of origin. My approach to marital therapy, based originally on my family therapy experiences (Framo, 1965a), has been more recently described (Framo, 1980).

I would like to clarify one other misconception about my approach. As I stated previously (Framo, 1975b), changing a family system is for me the ultimate professional challenge, and my therapeutic philosophy is to learn as many kinds of treatment approaches as possible in order to have a full repertoire of techniques available to shift a system. Consequently, I have attended workshops on Transactional Analysis, gestalt, encounter groups, behavior therapy, rational-emotive, EST, existential therapy, and other methods. I have used methods of working with families from a number of different schools (communicational, paradoxical, strategic, sculpting, and so forth), and believe it is necessary to be eclectic in dealing with the tremendous variety and kinds of difficulties presented by families and couples. It takes years of experience to be appropriately and selectively eclectic in the sense of choosing a specific method for a particular problem.[2] One cannot apply one's theory to all problems. I do not use object-relations theory and family-of-origin sessions with all my couples. There are aspects of marriages and families that are unrelated to problems hanging over from the families of origin, such as those reflecting social and cultural changes. Furthermore, some uncomplicated marital problems can be treated by "conventional" marital therapy techniques, focusing on the marital interaction in the here and now. These couples' marital difficulties are temporary, not deep-seated, largely situational, a function of the stage of marriage they are in, and for the most part based on misunderstandings which can be untangled in a few sessions. (In a later section [of this chapter], when I specify different types of marital problems, this point will be further

---

[2]Every therapist comes up against unique kinds of problem situations for which there are no known techniques; the art of psychotherapy often consists of on-the-spot improvisation.

elaborated upon.) It is the more serious marital problems which require depth exploration of the conflict paradigms from original family and how they get played out in the marriage. Having said that, however, I believe that everyone can profit from meeting with their parents and brothers and sisters; the family members get to know each other better and can work toward more differentiated intimacy.

The Healthy or Well-Functioning Marriage or Family

There are a number of considerations to be taken into account in determining what is a healthy or well-functioning marriage or family. First, most clinicians have been trained to recognize or deal with abnormality and therefore have a tendency to miss the adaptive features of individual's personalities or family/marital relationships. Little is known about the self-corrective mechanisms that all families have. Since family therapists usually see families and couples when they are under stress and behaving at their worst, therapists often get distorted views of the positive sides of the relationships. Besides, most people think of therapy as the place where one talks about what goes wrong rather than what goes right. (I have observed couples being intensely hostile to each other during treatment sessions, and then, as soon as they leave the office, walking away arm in arm.) Finally, under the intensive scrutiny of the therapy microscope almost every individual, family, or couple can look sick. I believe that nearly every person, family, and marriage, over the course of their lives, goes through periods of turmoil and disorganization that at the time appear pathological.

Little systematic work has been done on the so-called normal family (Lewis et al., 1976); I am not aware of any family theoretician or family therapist who has developed a comprehensive theory of healthy marital or family functioning. Most family researchers have used minimal operational criteria for defining normal families—such as that a normal family is one that has not come to community attention for a problem (been arrested, in therapy, school problem, and so forth). Most family therapists, myself included, however, have indirectly alluded to aspects of healthy functioning, largely in contrast to descriptions of pathological families and couples. Accordingly, I have gleaned out of my various writings some ideal principles of healthy or normal family and marital functioning:

1. That partners each be well-differentiated, having developed a sense of self before separating from their families of origin.
2. Clear separation of generational boundaries within the family. The children should be free of the role of saving a parent or the parental marriage.
3. Realistic perceptions and expectations by parents of each other and of their children.
4. The loyalty to the family of procreation is greater than to the family of origin.
5. The spouses put themselves and each other before anyone else, including the

children; the marriage, however, is not a symbiotic one which excludes the children. The children do not feel that to be close to one parent means they are alienating the other.

6. Encouragement of identity development and autonomy for all family members. Successful development in the children will mean that they will leave home at some point to start families of their own.
7. Nonpossessive warmth and affection be expressed between parents, between parents and children, and among the siblings.
8. The capacity to have open, honest, and clear communication, and to deal with issues with each other.
9. A realistic, adult-to-adult, caring relationship between each parent and his or her parents and siblings.
10. An open family in the sense of involvement with others outside the family, including extended family and friends; allowing outsiders inside the family.

Insofar as the marital relationship is concerned, in a recent publication (Framo, 1980), I specified criteria for improvement in marital therapy; these criteria have implications for a healthy marriage. They are:

1. The partners are more personally differentiated, and dependency on each other is voluntary.
2. They have come to terms with the roots of their irrational expectations of marriage and of the spouse derived from the family of origin.
3. They have developed a more empathetic understanding of their mate.
4. They can meet each other's realistic needs in the face of their differentness.
5. They can communicate more clearly and openly.
6. They like each other more and they enjoy sex with each other.
7. They have learned to deal with the issues between them.
8. They can enjoy life more, and get pleasure from work and from their children.
9. They have developed flexibility in dealing with situational stresses and crises.
10. They have adjusted to the disenchantment of romantic love and have more realistic appraisals of the vicissitudes of mature, de-idealized love.

As I said, the foregoing criteria are ideal ones; I am sure no family or marriage meets all of them. In addition, in light of the fact that 40% of new marriages are likely to end in divorce, I should make a statement about families that break up. In my judgment some divorces are steps of growth, whereas others I perceive as manifestations of unresolved problems from original family. In a paper on divorce therapy (Framo, 1978a), I specified its goals as helping the couple to disengage from their relationship with a minimum of destructiveness to self, the partner, and the children, and with the freedom to form new relationships. I do believe that, although difficult, it is possible for divorce and remarriage to occur without enduring cost to the children or parents. In other words, a stepfamily can be a healthy, well-functioning family (Visher and Visher, 1979).

The Pathological or Dysfunctional Marriage or Family

My main conceptualizations and ideas about dysfunctional families and couples are contained in previous publications (Framo, 1965a, 1970). I postulated that symptoms are formed, selected, faked, exchanged, maintained, and reduced or extinguished as a function of the relationship context in which they are naturally embedded. Children's symptoms are frequently the outcome of irrational role assignments which one or both parents ascribe to the child; these designations usually have nothing to do with the inherent nature of the child. Children who are assigned the role of "the troublemaker," "the crazy one," "mother's protector," or "the stupid one" may incorporate and *become* their assigned role, may spend a lifetime disputing the role, may play-act at the role, or the child may learn to become his own person, independent of the role.

Examples of other factors which create or affect symptoms are: blurring of generational boundaries (as when the mother goes to her son to complain about her husband); family traumas (the death or absence of a parent, divorce, or the unemployment of a parent); maintenance of symptoms for system purposes (the child is being sick so mother will have someone to take care of); scapegoating ("Our marriage would be fine if it weren't for that kid."); emotional overburdening of the child (the child being expected to be marriage counselor for his parents); and overt/covert rejection or infantilization of the child. The particular type of symptom developed depends, in general, on what the system requires. Some dangerous symptoms of children are ignored by parents, although the school or others may recognize their seriousness. On the other hand, a child's "symptom" may be trivial as seen by outsiders, yet the parents may exaggerate its importance and may want to use drastic measures for handling it (such as wanting to institutionalize a child because "he lies.")

Among the factors that enable some children to survive and be relatively untouched by the family pathology are the following:

1. These children, for reasons having to do with the parents' backgrounds, did not become the focus of concern. Even their physical appearance could play a role in not being selected as special.
2. These siblings used the identified patient as a model of what to avoid.
3. These children may have had resources outside the family (such as an aunt, friend, or teacher), and therefore established wider emotional investments.
4. These children were more successful at utilizing defenses of isolation, but paid a price by having constricted personalities.

I have not developed any system for typing or classifying families, although I have recently (Framo, 1980) devised an informal scheme for classifying marriages. This very crude classification system is based on responsiveness to therapy; that is, those in the early part of the list I find, in general, less difficult to treat than those toward the latter part. The scheme is not precise enough to call it "marital diagnosis." Diagnosis suggests that specific treatment strategies have been devised for each discrete category, which is certainly not the case.

1. Couples whose marriage relationships are basically sound and whose problems largely stem from communicational misunderstandings. These couples essentially rehabilitate their own marriage, needing only a couple of therapy sessions.

2. Marriages where the partners love each other, are committed to the marriage, but "can't get along." Some of these couples are responding to the impact of parenthood, others have in-law complications, some argue a lot, and others avoid conflict.

3. Brother-sister marriages where the spouses care a great deal for each other, but there is little excitement in the relationship. Sex is routine and marital life is comfortable but dull.

4. Conflictual marriages where the spouses feel markedly ambivalent about each other. The partners are engaged in a power struggle and are in conflict over a variety of issues, ranging from feminist issues to sex, disciplining of the children, dual-career conflicts, in-laws, money, and all the other "cover" issues.

5. Marriages in which one partner is symptomatic. Involving both partners in conjoint treatment can move this kind of marriage into the "conflict" category. The symptoms (such as depression) may become unnecessary as the couple begins to deal with their issues.

6. Marriages whose problems are a consequence of incomplete marital maturation. These partners have never really left home and are overinvolved with one or both families of origin.

7. Marriages of mental health professionals or of "professional patients" are not easy to change. For some of these couples, being in therapy is a way of life. The professional therapist-spouses have been doing bad therapy on each other, sometimes for years; each is an expert on the partner's dynamics.

8. Second or third marriages are usually complicated by ghosts of the previous marriages, children, and obligations to the former spouses. Loyalty rearrangements, problems of step-parenting, financial stresses, and grandparents all present difficulties.

9. Older couples whose relationship problems have calcified and whose options are limited. These couples came to therapy too late.

10. "Pseudo-mutual" couples who deny all problems in the marriage and present a child as the problem. These couples cannot admit to the ordinary difficul-

ties all couples can acknowledge. The therapist may reach these couples indirectly by accepting the child as the problem (Montalvo and Haley, 1973). An alternative method of working with child-focused families is offered by Bradt and Moynihan (1971).

11. The marriage that is in extremis, where the couple come to therapy as a last resort before seeing lawyers. One partner may be finished with the marriage and the other is trying to hold on. Some of these couples can be engaged in divorce therapy.

12. Finally, there is the kind of chronically unhappy marriage where the partners "can't live with and can't live without." These couples may have had many unsuccessful individual or marital therapy experiences; they should have divorced and could not because permanent separation means psychic death.

The Assessment of System Dysfunction

My unit of treatment is the whole family when there are problems involving the children. As I stated earlier, sometimes I do family therapy (parents and children together) from beginning to end. Other times, when the problems in the children have been alleviated, I dismiss the children and work with the parents' marriage. Still other couples enter therapy explicitly for marital problems and either do not have children or state that their marital relationship is the problem.

I no longer do individual therapy. When I treat a couple I insist on seeing them together, usually with a female cotherapist. If one spouse wants to be seen alone first or wants the partner to be seen alone, and either one refuses to come in for a conjoint interview, I will refer them elsewhere. During therapy I refuse interviews with a single individual, although during ongoing couples group therapy I will see a couple unit for emergencies. I am aware that there are therapists who find it diagnostically valuable to have separate interviews with a single spouse, but in my experience the advantages of individual sessions (such as learning about secrets, affairs, and so forth) are not worth the suspicions of the absent partner, the temporary relief of the confiding spouse, or the conflicts of loyalty and confidentiality in the therapist that such sessions promulgate. Furthermore, each spouse lives in the context of an intimate relationship, and separating the partners for private sessions negates the context, obscures the interactional collusiveness, and violates the integrity of the marital unit. The only exception made to my own rule is when I may separate divorcing spouses in the later stages of divorce therapy, although even under this circumstance I consider that the person who cannot tolerate the presence of the partner has not emotionally divorced that partner.

The only method of assessment I use is the clinical interview, which I find far superior to any formal questionnaire, guided interview schedule, situational test, or experimental procedure. Questionnaires and formal tasks do not give an observer the opportunity to follow up on leads or observe reactions. It is much easier to deceive a questionnaire than it is to fool an experienced clinician. Besides, questionnaires tell you nothing about how partners typically behave with each other, because people do not know how they interact with their intimates. Previously, I have stated my objections to the use of questionnaires in family research (Framo, 1965b).

Initial interviews, on the other hand, can also be misleading; it takes several interviews to get a fairly clear picture of what is going on.[3] Generally speaking, I do not make interventions in the first few sessions, as my cotherapist and I assess the couple, and while they, to be sure, assess us. The reason for early nonintervention is that I want to get maximum information without deliberately affecting the process. To be sure, assessment and treatment are inseparable, even when the therapist does not make a purposeful intervention. Among the factors that have therapeutic or antitherapeutic effects in the initial interviews are: history of previous therapies, therapy expectations, reputation of the therapist, the basis for the decision to come to therapy, the physical setting of the office, the therapist(s) physical appearance, the kinds of questions asked, how they are asked, amount of the fee, degree of "connectedness" between clients and therapist(s), a sense of hope or despair stimulated by the first interview, and so forth. When I see a couple I consider there are three main areas of inquiry: the husband and wife as individuals, and their relationship—how their intrapsychic spheres intermesh. More specifically, I attempt to cover such topics as the following in the early interviews: referral source, brief statement of problems from each spouse, age, occupation, length of marriage, ages and gender of children, previous therapies, prior marriages, basis of mate selection, family's reactions to choice of partner, the partners' fight styles, whether the spouses basically love each other, whether they ever had a good relationship, commitment to the marriage, the quality and quantity of their sexual relationship, a brief history of each family of origin, current relationship with parents and siblings, how they relate to each other in the interview, motivation for therapy, and so forth.

Goal-Setting

One of the ways that family and marital therapy differ from all other psychotherapies is that there are varied and sometimes competing vested interests at play during treatment sessions. In individual therapy the therapist is dealing with warring elements within one person, but when there are issues between people, their goals of therapy will vary. For instance, a wife's goal might be to get out of the marriage without guilt, whereas the husband's goal might be to make the

---

[3]I have had the experience of thinking in the first interview that a husband was crazy or unreachable, and wondering to myself why this lovely woman ever married a guy like that. By the end of the second interview he would seem reasonable and she would turn out to be impossible to deal with.

marriage relationship better; if the marriage ends in divorce the wife may consider the therapy a great success, and the husband may consider it to be a failure and may refuse to pay for the treatment. In family therapy a divorced woman who feels she has a second chance for happiness with a man who does not want her child, may have the goal of institutionalizing the child with the blessing of a mental health professional; the child, of course, has the goal of staying with the mother.

In the first interview I routinely ask each person what his or her goals of therapy are: What would they like to accomplish in therapy? One complication surrounding treatment goals is that the husband and wife may openly state goals that are at variance with their secret agendas for therapy outcome. For example, the husband may profess interest in saving his marriage, yet all the while be hoping the therapist will pronounce that the marriage is over. Some of the secret agendas are unconscious: a wife may unwittingly be attempting to prove to the therapist how cruel and heartless her husband really is, while praising his generosity. A husband may punish his wife for each step she takes toward autonomy (such as by not speaking to her for several days when she goes back to school), yet may state that he wants a wife who is independent. Finally, clients' goals almost always change as therapy progresses. They shift goals to accommodate to their widening awareness and changing perception of their problems. For instance, in the early part of therapy a couple may state as their problem the cliché, "We do not communicate," and later they may realize that their problems are not only more complicated than communication ones, but that they have entirely different values about the meaning of marriage. Goals of therapy, moreover, may clash not only among the family members, but with the goals of the therapist as well. Perhaps part of the skill of a therapist resides in finding the appropriate balance between the conflict of goals and expectations of all the family members as well as those of the therapist. (Not under discussion is the subject of differences between cotherapists about treatment goals.) I have often wondered whether, in some situations, it is not necessary for someone in the family to lose if someone is to gain. For instance, if a 40-year-old man finally gets to the point where he can leave his suffocating, widowed mother and get married, from his and the therapist's point of view, he is better, but from his mother's point of view he is worse.

Since my treatment model involves different settings and interventions at different stages as the typical couple progress through single couple therapy, couples group therapy, and family-of-origin sessions, my own goals of therapy change from one sequence to the next. My long-range goals of marital therapy were stated earlier in this chapter. In the early phases the first goal is the establishment of a working relationship between the couple and cotherapists; without trust therapy will never get off the ground.

The great majority of couples that I see enter a couples group following several diagnostic interviews (Framo, 1973). My goal during the couples group sessions consists primarily of utilizing the group process to further the therapy of the couple. The feedback the members get from each other is quite therapeutic;

feedback from group members often has more impact than the statements of the therapists. Some other benefits of the group format are: the partners come to recognize the universality of certain marital problems and do not feel so different from other couples; the couples usually develop trust of each other and consequently become more open; in a "good" group even deep secrets will be revealed; problems across couples are contrasted or are found to be similar, so couples use each other as models of what to imitate or avoid; observations of each other become sharper as treatment progresses; the couples usually come to care for each other, and caring is always therapeutic; the goals of the spouses usually undergo modification in response to therapists' activity and feedback from the group, and other benefits. Consequently, during the couples group sessions, the spouses become much more aware of their unrealistic expectations of marriage and of their spouse. These realizations bring about curiosity as to the genesis of their irrational expectations—which provides the opening for me to suggest anew that working things out with original family is one way of getting beyond the marital impasse. The group process helps individuals to become less resistant to bringing in their family, especially since this goal of mine becomes the group goal; family-of-origin sessions come to be perceived by the group as a sort of final examination or graduation ceremony. The two major goals for the family-of-origin sessions are discovering what, from the old family, is being projected onto the spouse, and having a corrective experience with parents and siblings. The ultimate payoff or goal is a more differentiated self, with consequent improvement in the marital or family relationships.

Treatment Applicability

Most of the couples I have treated were seen in my private practice and therefore were, economically at least, upper middle class. However, I have used these methods in a community mental health center where the social classes of the clients spanned the entire spectrum. I have seen couples conjointly, done couples group therapy, and had family-of-origin sessions with clients who were severely disadvantaged, poor, and nearly illiterate.

There are certain universals of family and marital life that exist with all human beings, in all classes and cultures. One family problem has been mentioned as being universal among those seeking treatment—that the loyalty of a spouse to the family of origin was greater than to the spouse and children. Almost everybody has a peer intimate relationship and has a parent, brother, or sister, and whenever there are intimates there are going to be relationship difficulties. Interestingly, those people who are not psychologically minded and who want something concrete, like a pill, when they are in distress often do not resist meeting with a spouse or with parents or siblings—although they have no concept of psychotherapy. Their very nonsophistication makes them more open to conjoint family or marital therapy since they do not know enough about therapy to know that that is not what is usually done.

In one sense I think everyone, people in treatment or not, can profit from family-of-origin sessions. Few people ever get to know their parents as real people, few families ever share, all together as a family, the really meaningful thoughts and feelings, and few people get to that last stage with parents, that of forgiving them and telling them that they are loved. So I see family-of-origin sessions as not being just a therapy method but as a kind of pandemic experience for people in general. As a matter of fact, in recent years I have been meeting the requests of family therapists to have one-time sessions with their original families. These sessions have been most productive.

Clinically, however, there are some marital situations where the family-of-origin sessions are more necessary, and still others where, although they are needed, there are certain unique circumstances which preclude their being held. Everyone transfers irrational attitudes and projects onto their spouse, including prominent people and professional marriage therapists; this phenomenon is part of being human and is a byproduct of the nature of intimate relationships. However, some people, who are more differentiated in Bowen's (1978) sense, have less need of fusion and can more accurately perceive the spouse as a person in his or her own right. These are the couples seen in marital therapy for relatively superficial problems, and for whom family-of-origin sessions are not necessarily indicated. At the other extreme are those people who view their spouses as plasticene objects to be molded to their own needs, who do not really know where they end and the spouse begins, who are overdependent (for example, one spouse cannot go to the bathroom without the other asking, "Where are you going?"), and who may exhibit intense transference rage toward the mate (culminating sometimes in spouse murder). These people are unable to commit themselves to anyone, because the deeper involvement is with the parents (thus, the only time they may come alive during treatment sessions is when they discuss their parents). Their marital relationship is unreal, shadowy, and dream like because where they "live" is in the old family. For these kinds of couples family-of-origin sessions are a must; but, as might be expected, they are also the most difficult to set up, to conduct, and to handle from the standpoint of subsequent emotional fallout.

From time to time when I have given workshops, I have been asked whether there are couples who should *not* be seen in a couples group. I have never had the experience of having a couple in a group and thinking they would have done better as a single couple. There are couples who are reluctant to enter a group, but once in the group their apprehensions vanish. I am usually able to get them to come into a group by telling them that in the group they will accomplish their goals quicker— which is true. The only couples I see as a single couple are those who need only a few sessions or those who are unable to arrange for the times that the groups meet. Although I have not yet met such a marital situation, it is possible that there may be some unique combination of circumstances and dynamics that would make couples group therapy contraindicated for a given couple. For instance, it is possible that a couple where incest with their children had occurred might not be able to deal with that event in the group. On the other hand, I have seen some pretty heavy secrets revealed in that setting, such as a man whose father was in jail for child molesting.

Contraindications for family-of-origin sessions is a topic that we know little about, largely because there have only been a few years' experience with the method. I consider family-of-origin therapy as the major surgery of family therapy, and, like major surgery, there are risks and there can be complications, especially short-term emotional upsets.

I have referred various family members for specific therapies, such as sex therapy, vocational guidance, behavior therapy, remediation of learning disabilities, group therapy, marathons, and even for individual psychotherapy. I prefer that an individual in marital therapy with me not be in individual therapy with someone else while the marital therapy is going on. The main reason for this stance is that these clients will frequently reserve important material for their individual sessions; besides, the outside therapist and I could be working at cross-purposes, especially if that other therapist is an adherent of the illness model. I do not feel that I have a right to tell clients to terminate their individual therapy or analysis before starting marital therapy, but I do inform them of the handicaps that their separate therapy could impose on the marital therapy. When the desire for more extensive work on self is expressed, or when I think it advisable, however, I do refer clients for individual therapy when the marital therapy has terminated.

The final point on treatment applicability concerns the question as to whether no treatment of any sort is ever recommended. There are couples, especially those who have had too much therapy, to whom I make the recommendation that the best thing they can do for themselves is not to be in treatment. I have also dismissed some couples from ongoing therapy who have been using therapy as a substitute for living. I tell them, "Go out and live your lives and stop examining yourselves."

The Structure of the Therapy Process

As stated earlier, couples are seen only conjointly, and almost all couples are seen in a couples group format after a few diagnostic sessions with the couple alone. There are no sessions with individuals. One major goal of the couples group setting is to prepare clients for the family-of-origin (intergenerational) sessions, which usually occur toward the end of therapy. The reasons for having the family-of-origin sessions late in therapy is that these sessions are more productive when the clients have changed in therapy, and are ready to deal with the difficult issues with their parents and siblings.

Occasionally I have family sessions with couples and their children, particularly if a couple in marital therapy expresses some concern about their children. These sessions are, of course, held outside the group. These family sessions have been valuable on several counts: the children are given the message that they are no longer responsible for handling their parents' problems, because that job has been taken over by the therapists; the children give the kind of ingenuous, truthful accounts of what is going on at home that only children can give; and if the session occurs toward the end of therapy the children can give a reading on how they perceive changes in their parents' relationship. Many couples at the end of successful marital therapy report "improvement" in their children even when I have never seen the children.

Insofar as combined therapies are concerned, the one form of treatment that I find does not interfere with family therapy is for adolescents to be in peer group therapy concurrent with the family therapy. The separate adolescent group and family settings have seemed to enhance each other. (I do not conduct the group therapy; that is done by someone to whom I refer the adolescent.)

Although I have had to work as a solo therapist at times, I prefer to work with a cotherapist, particularly a female. Through the years I have worked with many cotherapists and I have come to see the value of having someone there to share responsibility, to notice things I do not see, to fight with me about what's going on, to provide more therapeutic leverage, to protect my flank, to make observations I do not think of, to allow me to remove myself psychologically, and to provide a reassuring presence during the kinds of chaotic or frightening events which can occur during family or marital therapy. Families and couples always respond more favorably to being seen by cotherapists rather than a single therapist, especially male-female teams. Women especially are pleased that another woman is present to understand a woman's point of view. Over the past 7 years, in addition to working with other cotherapists, I have worked with my wife (Mary Framo, M.S.S., family therapist), in our evening private practice. The subject of husband-wife cotherapy is a large, rather complicated one that must await a separate publication. The only disadvantages I have seen with cotherapy is when there is a poor match between the personalities of the therapists. A cotherapy team can become like a marriage, and differences will inevitably arise—about strategy, interruptions, status, and who is chief honcho. If the cotherapists do not have the mechanisms for working out their differences, then they should divorce, because couples and families will exploit their alienation, try to cure the cotherapy rift, or terminate prematurely.

The physical arrangement of sessions is as follows: swivel chairs are used (so partners can turn and face each other) and the chairs are arranged in a circle. I cannot imagine conducting family or marital therapy sessions from behind a desk. All my sessions are audiotaped, and clients are free at any time to borrow the tapes to listen to at home. Many people take advantage of this offer, or bring their own cassette recorders to sessions. Sessions listened to at home can add an important dimension to the treatment in that, with anxiety being less, the observing ego is more operative at that time. Many clients report that while listening to sessions at home they noticed aspects of themselves (anger, sulking, conning, phoniness, obsequiousness, contempt, and so forth) that their defensiveness during sessions blocked them from seeing. I make no apologies about taping, the microphone is clearly present, and I communicate, in effect. "This is the way I work." Almost never does anyone object to being taped. (In those early days, when we used to ask permission and apologize for taping, there were many objections). After every session a summary of the session is written up; if you do not do this you will never remember what is on the tape, and the tape will be useless.

Marital or family therapy, as I conduct it, is not time-limited; it does not seem appropriate to me to specify arbitrarily how many sessions are needed for a given problem. However, when I calculated the average number of sessions that couples come for marital therapy, the average turned out to be 15 sessions. This figure is an average one; the range was from one session to about 50 sessions. Sessions are generally held once a week; with interruptions for holidays and vacations; the average length of treatment is about 5 months. Occasionally some families and couples are seen on an irregular basis; some people seem to profit more when there is more than one week between sessions, whereas others come irregularly because they cannot afford to come more frequently. Decisions about therapy structure are made explicitly by the cotherapists, subject to occasional negotiation with the clients.

The Role of the Therapist

Like practically all family therapists, I am rather active in therapy sessions; I cannot conceive of doing marital or family therapy in a passive, nondirective way. Because of the multiplicity of events on numerous levels, some degree of control of sessions by the therapist is necessary. For instance, since there is such deep and abiding resistance to bringing in family of origin, and because of my convictions about its value, I tend to come down rather hard on that subject; that is the one area where I am most directive.

Following the initial diagnostic sessions, where I abstain from making interventions, my conversational style usually consists of a fluid blend of questioning, empathizing, challenging, stage directing, avoiding snares, confronting, balancing, supporting, reflecting, disagreeing, and, when relevant, judicious sharing of some of my own life experiences. On the subject of self-disclosure, I think it important that the therapist convey in some form that he has experienced pain and loss, shame, guilt, and disappointment, as well as the exhilaration and joys of living. I even think it is helpful at times to communicate the reality of one's own parenting difficulties as well as of one's own marriage as going through up-and-down phases. It is just as unwise to support the fantasy of the therapist's life as ideal as it is to overburden clients with one's own problems.

In our efforts to read the punctuation of the couple and raise concealed intrapsychic and interpersonal conflicts into open interactional expression, I and my cotherapist will move in and out of their orbit and emotional field. While one therapist is "inside" it is better for the other to be "outside," and be in a position to rescue the one who got caught up in the couple's or the group's irrationality. When partners will not talk to each other and only want to talk to the therapist(s), I insist they talk to each other; when they only will talk to each other, I insist that they talk to me. Any behavior can be used as a defense.

My role as a therapist is fairly consistent throughout the course of treatment, although there may be times when the cotherapists will flexibly alternate roles. That is, the one who has usually been the rescuer may become the confronter, and vice versa. By the time the end of therapy has approached, I have noticed there is a tendency for me to become more personal and social with clients. Some couples groups after termination have had parties in one of the couple's homes, and although there was a time when I would never mix with clients socially, these days I do go with my wife, on a selected basis, to some of these social events. While it would be risky or inappropriate to mix socially with some clients, I have found no problems arising from social contact of this sort with the great majority of couples following termination. Family therapists have tended to break down a number of traditional professional taboos without the sky falling in.

Techniques of Marital–Family Therapy

In my earlier writings on therapy techniques in *Intensive Family Therapy*, (Framo, 1965a), I dealt with the phases of family therapy as well as such technical problems as resistance, marriage problems, the "well sibling," transference/ countertransference, and cotherapy. At that time most of my experience was with families with a schizophrenic member. Although some of those observations and techniques have held up over time, others have been modified; an update on my techniques can be found in an informal paper written in 1975 (Framo, 1975b).

My techniques vary according to whether I am seeing a couple, a couples group, or family of origin, not only because of the number and kind of people in the room, but because of the variation in goals, the nature of the therapy contract, and the psychological set of the clients. When couples first enter therapy they are intensely preoccupied with the fate of their relationship. Standard marital therapy techniques are used to deal with the relationship itself, such as accepting the couple, both as individuals and as a relationship, no matter how strange or unusual they seem at first; helping them develop congruent communications; the feedback technique (partners repeating back to each other what they think they heard); quid pro quo negotiations; work on differentiation; changing the rules of the relationship; teaching the couple how to "fight" or deal with issues with each other (Bach and Wyden, 1969); audiotape playback; as well as such conventional techniques as reflection, confrontation, interpretations, eliciting of affect, and so forth. On occasion, paradoxical tasks are assigned, but this sort of "homework," as well as some Masters and Johnson sex-therapy exercises, are used sparingly.[4] Techniques will differ according to the kind of marital problem being presented; see Section III of this paper for types of marital problems. The greatest mistake made by beginning marital therapists, in my judgment, is that they are often misled by spouses' rage or apparent indifference toward each other, and they conclude that the marriage is unworkable. I have learned to respect the integrity and the tenaciousness of bonds in marital relationships, even in the most alienated of couples or unlikeliest matches.

I originally put couples together in a group in order to free myself from the transference/countertransference logjam that occurs with certain kinds of couples (Framo, 1973). While some couples are a pleasure to work with, there are others who "triangle-in" the therapist as judge or prosecutor, those incapable of hearing anyone but themselves, those who become overdependent and helpless, and still others who try to solve their marital problems by joining in an attack on the therapist. In order to handle my own reactions of frustration, impotence, or exasperation, I began putting my difficult couples together. It was only later, after experience with the couples group format, that I recognized the power of this form of treatment. I now believe that couples group therapy is the treatment of choice for premarital, living-together, marital, and separation or divorce relationship problems. Indeed, all the couples I see come into a couples' group unless there are scheduling difficulties or unless the relationship problem does not require more than a couple of sessions.

The group contains three couples, and the method, in brief, consists of focusing on one couple at a time while the other two couples observe, and then eliciting feedback from everyone in the group; then the next couple is attended to, and then the next, all of the individuals getting and giving feedback. Sessions last for 2 hours and are conducted with a female cotherapist.[5] The couples groups are open-ended, in that as couples terminate, new ones are added. The focus is on the marital pair within the group context; it is recognized that other therapists conduct couples groups more like conventional peer group therapy where anyone can talk at any time. My primary focus is on the couple rather than the group because that pair had a history before the group started, and are likely to have a future together long after the group has disbanded. I am particularly interested in the transference distortions which occur between partners, not so much in the transference reactions across couples. Although I place the group as secondary to the couple, a

[4]Most sexual problems disappear as a function of working on the relationship difficulties of the couple. Those couples who still have a sexual dysfunction after their relationship improves are referred elsewhere for sex therapy.

[5]Cotherapists I have worked with in recent years have been: My wife, Mary D. Framo, M.S.S., Ph.D. candidate, Cheryl Keats, M.S.W., Joann Gillis-Donovan, Ph.D., Ann Gravagno, M.F.T., Peggy Tietz, M.S.W., and Gail Hogeboom Wilson, M.A., Ph.D. candidate.

group process is inevitable and must be managed and utilized to therapeutic advantage.

I find that couples do better when they are with couples who are not too far removed from them by age or stage of the life cycle. That is, I tend to put together couples recently married or with young children, and have other groups with older couples whose children are grown. It has not worked too well when I have put, say, a young couple with two older couples; the latter would often lecture the young couple about the troubles that lay ahead. The couples are usually seen alone for several sessions before coming into a group. Some people are fearful of entering the group, and I am usually able to get them in by saying, truthfully in my experience, that whatever goals of therapy they have they will accomplish faster in the group.

The rules of the couples group are stated in the first session: Violence is not permitted; partners are not to discuss the other couples where they can be overheard by others; when one partner cannot attend, the other should come to sessions; terminations should never occur on the telephone, and should be announced a week in advance; and individuals should try to give feedback in a constructive way. Unlike most therapists, I do not discourage the couples from having social contact with each other outside the sessions; during the 10 years I have conducted couples groups I have seen only benefits arising from the couples becoming friends with each other. Indeed, one of the curative factors in couples groups is the caring that the participants come to have for each other. I once had in a class a psychiatric resident from Ghana who said that in his country, when a couple had a serious marital problem, the two extended families would gather together in a circle and help the couple work it out. It is unfortunate that in our country people have to pay for supportive networks. One resource rarely used by therapists in treating marital problems is the extended family of each partner; my work with family of origin is designed, in part, for this purpose.

When the couple is seen in the context of the couples group, the presence of other couples and the group process add another dimension to the therapy. Now there is a wider audience for the interactional behavior; in this atmosphere there is less blaming of each other and more focus on self. At a certain stage in the course of a couples group, each individual usually hits a plateau and starts questioning his or her own behavior or attitude toward the spouse; some even start wondering about the source of their irrational perceptions and beliefs. There is considerable variation in the readiness of people to get to this point, depending not only on the differentiating capacity of the individual for insight, but on what is happening in the marital relationship as well. Some people, of course, never get beyond blaming the spouse; some couples become stalemated this way, and treatment can only progress by avoiding their interaction and focusing on the individuals. In any event, the person starting to examine self provides my entry into trying to get the client to bring in family of origin as a way of dealing with his or her unrealistic expectations of the partner or the marriage.

Early in the work with a couple, I indicate that I make it a practice of having each individual meet with his or her own family of origin, without the spouse being present. Anticipating the anxiety that this statement precipitates, I state that the sessions are usually held toward the end of therapy, after the clients have been prepared for the family conference and can see its value. During the couples group sessions, while working directly on the marital problems, I will occasionally ask direct questions about what is happening between a spouse and his or her parents and siblings. I have noticed that although all sorts of important things may be going on in the family of origin, if you do not directly ask, clients do not tell you; they consider such events to be extrinsic to their marital problems. (I recall one fellow who said, "I don't see why you ask about my stopping at my mother's house everyday. What does that have to do with my relationship to my wife?") In addition to asking about current relationships to family-of-origin members or about the in-law relationships, from time to time I remind group members that everyone is expected to bring in original family. There are usually members of the group who, although frightened at the prospect, plan to follow through and bring in their family. Some of them report that they have even mentioned the session to selected family members who might be receptive to the idea. There are other members of the group who firmly rule out ever bringing in their family of origin. The therapists' expectations along these lines, and the varying degrees of readiness to meet that expectation on the part of the couples group members, becomes part of the culture of each group. Usually the more willing members ally themselves with the therapists, and attempt to persuade the reluctant ones to consider doing it. Some individuals become strongly motivated to work things out with a parent or sibling. After some clients have had their family-of-origin sessions they can present more convincing evidence of their value; some of the most intransigent clients have reconsidered their negative positions upon hearing these accounts.

Over the years I have developed certain techniques for dealing with the aversive response of most people to the prospect of sitting with their parents and brothers and sisters and discussing openly the heretofore avoided hard issues. The resistances assume manifold forms. An early one is when clients state that they get along fine with their family and there are no issues to be dealt with. When I get a detailed family-of-origin history, however, which disassembles the global characterization, issues become apparent in nearly every sentence. Gradually, most clients begin to see that the family-of-origin sessions not only have the potential of benefiting themselves or the marriage, but other reasons begin to emerge for having the sessions. As the agenda for the session is prepared, the marital problems recede in importance and clients gradually are induced to deal with past and present issues with their family. It is fascinating to observe how the marital conflicts, which totally preoccupied the client several weeks earlier, fade away and are replaced by the dawning realization that maybe something can be done about that longstanding guilty overcloseness or alienation from a mother, father, or sibling. Working out a better relationship with family of origin frequently becomes a goal in its own right. Some clients, however, resist the endeavor to the end, either saying that their family situation is hopeless or indicating that meeting with the family could make things much worse by "opening up a Pandora's Box." Especially difficult to deal with is the client who describes his or her family as "close and extremely loving," with the implication that it is not possible for people to love too much. Spouses' reactions to their mates' accounts of family history frequently reveal undisclosed facts. For instance, one client never mentioned the suicide of her father until her spouse brought it up. On the basis of the family histories the client is assisted in developing an agenda of issues to bring up with each and every member of the family. Each concrete issue becomes anxiety-laden. When the adult male says he always longed for affection from his father, and I suggest he tell father that in the session, his apprehensive reaction is predictable. An adult daughter preparing to tell her mother that she can no longer be responsible for mother's happiness approaches that confrontation with great fear.

I do not have spouses present in the session because the focus is on what transpired in a given individual's family as that person was growing up, long before the spouse was met. If the spouse were present, the incoming family would be inhibited from discussing sensitive issues in the presence of an "outsider" or could not resist triangling in the client's marriage instead of dealing with the relationships in *this* family. (There are occasions when I have included the spouse in order to deal with problems in the in-law relationships, but I do not consider these sessions "family-of-origin" work in the sense in which I use it.) Usually one spouse is more ready to deal with his or her family than is the other. Most of the time partners urge each other to do it even if they themselves are unwilling; as a matter of fact, I have seen some partners threaten divorce if the spouses do not attempt to work things out with their family. Only once did I have a spouse oppose the partner meeting with his family.

Most of the resistance to bringing in family of origin resides in the client, because usually when he or she becomes motivated the family follows. The reasons given by clients for not wanting to bring in original family are infinite, each one sounding most convincing and legitimate to the therapist unfamiliar with family-of-origin work ("They live too far away," "I know they would never come," "My mother is in bad health," "My father doesn't believe in psychiatrists or psychologists," and so forth). Occasionally, despite all the efforts of a client to get his or her family in, some families refuse; some of these refusals are based on clients' sabotaging the session by implicitly presenting it to the family as punishment, whereas other times there are circumstances peculiar to a given family situation that preclude such a session. I have the clients themselves take responsibility for writing and phoning and gathering their family members together to come in. Some families are scattered around the country, but in this age of jet travel, geographical distance does not present a serious barrier. Family members come in from all parts of the country, and some have traveled from overseas. The emotional barriers are far more critical, and when these are overcome the reality problems are not difficult to deal with. As the session approaches, anxiety starts building up in the client, and usually starts spreading to the family outside. I begin to get calls from various family members about a parent's poor health and whether the emotional strain of such a session could bring about a medical disaster. One message I attempt to communicate, both to the client and the family members, is that the parents or siblings themselves have issues they might like to bring up with the client or other family members.

Techniques must be modified for the family-of-origin sessions inasmuch as the parents and siblings are usually not coming in with an acknowledged need for help. Similar to when I interview a family at a workshop in front of an audience, I find it necessary to tread a fine line between dealing with meaningful things and yet not explicitly treating the incoming family members like patients. In my experience in working with many families of origin I have found that there are certain tactical and strategic errors which should be avoided. Historically, one of the earliest identified resistances in family therapy was that of the "absent member maneuver," a process whereby the family members collude to keep a significant member out of the session (Sonne, Speck, and Jungreis, 1962). This resistance is especially likely to come into play when planning family-of-origin sessions. For instance, sometimes the client is willing to bring in parents but refuses to bring in a brother or sister. Or the family shows up without an important member despite assurances that everyone would be there. Generally speaking I will not hold the session without a significant family member; the session is postponed until that person can make it. The presence of siblings is especially critical in family-of-origin sessions, and they are the ones most likely to be absent.

I believe that a male–female cotherapy team that is congruent is a potent therapeutic force; especially is this true in working with families of origin. Whenever by necessity I have had to conduct these sessions alone, I have felt undefended and powerless. Part of the reason for this is that family-of-origin sessions are so unpredictable; you never can tell what they are going to be like. Families described by clients as docile and passive sometimes turn out to be hostile and difficult, and families described as impossible sometimes create a "love in." The incoming families find it reassuring that a man and woman are seeing them, not only because both sexes are represented but because that arrangement seems to remove the session from the stereotype of psychiatry, which most people distrust. The cotherapy arrangement allows the initial human contact to take place more easily and then, throughout the session, can bring to bear the kinds of bilateral, complementary, and opposing interventions that only a well functioning cotherapy team can do.

There is considerable variation in these family-of-origin sessions; they differ in intensity, time focus, issues, degree of relatedness, amount of fusion, content, pace, awkwardness, defensiveness, and every other dimension that can occur when family members are brought together for the purpose of getting to know each other better and dealing openly with each other. One error that can be made is to accept the client's anger toward the parents or siblings at face value, and miss the positive feelings and yearnings. The natural feeling toward parents is one of ambivalence, and if the therapists support the client's bitterness toward parents, the session will rapidly go downhill. Indeed, the anger in these sessions sometimes goes in all directions (parents to their children, siblings to each other, parents to their own siblings or parents), but the deeper levels of caring almost always eventually emerge in these sessions.

The sessions are audiotaped and it is suggested that they be listened to later by all the family members, including those who could not be present, as well as the spouse. Although most of these sessions are one-shot ones (lasting now for 4 hours in two separate sessions, with a break in between), some families return for several sessions. A detailed account of a full-length case study of a couple, including couples group and family-of-origin therapy, is contained in Framo (1978b).

Following the family-of-origin sessions of both partners, most marriage relationships improve, since some of the mythologies have been cleared away and the transference distortions diminished. My theoretical formulation of change, based on the object-relation inner and outer interchanges, is in the earliest stage of hypothesis formation. Empirically speaking, however, these sessions usually work; there is something about facing and dealing with old issues with original family that seems to take the charge out of the negative reactions to the spouse. Some partners, however, following the family-of-origin sessions, having more fully discovered who they were really married to, begin to consider seriously whether or not to stay in their marriage. They agonize over such questions as the effect on the children, what a single life would be like, the financial aspects, and all the other difficult reality consequences of divorce. Some of these couples then become engaged in divorce therapy (Framo, 1978a).

The best terminations, to be sure, are those that are mutually agreed upon. Some couples terminate prematurely for various reasons, whereas I have had to terminate others unilaterally when I estimated that the couple were going nowhere in therapy. Terminations are always prepared for, and all clients are always told that my door is always open for needed sessions in the future.

Curative Factors

Despite the thousands of articles written on how and why psychotherapy works, when it does, definitive answers have not been established. Many ideas have been put forth about the root therapeutic factors, depending on the theoretical orientation of the proponent. Among the various curative elements which the more than a hundred kinds of psychotherapies have proposed are the following: the relationship to the therapist; acceptance and sensing that someone cares; emotional insight; modeling; power influences; unconditional positive regard; conditioning; systematic desensitization; corrective emotional experience; awareness of body

sensations; analysis of the transference; game-free training; restructuring; paradoxical or "illogical" problem resolution; and so forth. I can only speculate about
what is curative in my methods of treatment; independent observers might arrive at
quite different hypotheses. In the second section of this chapter I stated some
criteria for marital improvement, and in the first section I suggested some ideas as
to why family-of-origin sessions are usually helpful. I will now elaborate on a few
of those points.

Insofar as marital therapy is concerned, spouses who report a successful therapy
experience seem to have become more separate as persons, have higher self-
esteem, are more tolerant of each other's regressive features and idiosyncrasies,
can communicate more clearly about formerly anxiety-laden topics, can fight less
destructively, can treat formerly loaded issues with humor, have more realistic
expectations of marriage and of each other, are more affectionate and sexual with
each other, manifest less hostility (in its various forms) to each other, are more
accepting of the zig-zag course that intimate relationships take, and are not deeply
disappointed that they are not wildly, romantically "in love." (At the end of marital
therapy one woman said incredulously about her marriage relationship, "You
mean this is *it?*") Just how the couples arrive at this final stage is not clear to me in
terms of what I do or do not do. Usually clients perceive therapist(s)' interventions
differently than they were intended. Greater understanding of what happened in
the therapy is not always achieved by asking clients either. Jay Efran, a colleague
of mine, is fond of telling the story that when he asked a client at the end of therapy
what really helped him the most in all those months, he expected to hear some
profound insight, and instead the client replied, "It was that time when I was
feeling low and you said something like, 'Behind every cloud there is a silver
lining.'" Carl Whitaker says that one of his clients reported his most successful
session as being one in which "nobody was up to anything." As someone once put
it, the damndest things help people.

One of the things which seems to help marriages, as I stated previously, is that
the partners have a more empathic understanding of each other. Having been given
the opportunity to hear each other's life history, and in the light of knowledge of
what the spouse had to struggle with, partners find each other's behavior more
understandable. (One wife said, "I still don't like my husband's rages, but after
learning what his father did to him I know where they come from and I don't take
them personally any more."). Furthermore, I have noticed that most married
people do not really listen to each other; they are like amateur actors who wait for
their cue to recite memorized lines and do not listen to the meaning of the words of
the other actors. In marital therapy the partners have learned to listen and to really
hear each other, thereby diminishing their own preoccupations, righteousness,
and self-centeredness.

I do not fully understand why an adult meeting with his or her family of origin,
in the special way I have described, should frequently produce such profound
changes, particularly the way such sessions often affect the problems for which the

couple or family originally entered therapy. Most psychotherapies focus on unscrambling the inner life of a client and then leave it up to that person to work things out with the parents or siblings on his or her own. Individual therapy or analysis may help a man gain insight into the unconscious reasons why he cannot get close to his father, yet in actuality he and father may remain distant. Psychoanalysts and other individual therapists will not get involved with healing the real problems in family relationships. Some otherwise very mature adults are currently enslaved in their relationship with their parents (such as the executive who must call his mother every day), or are completely cut off from a hated brother or sister. The family-of-origin method is designed to deal with these kinds of problems—which certainly have their effects on the marital or parental functioning.

In addition to adults hurting from difficulties with their parents and siblings in the present, they are also locked into the fantasy family of the past. As a matter of fact, the real source of marital conflicts of today, in my view, has to do with unconscious attempts to deal with and master that fantasy family, using the current intimates as stand-ins.[6] Something happens to that repressed fantasy family when the adult meets with his or her actual, real original family and confronts them with the heretofore avoided issues which had existed between them. Dealing with the real, external figures seems to loosen the grip of the introjects of those figures and exposes the past to current realities. Following the sessions the old family can never go back to the way they used to be, and the adult client frequently begins to perceive the spouse and children in a more realistic way. Family-of-origin sessions change marital relationships in many different ways. For instance, the wife whose husband complained of her being "bossy, super-independent, and not seeming to need me," in her family-of-origin session told her parents she was giving up her role of taking care of them and instead wanted them to take care of her. When her parents at least tried to meet this need, she could allow herself to be more vulnerable with her husband. See the case history in Framo (1978b) for a more complete account on how working things out with family-of-origin directly can help a marriage.

My interpretations to a couple do take historical factors into account, but in vivo. That is to say, since I have seen the actual parents and siblings I am in a better position to point out how patterns and behaviors from the old family are being inappropriately played out with the spouse and children. Some of these interpretations catch hold on the basis of what is customarily called "insight." Insight is a much abused term, particularly under attack by those who claim that "understanding" never really changed anybody. Insight, as I see it, is an extraordinarily

---

[6]It is not surprising that among the anger-provoking insults spouses will hurl at their partner during an argument are such statements as the following: "You're just like your mother," or "You're not going to treat me the way your father treated your mother," or "You keep forgetting I'm your husband, not your father."

complicated phenomenon combining cognitive, emotional, and motoric elements. From my viewpoint, unless insight leads to behavioral or attitudinal change, it is not insight.

Although ideally it is best if each member of a family or both marital partners change, it is not necessary for each individual, qua individuals, to change if there are to be relational alterations. Small system or interactional changes can have powerful effects, such as an excluded father being more involved in the family, or a couple's fight style not having such deadly intensity, or the children being able to deal with mother directly instead of having to go through grandmother, and so forth.

Transference is a ubiquitous human phenomenon and will develop over time in any significant relationship. Over the years, as my experience accumulated, however, I have come to deemphasize the transference to the therapist(s) and instead I now focus attention on the transference distortions which occur between the intimates. While transference to the therapist(s) will always be present, a therapist can choose not to deal with it explicitly, unless it is seriously getting in the way of therapy. For example, when a couple insist on my telling them how I feel about them, I indicate that my feelings are not as important as their feelings about each other, since they will be dealing with each other long after I have been forgotten. One of the reasons I started doing couples groups was to dilute the transference to me, since some couples had such strong needs to view me as judge, rescuer, or persecutor that they were unable to move in treatment.

Family or marital therapy is much more likely to elicit countertransference feelings than is individual or group therapy because of the ways in which the ghosts of the therapist's own family intrude into the treatment room (Framo, 1968). I agree with Bowen (1978) that the best safeguard against inappropriate reactions to a family or couple is for the therapist to get his or her own house in order and improve his or her own functioning. This goal can best be accomplished by working out problems with one's own original family, as well as family of procreation.

Effectiveness of the Approach

Any theoretician always feels somewhat abashed when he has to admit that concrete, hard data has not been provided as evidence for the effectiveness of his conceptual approach to psychotherapy. The discipline of psychology is more committed to research than any of the other mental health disciplines; as a matter of fact, in some quarters any psychologist who does not do numerical studies with proper experimental design and probability statistics is regarded as not really being a psychologist. Having been originally trained as a clinical psychologist, my mortification should be complete because I have done no systematic research on my treatment methods. In a recent paper, Wells and Dezen (1978) stated, ". . . a number of these [family therapy] schools (in some instances led by major figures in the family therapy movement, the very role models for the aspiring practitioner) have never submitted their methods to empirical testing and, indeed, seem oblivious to such a need." p. 266

Still, I am not yet deserving of being drummed out of the corps. In demonstration of my not being oblivious to research needs not only did I prepare a lengthy survey of family interaction research in the early days of family therapy (Framo, 1965b), but in 1967 I organized the first national conference on family interaction research with 29 family researchers and family therapists, the proceedings of which were published in a book (Framo, 1972). In the introduction to that book I stated the perennial basic conflict between the clinician and the researcher:

> (S)ystematic researchers would argue that, while clinicians can provide vital information and inspiration for the formulation of hypotheses via hunches and impressions, opinions are still opinions, unable to be proved or refuted by any scientific standard . . . there is general agreement that observations must be organized into theory, that theories should be operationally stated and put in the form of testable hypotheses, and that variables should be manipulated by certain rules so as to permit the data to confirm or disprove the hypotheses by other than personal means. Only in this way, the researchers state, can laws of broad applicability be abstracted from the individual instance. The clinicians dispute this thesis, saying that problems are defined by researchers in terms that are most convenient to research, and that experimentalists, in their quest for scientific objectivity, end up measuring pallid, trivial variables and distill all humanity from their investigations.

The dilemma between studying "the significant or the exact," as someone put it, keeps many clinician-theoreticians from doing research. As soon as one starts converting theory into operational definitions, much is lost in translation, and one ends up measuring something that bears little resemblance to the original.

There are many other intricate problems associated with doing research in this area, particularly therapy outcome research. There are such technical problems as adequacy of control groups, how to handle no-treatment groups who seek help on their own, the homogeneity of samples, the size of a sample, finding sophisticated measuring instruments, and so forth. It seems to me that the field needs some creative designs for studies that will take into account the unique features of marital and family therapy. From whose vantage point do we evaluate success or failure? Marital and family therapy differ from all other psychotherapies; each person has a different agenda for therapy goals, both stated and secret, and the goal usually is that someone else should change. How can client satisfaction be the sole criterion of change? If a divorced woman feels she has a second chance for happiness with a man, but if the man says he wants to marry her and does not want her child, would the therapy be successful if the clients were pleased that the family therapist went along with institutionalizing the child?

In addition to the enormous complexity of the treatment situation, which can create formidable barriers to systematic investigation, there are also the practical obstacles to doing research in clinical settings, especially the problem of staff cooperation. There are very few clinical settings where the clinical director will allow interference in the routine; psychotherapists generally do not want any researcher examining ("tampering with"?) their treatment. Gurman and Kniskern (1978), in a comprehensive review of over 200 marital and family therapy outcome studies, have performed a valuable service by specifying criteria for evaluating the adequacy of outcome studies. The problem with these criteria is that they would be nearly impossible to meet in a clinical setting (such as random assignment of families and couples, or, more difficult to meet, random assignment of therapists—a criterion which would require a huge clinic).

In the academic setting where I now work, a doctoral program in clinical psychology, the students are rightfully preoccupied with getting their doctorate as quickly as possible. A problem exists in communicating about systems in an academic clinical psychology setting, as in most psychiatric settings (Framo, 1976b), where the study of the individual is paramount. More traditional studies in clinical psychology are favored by students over family interaction research because, frankly, the latter are more difficult to do and take more time. A few motivated students have done their dissertations in this area, but they are exceptional and, besides, they selected the kinds of studies that were feasible within their doctoral time frame.

I am the kind of clinician who needs to step back from his practice and conceptualize about what has been observed. One quandary of a theoretician–clinician is how to treat and conceptualize, teach, write, give workshops, and still have time to do systematic studies. I have had fantasies of having a support staff to handle all the inquiries and requests that I get, and a large group of research assistants who would study and evaluate my treatment methods. There are very few family therapists in the country who work with family of origin as I do, and I think it necessary to confirm with hard data my clinical impressions on how powerful such sessions can be in producing change. Not only treatment results need to be examined, utilizing systematic follow-up, but greater understanding is needed on why and how sessions with family of origin can break up deep-seated attitudes and behavior patterns.

Training of Marital-Family Therapists

I believe that family therapists were "trained" by their original families, and the formal training they get today refines that lifelong process. In my judgment, while there are certain kinds of family problems that can be handled by any reasonably intelligent person or paraprofessional trained in the problem-solving method, there are other, more complex situations, which require the kind of "natural" who has been trained as a general psychotherapist first and later as a family therapist. That is to say, I believe that every family therapist should have had individual and peer group therapy experience as well as experience with the whole range of emotional disturbances in varied clinical settings. Intensive supervision by a supervisor who knows what he or she is doing is also a must in the training of any therapist. Whether or not those individual or group therapy experiences should occur prior to or concurrent with the learning of marital or family therapy is a moot question, open to study. This viewpoint of prior individual and group therapy experience is consistent with my theoretical perspective of exploring the relationship between the intrapsychic and the transactional. There is something about working through people's internal and interpersonal defenses, it seems to me, that helps one know how to deal with the intimate system operations. If, for example, a man has an internalized fear of women which he handles by projection of anticipated attack from his wife, we are in a position not only to understand why he beats up his wife, but to help him deal directly with his mother about his earlier fear of her.

It is interesting that several family therapists have recommended that family therapy trainees have a personal therapy experience (meaning individual therapy), but no one recommends that trainees should have marital or family therapy with his or her spouse, family of origin, or family of procreation. While I do not think it should be a requirement, I personally believe such experiences to be among the best preparations for becoming a family therapist (Framo, 1979). Bowen's method of training includes having trainees conduct geneological searches in the quest for self, an extremely valuable method of training. In my classes there are no formal examinations; the only requirement is the writing of a family biography. Students have reported that this was the most painful and difficult, yet the most meaningful assignment of their lives. I have become aware, further, of the high rate of divorce among family therapy trainees, a phenomenon insufficiently studied. One could speculate that the trainee and the spouse are living in such different worlds that they lose touch with each other. The foregoing is one of the reasons I encourage trainees to include their spouse or other family member in certain aspects of my training program.

There is insufficient space to go into detail on the didactic and experiential aspects of my training program. I believe that trainees should be exposed to the various theories and methods of working with families so that eventually they will develop a style that is comfortable for them. In addition to becoming familiar with the classical literature in the field, I think trainees can learn a lot about marital and family dynamics from plays, movies, and novels. Another area that is neglected in family therapy training programs is knowledge about ethnic family cultures. Other aspects of training, such as group supervision, live supervision, simulated families, videotape, program evaluation, and so forth each would require separate treatment, a task beyond the purposes of this paper. Although I stress the value of students working things out with their own family, I do believe they must learn skills. Overall, however, it is the personal development of trainees, rather than *just* their technical skill alone, which will determine their effectiveness as family therapists in dealing with what I have called the "gut" issues of family life—the passions, hates, loves, injustices, sacrifices, comforts, disappointments, frustrations, ambivalences, and gratifications of family life. These are the universals that everyone raised in a family has had to struggle with.

10

In-Laws and Out-Laws: A Marital Case of Kinship Confusion[1] (1977)

After 5 years of working together in cotherapy in our evening practice, my wife and I should have arrived at the point where we could predict after the first few sessions which couples were going to make it in marital therapy. In all honesty, however, our predictions have turned out to be pretty lousy. Couples who looked hopeless in the beginning often ended up with a new, vital marriage with the same partner, and others we were sure were going to put their marriage together got nowhere in therapy or later divorced. Considering that behavioral scientists have isolated only about 50 out of the million or so dimensions of marriage, maybe we do not have to turn in our credentials.

In any event, we were most pessimistic initially that Fred and Lynn's marriage had much of a chance of lasting in any meaningful way. Lynn had a whiney, high-pitched, irritating voice with which she righteously harangued her husband, and Fred had that maddening, smiling passivity that drives people up walls. Although on one level we liked them, we both had fantasies of choking them; evidently they stimulated some aspect of *our* shared introjects. Lynn was highly motivated for therapy *for* her husband; she was not only defensively impervious to any point of view but her own but was incapable of looking at her part in any transaction. It was more difficult to get Fred to commit himself to therapy because he had had a bad experience with a psychiatrist where each had engaged in a

Reprinted with permission from P. Papp (Ed.) *Family Therapy: Full-Length Case Studies*. New York: Gardner Press, 1977. Copyright © 1977, Gardner Press, Inc.
[1]Mary D. Framo, M.S.S., my wife, was cotherapist with me in the treatment of this couple. Views of this case were exchanged back and forth during the therapy and Mary also contributed her impressions to this writeup. Both separate and concurrent opinions are specified in this paper.

contest as to who could keep silent longer. Besides, Fred was weakly motivated to stay married, whereas Lynn desperately wanted to keep her husband. I do not know whether it was these challenges or the tangled relationship between Lynn and Fred's family that intrigued me conceptually that made me decide to continue with them. Furthermore, I planned to put them in a couples group, where a lot of help would be available in handling them (for a description of my method of conducting couples' groups, see Framo, 1973).

Fred and Lynn's problems were rather interesting. Both in their thirties, physically attractive, and moneyed, they were married 3 years and had a 2-year-old girl and a baby boy. Fred, very successful with his own business, had recently left his wife and children and moved into his parents' house because "I wasn't sure I wanted to be married." After a few days he had decided he did not want to break up his family, and when he returned home he agreed to come for therapy. When asked how she saw their problems, Lynn poured forth the following story, insinuating that once the therapists heard it they would look at Fred in astonishment and start therapizing him forthwith. Lynn said that they married in another city, where her own family was, and moved here, where his family was. Although Fred's sister Elaine vehemently opposed his marrying Lynn, she and Fred's mother, Ann, actively tried to ingratiate themselves with Lynn by buying her gifts, inviting her daily to go shopping with them, and dropping in to see her every day. Lynn said that initially she was flattered and pleased to have another family to take the place of her own; she had not recognized that her acceptance was based on being adopted and absorbed into the old system. Lynn said, however, "All that togetherness got to be more than I could handle. We had no life of our own because his family members were always under our feet." But Lynn said she was less bothered by the overcloseness than she was by the unusual displays of affection between Fred and his mother and sister. She said that Fred kissed his mother and sister "full on the lips, and they sat on his lap often and he patted their rear ends and caressed their legs. It's positively disgusting the way they slobber over him; everybody notices it and comments on it, and when I mention their behavior to his mother and sister they say, 'But we *love* him; we're a close, affectionate family.'" Lynn went on to say with intense feeling, "He knows I can't stand it; it eats me up alive. I told him to stop it for my sake. I want to fight for my husband and get him away from them." Lynn said she could not understand why Elaine's husband (Elaine had recently married) did not seem to be bothered by the near-incestuous relationship between his wife and brother-in-law. Lynn began withdrawing from his family, yet she manifested increasing preoccupation with them, becoming furious whenever Fred visited his family. She was giving contradictory messages, however; she felt spurned and hurt when Fred's sister did not invite her to be maid of honor at her wedding. Fred felt he was being forced to choose between his original family and his wife and he was resentful over having to sneak around to see his mother and sister. I did not realize Fred even had a father until Lynn said, "Fred's Dad is a nothing, a zero, completely dominated by his wife." The incident which precipitated the open rift occurred when Lynn approached her mother-in-law for help in handling her problems with Fred, and her mother-in-law asked to speak to Fred alone, at which point she advised her son to get a divorce. Lynn had not realized that not only is blood thicker than water but that it is wise in this world to know who your friends and family really are. Fred's private conference with his mother made him leave Lynn, but after he told us some history of his family we understood why he again left his parents' home to return to his wife.

Fred said that while he was growing up he hardly knew his parents. Since his parents had a business in which they worked together 18 hours a day, he and his sister, who was 5 years younger than he, spent a great deal of time together and were "very, very, very close." With the utterance of each "very" I got an image of one intertwined body of fused parts. He said, "She came to me for everything, I tucked her in bed and read her stories and gave her baths and listened to her; I guess I was like a father to her." Fred's mother was 18 years older than Fred and his father was 15 years older than his mother, age gaps which promoted the realness of being an oedipal victor. As a matter of fact, Fred's mother became openly involved with another man and when Fred was 15 years old she asked him if she should leave his father. Fred said he was flabbergasted at being placed in this position, and finally asked mother to stay because of the younger sister. Mother's boyfriend became like a member of the family and Fred said he felt closer to that man than he did to his own father. He was bewildered by his father's indifference about the situation and infuriated at him for doing nothing about mother's affair, but he said nothing. Although the other man died some years ago, to this day nobody has ever said anything about this affair, which went on for years; Fred said it was like an elephant in the living room with everyone pretending it was not there. He and his father became so alienated in subsequent years that when one entered the room the other would leave. In more recent years, Fred said, he and father had made some sort of peace with each other and they were now partners in the business, although one got the impression listening to Fred that his father, in effect, worked for him. Early in the therapy Fred said, longingly, "My father and I get along now, but I don't really know him and I'd like to have a relationship with him before he dies." This kind of statement is always my cue to state that our therapy includes bringing in the family of origin of each partner for a session, usually toward the end of therapy, after they have changed and are ready to deal with their parents and siblings when they bring them in. (This method of involving adults in sessions with their family of origin is explicated in Framo, 1976a). Although most people fervidly rule out such sessions for themselves, invariably they encourage the spouse to bring in his or her original family, reasoning that all the stuff the partner had been dumping on them would revert back to the original targets. In Lynn's case it was different: She strongly opposed Fred's bringing in his family. This position made us recognize that she had an investment in his

family which went beyond her surface complaints. Her family background provided the clues for understanding her secret agenda of wanting to be the daughter
in his family, something which could never be.

Lynn's parents divorced when she was 2 years old and she was raised by her
mother, grandparents, and mother's three sisters. She spoke glowingly of her
relationship with her mother, saying they were very close and mother was "a
perfect mother." Lynn was extremely bitter toward her father, saying that he had
nothing to do with her when she was small, and that when she was a teenager he
would only see her every few years when he went to her city for a convention.
Their relationship was characterized primarily by conflict followed by long
periods of hurt withdrawal on both sides. She knew little about the causes for the
divorce because her mother did not want to talk about it; for years her father had
been trying to tell "his side of the story but I refused to listen to it because he'd tell a
bunch of lies about my mother. I owe her a great deal and I owe him nothing." I
initially got the impression that Lynn had had almost no contact with her father
through the years, and it was only when pressed for more details that she
reluctantly indicated that he sent her gifts, telephoned and wrote her frequently,
and at one point took her to Europe with him and one of his daughters from his
second marriage. Then Lynn added, acidly, "He never came to my wedding or
invited me to his, and he never introduced me as his daughter to his second wife,
who threatened to leave him if he had much to do with me." Lynn's mother
remarried when Lynn was 13, and after that man was killed in an accident her
mother married for a third time, this present marriage being described as "disastrous." When we suggested that at some point we would have a session with her
and her parents she said, as anticipated, "No way. If you insist on that you'll never
see me again. My father still hates my mother after all these years and feels I have
sided with her, which I have because I have good reason to." Then, crying, she
said, "Do you think I give a damn about that man who's supposed to be my
father?" I indicated that if she could ever bring herself to deal with her parents, and
if I could give a father back to her, she would be less hooked into her husband's
family and she and Fred might have a chance to have a real marriage. Her
uncharacteristic silence for several minutes following that intervention gave us our
first hope that maybe change was possible in this situation. Insofar as Lynn
rejected her own yearning for a father, she attributed to her husband an attachment
to his family which she endlessly complained about but envied. Fred was also the
target of her displaced fury. The fact that Fred's primary loyalty was indeed to his
original family does not negate the validity of her dynamic efforts. For me, the best
way of resolving this problem was to take Lynn's problems back to where they
began, to bring her and her father together and to strengthen that relationship. At
this point in the therapy, however, she was nowhere near ready to do this.

When Fred and Lynn joined a couples' group with two other couples, Lynn
proceeded to impress them with the juicy details of Fred's sexy relationship with
his mother and sister. She went on and on about Fred's family, expecting the other

two couples to be sufficiently shocked to tell Fred he should renounce his original family. However, the other two couples had been in a group for some time and were too sophisticated to take Lynn's words at face value; as a matter of fact, one group member picked up quickly how obsessed she seemed to be about his family. No matter where a discussion started in the group she referred the topic back to his family. Mary and I and the group made valiant attempts to get Lynn off his family and onto herself. It did not work; we would get a flood of self-justifying words. I then used an intervention that had been quite effective in the past with people who were openly critical of their in-laws: I told Lynn that by carping about his family she was doing herself a disservice and sabotaging her own goals. So long as she criticized his family, he, of course, had to defend them and never had to get in touch with his own anger toward them *because she was expressing it for him*. I had not reckoned with Lynn's formidable defense; that confrontation brought a change in her behavior for only 2 weeks, and when Fred still could not acknowledge any negative feelings about his family, she went back to her broken record. I began to feel helpless. I was supposed to be the expert; besides, all those assistant therapists in the group could not budge them either.

Now to be sure we knew that the sexual overtones in the behavior between Fred and his mother and sister would have given a psychoanalyst a field day; the oedipal interpretations were so obvious you could get them for half price. But we wanted to deal with this material on our terms and with our timing, not his wife's. Moreover, since this "sexual behavior" was so egosyntonic for him we had to discover another route to changing the order of Fred's priorities. Luckily, Fred's family provided an incident that for the first time made Fred deal with them in a different way. They did something which really got him mad at them; these are the serendipitous things that sometimes help the therapy to go. Fred was much better off financially than his sister and brother-in-law, and his parents, feeling their two children should have equal material advantages, would buy things for Elaine and charge them to the business where Fred and Dad were "partners." On the occasion of this particular incident, while Fred and Lynn were out of town, his parents went into Fred's house and removed some valuable items to give to his sister. Fred said that not only did they violate the privacy of his home, but they lied to him, saying they took the items for themselves rather than his sister. (It should be mentioned that in recent months, since Elaine and Lynn had had a falling out, there had been no contact between Fred and his sister. Fred's parents acted as the communicators between their two children.) On seeing Fred's anger to his family Lynn was triumphant, but we all had to sit on her to get her to keep her two cents out of it. When Fred hinted that he could get back at his family by cutting off their funds we began to get some sense of the power he had in that original family, in contrast to the relative impotence he manifested in dealing with his wife. At this stage of therapy the most Fred could do relative to his original family was to ask his parents not to come into his house when he was not there. He was not yet ready to deal with his family about the real issues.

Because the sexual relationship is extremely sensitive to other difficulties in a marriage, it was no surprise to discover that this couple had sexual problems. In one session Fred said that one reason he left Lynn was because of his dissatisfaction with their sex life. This statement made Lynn very angry; she said she was the one who had to approach him for sex and, besides, how dare he bring this up in the group without first discussing it with her at home? This interchange confirmed further Fred's reluctance to confront Lynn, except in the sanctuary of the group; Lynn, too, often said she had to come to group to find out what Fred was thinking. I have seen this phenomenon many times and have come to believe that one of the reasons people go to conjoint marital therapy is to provide a safe setting to tell their mates what they really feel or think. Husbands and wives, I have learned, are often afraid of each other. When they can level with each other, on all levels, on their own, they are probably ready to terminate therapy, or perhaps the marriage. In any event, Fred related that in the past he had always been attracted by "showgirl, trashy broads," and one of the reasons he was uncertain about being married was that he was not sure he wanted to give up a swinging bachelor life. Lynn, he said, was more refined, like his sister and, moreover, she had a habit of compulsively washing her genital area before and after sex, which turned him off. The material that Fred had given was rich. I wondered to myself whether Fred split the erotic introjects of mother and sister into the familiar whore-nun dichotomy that men fantasize about women, and I thought he was bound to have difficulty relating sexually to a wife who chastely washed away dirty sex. I could not resist the temptation to communicate a piece of this thinking to him by wondering aloud whether he did not feel unfaithful to his mother and sister when he married Lynn. Following that observation Fred started giggling and then went into paroxysms of laughter he could not stop. His uncontrollable laughter contagiously spread to the rest of the group, suggesting that a universal theme had been triggered off.

In addition to exploring the deeper cross-currents in the marriage, I also dealt with the more external manifestations of the disturbed relationship. From time to time I used such techniques as quid pro quo negotiations, paradoxical instructions, task assignments, clarifying of communication, and the feedback technique (where one partner must listen and repeat back the other's message until the content and emotional meaning are heard correctly). Fred and Lynn had to repeat the messages many times before the partner agreed that it was right. Fred's withdrawal and inability to share opinions or feelings was based in part on his feeling of being overwhelmed by her barrages and his inability to match her clever use of words. Audiotape playback of Lynn's monologue sometimes helped her realize how she must sound to others and why people often closed their ears to her; Fred also came to see how silence can be more devastating than screaming. Closely connected with their style of communication were their fight styles (Bach and Wyden, 1969) and their difficulty in reconciling the natural ambivalence of love and hate that exists in all intimate relationships (Charny, 1969). Compared to her Howitzers, Fred felt he had a pop gun; besides, her belt line was so high and she was so sensitive to criticism that Fred had to be most circumspect in dealing with issues with her. On the other hand, Fred's dirty-fighting technique of avoidance of fights and being Mr. Nice Guy did not change until he observed the angry interchange in other couples and came to learn that intimacy without conflict is impossible.

As the sessions progressed Fred became more assertive and unwilling to tolerate Lynn's onslaughts. His anger grew to match hers, culminating in a fist fight between them at home followed by Fred again leaving her to live with his parents. I was discouraged anew by this turn of events, although the fist fight in their case was at least an indication that Fred was relying less on camouflaged and silent hostilities. Mary was more hopeful about them than I, and the group's impressions were mixed. I myself learned from this experience that sometimes physical violence can paradoxically communicate that important matters are at stake; it can show deep concern and can represent a desperate bid to be taken seriously. Fred kept telling Lynn that she was too needy and demanding; he was alluding to what Martin (1976) has described as the "lovesick" wife. Lynn got very upset at this, saying, "I want to give him so much and he wants to give me so little." Group members kept telling her that she sounded like she wanted to possess him 100%, and that the hungrier she was, the more he moved away from her; they felt Fred could give more if she stopped pushing. With respect to her obsession with his family, she was repeatedly given feedback that it was his family, not hers.

Among the reasons I've come to believe that couples group therapy is the treatment of choice for premarital, marital, and separation and divorce problems is that the other couples provide not only models of how marital struggles can be worked out but also models of what to avoid. An event took place in the group that had the serendipitous effect of stimulating their movement in the therapy. Another couple in the group was planning to divorce, and the turmoil this couple was going through really shook up Fred and Lynn. For the first time they faced the real possibility of divorce, with its attendant pain. At this time another therapeutic dimension of couples groups emerged. Certain events in a group can create a contagion of affect which reawakens in full force early, forgotten feelings. This phenomenon seems to have the same effect as Paul's (1976) cross-confrontation technique in reviving old suppressed or repressed feelings. The transactions of the other couple put Lynn in touch with her unremembered anguish surrounding the divorce of her parents, and Fred connected with the shock and anger about his parents' near-divorce of many years ago. Both of them, like everyone else whose parents had had bad marriages, consciously wanted better marriages than their parents. Furthermore, basically, neither partner wanted to lose the other. I myself became convinced again of the old adage about psychotherapy—that people do not change unless they *have* to, when they feel it in the gut, and when the consequences of not changing are unacceptable. Shortly after their fist fight, Fred moved back with his wife again and they arranged to go away together to a resort area for a few days where they planned to "talk over our problems." Fred said he wanted to tell Lynn how difficult it was for him to balance all his roles of son, father, brother, and husband, and Lynn had wanted to tell him she could more see how she was driving him away. "Instead of talking, however," Fred said, "we swam, had some great meals, slept late, made love, and then we didn't need to talk." (Remember the old advice of family doctors to "take a vacation"?) They were both, by now, strongly motivated to work on self, and the enormous resistance to bringing in original families had faded. Now I was ready to bring to bear that most powerful of therapy techniques, family-of-origin sessions.

I have become convinced, as have Bowen (Anonymous 1972, and Bowen 1974), Boszormenyi-Nagy and Spark (1973), Haas (1968), and Whitaker (1976), that working things out directly, face-to-face, with the family of origin, rather than via the transference with a therapist, can have a powerful effect on the original problems for which people come to therapy. Verily, my experience with this method has persuaded me that one session with the family of origin, conducted in a specific kind of way, is usually far more potent and effective than numerous regular therapy sessions. It needs to be kept in mind that this method does not just consist of bringing in family of origin; clients need to be prepared to really deal with and confront their original family members in special kinds of ways (see Framo, 1976a).[2] The clients' inordinate unwillingness and outright refusal to involve their parents and brothers and sisters in the treatment process testifies to the great power of this approach. Considerable experience is needed with the method before a marital or family therapist learns how to deal with the resistances. One of the reasons I integrate couples group therapy with family-of-origin work is that in attempting to overcome the nearly instinctive aversion to bringing in original family I will use whatever help I can get. I push in this direction forcefully because of my convictions about what these sessions can do. An atmosphere develops in the groups whereby everybody is expected to bring in their original families. Bringing them in has become almost like a final exam before graduation, and the group members exercise considerable pressure on others to do it, even while they are frightened to do it themselves. When the reluctant members see the leaps in progress made by those who have their sessions, they become more willing to consider it.

While Lynn was now intellectually prepared to consider bringing in her parents, when we got right down to it she was terrified of having her parents come in together. She said that her father would not sit in the same room with her mother. In addition, she was not sure her father would even come in with her alone. I told

[2]In recent years I have had a number of requests from family therapists to have sessions with their families of origin. Although the preparation for these sessions has to be foreshortened, since these therapists are not regular clients in ongoing couple or family therapy, even these brief encounters, according to those who have had them, have proved worthwhile and productive. No other publication of mine has prompted so many letters from professional therapists in terms of how the family-of-origin paper has affected not only their professional practice but their personal lives as well. There is, I believe, a universal longing to try at least to come to terms with parents before they die.

her I had confidence in her and that when she herself really wanted him in she would find a way. Late one night I got a call from Lynn and she said, "Waddaya-know, my dad said he'd be glad to come in. I'm surprised." Further preparation of Lynn for the session consisted of going over her family history again, this time in more detail. She was again resistive to the suggestion from all of us that she listen to her dad's side of the story, saying that she could not do that to her mother. I said that listening to him did not make her a disloyal traitor to her mother. Her fixed view of her father seemed so immutable that I wondered whether the session would accomplish much. Mixed in with her resentment and defensiveness, however, were the detectable signs of great foreboding that are prodromal for family-of-origin sessions. I have speculated that perhaps one basis for this intense fear is that people must feel they were loved by their parents, and there always exists the risk that they will discover otherwise, so they are afraid to expose themselves to this last chance to find out the truth. The group was supportive of Lynn around her anxiety about the session, and they helped her delineate the issues she would take up with her father. Lynn knew that she would be on her own in the session with Dad, that even Fred would not be present.

Mr. T., Lynn's father, was a prominent research scientist in a nearby city, and when we met him we were struck with his obvious interest in Lynn and her welfare, contrary to her statements about his disinterest in her. In the early part of the session Lynn could not contain herself and told her father how she had felt rejected by him all her life, that he had abandoned her as a child, and that through the years had little to do with her. She said the rejection got confirmed when he did not come to her wedding and did not invite her to his when he married again. Her father was taken back by this onslaught, and keeping in mind our belief that incoming parents need support, we cautioned Lynn to slow down and listen. Obviously relieved that finally Lynn agreed to listen to his version of past events, he told the following story. He said that his marriage to Lynn's mother failed because his wife put her own family before him (sound familiar?). He said that they lived with his mother-in-law, and when his marriage relationship worsened his wife and mother-in-law teamed up to get a court order evicting him from the house. Furthermore, they had the money to hire "tough" lawyers who managed to legally block all his efforts to see Lynn. Mr. T. cried as he remembered, not only the humiliation of the experience, but the torment over being cut off from all access to his little girl. Lynn was astonished at this story. She went through a period of great confusion, trying to reconcile her lifelong animosity toward her father with this new information that made the bitterness untenable and inappropriate. She had never seen her father cry before and she did not know how to deal with it, except to cry herself with a perplexity that seemed to say, "Damn it, I'm not supposed to care for you. You're my pet hate." They went on to talk about the misunderstandings and miscommunications that had occurred through the years, but Lynn kept going back to that stunning realization: "You mean you didn't see me when I was little because you were legally *prevented* from doing so? My God, do you know what this means to me?" A number of other issues were discussed during the session but the foregoing interchange overshadowed everything else. However, another issue came up that was important. Mr. T.'s present wife could not tolerate any mention of his previous wife or child, and whenever Lynn visited him she could not stay at their house and instead had to stay with Mr. T.'s sister. Mr. T. decided at this session that he was no longer going to allow his present wife to determine the kind of relationship he was going to have with Lynn and that she would be welcome in his home any time. Before he left the session he asked me for the name of a marital therapist in his home town because he wanted to work on his problems with his present wife.

Following the session with her dad, Lynn had to face her mother with the truth; and for the first time she got angry at her mother, not only for what her mother and grandmother did to keep her father from her, but for concealing the facts all these years. The rigid dichotomy of father-devil and mother-saint began to dissolve, and this external shift was reflected in an inner rearrangement which in turn created some new behaviors in Lynn. Her voice lost much of its stridency, she began talking with her father for the first time about what was going on between her and Fred and his family, and everyone in the group noticed her lessening preoccupation with Fred's family. Since people fear not only change in themselves, but also a change in their intimate other, it was not surprising that Fred subtly began trying to nudge Lynn back to some of her old ways. It became obvious that Lynn's behavior had served a defensive function for him vis-a-vis his family, and when this time she did not cooperate he was forced to face his own conflicts about them. Fred, furthermore, had progressed so much in therapy that only a few interpretative comments were needed to block these efforts to use Lynn. There was now no escaping the need for Fred to deal with his family. He handled his anxiety about the session by doing a lot of preliminary work with each parent alone prior to the session. Although he did not want to be met with any surprises in the session, the one person he did not speak to was his sister Elaine. He had not seen her for a long time because of the hard feelings between his sister and his wife, and also because, as he put it, "Elaine's so damn spoiled I really didn't want to see her myself." Since his parents were the go-betweens, his mother informed Elaine about the session. Some members of the group developed hypotheses about what would happen during Fred's family conference (such as whether the family would discuss the other man in mom's life), and Lynn said she was really looking forward to listening to the tape of the session.

Both of Fred's parents and his sister Elaine were present for the session. Elaine and Fred were polite to each other, with the kind of controlled wariness that old lovers display when they have not seen each other for a long time; they had to be careful not to let the other know they still cared. Dad, looking like the grandfather of Fred, said almost nothing, and Mom, a handsome, well-dressed woman, did most of the talking. It quickly became apparent that Fred called the shots in this family, however; whenever he started to speak everyone deferred to him. This was a Fred we had never seen before. Mom, early in the session, brought up the subject of her relationship with the other man. (Fred, it will be recalled, had prepared his mother to do so.) She attempted to justify it by saying that she came from a family where money was extremely important. She had married Fred's father, a much older man, because he had money, but shortly after they married he lost his business and in order to regain his wife's love he worked 18 hours a day in a new business. She said, "My husband came from humble beginnings and would have been satisfied with less, but I spent the money faster than he could make it. So I don't blame him in a way. Still, he was paying more attention to the business than to me and finally I told him, 'You either stop being married to the business or I'm getting a divorce.'" It was apparently at that point that she asked Fred, at the age of 15, whether she should divorce, and also at that time she got involved with this other man who had money. The tension in the room began to rise at this point, and Fred confronted his father with how angry he had been for tolerating having this other man living in their house. Fred's father, paralyzed with feeling at that point, could not speak. Recognizing his inability to deal with this loaded area, we moved on to the relationship between Elaine and Fred. Elaine said that all she remembered about her childhood was being alone, except for Fred. She cried when she remembered the day Fred told her he was getting married. She was quite open about her jealousy, but we were startled when Fred said he had the same feelings of shock when she got married. At that point in the session Elaine switched from tears to intense anger, saying that Lynn was responsible for the alienation that existed in their family. Other issues were discussed, such as the open display of affection between Fred and sister and mother, the resentment over Fred "ruling" them, and Fred's trying again, unsuccessfully, to reach his father. When the session ended we knew there would have to be another one, the next time including Lynn and Elaine's husband. In addition to the unfinished business from this session, there was the issue of the parents trying to push Fred into taking Elaine's husband, Barry, into his business. We also knew that the two natural enemies, Elaine and Lynn, had to work out some rapprochement in order for their respective marriages to survive.

Following Fred's family-of-origin session, Fred's mother got in touch with Lynn and the two of them became friendly again. Lynn was very pleased by this development but several members of the group cautioned her that perhaps her mother-in-law was using her in a tactical maneuver to gain favor with Fred. Besides, this alliance was an unstable one since Elaine was now on the outside of the triangle and could not stay out. Lynn had changed considerably by this time and had more objectivity about the situation. Fred felt that while his session with his family had accomplished much, he was concerned about the rift between him and his sister, as well as his inability to get through to his Dad. When he mentioned that he hardly knew Elaine's husband I suggested he have lunch with Barry to get to know him. The following week, coincidentally, Barry invited him to lunch and Fred reported that when they got together he realized for the first time Barry's resentment of him.

In preparation for the session to include Fred, his parents and sister, Lynn, and

Barry, Lynn was warned to play it cool. She had a lot of feeling about being scapegoated, but did manage to be less reactive. In this session several important things happened. Barry told Fred in no uncertain terms that Fred was arrogant, that he treated his parents badly, and he said, "Everybody in this family is supposed to cater to you." He went on to say that Fred's worship of money indicated a distorted sense of values about life. Fred's dad, speaking up for the first time, noted that Fred had some of his mother's preoccupation with money. Fred said that before he would take Barry into the business Barry would have to prove himself. Barry said, "Don't do me any favors." Mom kept deploring in the background the possible breakup of the family. Barry knew the history of the relationship between his wife and Fred, yet denied any feelings of jealousy. I then told him the story of a Sid Caesar skit I had once seen where Sid Caesar comes into a room and catches Carl Reiner kissing his wife. They all agree to handle this matter in a civilized manner and discuss it rationally, but a few minutes later Sid Caesar gets furious with Carl Reiner over the way the martinis were mixed. Barry got the point even if he could not respond to it. The highlight of this session, however, was that Fred and his father were finally able to have a dialogue about the important things that happened between them through the years. We had to exert some effort to keep mother out of that interchange. What really touched father was when Fred said he had longed for more closeness with him. Fred, like Lynn, was surprised that parents can feel rejected too. They broke through to each other when Fred told his dad that he had never wanted to be passive like him and that he also paradoxically wanted to beat him out and be more successful. While Fred felt he had turned out to be a better businessman, it was a hollow victory because he realized that he did not want to lose a father in the process. He also said he had come to admire many fine qualities in his dad, qualities that he himself did not have. The entire family then witnessed an event they had never thought they would see—a withdrawn, isolated father deeply sobbing about all the disappointments in his life. They were even more stunned when he pulled himself together and began, at long last, to take charge of all the squabbles in the family. He even mediated some agreements between Fred and Barry, and Elaine and Lynn.

Only a few more sessions were needed with Fred and Lynn following Fred's second family-of-origin session. Fred said that some pervasive, nameless dread that had always been present in his family of origin (a dread that other clients had reported in previous family-of-origin sessions) had disappeared. He felt he could love Lynn and his own family without feeling untrue to either. Fred said that he and Dad had continued to talk personally, ever since the family session. He was enormously pleased to have a relationship with his father, at long last. Lynn recounted an event that had enormous significance to her. On her birthday, her parents were together with her for the first time since she was a little girl, and she took a picture of the two of them together. Her father's bitterness toward Lynn's mother had vanished after he felt Lynn had forgiven him. Lynn also reported that she and Elaine had gone shopping together for their children (Elaine was pregnant); Lynn's involvement with Fred's family appeared to be on a realistic basis. On their way to the last session Fred and Lynn had an argument, which I saw as the usual termination regression. When I called them 6 months later they said they were doing "just great and felt truly married for the first time." I thought to myself, considering where they started, "not bad for 25 sessions."

Summary Evaluation

Although in some respects the marital problems that Fred and Lynn brought to therapy were of the garden variety, I selected this case to write about in order to illustrate the powerful effects that extended families have on a marital situation. We all know of the past dynamic forces that families of origin exert in shaping people and marriages (best exemplified in Dicks' work at Tavistock, 1967), but less widely realized are the *current* influences of both families and both sets of in-laws on the husband and wife. If you are treating a couple and you do not specifically ask what is going on in their relationships with parents, brothers, sisters, aunts, uncles, and in-laws, they usually do not tell you. Individual therapists focus on their patients and tend to ignore the marital partners or the children. Family therapists and marriage counselors all too frequently ignore the families of origin, both from the standpoint of understanding the marital struggle or utilizing extended family as a therapeutic resource. It is possible that Fred and Lynn's marriage relationship would have improved just from marital or couples group therapy. (I do believe, however, that they would have had a destructive divorce without treatment.) Most of the marital cases I have seen, nevertheless, made their breakthroughs following the family-of-origin sessions. Through most of the therapy Lynn was not willing to bring in her father, and we had to clear away some other aspects of the troubled relationship before she could deal with that dimension. Once the more superficial aspects of their difficulties were handled, and under the threat of losing her loved-hated husband, her antipathy to dealing with her father was surmounted. When she got her father back, the force of her need to work out her intrapsychic conflicts *through* Fred nearly dissipated.

One aspect of Fred's role in his original family was that of the parentified one; his being an apparent winner resulted in a thin triumph, which exacted a high price. His exalted position in that family created a sense of confidence that enabled him to be successful in the outside world, but, like many prominent and socially successful people, he was severely damaged in dealing with intimate relationships. His emotional radar signaling system chose a mate who would fight the battle with his family that he could not; Lynn expressed his anger *for* him. His family-of-origin sessions had many aspects, but the critical event, like that of Lynn's, was getting the father he felt he never had. Both Lynn and Fred shared the introject of the longed-for father.

The couples group format provides many more therapeutic benefits than just serving as leverage to bring about family-of-origin sessions. In the group sessions the partners learn by identification, get support and understanding, and profit from the confrontations from the other group members. Since marital interactions are often driven by strong, often overwhelming emotions, the group helps in tempering these, leading to more reality thinking. One part of my method of conducting couples group sessions consists of every member of the group of three couples, in turn, giving feedback to the couple that had just been focused upon. By alternating in the "patient" and "observer" roles the individuals often treat themselves through others, and they also gain a sense of adequacy and competence. Spouses, moreover, get to see how other people respond to their partners, and this helps loosen the fixed, distorted views that all people have about their mates. In Lynn's and Fred's case, the group did not see either partner as crazy and unreasonable as each saw the other.

Lynn's and Fred's therapy was an instance when the treatment worked the way it is supposed to, according to my conceptual outlook (Framo, 1965a, 1970). It should go without saying that not all my cases do. Too often case reports in the literature make the treatment sound smooth and easy, as if therapy progressed evenly and barriers were easily overcome. Someday a book should be written on treatment failures, because I think we can learn a lot from them. I was glad to participate in this volume, which is a first in requesting contributors to describe the process of treatment as it really happens, like marriage, with its ups and downs, backsliding, treatment errors, despair, hope, times when nothing seems to be happening, and times when those occasional bursts of movement occur that make it all worthwhile. I happen to believe that it is extremely difficult to change oneself or other people, and one is damn lucky when it happens.

Part Five

Professional and Personal Issues

"Personal Reflections of a Family Therapist" was originally given as the guest lecture at the Ninth Annual Georgetown Conference on Family Psychotherapy in 1972, and then was published in the January, 1975, inaugural issue of the *Journal of Marriage and Family Counseling* (presently the *Journal of Marital and Family Therapy*)—the official journal of the American Association for Marriage and Family Therapy (AAMFT). Subsequently the article was reprinted in 1979 in *Advances in Family Psychiatry*, of which J. G. Howell was the editor. In this chapter I recount, in an informal, chatty style, some of my own experiences over the years as a family therapist. I discuss my early years as a family therapist, my perception of some of the changes in the field that have occurred over time, and finally I attempt to deal with the subjective, personal side of treating families and couples—in which section I reveal some of my feelings about doing this kind of work that are ordinarily reserved for private conversations with close colleagues.

After 13 years at the Eastern Pennsylvania Psychiatric Institute, I moved in 1969 to the Community Mental Health Center (CMHC) of Thomas Jefferson University with the goal of establishing an independent family therapy unit. I was ultimately successful in getting federal funds to set one up, which was a first; to my knowledge, there has not been another independent family therapy unit within any other CMHC in the country. In "Chronicle of a Struggle to Establish a Family Unit Within a Community Mental Health Center" I tell the story of the ups and downs, the frustrations, pitfalls, organizational problems, and conflicts between paradigms and professions, as well as the minor victories and fulfillments of this venture. One conclusion I did end up with, however, is that I question whether a systems model of therapy can be integrated with the kind of individual illness model that is being taught in medical schools and universities. As I say in that chapter, "When some of the full implications of the systems viewpoint become apparent—in terms of their effects on diagnoses and treatment procedures, admission policies, status, and so forth—establishment mental health finds it too threatening." Following publication of this chapter in 1976 in its original form as a paper in the book *Family Therapy* edited by Phil Guerin, I received a number of letters from family therapists who told me that the paper reflected their own experiences in attempting to introduce family therapy into their particular work setting. I believe that a portion of family therapy training should include discussion of the problems likely to be encountered when one sees families in traditional work settings. The politics of the work context should be included in family therapy training programs.'

"A Personal Viewpoint on Training in Marital and Family Therapy" was originally presented as part of a symposium on family therapy training at the 85th Annual Meeting of the American Psychological Association in 1977, and was published in that form in *Professional Psychology* in 1979. Again, in informal, unsystematic, and incomplete fashion, I gave some of my views on training in this field, the opinions offered being preliminary and impressionistic in nature. Along with other family therapists, I have been concerned about the quality of training available in a field that has become so popular and has had such astonishing growth. The training programs around the country (indeed, now around the world) vary considerably in quality and comprehensiveness, from the excellent to the very poor. In some places, such as California, "Marriage and Family Counselors" are being turned out by the thousands, and although some of these MFC's get adequate training, others see families and couples without ever having worked with different population groups (such as children, adolescents, or the aged), or without ever having seen a psychotic person. Worse yet, some mental health professionals go to a weekend workshop, learn a few "tricks" to use with families, and thereafter refer to themselves as "family therapists." I emphasize that there is very little in the conventional training of a psychiatrist, clinical psychologist, or social worker that qualifies him or her to treat families and couples. Part of the problem is that little thought has gone into standard-setting in this field, a rather difficult task considering the heterogeneity of viewpoints and schools in family therapy. The American Family Therapy Association (AFTA) was, in part, formed in order to attempt to set some standards. I served for several years on the National Advisory Committee to the Commission on Accreditation for Marriage and Family Therapy Education, established by, but independent of, the American Association for Marriage and Family Therapy (AAMFT). While on this committee I came to appreciate the enormous complexity involved in setting standards for family therapy training. Until some standards are established, however, it will be difficult for family therapy to be recognized as the independent profession it is. I have been impressed with the progress that has been made along these lines by the two family therapy organizations.

This book concludes, and rightly so, with my favorite piece, "My

Families, My Family." Writing this paper was, for me, a needful abreactive experience, helping me to cope with a crisis in my own life. In this paper, I tried to deal with how the ghosts of my own family came into the treatment room, and how I sometimes had difficulty distinguishing clinical families from my own, giving rise to flashbacks "at once compelling and fearsome, fascinating and despairing, growth-promoting and regressive." Nat Ackerman told me after he read this paper that this dimension is always present to some degree and can be critical to the outcome of treatment, even though nobody talks about it. Carl Whitaker told me that in my disclosures about my family I stopped just short of being self-destructive. The paper was finally published in *Voices*, the journal of the American Academy of Psychotherapists; this journal is about the only one in which professional psychotherapists can share thoughts about the human, personal side of being a therapist. A rather strange series of events followed the publication of this paper. Wherever I go in the United States and in foreign countries people show me a tattered, xeroxed copy they have been carrying around; it has apparently been reproduced thousands of times. However, to my knowledge, it has never been cited in anyone's list of references. Someone explained this phenomenon thusly: "It is too personal to be cited; it seems that people incorporate this paper and own it as part of themselves." Could be.

11

Personal Reflections of a Family Therapist (1975)

I would like to share some of my thoughts about and experiences with the field of family therapy over the past 16 years, especially since the publication of *Intensive Family Therapy* (Boszormenyi-Nagy and Framo, 1965).

The Early Years

Let me start with telling you a little bit about where I've come from. For about 6 years after I got my Ph.D. I was a conventional clinical psychologist who gave several thousand Rorschachs and Wechslers, looked for signs of psychopathology, and sat in case conferences where everybody argued about diagnoses. (I can no longer sit in the same room where this is happening.) I did some research, individual psychotherapy, and group therapy, but always with a sense of vague unease about the worthwhileness of what I was doing.

When I joined Ivan Nagy at the Eastern Pennsylvania Psychiatric Institute in 1957 on a schizophrenia project, and we started working with families, we felt a sense of excitement of discovery of a wholly new way of viewing and conceptualizing emotional difficulties. For us it was somewhat akin to the discovery of the microscope in that phenomena were revealed that had never been seen before. We couldn't wait to get out of bed in the morning to get to work to see what we'd find out that day. We were sure then, as I am even more convinced today, that we had hold of something damn significant in the transpersonal–intimate view of

Reprinted with permission from the *Journal of Marriage and Family Counseling*, 1975, *1*, 15–28. Copyright © 1975, American Association for Marriage and Family Therapy.

man. Revelation of the phenomenon of interlocking, multi-person motivational systems was a genuine breakthrough. Many heretofore inexplicable paradoxes and symptoms began to make sense; the family-systems approach helped decode age-old human dilemmas. How to *change* a family was another story. There was nobody around to teach us, of course; we watched each other and supervised each other and we used cotherapists to keep from getting overwhelmed. In the light of what we know today about working with families, our efforts were crude and fumbling, but I will always remember the exhilaration and joy of creation of those days. It was pretty lonely in those days, too, especially when we wanted to share ideas with colleagues. I remember we had to be surreptitious about seeing families; we'd whisper to friends at conventions in hallways, "I'm seeing families; what about you?" In those days it just wasn't done; there were both professional and cultural taboos.

Since those early days there has been a tremendous growth in the field. The literature has expanded enormously, training programs have proliferated, local family institutes have been organized around the country (although family therapists for various reasons still resist forming a national organization), and workshops and seminars on family therapy at conventions continue to be crowded. Family therapy is being used in many different settings. I myself have given over 100 workshops around this country and in Italy, the Netherlands, and Mexico. There is no question that family therapy is here to stay; it is now even listed in traditional textbooks as an "acceptable" form of treatment. Many mental health professionals latched on to family concepts and practices because of the ring of truth that it is very difficult to change individuals solely through the one-to-one relationship with a professional; it is necessary to change contexts, especially intimate ones. For the first time practitioners, dissatisfied with puzzling treatment failures using traditional approaches, found a way to deal with the *real* problems of people, the relationships with those who matter most to them. A son, for example, could work directly on his real relationship *with* his father rather than talk *about* this relationship to professionals or make a father out of the therapist. A wife could deal directly with her real husband rather than "a paid friend." Symptoms came to be viewed as byproducts of pathological relationship events.

The situation, however, is much more complicated and tricky than the picture I've just painted. Paradoxically, in the midst of all this growth and acceptance and admiration, a systems approach is still quite threatening to the psychiatric, psychologic, and social work establishment—those who have the power to give grants, establish policy, train, set salaries, and appoint to positions. For example, I wrote up a National Institute of Mental Health (NIMH) grant to establish the first family therapy unit in the country as an independent service within a community mental health center. The grant was approved in 1969 but took 3 years to be funded. I could write a book on the hurdles that were placed in the way of this grant, at the federal, state, and local levels, from the medical university, and even from the community mental health center where I worked. Those resistances ranged all the way from the federal government wanting to know why I couldn't rewrite the grant and orient it toward children or drugs because there was money there; through the state office that said they couldn't give matching funds to a program that violated the CMHC act which requires treatment•for psychiatric illness[1]; through a message from the city office of mental health that local matching funds could only be granted to proven treatment programs, and, besides, why have an independent service for a specific form of treatment? If they set up a unit for the family, why not set up one for group therapy? At the medical university I was called in by the person who set my salary; I was told that some of my publications implied that established psychiatric practices were sometimes less than therapeutic, and would I please tone down my papers. As I was leaving the office, I was told, "By the way, Jim, I've begun doing family therapy, and have been doing it for years." I might mention that although I was chief of the unit, my assistant chief, a psychiatrist, was paid a much higher salary. Within the CMHC it was difficult to get referrals from other services, so we had to go outside the center and deal with such people as the clergy, nonpsychiatric physicians, the courts, schools, welfare and child protective agencies, and so on. The ambivalence of the other services in the CMHC about our unit was striking. On the one hand the unit was viewed with envy as the glamour outfit, but the sabotaging was fascinating to observe, using the unit as a dumping ground for all the impossible situations. You know the story: "Send them to family therapy; it can't do them any harm." We rarely got fresh crisis situations. I used to think it was just the psychiatric establishment, but later I joined the faculty of an academic department of psychology, and at one of the case conferences of the psychological service center I suggested that the patient be seen with her family. Despite the fact that this staff had recruited me because they wanted a family therapist on the staff, it was interesting to observe all the dubious and avoidant remarks that followed my suggestion.

Family therapy cannot be ignored, but it can't be digested either. Someday I'll take Murray Bowen's advice and suggest to my staff that they go around "bad mouthing" family. I have learned that one should not try to sell this approach; what I find happening is that people come over to observe treatment sessions through the one-way mirror, and then they get hooked.

Family Therapy Today

Pressure from students is forcing some departments of social work to give a course on family therapy; as far as I know there are only a few doctoral programs in clinical psychology that offer such a course, but the most interesting development

---

[1]When the unit was established we were required to give a psychiatric diagnosis to every member of the family, including babes in arms. What we did, of course, was to give mild diagnoses; the babies were all labelled "infant adjustment reactions."

is occurring in psychiatric training. Because family therapy is "in" these days it is felt it ought to be included in psychiatric residency training programs, but this gesture is often merely lip service. When some of the full implications of the systems viewpoint begin to seep through—in terms of its effect on diagnosis and treatment procedures, admission policies, status, and so forth—we may witness the termination of these training programs. It is a mystery to me that the new medical discipline of Family Medicine rarely includes any teaching about family dynamics in its training programs.

One wonders in this connection whether it is best for family therapy to exist in a setting of competing viewpoints or mixed models, or if it should do what psychoanalysis did and set up its own institutes and standards. That course led to psychoanalysis becoming isolated, and you can note how psychoanalysts are trying to get back in, for instance, the movement of analysts into universities, medical schools, and community psychiatry. I can see the validity of the arguments on both sides, and I don't have an answer for that question. In fact, at the present time practically all training in family therapy is being done by local family institutes in the major cities around the country. While there are a few service centers that are exclusively family oriented, most family therapy is practiced in settings that use many treatment modalities.

I do see the family approach as a philosophy and an orientation to the human condition, not as just a technique or a form of therapy. I've even wondered if this work is therapy at all and whether it isn't a special form of experience, one that belongs outside the framework of the helping professions, perhaps in education. A lot of people are hopping on the bandwagon; some have over-bought the family approach and use it inappropriately. For instance, bringing a family together in one room to talk about the patient is considered family therapy by some people. Viewed as a theoretical orientation, it matters less who is actually in the treatment room; the Bowen group does family-oriented work with individuals. Virginia Satir has said she can find out in 30 seconds' discussion of a family whether someone understands the systems approach. I do not mean to imply that there is only one right way to treat families. Indeed, one of the main developments in the field is the existence today of many schools of family therapy, all the way from work with single family members (Anonymous, 1972) to social networks (Speck and Attneave, 1973) and Auerswald's focus on ecological systems and the interfaces between systems (1968). Already there is talk of the old and the new family therapies. In a paper on the future of family therapy (1970), John Bell correctly predicted that the field would move into working with black-ghetto families, communal families, and the multi-families created by divorce and remarriage, and foresaw the field moving into industry and business (not only with families dislocated by reassignments but with work systems themselves); he envisioned more transcultural family work, and movement into a variety of settings and institutions such as prisons, homes for the aged, foster homes, and group living homes, as well as movement in the direction of preventative and family-life education programs.

Speaking for myself, changing a family system is the ultimate professional challenge; it is perhaps the most difficult of all therapeutic tasks, but also has the greatest payoff. My own therapeutic philosophy is to learn as many kinds of treatment approaches as possible in order to have a full repertory of techniques available to shift the system. Consequently, I go to workshops in transactional analysis, gestalt therapy, encounter techniques, behavior therapy, rational-emotive therapy, existential therapy, as well as to those using methods of working with families that are outside my own orientation, such as family sculpting. I use techniques from psychodynamic theory, communication theory, group therapy, parodoxical instructions, audio and video playback—whatever I need to use to move a system. Shifting a family system just a notch increases by multiple ratio, much like a pebble dropped in water has a rippling effect. In my training programs I try to acquaint students with as many different schools of family therapy as possible; after being exposed to many different ways of working with families, eventually the trainees can develop a style that is most comfortable for them.

We've learned a lot about the nature of working with families as the years have gone by. Following those early years of working with schizophrenics and their families, we moved into work with many family types and throughout the range of manifest symptoms. Most family therapy today is of the short-term crisis variety, I would suspect; I'm uncomfortable when I remember that the first family I saw was seen for 5 years. Undifferentiated families usually will come forever without significant change beyond symptom improvement, but the more differentiated families seldom stick beyond the crisis resolution. Perhaps this is as it should be, in that families should only be helped to the point where they can rely on their own self-corrective mechanisms. The dropout rate in family therapy is quite high, but there are good reasons for this, I think. First of all, the sources of resistance in families (as compared with individuals) are greater and can come from many more directions. A family can dropout or prematurely terminate for reasons that have nothing to do with the way the therapy was conducted: A husband and wife can have a fight before a session and one refuses to attend; a child might not want to return and the parents go along with the refusal; the parents may have too much invested in scapegoating a child and sense from the first session that this mechanism might change; an extended family member or outside psychiatrist, lawyer, or clergyman may dissuade the family from returning, and so on. Events go on outside sessions that the therapist knows nothing about. Another reason for early dropouts, in my judgment, testifies to the very power of family therapy. *Because* it can bring about fundamental changes (and this can happen as a result of just one session) many families are very threatened by the anxiety of change and, therefore, don't come back. *When people don't really want things to change they find methods other than family therapy to deal with them.* This high early dropout rate or "no-shows" is a source of disappointment that beginning family therapists have to learn to deal with. I am intrigued by Murray Bowen's experimentation with nonregularity of sessions, whereby sessions are timed to system changes, or gauged by the anxiety level, rather than being spaced for the convenience of the therapist's schedule. Such a procedure may cut down on dropouts. Family process is a continuous dynamic force that may not be geared to once-a-week intervention. We have a lot to learn about the timing of sessions as well as many other matters that bring about change.

I still struggle with one of the oldest dilemmas in family therapy, namely, that the different family members come in with varying secret agendas and expectations, and these often clash with each other and the goals the therapist sets for them, at least implicitly. Perhaps part of the skill of the therapist resides in finding the appropriate balance between the clash of goals and expectations of all the family members as well as those of the therapist. This problem existed in individual therapy when the patient wanted to stop his suffering but did not really want to change his exploitation of others. With whole families it gets more complicated because motivations vary; people come in for somebody else and not for acknowledged help; some members are dragged in, others act out their problems through other people and they are either not suffering or they endure bearable hurts. Some family members give family therapy superficial commitment, go along with it for a while, and then later on say "Yes, doc, we understand we have a part in this but what about Johnny, really?" It's true that most of the time the designated patient is the first to change, but sometimes he's the last, or doesn't seem to change at all, even when a part of the system has changed (as when the marriage relationship is better). As Tony Ferreira once said, we had to discover that the family is a system first, before we could recognize that it does not always behave as a system.

Most families are very fearful of coming to sessions, but there are some I've seen who asked for family therapy and were eager for it; some of these families use its very rationale to subvert the therapy. They'll say, "It's a family problem," but nobody takes responsibility for anything. When I see families or couples I make clear my expectation that each person has to take responsibility for his own life; yet this is a paradox in a way because asking them to come in together implies shared responsibility, that all their fingers are in this pie. When are you responsible for someone else, and when only for yourself? I wrote a long time ago that families essentially come to therapy to restore or maintain the status quo, despite their words and their pain, and I still think this is so. A key question I ask myself is: Why, since the problem has usually existed for some time, is the family coming in *now*? What in the system is not working? The presented problem usually has little to do with the real problem. (For example, the presented problem may involve concern about a teenager's school problems or loneliness, whereas, actually, the teenager's growing autonomy is perceived by the parents as rejection of them.)

I still occasionally get feelings of failure and helplessness when I've tried everything I know, and they are still stuck. So you bring in a cotherapist as a consultant, advise a break in treatment, or refer them elsewhere. When do we let families go—when their games are better than ours? When you're tired of them? When you realize that you want more for them than they want for themselves? When your case load is high do you increase your expectations with the families who are dragging? You cannot always expect appreciation for your efforts; as a matter of fact, there are times when expressed appreciation is a sign that no change has taken place. There are some people you just can't connect with and you realize later when you listen to the tapes that you just didn't like them, or sensed they didn't like you, and that you kicked them out. I've wondered, those families or couples who do change a lot, are they the ones we liked?

Another phenomenon I've noticed is that some people cannot tolerate success (one father said, "I can't stand it; my wife is nice to me and even my car is working.") Occasionally one has to work with families around the issue of accepting the improvement. For example, when the marital relationship improves, sometimes the children (who presumably have much to gain) become more resistive in family therapy. The parents, who wanted medals for their progress, are then disappointed. What will be provided as replacement for the unhappiness? While the family or couple are regrouping and finding new ways, depression may follow the stopping of the "acting out;" this phenomenon has a parallel in the way psychoanalysts speak of the sense of regret over the loss of symptoms.

Evaluation: Success and Failure

I'd like to discuss briefly this question of success and failure because it's related to the important question of research evaluation of family therapy. Does family therapy work, and what do we mean by working? The question is enormously complicated, and I'll just touch on a few aspects. On what level should we look for change? On the level of symptom relief? (This is the least of the family therapist's goals.) Do we seek greater differentiation among family members, greater intimacy, less family distress and unhappiness, more open and clear communication? Do we seek changes in attitudes, in behavior, on the level of deep needs, homeostatic balance, shifts in alliances? Do we pursue better social functioning outside the family? If we help resolve interpersonal conflicts will intrapsychic conflicts become lessened; if we resolve intrapsychic conflicts will the relationships improve?

Incidentally, on this question of the interplay between family-group defenses and individual defenses against depression and anxiety, I see the real task of the psychological sciences over the next century as a deepening understanding of the extraordinarily intricate relationship between the intrapsychic and the transpersonal. I've made a tentative beginning along these lines in my paper, "Symptoms from a Family Transactional Viewpoint" (1970) where I explored the object relationship theory of Fairbairn as a link between the personal and the social.

Continuing with this question of evaluation of family therapy results, we have to keep in mind parameters of social class, types of families, and the all-important factor of the particular stage of the family life cycle the family is in when they come to us. We plug into a continuous family-natural-force at a particular phase of the family development, and only deal with pieces of a larger context at any given point in time. How many of us in dealing with a given family wish we could have seen them years ago, before the patterns became calcified? (How many of us, for that matter, have wished family therapy was in existence when we ourselves were children, and felt that if we'd had it for ourselves how our lives might have been so different?)

Nat Ackerman has commented on still another dimension of this evaluation problem. Unlike most forms of therapy, family therapy does not aim so much at merely taking something away, such as pathogenic conflicts, but often achieves a surplus, positive, actualizing sense of enrichment in family life (Ackerman, 1966, chapter 2). How do we go about measuring this dimension? Many families report that they really enjoy each other more and get more out of life than was ever thought possible. What about the bad and good side-effects of family therapy on extended members? For example, should we include in our evaluation the fact that we produced no change with a given family, but that the married sister who came to sessions originally to help her delinquent brother reported that her own marriage got so much better as a result of attending sessions? On the other hand, doesn't it sometimes happen that somebody has to lose for the rest of the family to gain? For example, a grandparent who has been tyrannizing a whole family may lose out to the autonomy forces of her children and grandchildren, and she may end up in an institution for the aged. Or a man finally gets to the point where he can leave his suffocating, widowed mother and get married; from his and the therapists' point of view he is better, but from his mother's point of view he's worse. Under what circumstances is a divorce an indication of improvement or growth and when is it not? In any discussion of favorable or unfavorable results you get involved with questions of values, not only value conflicts between the family members but between the therapist and various family members, as well as societal value dissonances. Take, for example, how the current social revolutions creep into the treatment room—the Black militant teenager castigating his "Uncle Tom" parents, the woman who wants to change her traditional housewife role and have an open marriage, the therapist struggling with his old value system when treating couples engaged in the swinging, group sex scene.

Recent Methods of Treatment

Shifting the topic a bit now, I'd like to discuss some of the treatment methods I have come to use in recent years. Take this question of combining other forms of treatment with family therapy. For instance, I have found that when one member of the family is in individual therapy or analysis outside the family sessions, that this arrangement forces the family therapy to labor under a handicap. That individual usually reserves the most significant material for his "own doctor" and filters his productions for the family sessions. I have found concurrent peer group therapy for adolescents or other family members as helpful and not interfering with the family therapy. Also, I have occasionally sent obsessive and uptight people to encounter or marathon weekends in order to loosen them up, and this is done for the overall purposes of the family therapy. Now and then I work with sibling sub-systems, without the parents, as well as other combinations of family members. Occasionally I will see individuals; for instance, when working with a married couple who cannot tolerate being in the same room with each other or cannot interrupt a repetitive interaction pattern, I will temporarily see them separately and then bring them back together when as individuals they have changed. I have used the structured separation method for couples where one or both partners cannot tolerate living together; the spouses live apart, continue to come to therapy sessions, and each person works on family of origin (Toomim, 1972). My method of working with adults and their families of origin will be discussed later.

Although in particular situations I believe it is necessary to do family therapy throughout the course of treatment (including the children), I have moved more in the direction of working with the marriage relationship of the parents once the originally symptomatic children have become defocused. Most of my family therapy these days, then, becomes marital therapy. In addition, of course, I see couples in marriage therapy who come in explicitly for marital problems; some of these couples do not have children and some with children do not present their children as the problem. I still believe a statement I wrote years ago that "whenever you have a disturbed child you have a disturbed marriage, although all disturbed marriages do not create disturbed children," (Boszormenyi-Nagy and Framo, 1965; p. 154)—some partners do manage to keep the kids out of their difficulties.

The next direction I moved into was to start doing couples group therapy, and I did this as a matter of clinical expediency. There are some couples who work beautifully by themselves, and utilize the therapeutic setting so effectively that the best thing you can do is stay out of the way and not do something stupid. With other couples I found myself boxed in by their triangulating efforts, or I couldn't tone down the emotional accusations to each other, or they'd move for a while and bog down, and I found my freedom of action blocked by feelings of anger, boredom, and frustration. So in the beginning I put couples together in order to handle my own feelings and free myself. Another reason I organized couples groups is that, as with a family, you need an ally, the most differentiated one, to help you deal with the system. I frankly felt I needed allies to help me deal with some of the couples. These "assistant therapists" serve a different function than that of a formal cotherapist. Like a lot of things that you do for one reason you find has serendipitous effects, I discovered that couples group therapy is a powerful form of treatment in its own right. As a matter of fact, I've come to believe that couples group therapy is the treatment of choice for premarital, marital, separation, and divorce problems (Framo, 1973).

This all leads to a major, most recent dimension of my work, family therapy involving adults with their family of origin. Before I deal with this clinical method, I'd like to make a few observations about some dynamics of family life. People are constantly repeating relationship struggles from their family of origin and they seek through marriage, children, friends, enemies, work colleagues, encounter groups, and psychotherapists the kinds of responses that will enable them to correct, master, or continue old, unfinished family business. The relational environment is manipulated such that others are maneuvered into being nurturant parents, servants, tormentors, or what have you, in order that more primitive conflicts will not come to the surface. In this sense, painful symptoms can be avoided by selective choice of relationship. But no one has any choice when it comes to relatives, to parents and siblings, grandparents, uncles and aunts; these are captive relationships. One's parent may not be the sort of person one would have chosen to have as a friend; even if one's father is a weak, lovable, neglectful failure and one's mother is unreal, unreachable, and always depressed, one cannot easily give parents up the way one could give up an acquaintance. Friends and mates are replaceable; nothing can change the fact that one's mother and father will always be one's mother and father.

The stakes are higher and the consequences graver when one deals with one's family members because they have the wherewithal to affect the core of one's being. Families are where we live, and, as Carl Whitaker said, "The family is the place where you are dealing with life and death voltages." These realizations help explain why disappointment, hostility, and frustration are so much more intense in the family setting, the rejection much more hurting, the loyalty and sacrifices so compelling, and the gratification so fulfilling. There is a special, real quality in dealing with one's parents, brothers and sisters, spouse, and children which does not apply to other social relationships. The psychology of intimate relationships is unique, has laws of its own, and reduces all people, whatever their station in life, to the same common denominator. For instance, when Franklin Roosevelt got married, his mother bought two contiguous houses in New York City, had the walls between the two houses knocked down, and lived in one side while Franklin and Eleanor lived on the other. In this way she could control every aspect of the newlywed's lives. One wonders where was Franklin, one of four world leaders and a president of the United States, in all of this?

We family therapists are in possession of a great and powerful secret. The Chinese Communists who brainwashed their enemies knew this secret; they forced prisoners to confess the wrongs they'd done their parents in order to put them in a more vulnerable position. In family therapy sessions, dealing with the most powerful needs in the human realm, the most commanding, socially influential people can be reduced to the status of a sobbing child.

Family influence persists through space and time, kept alive by "programming" and family ghosts of the past, and lived through other people in the present. Family primacy does not affect geography, as adults discover when they try to break off contact and put physical distance between themselves and their families of origin. One pretty much *has* to be involved with one's family whether one wishes to or not, even if one doesn't actually see the family very often or at all. The long arm of family loyalty, loves, and hates stretches beyond death and grave unto succeeding generations, creating unseen forces which influence the destiny of many lives.

I began bringing in families of origin on the basis of my clinical experience with family and marital therapy. Of all the methods I have used, involvement of the family of origin is the most effective; I've found that one session of any adult with his family of origin can take the place of many regular therapy sessions. I should mention that people usually strenuously resist bringing in their family of origin initially, and it takes considerable therapeutic preparation before they are ready to deal with their family.

Early in my experience with families and couples it became apparent that the relationship problems that adults have with their mate, children, and others are reconstructions of earlier conflicts with their families of origin. It seems almost naive to state this truism, but when I began searching the literature for those who had a systematic theory for using family of origin as a therapeutic resource there was no one to add to Murray Bowen (Anonymous, 1972). My method of involving adults with their family of origin differs from Bowen's. Murray Bowen sends his adult clients home on timed visits to their families of origin and coaches them in their differentiating efforts. He uses the same method in training family therapists, supervising his trainees to conduct family voyages. Whereas Bowen rarely has the adult bring in his family of origin for therapy sessions with him, I do just that, since I'm working toward somewhat different goals.

This practice has been so productive that now I routinely have at least one session, if at all possible, with each adult and his or her family of origin. I have found this procedure to be valuable, in a different way, for the married adult who is overinvolved with family of origin, the one who has infrequent superficial contact, and the adult who is totally alienated from his parents or siblings. In these sessions the mate or children are not present. I usually do not allow much talk about the adult's marriage to take place when he or she is meeting with the family of origin (another method of triangling which diverts from the main purpose). The focus is on the adult's past and present relationship with his parents and siblings—what went on in the history of that family, how the roles were distributed, the alliances formed, nodal events, tragedies, secrets—in short, the usual things looked for in a family diagnostic interview. Important diagnostic information is obtained on how past family problems are being acted out in the present. More to the point, however, in these sessions opportunities are available for genuine corrective experiences, clarifying of old misunderstandings, and the possibility of establishing an adult-to-adult relationship with one's parents. This kind of experience gives people the chance to get to know their parents as people rather than as fantasy figures who have to be inflated or deflated.

Incidentally, in recent years I have been doing family, marital, and couples group therapy with my wife as cotherapist. In these family of origin sessions her presence has come to be especially meaningful, particularly for the parents and siblings as well as for the adults who had been in treatment. Her being a woman and parent gives her a special role that helps ease the natural gap between generations and sexes.

The Subjective Side of Doing Family Therapy

Turning now to the subjective side of doing family therapy, back in 1968 I went through some personal experiences whereby the boundary between my work with clinical families and my relationship with my family of origin and my wife and kids was becoming more and more permeable and diffuse. It was becoming increasingly difficult for me to keep the two separate. One way I handled this struggle was to write a paper (chapter 14 in this book). It was called, "My Families, My Family" and was published in *Voices,* the Journal of the American Academy of Psychotherapists (1968). I wrote this paper in 4 days and I wrote it in blood; I think it's the most honest piece of writing I've ever done. The paper has had a strange reception. I've received many letters about it from all over the world, it has been xeroxed hundreds of times for training programs around the country, yet it has never been cited in any reference list. This phenomenon is a mystery to me. I wrote in this paper:

> I don't know when I first became aware of the phenomenon that treating families not only revives the specters of one's own past family life, but also has subtle, suffusing effects on the therapist's current family relationships. After doing family therapy, and seeing what emotional systems can do to people, I take my own family life more seriously. In the living presence of a mother, father, brothers, and sisters, the constellation in which most of us grew, one finds oneself transported back to old thoughts, longings, disharmonies, and joys in a way which can be more moving and reintegrative than one's own personal therapy or analysis. Each family we treat contains a part of our own. As I saw more and more families I have become used to reliving each stage of my own family life cycle during sessions, in a series of flashbacks at once compelling and fearsome, fascinating and despairing, growth-promoting and regressive. While I am conducting treatment sessions, with my surface calm and important, hiding behind my degrees and the trappings of my profession, evaluating the dynamics of the family before me, figuring out the strategy, avoiding the traps, I communicate to the family only a small portion of the emotional connections I make with them, the places where we touch.

The rest of the paper consists of statements made by family members during sessions with different families, and then, in parentheses, my personal and verbally uncommunicated associations to the material (such as the time I heard a teenager tell his parents, "Go fuck yourselves" and I got the uncanny feeling that his parents suddenly looked like my parents and I wondered if this boy was saying for me what I never dared to say). And I also recounted moments of tenderness, nostalgia, regrets, loving feelings, disappointments, and lost opportunities, culminating in the realization that I was trying to refashion all my clinical families into the kind of family I always wanted mine to be. When a family member said to me, "Doc, I keep getting the feeling that you have some kind of ideal family image you expect us to live up to and that somehow we should be like your family," I shuddered with the thought, "My God, can it be true?" But my point in bringing up this paper is that I barely scratched the surface then on the personal side of being a family therapist.

Family therapists are a curious, distinctive breed among mental health professionals. They have broken down a number of professional taboos, especially concerning secrecy and confidentiality, and they practice openness, direct observation of therapy and each other, live supervision, and the sharing of experiences, and they treat people as persons rather than as patients. They view symptoms as epiphenomena of relationship struggles and they focus on the human context rather than psychopathology. They keep looking for some word other than "patients" to describe the people they see professionally and some word other than psychotherapy to describe the process. Mavericks that they are, they are relatively unconcerned with the degrees its practitioners have. Most try to practice what they preach, and are relatively frank about their own family struggles, thereby decreasing the usual distance between professional and seeker of help. Family therapists have strong convictions about the validity of their work and firmly believe that they are where the action's really at. Innovative and creative in theory, therapy techniques, and methods of training, they nonetheless run into trouble at times in their professional and personal lives. Professionally, they are concerned with such questions as: Should family therapists be certified or licensed; should anyone who has a feel for this work practice it, and what kinds of standards should there be? Are family therapists born and not made? Should they have had prior experience in individual and group therapy? What is the best way to train family therapists, assuming they have the necessary personality equipment? (I find that some mental health professionals can never become family therapists no matter how much training they get.) How much do we really know about changing families? How comprehensive are our theories, how effective our techniques, and why is there so little systematic research on family interaction or therapy outcome studies? Do we need a national organization or confederation of local family institutes?

The personal side of treating families and couples is even more important because these private matters have a strong effect on professional and treatment issues even if they are not recognized and acknowledged. I'll plunge directly into one of the touchiest. My sampling is limited and may be off, and I do not know the statistics for other mental health professionals, but among the family and marital therapists I know of, I see a high rate of divorces, separations, accidents, emotional crises, and even premature deaths. Assuming that the frequency of these events is beyond chance, one wonders why? I have speculated about several possible explanations. Foremost, I think there is a selective factor in people going into this kind of work. Although all family therapists, I believe, continue their struggles with their own families of origin with their clinical families, some have mastered or resolved or have come to terms with (or whatever words you want to use) their own past so that they can use the experiences adaptively. Others, I fear, do use families in order to work out their own problems. (I am not discussing here the kind of highly sophisticated way that Carl Whitaker exposes his child self and asks the family to take care of him; he knows exactly what he's doing.) What I'm trying to identify here is that those family therapists who become casualties of one sort or another probably have serious family problems themselves, either from the old family or with their current family, and it's likely these events would have occurred even if they had never become family therapists.

Another factor may have to do with the fact that treating couples and families is extraordinarily stressful work. How hazardous is this occupation? While the transactions of a family session may sustain us, at the same time they drain and exact a toll. I'm sure you have all had the experience of having observers behind the one-way mirror needing a reentry experience with you at the conclusion of a treatment session; they are often so overwhelmed with feeling that nobody has anything to say. Have you also noticed how, during sessions, observers behind the one-way mirror will joke, laugh at, kibitz, and make hostile remarks about the family members or therapist? Do observer therapists need this release to get back at families for what they do to us? Many a time after a particularly heavy session I need a drink or need to unload with my cotherapists, a friend, a group of observers, or I need to talk with my wife at night when I can let all the feelings out and get feedback that I did the right thing or that I didn't fail or that I'm a pretty wonderful guy. Sometimes I work it out vicariously with a good TV show, play, or movie, or by chopping wood or gardening on weekends, writing an article, building a bookcase, painting an oil, making love.

A wide range of support systems, personal and professional, for doing this work is vital, and when these support systems are not working there's going to be hell to pay (Whitaker, Felder and Warkentin, 1965). When your own marriage is seriously troubled, or you're having difficulty with your kids, or if you haven't worked out a self with your family of origin, or if your work system is hostile to a systems approach, it's going to be especially difficult to conduct marital or family therapy sessions. This whole question of whether therapists in deep distress can be of help to others is a very intriguing one. I've seen therapists whose own marriages and families were falling apart who nonetheless managed to still be effective as professional therapists; somehow they were able to dissociate themselves from their own personal lives and still be objective. Others, of course, bring their own personal unhappiness, biases, and distortions into the treatment room—with uncertain effects. But who's to say? Sometimes the sharing of a personal tragedy or a vulnerability can be just the thing that establishes a human contact.

A great book on psychotherapy was written in the 1950's by Carl Whitaker and Tom Malone called *The Roots of Psychotherapy* (1953). Some important things were said in that book, but I don't think therapists were ready for them. The book dealt with something that is coming up now in family therapy, the subtle interplay of professionally helping people and being helped by them. Are some family therapists getting divorced because they discover with clinical couples what expanded dimensions of relationship are possible, and they decide they want more than they themselves have? As you know, all marriages go through up and down phases. What do you do during a down phase in your own marriage when you're treating a couple whose marriage relationship is in better shape than your own? Or this can go the other way: you are likely to write optimistic articles about the viability of marriage or set different standards for treatment couples when your own marriage is in an up phase. How unsettling is it when couples or families or individual family members you are treating are way ahead of you and working on their growth better than you are? How do you deal with your jealousy when you help kids get more from their parents than you yourself got from your own parents? What do you do when you see a man be cruel to his attractive wife and you feel you wouldn't treat her that way if you were married to her? How often are you able to have moments of more authenticity with clinical families than you are able to with your own family? How do you handle observing a man on his knees crying and begging his wife not to leave him? How tough is it for you to deal with incest or parents who have literally murdered their children, or a dying father who's mean to his family because he doesn't want them to miss him when he's gone? *Does tragedy toughen you or chip away at you?*

How many of us are amateurs who carry over into our own personal lives the turmoil of the families we treat, and is a true professional one who learns to take distance and cut off? Although in general I have pretty good control over my own feeling system, there are family phenomena I still have difficulty handling: marriages where one partner desperately wants out and the other just as desperately wants to hold on; men who smile at everything; snotty kids; stagnation; lying and dishonesty; dealing with child abuse; cloudlike vagueness in people; people who make you feel helpless or those who appreciate nothing you do or who are too appreciative; overly suspicious people; valid family secrets; men humiliated by their wives and wives humiliated by husbands; letting my theories get in the way of my listening; massive scapegoating; passive-aggressive people; depressed families; parents destroying children and children destroying parents; families where someone in the family is dying, especially a child.

Family phenomena I enjoy dealing with: resuscitating a dead marriage to the point where they are really married and "in love"; helping kids get unhooked; bringing together an alienated father and son or mother and daughter and observing the "high" when they become more real to each other; helping a mother or father feel like a parent for the first time; watching a whole family move from despair to an enriched life; seeing dangerous or painful symptoms disappear; getting baby-card announcements; seeing people make use of their potential; enjoying children who cut right through adult pretensions; realizing that the beneficial effects of the family therapy today may carry over into the next generation; sensing a real system change; doing a follow-up and learning that the changes lasted.

Professional psychotherapists are just like anybody else when it comes to dealing with their own families, and some people say they handle intimate relationships even worse than others. One family therapist I knew used to tell couples all the time how important it was to go to marital therapy together, yet when his own marriage was breaking up he and his wife went to two therapists separately. One therapist I knew told of how her children used to slip notes under the door to her office at home, asking for an appointment. I believe that the first obligation of a therapist is to improve his own functioning and get his own house in order.

This discourse leads to the question of whether family therapists should get family therapy for themselves; should it be a requirement, as the analysts require analysis to be a psychoanalyst? Although I'm not certain whether it should be a requirement, I do feel it's highly desirable. I can tell you firsthand that it's damn important to know what it's like to be on the other side. In the family sessions I've had with my own current family I came to appreciate the fear and anxiety that people have when the system is under examination. Before the sessions started I fooled myself into thinking I would not be therapist in that situation, that I'd just play from myself, be open and sincere, be a husband and a father. I realized later that I'd had it all planned how the sessions should go. But it went in unexpected directions as I learned what my kids and wife really thought about some things. When I heard the tape later I heard myself telling everyone what they *should* think. And I discovered that 48-hour delayed anxiety response that other family therapists have mentioned. Believe me, it's real and it's scary, you get to identify what's really going on, and it can really change things, and by change I don't mean just feeling better. In that situation you are like every other family member who comes for help. If you really want to find out what family therapy is all about, try it yourself.

12

Chronicle of a Struggle to Establish a Family Unit Within a Community Mental Health Center (1976)

In June of 1972, three years after application, the first family therapy unit as an independent service within any community mental health center in the nation was officially funded by NIMH. The community mental health center (hereafter referred to as CMHC) was part of a major medical university in the city of Philadelphia. I will document here the sequences of events surrounding this experiment in establishing a Family Unit in this setting, and describe the frustrations, difficulties, and satisfactions that were part of this attempt to integrate a systems service model with one based on the conventional model of individual psychiatric disorder. In doing so I am, of course, expressing only my own point of view.

Since 1957 I had been working with Ivan Boszormenyi-Nagy at the Eastern Pennsylvania Psychiatric Institute; our theoretical and clinical work with families was reported in *Intensive Family Therapy* (1965). Preliminary discussions were begun in 1967 with Dr. Daniel Lieberman and Mr. Jerry Jacobs, the Director and Assistant Director of a Philadelphia CMHC, which was in the process of being organized. Without their support, the enterprise would not have been possible. Indeed, without the support of the director of a mental health organization, no family unit anywhere has a chance. Dr. Lieberman had already established some innovative programs in California and Delaware, and is the sort of person who is receptive to new ideas. We discussed the possibility of having an independent Family Unit within the Center, and although it was not possible to include the project in the initial staffing grant request, it was decided to prepare a later

Reprinted with permission from P. Guerin (Ed.) *Family Therapy: Theory and Practice*. New York: Gardner Press, 1976. Copyright © 1976, The Gardner Press, Inc.

proposal to NIMH as an expansion grant. I came on board in 1969, after the Center had been established, but without official status. In that same year, at the American Psychological Association annual meeting, Edgar Auerswald, Frederick Duhl, Matthew Dumont, Alan Levenson, Daniel Lieberman, Marshall Minor, and myself presented a symposium on "The Systems Approach to Community Mental Health."

"The Family Transactional Approach as a Central Integrative Model for Community Mental Health Services: A Bold, New Approach" was the title of my grant proposal to NIMH. Its grandiosity is immediately apparent. "Bold, new approach" is President Kennedy's phrase, used when he presented to Congress his proposal for the establishment of nationwide comprehensive CMHC's for "the prevention and treatment of the mentally ill and retarded in their home communities." The rationale of CMHC's was that all services for the mentally ill—emergency, outpatient, partial hospitalization, community, diagnostic, rehabilitative, pre- and aftercare services, training, research, and evaluation—were to be placed under one umbrella in each local community. A considerable amount of planning and thinking was done in each state; I served on a task-force that was planning CMHC's for the state of Pennsylvania. By 1971, about 450 CMHC's had received grants; 304 were in operation throughout the country, serving areas inhabited by some 65 million people. Great progress was made in meeting financial, administrative, staffing, and physical facility problems, but much confusion existed concerning the basic philosophy or theory of the community approach. As Gerald Caplan (1965) stated, "The first problem which confronts the community psychiatrist, who wishes to guide his professional operations in a consistent and meaningful way, is the need for new theoretical models." Most CMHC literature dealt with organizational and empirical matters. Some articles described specific models for particular community situations, but only a few were devoted to the fundamental question of basic rationale and concepts (Blackman and Goldstein, 1968; Feldman, 1971; Howe, 1964; Klein, 1965; Mayo and Klein, 1964; Sabshin, 1966; Whittington, 1968). Furthermore, the CMHCs had an enormous mandate that was probably impossible to fulfill.

Some mental health workers had moved toward dealing with problems of living and functioning in the life situation; however the helping professions still put their major emphasis on central illness processes inside individuals. The possibility was very real that CMHCs would operationally become just a continuation and redistribution of traditional practices. As Reiff (1966) observed, "The concepts of community mental health have the potential for introducing revolutionary innovations, but a sober look will reveal that institutionalized community mental health under the federal programs tends to become an extension of professional ideology over that part of society from which it has been hitherto alienated." Yolles (1965, 1967), then director of NIMH, sounded the call for "creative generalists" from all the behavioral sciences to develop "new departures in looking at problems of mental health" and "flexible, innovative programs" in order to meet the unique challenges of community mental health.

That challenge was clearly there for me. As one of the early workers in family theory and therapy, I envisioned the profound implications of a systems approach as an organizing principle for delivery of mental health services. As I saw it then, and still do, the family model deals with the real problems of people, instead of the symptomatic consequences of family disturbances. Moreover, the family approach offers the opportunity for secondary and tertiary prevention, helps avoid duplication of services, and delivers more efficient and rapid help at reduced cost. Take, for instance, the experience of a family crisis unit in Colorado (Langsley et al., 1968; Pittman et al., 1966): they found that by treating whole families in crisis they were able to avoid hospitalization of a "psychotic" member over 85% of the time, at one-sixth the cost of hospital treatment. Follow-up several years later showed that these "psychotic" patients were functioning in a way far superior to a control group of patients who had been admitted to the hospital.

Many aspects of family theory and therapy are relevant to community mental health. Developments in psychoanalytic ego psychology, child development, group dynamics, social–psychological theory, communication theory, cultural anthropology, general systems theory, social psychiatry, and family sociology coalesced in the 1950's into a family transactional approach that promised to lead to a revolution in psychopathological thought. Don Jackson (1947) explicitly recognized the movement when he wrote:

'We are on the edge of a new era in psychiatry and the related disciplines of psychology, social work, anthropology, and sociology. In this new era we will come to look at human nature in a much more complex way than ever before. From this threshold the view is not of the individual *in vitro* but of the small or larger group within which any particular individual's behavior is adaptive. We will move from individual assessment to analysis of contexts, or more precisely, the *system* from which individual conduct is inseparable.'

The view that psychiatric illness, craziness, odd disordered behavior is a socially intelligible response orchestrated to an odd, crazy, or disordered context marks a significant and momentous shift from demonological thinking.

I emphasized in my grant application that the family approach was not just another form of treatment that would take its place along with other therapies, such as individual, group, child, and other treatment methods. I tried to explain that it is a new philosophy and orientation to the human condition. I suggested that a family therapy unit could provide a meaningful service for members of the community, not only where they lived physically, but where they lived emotionally. That is to say, that while such social systems as the school, the work situation, and the neighborhood are important, the effects of family emotional systems on people are much more powerful. (I remember once a man in family therapy told how he had been in a concentration camp in Germany during the war. When I said that that must have been pretty rough, he replied, "As bad as it was, it doesn't even compare to the damage my family did to me.") Even the layman knows that when someone is manifesting a problem, that person's difficulties are usually related to what is going on in his or her family. However, although everyone in the mental health professions agrees that family relationships are important and highly influential, in actual practice only "sick" individuals are usually treated.

In my application I also pointed out that a systems viewpoint had many practical implications for community mental health. For instance, the symptoms of one or more family members may involve many community agencies and professional helpers, each dealing with a limited sector of the family process, leaving the system untouched. A marital difficulty, for example, may spill over into the children's presenting problems in school or in the community; it may involve the police, juvenile court, domestic relations court, social service agencies, psychiatrists, visiting nurses, Alcoholics Anonymous, religious organizations, and medical hospitals. In essence, the helping professions deal only peripherally with the effects of pathological family processes. Because they lack awareness of the total family situation, there is inefficient duplication of services, and sometimes the various agencies and helpers work at cross purposes: one family I know of had various family members simultaneously involved with 18 agencies. By treating whole families, furthermore, contact can be made with asymptomatic people who bring others into treatment; these people may never seek treatment for themselves, and yet have great pathological impact on their intimates. The family approach, then, could move the helping professions into a heretofore unreachable part of the population. Moreover, since problems in families tend to repeat themselves from one generation to the next, treating the whole family gives us a chance to abort the problems in this generation—a truly preventive method. Rather than perceiving the family as an interference in the treatment of a "patient," or as a noxious influence, we can recognize it as needing help itself, and as containing the potential for possible change.

The mental health professions have traditionally dealt with emotional problems through programs set up for different population groups—children, adolescents, adults, the aged—and for various diagnostic categories: schizophrenia, learning disabilities, drug abuse. As a matter of fact, the NIMH is organized in this way, and funds its programs along these fractionated dimensions. By its very nature, family therapy cuts across population groups by simultaneously treating the several generations of the family; and since family therapists regard a "patient's" symptoms as an indication of a family-wide disturbance, diagnostic categories become somewhat irrelevant. Consequently, a Family Unit within a CMHC requires autonomy and a clear self-identity, since it serves across all the services of a Center.

I proposed the following programs as functions of the Family Unit:

Family Diagnostic Intake Evaluations

Family therapy experience has indicated that mental health professionals cannot rely on the school's, or the court's, or the family's, or even on a referring professional's definition of what the problem is, and who the patient is who alone needs evaluation or treatment. When a child is brought in for help, or an adult comes in for help, family therapists regard that person as the representative of the family group. He or she is the symptom-bearer, the consequence of the balance of forces in the family at any given time. A long-term, continuous, often hidden, dynamic family struggle has preceded the outbreak of that person's symptoms. Symptoms are formed, selected, faked, shared, perpetuated, carried vicariously for someone else, or extinguished on the basis of the family relationship struggles. Symptoms may be bribes, manipulations, games, the result of genuine intrapsychic conflicts, blackmail efforts, nonspecific attempts to introduce excitement or variance into a rigid, dead family, tactics in achieving a family advantage, and so forth (Framo, 1970). Unless the whole family is observed interacting together, it is very difficult to tell what the symptoms mean and who or what needs changing. Not the psychiatrist who does a consultation, or the clinical psychologist who administers tests, or the social worker who interviews a relative is in a position to understand the meaning of the presenting symptoms he is called upon to diagnose or treat.

Sometimes the dynamics of a particular family situation may require that one of its members be put out of the family. For example, a mother, married a second time, is forced to choose between her child and her second husband who can't stand her child. Not wanting to lose her second chance at happiness, yet not being able just to give up her child, she focuses upon some disability in the child, who is then taken to a professional for diagnosis and possible placement "for the child's sake." It is a bit frightening to realize how often mental health professionals officially certify the family's process of designating a patient. One wonders how many psychiatrists, clinical psychologists, and social workers have lent themselves to family extrusion processes, the rejects of which populate our institutions for mentally ill children, delinquents, and aged, and our mental hospitals, boarding schools, prisons, and military academies. Family diagnostic evaluations were proposed as the best way to determine what really produced the manifest symptoms in one or more family members, and indeed, whether there is a "patient" as such. Some behaviors are labeled by the family as mental illness which to outsiders are clearly not abnormal, and may even be adaptive. Other behaviors, which are clearly disordered or dangerous from a psychiatric or social adjustment point of view, are denied, blocked out, or minimized by the family. Parents may be disturbed by their child's stealing, and remain oblivious to his suicidal gestures, or to the consequences of the child's being their marriage counselor when they fight. Or a husband may prefer to see his wife's depression as her "illness," rather than as her response to his extramarital affairs or his refusal to talk with her.

In order to provide more efficient service which could lead to lasting and fundamental change, I claimed, practitioners must widen their conceptions of the problems they are called upon to treat, and consider how they do influence and could influence the decisive intrafamilial struggles fought just behind the manifest front of clinical symptomatology. A number of advantages for CMHC purposes in evaluating whole families, including the so-called "well" siblings, on initial consultation, were cited.

1. By evaluating whole families, more patient-community needs are met, not only because more people are seen, but because treatment and remedial efforts can be aimed intelligently and consequently given more rapidly than by traditional methods.
2. Family evaluations help avoid the "sickness-patient-diagnosis-treatment" sequence for one person. They also help other family members to take responsibility for the process in which they all share, so that these other members no longer have to expiate guilt through a variety of maneuvers.
3. Some people, especially adolescents and asymptomatic spouses, are often resistant to psychotherapeutic exploration. However, the involvement of the family increases motivation in truly symptomatic individuals, and may avoid desperate acting out or graver symptomatology as a means of forcing relatives to do something. Scapegoated family members then no longer have to feel that everything is being dumped on them.
4. Family evaluations help avoid hospitalization or institutionalization. This means there is no need to label someone a "mental patient," which can mark or scar a person for life and help make the problems irreversible. Occasionally a disturbed person thrusts forward someone else in the family as the patient, who, because it suits the family system, accepts the designation. Some "well" siblings have been found to be more disturbed than the labeled patient. And when the siblings are healthier, their presence in sessions is vital because they can usually give objective views of family events.
5. Caplan (1965) has stated that the goal of community psychiatry "demands the smallest possible intervention in each instance, consonant with getting the sufferer back onto the track of adjustment and adaptation in the world of reality." Whenever a family is seen for evaluation, diagnostic and therapeutic functions overlap. Sometimes opening up family communication in just one session can unfurl a process that afterwards makes it unnecessary for the family to return. Even small system changes, such as involving the father more in the family, can make a great difference in total family functioning. Insistence on seeing fathers fills a gap in the traditional approach which tends to exclude them from participation.

What if the rest of the family, other than the symptomatic one, refuses to come in for family sessions? Although this does happen, in my experience it is rarer than one might think. If the professional has convictions about the family approach and presents it as "This is the way we work," most families will come in. Those professionals who have mixed feelings and doubt convey their uncertainty; or they apologize, rather than offering the session as a real opportunity. Most families are willing to come in, if for no other reason than to express their concern about the "patient." The family is defined, for these purposes, as those members of the immediate, extended, or psychological family who exert a demonstrable influence on the family system.

Short-Term Family Crisis Therapy

The practice of seeing families as soon as possible for emergency situations may mean well-aimed therapeutic intervention in families who are in the midst of an acute crisis. Acute crises develop around such events as suicide attempts; sudden personality changes in a family member; a death in the family or a successful suicide; an adolescent who has been arrested, run away from home, been truant, been taking drugs, or has become pregnant out of wedlock; someone's dropping out of school; premarital conflicts with in-laws; marital conflict where separation or divorce is imminent; post-divorce crises; squabbles about a will; the institutionalization of an adolescent or an aged grandparent; a parent is going to prison; situations where a parent is out of work or cannot take care of the house or children. Short-term family therapy (1 to 10 sessions) can help resolve such emergencies because families in crises are usually more open to exploration and change. Therapeutic intervention is being introduced at a decisive time and in ways which can critically influence the later course of the family.

Clinical experience with brief family therapy shows that alleviation or removal of disorganizing stress situations usually results in a continued process of improvement, even in the absence of prolonged psychotherapy. Family sessions frequently break chronic cycles of uncommunicativeness and start a process of snowballing whereby the family can come to rely on its own self-corrective mechanisms. Kaffman (1963) evaluated the results of 70 families seen in short-term family therapy, and found that in 75% of the families there was a high degree of improvement, as shown by disappearance of symptoms and referral problems, with only 5% showing no change; follow-up checks revealed that the changes were sustained. Changes in family dynamics may ameliorate individual disturbances even in the absence of individual therapy; on the other hand, prolonged individual psychotherapy may fail to bring about clinical improvement due to the absence of parallel changes in the family system. Short-term therapy methods, moreover, fit into the expectancies of the great number of people who have no sophistication about psychotherapy, and are often surprised that more than one session may be necessary to help solve their problems.

Multiple Family and Couples Group Therapy

Multiple family therapy (MFT), consisting of the simultaneous meeting of several families together, has a number of advantages. Laqueur et al. (1964, 1973) and Davies et al. (1966) are among those who have reported on their experiences with MFT. This treatment method has been found to be especially helpful with disorganized families who could not tolerate the intensity and depth of single family therapy; the presence of other families and consequent diffusion often enables them to participate more freely, especially when there are common problems. And there are almost always common problems. Every family has to deal with parent–child relations, marital conflicts, who does what around the house, disciplining of children, relationships with extended family, expression of feelings, privacy, and similar matters. MFT enables each family to compare itself to other families, and they do learn from each other, by pointing things out to each other and by identification. Mothers, fathers, teenagers, smaller children, and grandparents have an opportunity to share and compare the ways other families handle conflict. Broken, one-parent families are especially helped by being with other families, especially if a father from one family is present as a model for fatherless children in other families. These "sheltered workshops in family communication" have been so successful that families who have been through the process have referred other families from their neighborhood or circle of friends—a circumstance which certainly has implications for a community mental health center.

Couples group therapy (Framo, 1973) is based on the principle that several married couples meeting together, usually with a male–female cotherapy team, can improve their relationship or get help in terminating the marriage. Couples get honest feedback from others, and benefit by observing how other couples work out their problems. Since there is a direct relationship between marital problems and problems in the original families of spouses, treatment sessions involving these adults and their families of origin can be held for motivated people (Framo, 1976).

Family Outreach Program

This sort of program may help the families in the catchment area who are either unable or unwilling to come to the Center. These are the indigent, unmotivated, often fragmented families who do not ordinarily seek professional help, cannot keep regular therapy hours, and are culturally unable to be treated by the usual psychotherapy techniques. Yet, this is also the population which has proportionately high rates of delinquency and crime, drug and alcohol addiction, infant mortality, unemployment, admission to state hospitals, and physical illness. All these disadvantaged families share, in common, poverty, despair, powerlessness, anomie, transiency of marital bonds with high rates of desertion, separation, and illegitimacy.

Nonprofessional indigenous family counselors were to be trained to see these families in their homes and help them with the emotional issues surrounding their real problems—housing, jobs, food, truancy, legal problems, public assistance, and marital conflicts.

Training and Research Programs

In addition to the foregoing clinical programs, we planned to institute training programs in family and marital therapy for CMHC personnel, and a program of evaluative research on the effectiveness of the clinical programs.

The projected training program was to be on two levels. One level of training in family dynamics and everyday family life problems was designed for pre- and nonprofessionals in the Center—medical students, residents, psychology and social work students, indigenous family workers, and nurses—and others outside the Center, such as general practitioners (GP's), police, pastoral counselors, teachers, and others involved with family problems. The second level of training was designed for CMHC professionals with prior experience in individual or group therapy. These professionals were to be trained in family and marital therapy, utilizing, in addition to other training methods, the observation of family therapy sessions through the one-way mirror.

An important part of any program is its research function, because without systematic evaluation there is no way to determine whether a program is doing what it is supposed to do (Framo, 1972). Accordingly, a research plan was formulated to study, codify, and evaluate the clinical programs of the family unit in order to appraise their effectiveness.

Out of my enthusiasm for what the family approach had to offer, and being unaware of the truly formidable difficulties involved in such an undertaking, in the proposal I recommended a daring concept. I proposed that CMHC's become family centers, and that diagnostic family evaluations, where possible, become a routine part of the admission procedure to a CMHC, no matter how the problem was presented or who presented it. I was not suggesting that family therapy be done in all situations, since that would be unfeasible and at times inappropriate. Rather, on the basis of several family evaluation sessions, once the symptom in its context was better understood, a team would be in a better position to determine which of a variety of treatment modalities was indicated and for whom; and referrals could be made to the various services of the CMHC—whether individual psychotherapy, conjoint marital therapy, peer group therapy, partial hospitalization, drug or alcoholic services, or family therapy. The family evaluation might also reveal that a psychiatric problem was not present; or that referrals were needed for specialized services like vocational guidance, homemaker service, remedial reading, parent effectiveness training, speech therapy, halfway house, employment services, homes for unwed mothers, or medical care. Family diagnostic evaluations, in other words, would constitute the primary admission procedure.

Governmental recognition of all the obvious (to me) truths contained in this proposal, I fantasized, would precipitate an immediate call from Washington to come down there and help reorganize the entire CMHC movement. The only official message I got from Washington, however, for 3 long years was silence. It was the beginning of my education on the mysterious workings of governmental and medical organizations. What now follows is a personal account of what actually happened later.

When I joined the Center in 1969, having no official standing (I was hired on paper, I believe, as a psychiatrist in mental retardation), I had to make do with makeshift quarters in the outpatient service. I had no staff or even a secretary, and started seeing families alone. In a short while I was able to get a secretary, and about a year later was moved to an old building which turned out to be a blessing in disguise. The building contained a large room with a fireplace that could be used as a treatment room; it looked more like a living room than an office—much better for family sessions. The director managed to find some money for installing a one-way mirror and for swivel chairs for treatment families. But we had no office furniture; so my secretary and I borrowed, expropriated, and scrounged around for old file cabinets, a typewriter, and a couple of desks. The women's auxiliary board of the hospital, after I gave them a hard sell about the value of the work we were doing, kindly donated money for drapes and decorations, so that the place looked fairly livable and not so bare. By writing to department stores in the city, we were able to get them to donate rugs. The director also squeezed money out of somewhere to set up a sound system and tape recorder so family sessions could be observed as part of a training program. In addition, a way was found for me to hire two staff members, a family therapist and a nonprofessional family counselor by letting them occupy unfilled slots from other services. We were nearly in business. Those days of having to get by on a shoestring were difficult, but nonetheless challenging and exciting. At the same time, I wished I had the plush quarters and video equipment they had in the medical college.

Having been used to the pace of a research and training institute for many years, I was unprepared for the rapid pace of a community mental health center. Memos, guidelines, announcements crossed my desk by the hundreds; written reports were constantly requested, and there were innumerable meetings with various services and agencies for sundry purposes. There was even a meeting once on why we had so many meetings. In any event, I got to know the people at the Center better, came to like many of them, and was learning how a CMHC worked. During meetings on delivery of services, when I would bring up the value of seeing whole families, I was listened to politely, but not heard. A curious dual attitude existed on the part of most of the professional staff: on the one hand, they were fascinated by family therapy and what it could do; and on the other hand, they continued to treat patients as they always had. In the Children's Unit, they operated from a child-guidance model of treating the child, with the social worker seeing the parents, usually only the mother. Now and again some therapists would come over to observe family sessions, and this created interest in starting the training programs. I pretty much had to bootleg families to treat; because of my reputation some families were referred from agencies in the community. We rarely got fresh crisis situations, and frequently had to deal with families whose problems had calcified and who shopped professionally for help. Marital problems had usually been handled by treating the partners separately, but when the advantages of conjoint treatment became more apparent, we started getting couples referred to us.

During this period several informal messages came down from the NIMH that if I rewrote the grant and oriented it toward the treatment of children or drug abuse, money might be available. I ignored these hints, determined to stick to my convictions. I got caught up in that syndrome familiar to those awaiting the outcome of a grant application—I anxiously followed the newspapers and news-letter reports on how much Congress would appropriate for the NIMH and on whether the President would cut NIH funds, and I worried about whether the application would get lost in the bureaucracy. The Vietnam War was still on, and I remember thinking bitterly that the Family Unit could be funded for the cost of one army tank. After an on-site visit from an NIMH committee, who were handled quite gingerly, we received word from the feds that the project was funded for an 8-year period for a million and a half dollars overall.

I had not, however, anticipated the roadblocks thrown up by the state and city mental health offices, who were required to give matching funds. The state informed us that they didn't know if they could support a project that seemed to violate the CMHC act, which requires treatment for psychiatric illness. In other words, a married couple technically could not get help from a CMHC for their marital relationship; each partner needed a psychiatric diagnosis, and if they were not "sick" they were not eligible for treatment. By treating people without symptoms the Family Unit would technically be breaking the law. Luckily, the director of the center knew the then commissioner of mental health for the state, and after repeated phone calls to him, we got state approval. The deputy health commissioner for the city office of mental health was a friend of mine, so I was surprised when he seriously questioned the value and even the legal status of a family unit. He wanted to know, why have an independent unit for family therapy in a CMHC? If they gave matching funds for a Family Unit, why not set up units for group therapy or other treatment modalities? Somehow I was able to communi-cate that the family approach was not just another form of treatment; and eventual-ly, with the assistance of the regional director of NIMH, who saw the merits of the proposal, the city office gave final approval. It should not have been necessary to use the help of friends.

Now we were legal! We could hire staff, put all the programs into operation, and, wonder of wonders, even get a videotape recorder—one of the most effective training devices and therapeutic tools via videotape playback to families. I discovered however that I could not hire staff until I prepared job descriptions. Job descriptions for family therapists did not exist, and so far as I could find out, they didn't exist anywhere in the country. So I had to devise job descriptions of various levels of responsibility: for my job of Chief, for Assistant Chief, Senior Family Therapist, Family Therapists II and I, and Indigenous Family Counselors II and I. Since family therapy is an interdisciplinary approach, I felt that family therapists should be paid according to their training, experience, and competence as family therapists, and not according to their basic professional designation. This idea was completely contrary to state regulations and salary practices of the medical school. Psychiatrists had to be paid more than psychologists, who in turn were paid more than social workers. I couldn't fight city hall and had to give in to that hard reality, but I did resent the fact that my assistant chief, a psychiatrist, with far less experience, got $3,000 more a year than I did.

It was not easy to recruit experienced family therapists. And many applicants, who would never have applied for individual or group therapy positions without prior training, felt sure they could treat families; after all, they grew up in a family. Eventually a staff of eight was recruited, including my former secretary who had left to get training and a master's degree, and returned to the unit.

The next hurdle was the requirement, which also exists with insurance companies, that we give an official APA diagnosis to every member of the family. CMHC regulations prescribed that these statistics be kept by the research section of the Center. We developed the practice of labeling babies as having "infant adjustment reactions," and adults were fairly routinely diagnosed as suffering from "anxiety reactions." After all, who does not have to adjust and who is not anxious in this world?

One cannot escape a numbers game in a CMHC. All the services had to report monthly how many patients they saw, and it was impossible not to compare the patient census of each service when we had our chief-of-service meetings. Although accountability in a CMHC is a worthy endeavor, nonetheless this procedure fostered competition among services to see the largest number of patients. It also accounted for the territoriality syndrome; that is to say, patients, with some exceptions, tended to get the kind of treatment which was available wherever they happened to enter the system. The various services tended to hold on to the patients they got in order to build up their census, except for the "impossible" patients they would try to unload. There seemed to be no way of evaluating quality or appropriateness of treatment. I too pushed my staff to see as many people as possible.

In the early days, we used to insist that the entire family come in. Several times we followed the usual family therapy practice of refusing to see, say, a mother who came in alone to complain about a child or husband. Then one day we learned that one of these clients called the city office of mental health to complain that we were denying treatment. After that experience, we started family therapy with whoever showed up for sessions, and built up to the whole family from there. There are certainly things you can do in private practice that you cannot do in a public agency.

Families and couples were usually seen by male-female cotherapy teams, an inefficient procedure by CMHC standards since it cut down on patient–staff ratio times, but a most effective therapy procedure that produced change. It was difficult to get referrals from within the Center, so we established relationships with, and got referrals from schools, the clergy, nonpsychiatric physicians, the courts, and so forth. In our first year we saw over 200 families containing over 500 individuals; however, I was always more interested in high treatment standards than numbers. The outreach program worked out fairly well because we had a dedicated nonprofessional team. Some problems did come up: some families did not want to be seen in their homes, because they did not want neighbors to know that people were coming to their home to help them; other families objected to getting help from those who were not "real doctors."

The other services of the Center seemed to have mixed feelings about the Family Unit. Perhaps they were responding to my earlier efforts to sell the family approach—efforts, I learned, that created defensiveness. Perhaps they resented the specialness of the Unit or our relative opulence, because many of the services had to struggle for staff and equipment. (The Center at one point nearly closed down due to insufficient funding). On the other hand, those who observed treatment sessions, and came to see psychopathology in an entirely different light, did request training. The training programs turned out to be very successful for the pre- and nonprofessionals; but very rarely did the professionals enroll, especially the psychiatrists. Some of the Center's professional staff started seeing couples and families conjointly, but lacking specific training, some of them did family therapy inappropriately; bringing the family together to talk only about the patient is not family therapy. I came to understand that these professionals felt that to come to the Unit's training program would have constituted some loss of face. Many of the difficulties of the Unit would have been obviated had I been a physician or psychiatrist.

Being in a medical setting had some advantages, because we were able to get involved with that vast, untapped area of family problems associated with medical wards. The family therapist–physician on the Unit became a consultant to pediatrics, the dialysis ward, OB-Gyn, and even to physicians dealing with families when someone died. Medical hospitals have not yet recognized the enormous potential of family work in the practice of medicine. I found the medical students in the training programs to be more receptive than the psychiatric residents, who by that time were firmly grounded in the individual view of mental illness. Another productive training program was one I gave for a group of policemen, who spend the majority of their time, I was surprised to learn, dealing with family disturbances.

The number of reports I had to write increased; there were progress reports, research reports, 1-year plans, and 5-year plans. Meetings with outside agencies and other services of the CMHC proliferated; we were seeking out sources of clients, coordinating services, monitoring continuity of care, and so forth. I frankly got the feeling that we spent so much time writing and meeting about what we were doing and were going to do that there wasn't enough time in which to do it. Never had I been so tired at the end of the day. One observation I've made about mental health organizations, not just CMHCs, is that when the census goes down and there is pressure of service to justify professional existence, the staff get more anxious, have more meetings, and end up treating each other.

After 4 years at the Center, a series of circumstances led to my leaving the CMHC and accepting an offer to enter academic life. Those circumstances are another story, but one contributing factor was the opportunity it gave me for more time in which to practice, teach, develop concepts, and write.

As I look back on my efforts to set up an independent family therapy unit within a CMHC, the perspective of time makes it possible to evaluate the whole experience. Firstly, I have serious question as to whether a systems model of therapy can be mixed or integrated with an individual-illness model. I do not intend to denigrate individual therapy. There are proper indications for individual treatment, and there will always be a need for it. But I believe that the premises, philosophy, and orientation of the two models are too different for a marriage to occur. Family therapy, I am sure, is now probably being done at most CMHCs; but I can understand why no other independent family therapy units have been set up in any CMHC in the country (to my knowledge). When some of the full implications of the systems viewpoint become apparent—in terms of their effects on diagnosis and treatment procedures, admission policies, status, and so forth—establishment mental health finds it too threatening. Various people around the country, when they heard about the Unit, got in touch with me and asked how they could do the same thing; I was not able to be too sanguine about their prospects, and promised that someday I would publish the reasons. A combination of this difference in philosophy with the way the laws are written, the bureaucracy of NIMH, the rules and regulations of CMHCs, not to mention the traditions of medical settings, add up to an awe-inspiring set of obstacles.

I do not know to what extent my own shortcomings led to less than striking success. My inexperience as an administrator was apparent in the way I felt I had to monitor everything myself, and had difficulty delegating duties. I discovered how easy it is to blame things on the boss until you yourself are the boss. For instance, I had great difficulty bringing myself to fire people. Possibly I could have been less doctrinaire and more tolerant of traditional ways of helping people, and not so imbued with a self-defined sense of revolution.

I also do not mean to criticize the Center, which in many ways was a fine model CMHC when compared to others. Nor do I wish to fault the sincere, conscientious, and competent people at the Center, the great majority of whom worked very hard to help the residents of the community they served. Indeed, statistical evidence exists that they ameliorated much human distress. However, most mental health professionals are bound by the concepts by which they were trained, and CMHCs are limited by ill-defined conceptual foundations. I emphasize that, as in a family, CMHCs are not "bad" systems, and no one, really, is to blame. People get caught up in organizational structures with their rules and guidelines, and these systems develop a life of their own, with their own regulatory powers. In any event, for me, overall, it was a good go, and I don't regret the experience.

Since I left the Center, I have learned that the CMHC has decentralized. The catchment area has been divided into five districts, each with its own team of specialists and generalists. Apparently decentralization has been found to be more effective in the delivery and volume of services. For example, whereas in the past only 20% of therapists' time was spent in face-to-face contacts with patients, with decentralization this figure has increased to 50%. The family therapy unit has continued in modified form, and the previous training programs must have had some effect, because many more people are now doing family therapy. I had apparently left some imprint after all.

13

A Personal Viewpoint on Training in Marital and Family Therapy (1979)

At the risk of sounding as if I am quibbling, I would like to say at the outset that I question the title of this program. From its beginnings the family movement has been interdisciplinary in nature, and I do not want that to change. I would also be against the topics "Family Therapy Training for Psychiatrists," or "Social Workers," or whatever. Admittedly, of the three major mental health professions, psychologists are most underrepresented in the field, and that may be why this topic was chosen—in order to see how a systems viewpoint can become a part of the mainstream of psychology. There is very little that I do today that has anything to do with the way I was trained as a clinical psychologist. Accordingly, I consider myself, foremost, a "family therapist and theoretician" and only secondarily a psychologist; when I am asked to state my profession I say "family therapist." These are the reasons I have not joined the organization called the Academy of Psychologists in Marital and Family Therapy. We have fought long and hard in this field to wipe out the professional differences, with all the hang-ups about status, salary, and who-is-in-charge. When cotherapists are working with families or couples, it matters little what their professional designation is and much more who they are. Besides, I happen to think there are too many different kinds of mental health professionals, which is very confusing to the general public. I like Kubie's old idea of selecting people to be trained specifically as professional psychotherapists. These people's profession would be that of psychotherapist—not that of psychologist, psychiatrist, social worker, or counselor.

In this article I will discuss some ideas about my philosophy of family therapy

Reprinted with permission from *Professional Psychology*, 1979, *10*, 868–875. Copyright © 1979, American Psychological Association.

training, the place of the contextual approach in psychology, some of my experiences doing training in different settings, and some thoughts about national developments in family and marital therapy training.

I personally believe that to some extent family therapists are born and not made. Some people, having mastered in some way the struggles in their original families, continue the process with clinical families. Most family therapists were healers or jugglers or manipulators in their families of origin, and when we train students formally, we continue the training they got from their parents, brothers and sisters, grandparents, aunts, and uncles. These are the naturals; they have an instinct for this kind of work and "know" family dynamics inside their skin. They are endlessly curious about figuring out family puzzles. These are the people I like to get as students; they are turned on to the field and are highly motivated. I do not like to train people who say, "They sent me here to learn family therapy." (On the other hand, not all family therapists can treat all kinds of family situations; we know little yet about matching therapists and families.) There are some people, I have found, who can never become family therapists, no matter how much training they get. I have been criticized for taking this stance, in the form of the statement that "If we only trained the naturals, we'd only have a select few. Don't you think your average bright mental health professional can be taught technical skills and thereby many more families can be helped?" I suppose certain kinds of family therapy can be practiced in a technique-oriented way. Haley (1976) and Minuchin (1974), who deemphasize the personal aspects of family life, stress a problem-solving approach. They have developed sophisticated training programs that prepare students to deal quite adequately with certan kinds of family situations. As a matter of fact, structural family therapy and the communicational or strategic schools have become the most widely practiced forms of family therapy, in contrast to dynamic approaches. I think this is so because they are readily understandable and teachable. I also happen to believe it is an excellent form of treatment for helping and defocusing a symptomatic child. There are other kinds of problems, involving only adults (marital, divorce, extended family difficulties), for which, in my judgment, these approaches are less suitable.

As you know, in this field there is no standard body of knowledge with agreed upon goals and defined limits; there is a diversity of approaches; there is no one right way to do family or marital therapy; there is no comprehensive theory; and there is no one way to train. In the past, outstanding clinicians found a way of working that was comfortable for them; they then developed a theory based on their clinical experience, and they trained students to think and act as they did. So we see a lot of "Ackermans," "Bowenites," "Satirs," "Whitakers," and even some "Framos" going around preaching their respective gospels of truth. Those of us who were early workers in the field never did get supervision, of course; we sort of supervised each other via the one-way mirror and going over tapes. So we do not know what it is like to be a student in this area. In order to help close the distance between me and my students, I talk about the struggles I personally go through in doing this work, how I consider myself a lifelong student who will always be learning and changing, and I play tapes of cases I failed with, showing that an experienced family therapist can get lost or overwhelmed.

There are now hundreds of training programs, many of them following the teachings of a charismatic leader. Very little family therapy training is being done in academic settings; most of the family therapy training is being done in free-standing family institutes in almost every major city in the country. In a recent issue of *Family Process,* I published a list of training facilities in family therapy (Framo, 1976c). Donald Bloch, editor of *Family Process,* is now in the process of developing a catalogue of training facilities around the country. There are some training programs, however—for example, the "Boston Model" originally developed by Frederick Duhl and David Kantor (Constantine, 1976)—that do not depend on a particular ideology and stress the learning experience itself. Liddle and Halpin (1978) have reviewed the family therapy training literature comprehensively.

Although training methods usually become an extension of how one conducts therapy, nonetheless I do expose students to the many varied theories and methods of working with families so that eventually they will develop a style that is best for them. My particular philosophy and bias in training is to deal with the personal development of the trainee as well as what I call the "gut issues of family life"—the passions, hates, loves, mysteries, paradoxes, joys, measureless sacrifices, injustices, jealousies, storms, comforts, bonds, patterns, and memories of family life that are burned into the cauldrons of the mind. As I see it, *the family, not anatomy, is destiny*. I think that people who have lived bland lives, who were raised in "nice, normal, dull, stable" families, are not as likely to become good family therapists as those who have suffered and struggled some. I believe that a family diagnostic has not gone well unless there was some pain and intensity of feeling. When you are unmoved by the family's crisis and have not been able to emphathize at all with them, the family diagnostic has gone poorly.

In my basic course on family systems theory for doctoral students in clinical psychology, I do not give an exam; the only requirement is the writing of a family biography (there are risks in this—two students discovered they were adopted). The students are offered the opportunity, on a voluntary basis, to present their families to the class, and I tread a fine line in not having this procedure become therapy. The focus is on how their old family business is getting in the way of their work with families or how it is affecting the cotherapy relationship. All of us have emotional blocks in dealing with certain kinds of people or problem areas, and there is something about treating couples and families that intensifies these countertransferences in ways that individual or even group therapy does not. Some family therapists have difficulty dealing with martyrlike or aggressive mothers; trying to bolster a passive father; or establishing a connection with a remote brother or sister. Some therapists overidentify with the children or go after the parents; others consistently avoid dealing with certain material (such as sex or aggression); others have a bias against women, men, divorce, marriage, or having children; and others have a blind spot about fighting or privacy because "that's not the way it was done in *my* family"—which was, of course, the *right* way.

It is hard for me to imagine, then, that one can treat families and couples without some firsthand knowledge and experience of one's own family. Although writing a family biography (which is a very different experience from talking about one's family) can be painful, it is one way of getting in touch with what families are all about. I might say that the students have said that this paper was the most difficult yet the most meaningful assignment they had ever had. The best way to become a family therapist in my judgment, however, is to have family therapy oneself. While I do not know if it should be a requirement, I think it is helpful to know what it is like to be on the other side. (I wish I had had family therapy when I was a child.) In this connection I find the idea appealing that, when possible, the spouses or other relatives of trainees be included in some aspects of the training. Every family therapist I know acknowledges the powerful effects on his or her own family and marriage from doing this kind of work. In my classes I extend an open invitation for students to bring spouses, parents, or siblings to class. I understand that other training programs do this, such as Phillips's program at the California Family Study Center (Phillips and Kelly, 1975). (I have also speculated about having trainees and their mates in couples' groups; I suspect the divorce rate among marital and family therapists is quite high.)

In addition to the foregoing, I do, of course, use other methods of training. Insofar as didactic material is concerned, I believe trainees should be familiar with the classical literature in the field, although the literature is growing so fast I cannot keep up with it. (The American Association for Marital and Family Therapy [AAMFT] is now distributing a bibliography I recently compiled; 10 years ago there were only several books in the field; now there are over 100 books on marital and family therapy.) But unless the reading is tied in with clinical material and the actual experiencing of doing therapy, it becomes an intellectual exercise. When I discuss a particular theoretical topic, I play an audio- or videotape excerpt from a treatment session, or we role play a simulated family to illustrate the point. Just reading articles on family therapy will do very little. I like to do supervision in a group, utilizing the group process. I also believe that a lot can be learned about family dynamics from plays, movies, and novels—such as *Death of a Salesman, Long Day's Journey Into Night, I Never Sang for My Father, Scenes From a Marriage, The Subject Was Roses, Who's Afraid of Virginia Woolf?*, and so forth. Furthermore, one area that is neglected most in family therapy training programs is knowledge about ethnic family cultures such as the Irish, Italian, black, Jewish, and "WASP" families. If you do not know the ways and style of a particular ethnic kind of family, you can interpret normal behavior for that culture as pathology.

One aspect of live supervision I should mention: I think it is very difficult for a trainee to sit in with a very experienced family therapist. For instance, I have sat in with Nathan Ackerman and Virginia Satir and had trouble finding a place for myself. I too am a high-powered guy who does not allow much room for a trainee cotherapist. So while I believe that cotherapy is a powerful method for both training and treatment, I have my trainees do it with each other rather than with me. I find I can serve a better function being behind the one-way mirror with the rest of the training group, alerting them to unnoticed interactions and strategies. When the cotherapists are of more equal experience, they can better fight and work through their problems with each other.

I have found Carl Whitaker's method of the supervisor-as-visiting-consultant to be useful—to sit in on a session and deal with the relationship between the therapists and family. I need this help myself sometimes in dealing with a transference-countertransference logjam. I also believe that male-female cotherapy teams are more effective. I know that when couples and families find that a man and a woman will be seeing them, they are always relieved. It makes the sessions seem less like "mental illness" or psychiatry, about which most people are suspicious and fearful. Husband-wife cotherapy teams are coming increasingly into practice; I have been working with my wife, who is a social worker-family therapist, in our evening private practice for the last 7 years. Other dimensions of training should include some awareness of the impact of changing sex roles on marital and family relations, as well as information about alternative family and marital life styles. Social changes are occurring very rapidly and are having profound effects on family relationships—most couples have many years left after the children are gone; and the women's movement, the rising divorce rate, and many more remarriages and reconstituted families are all examples of social changes affecting the family. Knowledge about contemporary changes, as well as ecological systems surrounding the family, is vital.

I would now like to say something about the place of family theory in psychology and some difficulties I have encountered doing training in an academic setting. My criticisms of the field of general psychology predated my family therapy experience. I could never quite understand why the human being was segmented by the subject matter of psychology into a series of isolated separate functions, such as cognition, affect, sensation, and perception. I remember the profound psychological discovery that need influences perception. Aside from Maslow and a few others, little mention was made about the study of the whole person as a set of interacting functions, much less the person in context. Indeed, philosophically, I have felt closer to social psychology than to clinical psychology, which still is exclusively concerned with what goes on inside people rather than what goes on between people. Actually, my main theoretical interest is in the *relationship* between the intrapsychic and the transactional (Framo, 1970).

In any event, following 13 years of work with Boszormenyi-Nagy at the Eastern Pennsylvania Psychiatric Institute, I attempted to organize a family unit in a community mental health center associated with the department of psychiatry of a medical school. I have already reported (Framo, 1976b) on the frustrations and difficulties of introducing a systems perspective into a traditional psychiatric department. Today I would like to tell you a little bit about some of the problems of doing this work in an academic psychology setting. It must be remembered that I entered academic life after 20 years of a very different kind of theoretical and clinical experience; I had been out of touch with academia since I was a graduate student at the University of Texas. In response to pressure from the doctoral students, I was recruited, and I accepted the position because, among other reasons, frankly, having the summers off would give me more time to write. I came in as a full professor and got tenure, so I have managed to avoid much of the competitive politicking that goes on in every academic department.

Since I have been immersed in the family movement, I was somewhat out of touch with developments in clinical psychology, although I soon discovered that most of the faculty in the clinical division were still teaching such traditional subjects as diagnostic testing, theories of personality, and psychopathology, and the psychotherapeutic orientation was primarily one-to-one. Some transactional analysis and encounter group work was being done; one staff member specialized in community psychology and one was an existentialist with whom I could communicate somewhat about a systems point of view.

I get many letters from people around the country asking to enter my family therapy program, and I have to tell them I do not have a program, but merely teach several courses within a clinical psychology doctoral program. I also tell the students in my classes that by no means am I training family therapists in this setting. The best way to become a family therapist is to treat families under intensive supervision; this training can best be done at a local family institute once one has completed training in one's basic profession. All I am doing in my courses is attempting to open students' eyes to a wider perspective and giving them a taste of this new field. It is my aim, I tell my classes, that by the end of the course they will never again be able to look at psychopathology in the same way—that even if they never do marital or family therapy they will always keep in mind the surrounding context of a client. I also state my conviction that the theory is far more important than the therapy—which has to do with "How do you change the situation?" Some of the students connect with the material and a few go on to become family therapists; the receptivity of other students is like that of psychiatric residents—they have been so grounded in intrapsychic psychology that it is too late. I find the undergraduates, like medical students, are more open to hearing the concepts.

Each doctoral student at Temple takes a different clinical practicum each semester; these practicum teams are run by a different faculty member who teaches his or her own kind of therapy. The students on my team are invariably confused by the dissonance between my orientation and that of the rest of the division. They say, "But my other supervisor said to do it another way," and I reply that one must learn in this world to live with paradox. Besides, I think mental health professionals ought to be familiar with the traditional theories and methods before they reject them. Still, occasionally, there are practical consequences that follow from the theoretical differences between me and the rest of the faculty. For instance, I rarely agree to have a child tested. (The bulk of the referrals to our clinic are children who are referred for testing.) If testing is to be done, the whole family should be tested by one of the interaction techniques. This stance does not mean that I would not refer a child for specialized help, such as for a bona fide learning disability or dyslexia—in the same way that I might refer a mother or father for vocational guidance.

I am viewed in my division as a kind of strange, radical professional who has lost his way. At division meetings, when we discuss the philosophy of training of a clinical psychologist, I have gotten tired of giving the same speech—namely, departing from the simplistic notion that human behavior is a function of psychological properties within the individual; family-systems theory emphasizes contexts, especially the intimate context of the family as a powerful motivating and organizing force in human affairs. I believe that the family is the most important (current, not just past) influence on your life, even if you have moved across the continent to get away from it. (People delude themselves into thinking they can solve problems with their intimates by geographical distance.) I stress my belief that unless clinical psychology moves in the direction of studying contexts and developing an ecological systems approach to human problems, it is doomed to extinction as a viable profession.

My speech is typically followed by a discussion about a safer topic, like who is going to teach abnormal psychology next semester, because the university needs the money and abnormal psychology is popular. The fact that family-systems theory is not a required course suggests how effective I have been. Shapiro (1975) has written about some of the problems inherent in teaching family therapy in a traditional setting. He states that some of the very techniques that are taught in other aspects of the program and that are effective in one-to-one therapy are inappropriate when working with families. (For instance, when whole families come in, the various members do not regard themselves as patients.)

Furthermore, I believe that part of the training of family therapists should be on the politics of the setting wherein their work will be practiced. Despite the enormous growth of family therapy, I still hear stories about guerrilla and infiltration tactics; in some places one still has to bootleg his work. At Temple University, counseling psychology is in a separate department, and there is a psychologist there who teaches family theory and therapy. He told me he has to come to my office to talk every now and then so he can get a sense of being heard and not feel so isolated. I have wondered whether family-systems theory can exist side by side with more mechanistic views of the human being and individual theories of psychopathology. Nathan Ackerman once told me that is why he set up his own family institute.

Stanton, in his survey of 1975, found that family theory and therapy was being taught in only 10 out of 130 approved clinical and counseling doctoral programs in the country. There are only a handful of internships in the county that are family oriented. I have seen only one book on theories of personality that included family theory. Compared to psychiatry and social work, psychology has been slow in catching up, but I think it will happen. Family theory has had a miniscule effect on the subject matter of academic psychology as a whole, but I think this will change, too.

Not many students in our program do dissertations on marital and family interaction and I can understand their decision to do a traditional study. It is more difficult to do studies in the family interaction area, and one has a better chance of getting the Ph.D. by sticking to the usual. I am supervising several dissertations being done by students who are really dedicated to the area. For example, one student is testing Bowen's hypothesis that people tend to marry those who are at the same level of personality differentiation, however different their social functioning level may appear. Another student is testing whether people who live together before marriage develop better marriages than those who do not live together first. Still another is investigating the impact of the firstborn on the marital relationship.

I would like to conclude with some news. After 25 years of resisting forming a national organization, a few of us have begun efforts in this direction. It is called the American Family Therapy Association (AFTA). Once we have a national organization, many things will follow—among them perhaps some research on evaluation of training methods. We will be able to have national meetings, and one outcome will be the exchange of information on training and, most controversial of all, the setting of some standards. It is going to be very difficult to determine who is, and who is not, a qualified family therapist.

14

My Families,
My Family[1] (1968)

I do not know when I first became aware of the phenomenon that treating families not only revives the specters of one's own past family life, but also has subtle, suffusing effects on the therapist's current personal family relationships. After doing family therapy, and seeing what emotional systems can do to people, I take my own family life more seriously. In the living presence of a mother, father, brothers and sisters, the constellation in which most of us grew, one finds oneself transported back to old thoughts, longings, disharmonies, and joys in a way which can be more moving and reintegrative than one's own personal therapy or analysis. And each family we treat contains a part of our own.

Perhaps the first time I transcended the time barrier was in the first family I treated when the mother and father argued, and I recognized that I'd heard *that* fight before. The rush of memories recreated the helplessness and anxieties of an 8-year-old marriage counselor, torn with divided loyalties and the question of which parent was right, mixed with the tart-sweet feeling of being "the important one." In my sense of urgency to find the caring for each other behind the bitter interchange I suddenly became the old family healer in my ambivalent efforts to marry my parents. (In this instance I had to rely on my cotherapist whose

Reprinted with permission from *Voices: The Art and Science of Psychotherapy*, 1968, *4*, 18–27. Copyright © 1968, Voices, Inc.

[1]I would hope that it would not be necessary to explain that this paper, a kind of self-indulgent labor of love and pain on my part, by no means is intended to give a rounded account of family dynamics or the process of family therapy, which can be obtained elsewhere. I am trying to highlight a dimension which I felt could no longer be ignored. I have tried to minimize the overdramatization to which all writings of this kind are subject. G. B. Shaw once said that all autobiographies are deliberate lies because no one is ungracious enough to tell the truth about his family. I've tried to tell the truth, but in a limited way because I have not opened the door all the way. Who really can?

boundaries, I hoped, were still intact, to help me to increase the distance and pull me back to today.)

During the intervening years, as these kinds of experiences accumulated, and as I exchanged confidences with other family therapists, I have wondered whether we are dealing here with reactions, associations, personal and reality factors, empathy, or what have you, which are not fully explainable on the basis of traditional concepts of transference of the therapist, countertransference, or parataxic distortions. As I treated more and more families I have become more used to reliving each stage of my own family cycle during sessions, in a series of flashbacks at once compelling and fearsome, fascinating and despairing, growth-promoting and regressive. While I am conducting treatment sessions, with my surface calm, official and important, hiding behind my degrees and the trappings of my profession, evaluating the dynamics of the family before me, figuring out strategy, avoiding the traps, I communicate to the family only a small portion of the emotional connections I make with them, the places where we touch, protecting the private part of myself which few can reach. I choose this opportunity, in a journal which allows it, to communicate to my colleagues what must be common, if largely unspoken, experiences. The format in which I present this material is as follows: First, statements from various family therapy sessions are presented, followed by my personal reflection or vicarious participation in parentheses.

Childhood

ME TO SON: "While your mother was crying I noticed you looked very upset. It's hard for you to deal with her unhappiness, isn't it? You feel you have to do something, don't you?" (Only if parents are happy can children be. Me to mom at age of 5: "Mom, don't cry . . . I love you; you still have me. When I grow up I'm going to buy you a washing machine, so you won't have to work so hard.")

MOTHER TO FATHER: "He's *my* son. Where were you when he needed you? You were never a father to him." (I bask in the pure innocence of the favored child, feeling the goodness of Mom who comes through and does the important, little things for me. Still, I'm haunted by the look on dad's face when this was told him.)

FAMILY MEMBER TO ME: "Doc, this is my *family* you're talking about." (Symbiotic family loyalty is the most powerful of human motives. You are used to your family and their style. Then as a child you go in a friend's house and compare families and the shock of realization that other parents, marriages, and families are different and can be better, but you defend your family anyway.)

ME TO FAMILY: "This family sounds dead, as if you have nowhere to go. Don't you ever enjoy yourselves? Don't you feel anything behind your faces?" (No response.) (Sometimes we had fun—like at Christmas dinner Dad would imitate Henry Armetta walking to the table and we shook with glee. And the time there was a peddler at the door and Mom answered the bell and said, "Nobody's home." And the peddler answered, "Nobody's home, lady?" And she replied, "No, nobody's home." . . . Well, anyway, it was funny to us.)

ME TO PARENTS: "You exploit, make parents out of, and psychologically murder your children." (How much of my anger rides on the back of old angers? With which of my undigested introjects was I dealing? Who was I trying to rescue? On whom, really, was I wreaking revenge?)

CHILD TO MOTHER: "Whenever I try to give you something or show you I care you always push me away." (I summon up these episodes: When Dad would try to kiss Mom she'd push him away and he'd wink at us with the message that he knew how to get around her. A more painful memory: My sister had bought Mom a large potted plant for Mother's Day and Mom said, disdainfully, "What did you bring me this for? It costs too much; take it back." My sister carried the plant back, crying all the way, and I wanted to hit Mom. Added frustration: If you didn't get Mom anything for Mother's Day she never let you forget it. At least my sisters, brother, and I could share things, refugees in a storm.)

CHILD IN FAMILY: "How do you sort out all your mixed feelings about your parents? When does this stop?" (When, indeed. Do we ever come to terms with this natural state of ambivalence: Did I love them? Did they love me? Did they love each other? What, pray tell, *is* love?)

SISTER TO BROTHER: "I don't understand what you're talking about. How can you say Dad was rejecting? I don't remember him that way." (You can feel a little crazy when someone reports only positive experiences with someone you feel has a negative transference fix on you, because no one is the same person with everyone. But then you have to ask yourself the critical question: Was it something in me or something in the other person?)

ME TO FATHER AND SON: "Didn't the two of you ever have a positive experience with each other? Was it always like this?" (Nostalgia: Dad was an entertainer; we kids felt pride that we had the only father on the block who went to work in a tuxedo. Dad would regale us with stories of the gangsters shooting up the nightclubs where he worked, and we were in the kitchen, late at night, fascinated and entranced. Why do I remember that?)

CHILD TO PARENTS: "As far as I'm concerned you people can go screw yourselves. I don't like your personalities: I don't like anything about you bastards!" (I'd never dared talk that way to my parents. Did I want to? Was this boy doing it for me? I recall the time my daughter told me to go to hell, and it jarred me.)

SON TO PARENTS: "Mom and Dad, I can't respect you. Mom, you go around in sloppy clothes and argue with the neighbors, and you, Dad, you always play the fool in public. How do you think that makes me feel?" (Triggered association: The shame when I first heard my parents lie—like the time the welfare lady came to check on our finances and all the kids were told to keep quiet, and Mom blandly denied that we had an automobile. Or the time we watched Dad con someone in such a likeable way that the cheated one didn't even seem to mind.)

MOTHER TO CHILDREN: "Your father is no damn good. He's a whoremaster, a liar and a cheat, and someday you'll realize it." (Funny, a lot of the things Mom said about Dad we knew were all too true, but somehow it didn't make a difference because he brought laughter into the household. We didn't respect him, but we loved him. Painful occasion in the past: Mom brought me once to peek at Dad's "girlfriend" and I hated her for that.)

SON TO FATHER: "How can I respect you when you let Mom walk all over you? What do you expect me to do?" (Dad to me: "What am I going to do about the way your Mother treats me?" Me, verbalized: "Gee, Dad, I don't know." Me, angry, unverbalized: "She's your wife, not mine.")

SON TO FATHER: "Dad, who were you to me? What did we mean to each other?" (A twinge of envy here. This son was accomplishing something with his Dad which I could no longer do because mine had died at just the point when it became possible. The first death in the family, this special grief of family-loss.)

FATHER TO SON: "You mean that time, many years ago, when I went away, you thought it was because of you that I left and that I didn't care? It was *because* I cared so much that I left. I used to hold you when you were little and feel such pride and love." (Son cries.) (Suddenly I remember the scene in *Death of a Salesman* where father asks about Biff, "Why is he crying? . . . He cried. Cried for *me!*" And the dramatic scene between father and son in *The Subject Was Roses*. Why haven't I written *my* play? Then I could tell all.)

CHILD ABOUT PARENTS: "My Mother and Father play a game with each other and all we kids know it. The tragedy for us was that when we were little we didn't know it was a game. They always hid from us the positive they had with each other." (One game I had witnessed: Dad gambled, Mom handled the money. Mom would hide the money and Dad always found her hiding places. Then the argument; then the making up; then the cycle would start again. So it goes.)

CHILD TO MOTHER: "Mom, just because you haven't talked to your brother for years is no reason I can't be friendly with him. I like him. You probably don't even remember what you argued about." (Family feuds, expected to continue from one generation to the next. Recollection: How we kids were made to feel like traitors because we liked Aunt Suzy, about whom dark hints of a lurid past were sent our way. We found out later she had disgraced the family by eloping instead of marrying in church. She had flaming red hair, noticed us, played with us, laughed a lot, and we thoroughly loved her.)

MOTHER TO CHILD: "You're very young. You don't know the heart-ache of life. Someday I'll be gone and then you may appreciate what I had to give you." (She is gone now, and I have to believe that she did the best she could with what she had to work with. What she did to us had once been done to her, by her own family. Occasionally there is that muted, panicky feeling that, no matter what,

Mom would have been the ultimate one to count on. But are the dead parents buried in the children?)

FAMILY MEMBER TO FAMILY: "We have a close family all right. Nobody listens to each other or really looks at each other. There's never time for that, and someday we're really going to regret it." (Why can't family members ever talk to each other about meaningful things? Remembered line from Wilder's *Our Town*: "God, it goes so fast . . . we don't have time to look at one another . . . Oh, Mama, please look at me as if you really saw me.")

FAMILY MEMBER TO ME: "Sometimes I wonder how many of the things you expect of our family you've been able to accomplish yourself." (Touché. Sometimes true. Settling the old family conflicts and improving the new family is a never ending process.)

PARENT TO ME: "Doctor, am I an awful parent? How would you feel if you were my son?" (Did this mother pick up my need for her? When is my child-self healthy and when is it destructive?)

Marriage

WIFE: "We have nothing to say to each other anymore. . . . It's empty and futile and I just don't care. After you're married awhile the desire is gone." (Malaise, disenchantment, and disillusionment in marriage is universal over time because romantic fusions based on internal images cannot be continually affirmed. How often does the average couple fall in and out of love over the years? One of the reasons you keep trying is because the marital relationship provides the ground for personality growth of the children.)

FAMILY MEMBER TO ME: "Just to look at you, doctor, I can't imagine you being a romantic person." (Remembering the exultation, the consciousness-expanding intoxication of that special brand of normal-craziness, "being in love." You became alive and music was richer and everything was brighter, and smiles came quicker, and you remember, too, the anticipation and feverish search for a place where you could be alone with her.)

IN MULTIPLE FAMILY SESSION, ONE HUSBAND TO THE OTHER: "What the hell are you complaining about? You got a good woman for a wife. Isn't she faithful? Isn't she attractive? There must be something wrong with you." (Plutarch is reputed to have told of the Roman who said, "See this shoe? It is not handsome? Does it not look well made? Ah, but none of you can tell where it pinches me.")

WIFE TO HUSBAND: "No one will ever know how much you have hurt me. You have been the ruination of my life . . . And when we die you kids better not bury me with him because this man never loved me." (How real is hate? Can you really only hate someone when they won't love you? We made sure we buried our parents together, united, and married at last, in death.)

HUSBAND TO WIFE: "I nag you because you're slovenly."

WIFE TO HUSBAND: "How can I be warm toward you, when you're always criticizing?" (Each marriage partner believes that the things he or she does is only in reaction to the mate's behavior. What would happen to our relationship if I did not play my characteristic role, give the expected, reciprocal response? Is this when symptoms develop?)

ME TO HUSBAND: "Why can't you give her up? Unless the two of you can entertain the possibility of doing without each other you cannot love each other." (Did I really believe this? Do I require of patients that which I might not be able to accomplish myself?)

MATES TO EACH OTHER: "I bitterly regret the day I ever married you. You're selfish, cruel, and try to dominate me and you're always critical of me in public. You give nothing to the marriage, but you have everything to give to your friends or to your own family." (This kind of sado-masochistic behavior has a special flavor and nip when there is an audience, telling others, "Look how ugly our wounds are." Do we use the kids as captive objects when we argue? Mutual projection in marriage is the mediating arena between the inner and outer worlds. Now I sound preachy. What is *my* "secret agenda" for marriage?)

HUSBAND TO WIFE: "Do you know what it's like to open up with a sincere, meaningful feeling and having it either ignored or brushed aside with a scornful or sarcastic remark? How I long for those days when we felt safe with each other, without having to weigh thoughts, and just poured them out, and we felt trust and the *response*." (What unremembered time does that evoke? But the affect is there.)

HUSBAND ABOUT WIFE: "My wife is disorganized, goes to bed in her clothes sometimes, won't wear sexy nightgowns, won't wear make-up or perfume for me, and let's herself go. It makes me furious."

WIFE TO HUSBAND: "If you really cared for me you wouldn't care how I looked." (Are they both right? Truth: Every married person secretly feels at times that the spouse is crazy and does not know how to love.)

HUSBAND ABOUT WIFE: "I'll tell you how my wife operates with sex. She feels everything has to be right before she'll come across—that sex is the dessert when everything is perfect, meaning everything is done her way. And then she says I have to listen first to how I made her angry that day. She can love only after she hurts. Shall I run through all the excuses my wife uses to avoid doing it? Well, there's 'I'm too tired!,' That's number one. . . ."

WIFE RESPONDING TO HUSBAND: "I don't think my husband is all that interested in sex. He'll wait until late at night to approach me and then he does it with the delicacy of a Sherman tank. Or he'll pick a fight with me during the day to make sure nothing will happen that night. . . . The sad part is that we'll lie there all night unable to sleep or touch each other and then we don't talk to each other the next day." (Mutual avoidance of intimacy, one of the basic problems in marriage. Does everybody have that problem?)

HUSBAND TO WIFE: "You're not angry at me; you're angry at your father."

WIFE TO HUSBAND: "Don't give me that crap!" (One of the unfortunate byproducts of therapy: the couple learn to use interpretations against each other. I feel uncomfortable, wondering if I have fed this tactic.)

ME TO HUSBAND: "You keep trying to please a wife who is impossible to please. So what do you do when you can't please someone?" (Do you stop trying to please the mate? Will she move closer if you do, or will she move further away? How much do you owe others, and how much do you owe yourself? What is mature selfishness?)

MATE ABOUT MARRIAGE: "Sometimes things go well between us, and it's a warm feeling." (Like the times a lot has happened that day and you rush home to share it. And the moments your eyes lock in a crowded room. Or in the middle of the night, reaching out and knowing she is there. We've been through a lot together.)

Parenthood

MOTHER TO CHILDREN: "Who wants children? I never wanted any. I wouldn't want them if they were covered with diamonds." (Admit it—adjustment to parenthood was tougher than adjustment to married life. There is a stress on the family whenever someone either enters the family or leaves it. But nobody prepared you for the way that little baby disrupted everything. Then the wondrous pride, the wanting-to-take-care-of and protect, the way you're sick with worry when they're ill, and how there is pleasure with each successive stage they go through and each successive child. You are given a second chance to live your own childhood again, and all the frustrations get balanced out.)

CHILD TO MOTHER: "Aw, Mom, I don't wanna come to these meetings anymore. I'd rather be out playing." (I feel jealous sometimes when I see my kids doing things I can no longer do, such as the jubilant feeling of going out to play.)

FATHER TO ME: "Oh, I just go along with things. I earn the money. Raising the kids is her department." (How tempting it would be sometimes to take the comfortable course of the abdicating father.)

MOTHER TO CHILD: "What did you ever do for me?" (Am I hearing right? Shouldn't it be the other way around? True, it's very difficult to be a better parent to your children than your parents were to you. Do I know what I really want from my kids? You will repeat with your children some of the same wrongs that your parents committed with you. Verily, you can count on it.)

MOTHER ABOUT TEEN-AGER: "She doesn't have time for us anymore, ever since she met that boy." (It's hard to let the kids go. I recall Ogden Nash's poem:

I . . . never see an infant (male),
A-sleeping in the sun,

Without I turn a trifle pale,
And think, is he the one? . . .
Sand for his spinach I'll bring,
And tabasco sauce for his teething ring . . .
Then perhaps he'll struggle through fire and water
To marry somebody *else's* daughter.)

FAMILY MEMBER TO ME: "You can never know how it tears you apart to lose a child." (High fidelity silence as I stare stonily at the family.)

MOTHER TO FATHER: "I've noticed how you talk to Jane (the daughter) more than you talk to me. This always happens everytime we're on the outs with each other." (Yes, the pull to form an alliance with my daughter is there at times. Another important lesson from family therapy: Keep separate the generational boundaries in my own family.)

FATHER TO DAUGHTER: "I'm sorry I'm not the kind of person you want me to be, I'm not the kind of person *I* wanted to be. Things happen . . . you compromise. . . ." (Idealistic principles of youth fall by the wayside with each successive compromise. Should they have been kept, though? Doesn't the super-ego get healthfully relaxed as you get older? I recollect that line from O'Neill's *Long Day's Journey Into Night*: "None of us can help the things life has done to us. They're done before you realize it, and once they're done they make you do other things until at last everything comes between you and what you'd like to be, and you've lost your true self forever . . .")

FATHER TO ME: "It took me a long time to realize how my wife used me as the baddy. Like she'll keep trying to please Tommie and even give him things he doesn't want, and then he'll have a tantrum and she calls me in to punish him, and then she steps out of the situation." (The Bad Father Syndrome. I had to learn how to avoid that ambush. Me to wife: "If you don't think she ought to go to that party you'd better tell her.")

MOTHER TO FAMILY: "I can't help it if my nerves are bad." ("My nerves are bad"—perhaps the oldest rationalization for avoidance of responsibility. When had I heard that line before?)

PARENT TO ME: "Oh, doctor, you know so much about families. You must have a perfect family life." (How false I feel when I do not dispute the idealization. Should I mention my own particular Furies and hang-ups?)

DAUGHTER TO FATHER: "Daddy, you never trust me. . . . You always think I'm up to something, even when I'm not." (My daughter to me: "Daddy, just because those teenagers in those families you treat can't be trusted doesn't mean you can't trust me." Does my own family come to have the characteristics of those I treat? Do I begin to see problems in my family that aren't there?)

MOTHER TO ME: "Oh, I never had to worry about Eloise or tell her what time to come home at night. She set her own limits and I knew she had good sense." (No wonder Eloise got in trouble. Incident: My 5-year-old insisted he did not want to wear his hat out in the rain and after a long struggle with him my wife said, "O.K., go out without a hat." Then he looked at her in astonishment and said, "Don't you care, if I get sick?")

MOTHER (crying): "I've done my best . . . I've tried to be a good mother . . . Heaven knows, I've tried . . ." (Sympathy for the older generation now that I know how damn difficult it is to raise kids. Whenever you feel guilty about this keep in mind W. C. Field's great line: "Anyone who hates kids can't be all bad.")

Adulthood

FAMILY MEMBER TO ME: "Everyone in my family sees me as dishonest and evasive and practicing trickery. Then how do you account for the fact that my friends say I'm the most honest and direct person they know?" (One definition of maturity: the extent to which your family self and outside self are congruent. Or do you need the safety valve of home regression to survive socially? Yet, you are not the same person with other relationships that you are with your family. Our families get our irrational child-self, anachronistically. We reserve for our family the best and the worst that is in us. Accept this.)

PARENTS TO ME: "We regard everyone in our family as equal, because that's the democratic way." (One of the most valuable lessons I've learned from family therapy: A family can never be a democracy; it can only function as a benevolent dictatorship. Democratic families have helpless parents and children who are full of rage. One of my children to me: "Just don't go too far with this dictator business.")

MOTHER TO TEEN-AGER: "You shouldn't do those things. It's not nice. What will people say?" (How important it is for a parent to take a personal stand—the Murray Bowen principle of a differentiated "I" position: "*I* don't like what you're doing and *I* want you to stop it.")

PARENT TO ME: "Doctor, you've got to do something. This is a terrible situation." (It takes a lot of experience before a family therapist no longer feels he has to do something when there is a family crisis.)

FAMILY MEMBER TO ME: "It's up to you, Doc, to straighten us out. You haven't done us a damn bit of good. If something looks like a duck and walks like a duck, then by Christ it *is* a duck. And that's what you are—a goddamn quack. You have ruined our family." (This particular family was undergoing good system change. But it is a myth that the therapist should be all-accepting, forgiving, and give "unconditional positive regard." When there are assaults on me as a person I must be guided at times by what is necessary for my own comfort and health. Tonight I think I'll go see a good movie, preferably a comedy.)

FAMILY MEMBER TO ME: "Doctor, we will always be grateful to you for giving our lives back to us. How does it make you feel to know that you've really helped somebody?" (Is it harder to accept praise than criticism? Which is more illusory?)

ME TO FAMILY: "You're not all the same person, on the same blood stream and same nervous system. You are all separate people, but you don't realize it." (Which of us manage to get unstuck from the morass of our own family emotional systems? Sometimes the alternative to family loyalty is craziness.)

FAMILY MEMBER TO ME: "Doctor, you cannot know what fear is. You've probably lived a nice protected life." (Come closer, chum, I'll tell you. The place was Cassino, Italy, and the time was 1944 . . .)

ME TO FAMILY: "It's very complex." Or, "You have to work it through." Or, "You won't feel this way after you get the problem resolved." (Why do I always feel so ill-at-ease when I hide behind those corny platitudes?)

ME TO FAMILY: "I sense that despite this talk about stopping therapy you are hoping I'll stop you from leaving." (When your practice is low you try to keep patients, and when your practice is full you take at face value the stated desire to terminate, especially if you don't like the family.)

FAMILY MEMBER TO ME: "Doc, I don't think that's *our* problem. That may be one of *your* problems." (Just as the patients you are treating while you are in analysis "happen" to have the same problems you are currently working on, how much carry-over to families is there from problems you are dealing with in your own family now?)

MOTHER TO DAUGHTER: "Why don't you tell your father we need new chairs in the kitchen?" (Straighten out the channels of communication and force the family members to deal with each other rather than through others.)

ME TO WIFE: "If you really don't think your father ought to stay with us, I suggest you tell him yourself."

FAMILY MEMBER TO ME: "If you knew me outside, socially, I'm sure you'd see me in a different kind of way." (He's probably right. We do have a different set of standards of pathology for those whom we know well and like.)

FAMILY MEMBER TO ME: "This is pretty tough going, and very personal. Would you bring in your own family for treatment?" (I reply, "If one of my kids got in trouble the way yours did, yes." But did I mean it? Can we expect of treatment-families what we cannot do ourselves?)

FAMILY MEMBER TO ME: "What do you want from me? What is it that I'm expected to give you?" (If you are not getting gratification from your own family you are likely to want more from the family you are treating, in an irrational way. You are more likely to feel helpless and useless and you feed on them.)

FAMILY MEMBER TO ME: "Who are you to say what the good family life should be?" (This is one question that disturbs all family therapists. Should we present ourselves as the model of family health? Is Carl Whitaker on the better track when he presents the child part of self to close the distance between therapist and family?)

FAMILY MEMBER TO ME: "There's something I resent in you, doctor. I keep getting the feeling that you have some kind of ideal family image you expect us to live up to and that somehow we should be like your family." (My God, can it be true?)

References

Ackerman, N., and Behrens, M. A study of family diagnosis. *American Journal of Orthopsychiatry*, 1956, *26*, 66–78.

Ackerman, N. Family-focused therapy of schizophrenia. In S. Scher and H. Davis (Eds.), *The out-patient treatment of schizophrenia*. New York: Grune & Stratton, 1960.

Ackerman N. *Treating the troubled family*. New York: Basic Books, 1966.

Ackerman, N., Boszormenyi-Nagy, I., Brodey, W., and Gioscia, V. The classification of family types; a panel discussion. In N. Ackerman, F. Beatman and S. Sherman (Eds.), *Expanding theory and practice in family therapy*. New York: Family Service Association of America, 1967.

Allport, G. *Becoming*. New Haven: Yale University Press, 1955.

Angyal, A. *Neurosis and treatment*. New York: Viking Press, 1973.

Anonymous. Toward the differentiation of a self in one's own family. In J. Framo (Ed.), *Family interaction: A dialogue between family researchers and family therapists*. New York: Springer, 1972.

Arlow, J. Conflict, regression, and symptom formation. *International Journal of Psychoanalysis*, 1963, *44*, 12–22.

Auerswald, E. Interdisciplinary versus ecological approach. *Family Process*, 1968, *1*, 202–215.

Bach, G. Intimate violence, understanding and prevention. Unpublished manuscript, 1967. (Available from Institute of Group Psychotherapy, 450 N. Bedford Drive, Beverly Hills, CA.).

Bach, G., and Wyden, P. *The intimate enemy: How to fight fair in love and marriage*. New York: Morrow, 1969.

Beckett, P., Robinson, D., Frazier, S., Steinhilber, R., Duncan, G., Estes, H., Litin, E., Grattan, R., Lorton, W., Williams, G., and Johnson A. The significance of exogenous traumata in the genesis of schizophrenia. *Psychiatry*, 1956, *19*, 137–142.

Bell, J. *Family group therapy*. (Public Health Monograph No. 64.) Washington, D.C.: U.S. Department of Health, Education and Welfare, 1961.

Bell, J. The future of family therapy. *Family Process*, 1970, *9*, 127–141.

Bell, N. Extended family relations of disturbed and well families. *Family Process*, 1962, *1*, 175–193.

Berman, E., and Lief, H. Marital therapy from a psychiatric perspective: An overview. *American Journal of Psychiatry,* 1975, *132* (6), 583–592.

Berne, E. *Transactional analysis in psychotherapy.* New York: Grove Press, 1961.

Blackman, S., and Goldstein, K. Some aspects of a theory of community mental health. *Community Mental Health Journal,* 1968, *4,* 85–90.

Blinder, M., and Kirschenbaum, M. The technique of married couple group therapy. *Archives of General Psychiatry,* 1967, *17,* 44–52.

Bowlby, J. *Attachment and loss: Attachment* (Vol. 1) *and Separation* (Vol. 2). New York: Basic Books, 1969.

Bolman, W. Theoretical and empirical bases of community mental health. Community Psychiatry Supplement to *American Journal of Psychiatry,* 1967, *124,* 8–13.

Boszormenyi-Nagy, I., and Framo, J. Hospital organization and family oriented psychotherapy of schizophrenia. Montreal: *Proceedings of the 3rd World Congress of Psychiatry,* 1961.

Boszormenyi-Nagy I., and Framo, J. Family concept of hospital treatment of schizophrenia. In J. Masserman (Ed.), *Current psychiatric therapies* (Vol. II). New York: Grune & Stratton, 1962.

Boszormenyi-Nagy, I. The concept of change in conjoint family therapy. In A. Friedman, I. Boszormenyi-Nagy, J. Jungreis, G. Lincoln, H. Mitchell, J. Sonne, R. Speck, and G. Spivack (Eds.), *Psychotherapy for the whole family.* New York: Springer, 1965. (a)

Boszormenyi-Nagy, I. A theory of relationships: Experience and transaction. In I. Boszormenyi-Nagy and J. Framo (Eds.), *Intensive family therapy.* New York: Hoeber Medical Division, Harper & Row, 1965. (b)

Boszormenyi-Nagy, I. Intensive family therapy as process. In I. Boszormenyi-Nagy and J. Framo (Eds.), *Intensive Family Therapy.* New York: Hoeber Medical Division, Harper & Row, 1965. (c)

Boszormenyi-Nagy, I., and Framo, J. (Eds.), *Intensive family therapy.* New York: Harper & Row Medical Department, 1965.

Boszormenyi-Nagy, I. From family therapy to a psychology of relationships: Fictions of the individual and fictions of the family. *Comprehensive Psychiatry,* 1966, *7,* 408–423.

Boszormenyi-Nagy, I., and Spark, G. *Invisible loyalties: Reciprocity in intergenerational family therapy.* New York: Harper & Row Medical Department, 1973.

Bowen, M. Family psychotherapy. *American Journal of Orthopsychiatry,* 1961, *31,* 42–60.

Bowen, M. Family psychotherapy with schizophrenia in the hospital and in private practice. In I. Boszormenyi-Nagy and J. Framo (Eds.), *Intensive family therapy.* New York: Hoeber Medical Division, Harper & Row, 1965.

Bowen, M. The use of family theory in clinical practice. *Comprehensive Psychiatry,* 1966, *7,* 345–374.

Bowen, M. Toward the differentiation of self in one's family of origin. In F. Andres and J. Lorio (Eds.), *Georgetown family symposia: A collection of papers* (Vol. 1, 1971–1972). Washington, D. C.: Georgetown University Medical Center, Department of Psychiatry, 1974.

Bowen, M. *Family therapy in clinical practice.* New York: Aronson, 1978.

Bradt, J., and Moynihan, C. A study of child-focused families. In J. Bradt & C. Moynihan (Eds.), *System therapy,* 1971. (Available from Groome Child Guidance Clinic, 5225 Loughboro Rd., N.W., Washington, D.C. 20016.)

Brodey, W. Some family operations and schizophrenia. *Archives of General Psychiatry,* 1959, *1,* 379–402.

Bryant, C., and Grunebaum, H. The theory and practice of the family diagnostic: II. Theoretical and resident education. In I. Cohen (Ed.), *Family structure, dynamics and therapy.* Psychiatric Research Reports #20. The American Psychiatric Association, 1966.

Caplan, G. Community psychiatry—Introduction and overview. In S. Goldston (Ed.), *Concepts of community psychiatry*. Bethesda, Md: U. S. Department of Health, Education and Welfare, NIMH, 1965.

Carroll, E. Treatment of the family as a unit. *Pennsylvania Medical Journal*, 1960, *63*, 57–62.

Carson, R. *Interaction concepts of personality*. Chicago: Aldine, 1969.

Charny, I. Marital love and hate. *Family Process*, 1969, *8*, 1–24.

Clausen, J. The marital relationship antecedent to hospitalization of a spouse for mental illness. *World Congress of Sociology IV, Stress*, 1959.

Colon, F. In search of one's past. *Family Process*, 1973, *12*, 429–438.

Constantine, L. Designed experience: A multiple goal-directed training program in family therapy. *Family Process*, 1976, *15*, 373–387.

Coser, R. Laughter among colleagues. *Psychiatry*, 1960, *23*, 81–95.

Davies, I., Ellenson, G., and Young, R. Therapy with a group of families in a psychiatric day center. *American Journal of Orthopsychiatry*, 1966, *36*, 134–146.

Davis, M. *Intimate relations*. New York: Free Press, 1973.

Dewey, J., and Bentley, A. *Knowing and the known*. Boston: Beacon Press, 1949.

Dicks, H. Concepts of marital diagnosis and therapy as developed at the Tavistock family psychiatric units, London, England. In E. Nash, L. Jessner, and D. Abse (Eds.), *Marriage counseling in medical practice*. Chapel Hill, N.C.: University of North Carolina Press, Ch. 15, 1964.

Dicks, H. *Marital tensions*. New York: Basic Books, 1967.

Ehrenwald, J. Family diagnosis and mechanisms of defense. *Family Process*, 1963, *2*, 121–131.

Erikson, E. *Childhood and society*. New York: Norton, 1950.

Fairbairn, W. *An object-relations theory of the personality*. New York: Basic Books, 1954.

Fallding, H. The family and idea of a cardinal role. In G. Handel (Ed.), *The psychosocial interior of the family*. Chicago: Aldine, 1967.

Feldman, S. Ideas and issues in community mental health. *Hospital & Community Psychiatry*, 1971, *22*, 325–329.

Fisher, L. Dimensions of family assessment: A critical review. *Journal of Marriage and Family Counseling*, 1976, *2*, 367–382.

Flugel, J. *The psychoanalytic study of the family*. London: Hogarth, 1921.

Foley, V. *An introduction to family therapy*. New York: Grune & Stratton, 1974.

Framo, J. The theory of the techniques of family treatment of schizophrenia. *Family Process*, 1962, *1*, 119–131.

Framo, J. Rationale and techniques of intensive family therapy. In I. Boszormenyi-Nagy and J. Framo (Eds.), *Intensive family therapy*. New York: Hoeber Medical Division, Harper & Row, 1965. (a)

Framo, J. Systematic research on family dynamics. In I. Boszormenyi-Nagy and J. Framo (Eds.), *Intensive family therapy*. New York: Hoeber Medical Division, Harper & Row, 1965. (b)

Framo, J. My families, my family. *Voices: Art and Science of Psychotherapy*, 1968, *4*, 18–27.

Framo, J. Symptoms from a family transactional viewpoint. In N. Ackerman, J. Lieb, and J. Pearce (Eds.), *Family therapy in transition*. Boston: Little, Brown and Company, 1970. (Also reprinted in C. Sager and H. Kaplan (Eds.), *Progress in group and family therapy*. New York: Brunner/Mazel, 1972).

Framo, J. Conceptual issues and clinical implications of family therapy. Discussion of J. Bell's "A theoretical position for family group therapy." In A. Mahrer and L. Pearson (Eds.) *Creative developments in psychotherapy*. Cleveland: Western Reserve University Press, 1971.

Framo, J. (Ed.), *Family interaction: A dialogue between family researchers and family therapists.* New York: Springer, 1972.

Framo, J. Marriage therapy in couples group. In D. Bloch (Ed.), *Techniques of family psychotherapy: A primer.* New York: Grune & Stratton, 1973.

Framo, J. Husbands' reactions to wives' infidelity. *Medical Aspects of Human Sexuality,* May 1975, 78–104. (a)

Framo, J. Personal reflections of a family therapist. *Journal of Marriage and Family Counseling,* 1975, *1*, 15–28. (b)

Framo, J. Family of origin as a therapeutic resource for adults in marital and family therapy: You can and should go home again. *Family Process,* 1976, *15*, 193–210. (a)

Framo, J. Chronicle of a struggle to establish a family unit within a community mental health center. In P. Guerin (Ed.) *Family therapy.* New York: Gardner Press, 1976. (b)

Framo, J. Family and marital therapy training facilities: Academic and non-academic programs. *Family Process,* 1976, *15*, 441–445. (c)

Framo, J. The friendly divorce. *Psychology Today,* February, 1978. (a)

Framo, J. In-laws and out-laws: A marital case of kinship confusion. In P. Papp (Ed.), *Family therapy: Full-length case studies.* New York: Gardner Press, 1978. (b)

Framo, J. A personal viewpoint on training in marital and family therapy. *Professional Psychology,* 1979, *10*, 868–875.

Framo, J. Marriage and marital therapy: Issues and initial interview techniques. In M. Andolfi and I. Zwerling (Eds.), *Dimensions of family therapy.* New York: Guilford Press, 1980.

Frank, L. Causation: An episode in the history of thought. *Journal of Philosophy,* 1934, *31*, 421–428.

Frank, L. Research for what? *Journal of Social Issues,* Supplemental Series, 1957, No. 10.

Franklin, P., and Prosky, P. A standard initial interview. In D. Bloch (Ed.), *Techniques of family psychotherapy: A primer.* New York: Grune & Stratton, 1973.

Freeman, H., and Simmons, O. *The mental patient comes home.* New York: Wiley, 1963.

Freud, S. *Inhibitions, symptoms and anxiety.* London: Hogarth, 1926.

Friedman, A., Boszormenyi-Nagy, I., Jungreis, J., Lincoln, G., Mitchell, H., Sonne, J., Speck, R., and Spivack, G. *Psychotherapy for the whole family.* New York: Springer, 1965.

Gaarder, K. The internalized representation of the object in the presence and in the absence of the object. *International Journal of Psychoanalysis,* 1965, *46*, 297–302.

Goffman, E. *The presentation of self in everyday life.* Edinburgh: University of Edinburgh Social Sciences Research Centre, 1956.

Gottlieb, A. and Pattison, E. Married couples group psychotherapy. *Archives of General Psychiatry,* 1966, *14*, 143–152.

Greene, B. Management of marital problems. *Diseases of the Nervous System,* 1966, *27*, 204–209.

Greenson, R. The struggle against identification. *Journal of American Psychoanalytic Association,* 1954, *2*, 200–217.

Grinker, R. (Ed.), *Toward a unified theory of human behavior.* New York: Basic Books, 1956.

Grunebaum, H., and Bryant, C. The theory and practice of the family diagnostic. Part II. In I. Cohen (Ed.), *Psychiatric Research Reports,* No. 20. The American Psychiatric Association, 1966.

Grunebaum, H., Christ, J., and Neiberg, N. Diagnosis and treatment planning for couples. *International Journal of Group Psychotherapy,* 1969, *19*, 185–202.

Guerin, P. *Family therapy: Theory and practice.* New York: Gardner Press, 1976.

Guntrip, H. The therapeutic factor in psychotherapy. *British Journal of Medical Psychology,* 1953, *26*, 115–131.

Gurman, A., and Kniskern, D. Research on marital and family therapy: Progress, perspective, and prospect. In S. Garfield and A. Bergin (Eds.), *Handbook of psychotherapy and behavior change: An empirical analysis*. New York: Wiley, 1978.

Gurman, A., and Kniskern, D. (Eds.), *Handbook of family therapy*. New York: Brunner/ Mazel, 1981.

Haas, W. The intergenerational encounter: A method in treatment. *Social Work*, 1968, *13*, 91–101.

Haley, J. Family of the schizophrenic: A model system. *Journal of Nervous and Mental Disorders*, 1959, *129*, 357–374.

Haley, J. Marriage therapy. *Archives of General Psychiatry*, 1963, *8*, 213–234.

Haley, J., and Hoffman, L. *Techniques of family therapy*. New York: Basic Books, 1967.

Haley, J. Why a mental health clinic should avoid family therapy. *Journal of Marriage and Family Counseling*, 1975, *1*, 3–13.

Haley, J. *Problem solving therapy*. San Francisco: Jossey-Bass, 1976.

Handlon, J., and Parloff, M. The treatment of patient and family as a group: Is it group psychotherapy? *International Journal of Group Psychotherapy*, 1962, *12*, 132–141.

Hastings, P., and Runkle, R. An experimental group of married couples with severe problems. *International Journal of Group Psychotherapy*, 1963, *13*, 85–92.

Headley, L. *Adults and their parents in family therapy*. New York: Plenum Press, 1977.

Hill, L. *Psychotherapeutic intervention in schizophrenia*. Chicago: University of Chicago Press, 1955.

Hollander, M. Selection of therapy for marital problems. In J. Masserman (Ed.), *Current psychiatric therapies*, Vol. II. New York: Grune & Stratton, 1971.

Howe, L. The concept of the community: Some implications for the development of community psychiatry. In L. Bellak (Ed.), *Handbook of community psychiatry and community mental health*. New York: Grune & Stratton, 1964.

Howell, J. *Advances in family psychiatry, vol. 1*. New York: International Universities Press, 1979.

Huxley, A. *Genius and the goddess*. New York: Harper, 1955.

Jackson, D. Family interaction, family homeostasis and some implications for conjoint family psychotherapy. In J. Masserman (Ed.), *Science and psychoanalysis, II. Individual and familial dynamics*. New York: Grune & Stratton, 1959.

Jackson, D., and Weakland, J. Conjoint family therapy: Some considerations on theory, technique, and results. *Psychiatry*, 1961, *24*, 30–45.

Jackson, D. The individual and the larger contexts. *Family Process*, 1967, *6*, 139–147.

Jahoda, M. *Current concepts of positive mental health*. New York: Basic Books, 1958.

Johnson, A. Factors in the etiology of fixations and symptom choice. *Psychoanalytic Quarterly*, 1953, *22*, 475–496.

Johnson, A., and Szurek, S. Etiology of anti-social behavior in delinquents and psychopaths. *Journal of the American Medical Association*, 1954, *154*, 814–817.

Jourard, S. Marriage is for life. *Journal of Marriage and Family Counseling*, 1975, *1* (3), 199–207.

Kaffman, M. Short term family therapy. *Family Process*, 1963, *2*, 216–234.

Klein, D. The community and mental health: An attempt at a conceptual framework. *Community Mental Health Journal*, 1965, *1*, 301–308.

Kobler, A., and Stotland, E. *The end of hope*. Glencoe, Ill: The Free Press, 1964.

Kubie, L. Psychoanalysis and marriage: Practical and theoretical issues. In V. Eisenstein (Ed.), *Neurotic interaction in marriage*. New York: Basic Books, 1956.

Kuhn, T. *The structure of scientific revolutions*. Chicago: University of Chicago Press, 1962.

Laing, R. *The self and others*. Chicago: Quadrangle Books, 1962.

Laing, R. Is schizophrenia a disease? *International Journal of Social Psychiatry,* 1964, *10,* 184–193.

Lampl-DeGroot, J. Symptom formation and character formation. *International Journal of Psychoanalysis,* 1963, *44,* 1–11.

Langsley, D., Kaplan, D., Pittman, F., Machotka, P., Flomenhaft, K., and DeYoung, C. *The treatment of families in crisis.* New York: Grune & Stratton, 1968.

Laqueur, H., Laburt, H., and Morong, E. Multiple family therapy. In J. Masserman (Ed.), *Current psychiatric therapies, IV.* New York: Grune & Stratton, 1964.

Laqueur, H. Multiple family therapy: Questions and answers. In D. Bloch (Ed.), *Techniques of family psychotherapy.* New York: Grune & Stratton, 1973.

Leary, T. *Interpersonal diagnosis of personality.* New York: Ronald Press, 1957.

Leichter, E. Group psychotherapy with married couples. *International Journal of Group Psychotherapy,* 1962, *12,* 154–163.

Levenson, E., Stockhamer, N., and Feiner, A. Family transactions in the etiology of dropping out of college. *Contemporary Psychoanalysis,* 1967, *2,* 134–157.

Levinger, G., and Raush, H. *Close relationships: Perspectives on the meaning of intimacy.* Amherst, Mass.: University of Massachusetts, 1976.

Lewin, K. *Field theory in social science.* New York: Harper & Brothers, 1951.

Lewis, J., Beavers, R., Gossett, J., and Phillips, V. *No single thread: Psychological health in family systems.* New York: Brunner/Mazel, 1976.

Liddle, H., and Halpin, R. Family therapy training and supervision literature: A comparative review. *Journal of Marriage and Family Counseling,* 1978, *4,* 77–98.

Lidz, T., Fleck, S., Alanen, Y., and Cornelison, A. Schizophrenic patients and their siblings. *Psychiatry,* 1963, *26,* 1–18.

Lorenz, K. *On aggression.* New York: Harcourt, 1966.

Loveland, N., Wynne, L., and Singer, M. The family Rorschach: A new method for studying family interaction. *Family Process,* 1963, *2,* 187–215.

Luborsky, L., and Schimek, J. Psychoanalytic theories of therapeutic and developmental change: Implications for assessment. In P. Worchel and D. Byrne (Eds.), *Personal change.* New York: Wiley, 1964.

Martin, P. *A marital therapy manual.* New York: Brunner/Mazel, 1976.

Maslow, A. *Toward a psychology of being.* New York: Van Nostrand, 1962.

Mayo, C., and Klein, D. Group dynamics as a basic process of community psychiatry. In L. Bellak (Ed.), *Handbook of community psychiatry and community mental health.* New York: Grune & Stratton, 1964.

Menninger, K. *The theory of psychoanalytic technique.* New York: Basic Books, 1958.

Menninger, K. *A manual for psychiatric case study* (2nd Ed.). New York: Grune & Stratton, 1962.

Midelfort, C. *The family in psychotherapy.* New York: Blakiston, 1957.

Minuchin, S., Montalvo, B., Guerney, B., Rosman, B., and Schumer, F. *Families of the slums.* New York: Basic Books, 1967.

Minuchin, S. *Families and family therapy.* Cambridge, Mass.: Harvard University Press, 1974.

Montalvo, B., and Haley, J. In defense of child therapy. *Family Process,* 1973, *12,* 227–244.

Murstein, B. The complementary need hypothesis in newlyweds and middle-aged married couples. *Journal of Abnormal and Social Psychology,* 1961, *63,* 194–197.

Napier, A. The marriage of families: Cross-generational complementarity. *Family Process,* 1971, *10,* 373–395.

Napier, A., and Whitaker, C. Problems of the beginning family therapist. In D. Bloch (Ed.), *Techniques of family psychotherapy: A primer.* New York: Grune & Stratton, 1973.

Napier, A. The rejection-intrusion pattern: A central family dynamic. *Journal of Marriage and Family Counseling,* 1978, *4,* 5–12.

Neubeck, G. Factors affecting group therapy with married couples. *Marriage and Family Living,* 1954, *16,* 216–220.

Nizer, L. *My life in court.* New York: Doubleday, 1961.

Otto, H. Criteria for assessing family strength. *Family Process,* 1963, *2,* 329–338.

Patterson, G., Weiss, R., and Hops, H. Training of marital skills. In H. Leitenberg (Ed.), *Handbook of behavior modification and behavior therapy.* New York: Prentice-Hall, 1976.

Paul, N., and Paul, B. *A marital puzzle.* New York: Norton, 1975.

Paul, N. Cross-confrontation. In P. Guerin (Ed.), *Family therapy.* New York: Gardner Press, 1976.

Pavenstedt, E. A comparison of the child-rearing environment of upper-lower and very lower-low-class families. *American Journal of Orthopsychiatry,* 1965, *35,* 89–98.

Perelman, J. Problems encountered in psychotherapy of married couples. *International Journal of Group Psychotherapy,* 1960, *10,* 136–142.

Phillips, C. E., and Kelly, B. J. *Innovations in training and supervision of marriage and family counselors.* Paper presented at the annual meeting of the American Association for Marital and Family Counselors, Toronto, Canada, November 1975.

Pittman, F., Langsley, D., Kaplan, D., Flomenhaft, K., and DeYoung, C. Family therapy as an alternative to psychiatric hospitalization. In I. Cohen (Ed.), *Family structure, dynamics and therapy.* Psychiatric Research Report #20, American Psychiatric Association, 1966.

Pollak, O. Design of a model of healthy family relationships as a basis for evaluative research. *Social Science Review,* 1957, *31,* 369–376.

Prout, C., and White, M. The schizophrenic's sibling. *Journal of Nervous and Mental Disorders,* 1956, *123,* 162–170.

Rainwater, L. Crucible of identity: The Negro lower-class family. In G. Handel (Ed.), *The psychosocial interior of the family.* Chicago: Aldine, 1967.

Redl, F. Resistance in therapy groups. *Human Relations,* 1948, *1,* 307–313.

Reiff, R. Mental health manpower and institutional change. *American Psychologist,* 1966, *21,* 540–548.

Roman, M., and Bauman, G. Interaction testing: A technique for the psychological evaluation of small groups. In M. Harrower (Ed.), *Creative variations in the projective techniques.* Springfield, Ill.: Charles C Thomas, 1960.

Rubinstein, D., and Weiner, O. Co-therapy teamwork relationships in family psychotherapy. (With collaboration of Boszormenyi-Nagy, I., Dealy, M., Framo, J., Lincoln, G., Robinson, L., and Zuk, G.) In G. Zuk and I. Boszormenyi-Nagy (Eds.) *Family therapy and disturbed families.* Palo Alto, Calif.: Science & Behavior Books, 1967.

Ryckoff, I., Day, J., and Wynne, L. Maintenance of stereotyped roles in the families of schizophrenics. *Archives of General Psychiatry,* 1959, *1,* 93–99.

Sabshin, M. Theoretical models in community and social psychiatry. In L. Roberts, S. Halleck, and M. Loeb (Eds.), *Community psychiatry.* Madison, Wisc.: University of Wisconsin Press, 1966.

Safilos-Rothschild, C. Deviance and mental illness in the Greek family. *Family Process,* 1968, *1,* 100–117.

Sager, C. The treatment of married couples. In S. Arieti (Ed.), *American handbook of psychiatry,* Vol. 3. New York: Basic Books, 1959.

Sager, C., Gundlach, R., and Kremer, M. The married in treatment. *Archives of General Psychiatry,* 1968, *19,* 205–217.

Sampson, H., Messinger, S., and Towne, R. *Schizophrenic women.* New York: Atherton Press, 1964.

Sargent, H., Modlin, H., Faris, M., and Voth, H. The psychotherapy research project of the Menninger Foundation. III. Situational variables. *Bulletin of the Menninger Clinic,* 1958, *22,* 148–156.

Satir, V. *Conjoint family therapy.* Palo Alto, Calif.: Science & Behavior Books, 1964.

Schaffer, L., Wynne, L., Day, J., Ryckoff, I., and Halperin, A. On the nature and source of the psychiatrists' experience with the family of the schizophrenic. *Psychiatry,* 1962, *25,* 32–45.

Scheflen, A. Regressive one-to-one relationships. *Psychiatric Quarterly,* 1960, *34,* 692–709.

Schmideberg, M. Parents as children. *Psychiatric Quarterly Supplement,* 1948, *22,* 207–218.

Schur, M., Zetzel, E., Loewenstein, R., Langer, M., Haas, L., Pedersen, S., and Arlow, L. Symptom formation and character formation: Discussions. *International Journal of Psychoanalysis,* 1964, *45,* 147–170.

Schwartz, C. Perspectives on deviance—Wives' definitions of their husbands' mental illness. *Psychiatry,* 1957, *20,* 275–291.

Searles, H. Positive feelings in the relationship between the schizophrenic and his mother. *International Journal of Psychoanalysis,* 1958, *39,* 569–586.

Searles, H. Integration and differentiation in schizophrenia. *Journal of Nervous Mental Disorders,* 1959, *129,* 542–550. (a)

Searles, H. The effort to drive the other person crazy—An element in the aetiology and psychotherapy of schizophrenia. *British Journal of Medical Psychology,* 1959, *32,* 1–18. (b)

Searles, H. Anxiety concerning change, as seen in the psychotherapy of schizophrenic patients, with particular reference to the sense of personal identity. *International Journal of Psychoanalysis,* 1961, *42,* 74–85.

Shaffer, P. *Five finger exercise.* New York: Harcourt Brace, 1959.

Shapiro, R. Problems in teaching family therapy. *Professional Psychology,* 1975, *6,* 41–44.

Singer, M., and Wynne, L. Thought disorder and family relations of schizophrenics. *Archives of General Psychiatry,* 1965, *12,* 187–212.

Skynner, A.C.R. *Systems of family and marital psychotherapy.* Chapter 11. New York: Brunner/Mazel, 1976.

Sonne, J., Speck, R., and Jungreis, J. The absent-member maneuver as a resistance in family therapy of schizophrenia. *Family Process,* 1962, *1,* 44–62.

Speck, R., and Attneave, C. *Family networks.* New York: Pantheon, 1973.

Spiegel, J., and Kluckhohn, F. *Integration and conflict in family behavior.* Report No. 27, Group for the Advancement of Psychiatry, Topeka, Kansas, 1954.

Spiegel, J., and Bell, N. The family of the psychiatric patient. In S. Arieti (Ed.), *American handbook of psychiatry* (Vol. 1). New York: Basic Books, 1959.

Stanton, M. Family therapy training: Academic and internship opportunities for psychologists. *Family Process,* 1975, *14,* 433–439.

Strean, H. A family therapist looks at Little Hans. *Family Process,* 1967, *6,* 227–234.

Szasz, T. A contribution to the psychology of schizophrenia. *Archives of Neurological Psychiatry,* 1957, *77,* 420–436.

Szasz, T. The classification of "mental illness." *Psychiatric Quarterly,* 1959, *33,* 77–101.

Toomim, M. Structured separation with counseling: A therapeutic approach for couples in conflict. *Family Process,* 1972, *11,* 299–310.

Varon, E. Defenses inherent in the group situation. *Jewish Family & Children's Bureau.* Baltimore (mimeo), 1958.

Visher, E., and Visher, J. *Step-families: A guide to working with step parents and step children.* New York: Brunner/Mazel, 1979.

Voiland, A., and Associates. *Family casework diagnosis*. New York: Columbia University Press, 1962.

Von Emde Boas, C. Intensive group psychotherapy with married couples. *International Journal of Group Psychotherapy*, 1962, *12*, 142–153.

Warkentin, J., Felder, R., Malone, T., and Whitaker, C. The usefulness of craziness. *Medical Times*, June, 1961.

Warkentin, J., and Whitaker, C. Serial impasses in marriage. In I. Cohen (Ed.), *Family structure, dynamics, and therapy*. Psychiatric Research Report No. 20. American Psychiatric Association, 1966.

Warkentin, J., and Whitaker, C. The secret agenda of the therapist doing couples therapy. In G. Zuk and I. Boszormenyi-Nagy (Eds.), *Family therapy and disturbed families*. Palo Alto, Calif.: Science & Behavior Books, 1967.

Weigert, E. Narcissism: Benign and malignant forms. In R. Gibson (Ed.), *Crosscurrents in psychiatry and psychoanalysis*. Philadelphia: Lippincott, 1967.

Wells, R., and Dezen, A. The results of family therapy revisited: The non-behavioral methods. *Family Process*, 1978, *3*, 251–274.

Whitaker, C., and Malone, T. *The roots of psychotherapy*. New York: Blakiston, 1953.

Whitaker, C. Psychotherapy with couples. *American Journal of Psychotherapy*, 1958, *12*, 18–23.

Whitaker, C., Malone, T., and Warkentin, J. Multiple therapy and psychotherapy. In F. Fromm-Reichman and J. Moreno (Eds.), *Progress in Psychotherapy*. New York: Grune & Stratton, 1956, 210–216.

Whitaker, C., Felder, R., and Warkentin, J. Countertransference in the family treatment of schizophrenia. In I. Boszormenyi-Nagy and J. Framo (Eds.), *Intensive family therapy*. New York: Hoeber Medical Division, Harper & Row, 1965.

Whitaker, C., and Miller, M. A re-evaluation of "psychiatric help" when divorce impends. *American Journal of Psychiatry*, 1969, *126*, 57–64.

Whitaker, C. A family is a four dimensional relationship. In P. Guerin (Ed.), *Family therapy*. New York: Gardner Press, 1976.

Whitaker, C., and Keith, D. Counseling the dissolving marriage. In R. Stahmann & W. Hiebert (Eds.), *Klemer's counseling in marital and sexual problems*. Baltimore: Williams & Wilkins, 1977.

Whittington, H. The third psychiatric revolution—Really? *Community Mental Health Journal*, 1968, *1*, 73–80.

Winch, R. *Mate selection: A study of complementary needs*. New York: Harper & Row, 1958.

Wynne, L., Day, J., Hirsch, S., and Ryckoff, I. The family relations of a set of monozygotic quadruplet schizophrenics. Zurich: *Congress Report of the 2nd International Congress for Psychiatry*, 1957, *2*, 43–49.

Wynne, L., and Singer, M. Thought disorder and family relations of schizophrenics: I. A research strategy. II. A classification of forms of thinking. *Archives of General Psychiatry*, 1963, *9*, 191–206.

Yi-Chuang Lu. Mother-child role relations in schizophrenia: A comparison of schizophrenic patients with nonschizophrenic siblings. *Psychiatry*, 1961, *24*, 133–142.

Yolles, S. *The role of the psychologist in comprehensive community mental health centers: The NIMH view*. Paper presented at the Conference of State Chief Psychologists and Psychologists in the U.S. Public Health Service, Chicago, 1965.

Yolles, S. Community mental health services: The view from 1967. Community Psychiatry Supplement to the *American Journal of Psychiatry*, 1967, *124*, 1–7.

Zilboorg, G., and Henry, G. *A history of medical psychology*. New York: Norton, 1941.

Index